THE HEIDEGGER CONTROVERSY
A Critical Reader

THE HEIDEGGER CONTROVERSY:

A Critical Reader

Edited by
Richard Wolin

The MIT Press
Cambridge, Massachusetts
London, England

First MIT Press Edition, 1993
© 1991, 1993 Richard Wolin

This book was printed and bound in the United States of
America.

Library of Congress Cataloging-in-Publication Data

The Heidegger controversy : a critical reader / edited by
  Richard Wolin. — 1st MIT ed.
        p.   cm.
  Includes bibliographical references.
    ISBN-13 978-0-262-23166-4 (hc. : alk. paper) – 978-0-262-73101-0 (pbk. : alk. paper)
    ISBN-10 0-262-23166-2 (hc. : alk. paper) – 0-262-73101-0 (pbk. : alk. paper)
    1. Heidegger, Martin, 1889–1976. I. Wolin, Richard.
  II. Heidegger, Martin, 1889–1976. Selections.
English. 1993.
B3279.H49H3515 1993
193—dc20   92-30027
                                       CIP

10 9 8 7 6

CONTENTS

Contents

PREFACE

One of the foremost conundrums of modern European intellectual history concerns the delusion to which Martin Heidegger—probably the century's greatest philosopher—succumbed in 1933: the belief that the National Socialist Revolution represented the "saving power" (Hölderlin) of Western humanity; a power capable of redeeming European culture from the dislocations of a rationalistic, modernizing, and nihilistic bourgeois *Zivilisation*. It seems likely, moreover, that well after his resignation from the position of rector of Freiburg University in May 1934, Heidegger remained convinced that, despite its historical excrescences and transgressions, a philosophically idealized version of National Socialism—whose "inner truth and greatness" had been perverted by ideologues promoting "racial-biological thinking"—was the potential savior of the Western tradition.

It would of course be foolish to suggest that, as a result of Heidegger's concerted, short-lived engagement on behalf of the Nazi regime, he would somehow forfeit his status as a significant contributor to the legacy of Western thought. However, at the same time, now that we know the extent of Heidegger's partisanship for the Nazi cause in the early 1930s, we cannot help but read him differently. This is true not only because Heidegger the empirical individual was a member in good standing of the Nazi Party from 1933 to 1945; rather, we now read his work with greater attentiveness insofar as we know that his enthusiasm for National Socialism, far from being a fortuitous political flirtation, was *philosophically overdetermined*. That is, as numerous documents and lectures from the 1930s and 1940s attest, the philosopher himself was convinced that there existed profound and enduring resonances between his own philosophical doctrines and Germany's National Revolution. Or, as the Heidegger scholar Otto Pöggeler has appropriately remarked, "Whoever does not want merely to judge Heidegger but also to appropriate initiatives and to learn from him must realize that in the 1930s, Heidegger himself placed the decision about the truth of Being as he sought it in a political context." Hence, to rethink Heidegger's philosophy requires reading his texts and treatises with special attention to those aspects of his thought that may have facilitated his fateful political engagement of the 1930s.

The present compilation of texts is partly intended as a documentary complement to my earlier study of Heidegger's political thinking, *The Politics of Being: The Political Thought of Martin Heidegger*. And thus, one of the volume's primary goals is to serve as a type of sourcebook and guide to the many fascinating interpretive questions that have arisen around the theme of "Heidegger and National Socialism." To this end, I have sought to present a number of key texts by Heidegger himself, as well as seminal documents and commentaries that situate Heidegger's political involvement both historically and in the context of contemporary scholarly debates. Although some of these texts have already been published in English translation, many have appeared in journals that are far from readily accessible to interested readers. Given the numerous controversies, disputes, and polemics that have arisen in the aftermath of "the Heidegger affair," the advantages of rendering many of the key texts accessible in one volume seemed self-evident. With the exception of chapters 4 and 5 ("Overcoming Metaphysics" and " 'Only a God Can Save Us': *Der Spiegel's* Interview"), all of the translations have been commissioned for this anthology.

I would especially like to acknowledge the assistance of the translators, without whose self-sacrificial labors this volume would have scarcely been possible: Steven Galt Crowell, Joel Golb, and William S. Lewis.

PREFACE TO THE MIT PRESS EDITION: Note on a Missing Text

The present edition of *The Heidegger Controversy: A Critical Reader* differs from the original in one significant way: the omission of a text by Jacques Derrida entitled "Philosophers' Hell: An Interview."

The text has been omitted at Derrida's insistence. In truth, the word "insistence" doesn't do full justice to the nature of the situation. Derrida and a French attorney threatened a lawsuit against the original publisher of the volume, Columbia University Press, in the event that "Philosophers' Hell" were reprinted in any future editions of the book.

Derrida's actions—above all, their vehemence—seem peculiar. The interview was originally published in the November 6–12, 1987, issue of *Le Nouvel Observateur,* a leading Parisian cultural-political weekly. He has contested the propriety of the interview's translation/publication. Yet a permissions letter from *Le Nouvel Observateur,* dated October 23, 1990, unequivocally granted "the nonexclusive right to publish an English language translation for all editions and for sale throughout the world."

As a result of Derrida's complaints, not to mention his threat of legal action, Columbia decided to abandon the volume as it was originally conceived. The situation was especially regrettable since the first print run of the book had sold out within a matter of months. I'd like to express my sincere gratitude to The MIT Press for their confidence in the project and their commendable efficiency in ensuring its prompt reissue.

. . .

One need not be a deconstructionist to appreciate the ironies and paradoxes that attach to this "affair within an affair." To begin with, there are the ironies of engaging Derrida in a dispute about the prerogatives of "authorship." Who, after all, has done more to call into question our inherited conception of integral authorial authority than Jacques Derrida? But in this case he invoked the entitlements of authorship in the most conventional and, one is tempted to say, "pre-critical" fashion. Is Derrida himself the only one left to whom the notion of unimpeachable authorial prerogative still applies?

During a sojourn in Paris in the mid-1980s, I frequented from time to time a seminar on the subject of authorship and copyright held by Derrida. The underlying theme seemed to be the utter untenability of such quaint logocentric conceptions. They were unquestionably atavisms of Western metaphysics; they expressed the naive pieties of a philosophy of subjectivity, of an anachronistic longing for self-transparency and "presence" that was in urgent need of deconstruction. But in the dispute over the propriety of including his interview in *The Heidegger Controversy*, it seems that the subtleties and nuances of such theories of textuality did not apply.

Since Derrida had intervened in the matter along with his lawyer ["avocat à la cour"], should I have addressed my response to "Derrida Inc." (an allusion, of course, to his brilliant response to John Searle in *Limited Inc.*)? Moreover, and to further compound matters, in the case of the text in question there is the problem of *joint authorship*: as an interview, "Philosophers' Hell," after all, is the product of a common effort between two individuals, and thus Derrida could hardly be considered its sole "author," let alone its sole "legal author." The text was, one might say, "initiated" by the French weekly that commissioned it. In what way, then, can it be said to "belong" uniquely to him?

. . .

Of course, behind every text there is a subtext, if not a series of subtexts, and the controversy within *The Heidegger Controversy* over "Philosophers' Hell" is no exception. Derrida and deconstruction—whose indebtedness to Heidegger's later philosophy is avowed and profound—had been placed on the defensive by the damning revelations over Heidegger's Nazi past. Thus, deconstruction, because of its proximity to the Heideggerian "critique of reason," seemed implicated—however unjustly—in the Heidegger affair. (As proof of this claim, one need go no further than the French preface to Farias' work by former *nouveau philosophe* Christophe Jambet. Jambet concludes that, outside of Marxism, no school of thought in post-war France has enjoyed such unquestioned acceptance ["effet d'évidence"] as that of Heidegger; whose ontology, moreover, culminates in "a methodical *deconstruction* of metaphysics as such.")[1] I regard such insinuations as prejudicial and unfounded. They proceed by an unfathomable logic of theoretical contagion, a type of guilt by association, which knowingly undermines all attempts at intellectual honesty and fair play. Were it the case that all species of thought that have come into contact with one form or another of Heideggerianism were so tainted—for example, the philosophies of Arendt, Gadamer, Marcuse, Merleau-Ponty, Sartre, and so many others —the legacy of twentieth-century thought would be greatly impoverished.

Derrida feared that, in the aftermath of Farias' book and the sensational controversy it had unleashed, deconstruction would be unceremoniously dragged into the fray. It was this fear, it seems, that compelled him to make an unambiguous public statement on the flamboyant indictment of Heidegger's work purveyed by Farias and others. (In the interview, Derrida's characterization of Farias' scholarship is far from charitable. As he observes at one point: "The reading that is proposed, if there is one, remains insufficient and contestable, at times with such crudeness that one wonders if the investigator has read Heidegger for more than an hour.")

Then, to compound Derrida's sense of embattlement, there occurred a few months later the "de Man affair," first triggered by a front-page *New York Times* article of December 1, 1987 ("Yale Scholar's Articles Found in Pro-Nazi Paper"), which exposed the most articulate North American advocate of deconstruction as a collaborator in Nazi-occupied Belgium during World War II.[2] The mass of pseudo-evidence against deconstruction seemed to be mounting. I say "pseudo-evidence" insofar as here, too, one must admit that the idea that a school of thought (if deconstruction is indeed that) could be permanently compromised by the youthful political misdeeds of one of its adherents—however heinous these may have been—is intellectually groundless.

I think that the foregoing account of "deconstruction besieged"—an account that will be readily familiar to many—forms the indispensable background or subtext of Derrida's discomfort with the appearance of

"Philosophers' Hell" in English. But when exaggerated or carried to extremes, a siege mentality can impair good judgment and lead one to overreact. It can induce one to divide the world into friends and enemies; in the case at hand, into friends and enemies of deconstruction. Perhaps this situation to a certain extent accounts for Derrida's recent fascination with the doctrines of the German political philosopher Carl Schmitt.[3]

But this Schmittian leitmotif—that all authentic politics is predicated on the "friend-enemy" distinction—also has its consequences and perils. Are our friends those who merely agree with us on every occasion? Are they those who tell us solely what we would like to hear? If that were the case, then we would, ironically, stand to learn little from our friends. They would be little more than an obedient troop of sycophants and flatterers. Conversely, would our enemies then be those who disagree with us, who fail to tell us what we want to hear? If so, then among our enemies would be many men and women of good will from whom we stand to learn much; men and women of different persuasions than ours perhaps, but who, by virtue of this difference, are capable of teaching us much about the parochialism and limitations of our own point of view.

Such insights of course are highly speculative. But throughout all the confusion concerning rights, permissions, and authorship, there remains one especially troubling, paradoxical fact about this "affair within an affair": by threatening legal action over the republication of "Philosophers' Hell," Derrida has in effect suppressed the English translation/publication of his own text. De facto, he has engaged in an act of self-censorship. Is there beneath the surface more than meets the eye to such an act?

I suspect there is. One cannot help but interpret Derrida's conduct—at least in part—as an act of self-criticism; that is, as an attempt to mitigate and distance himself from a standpoint that he himself in retrospect views as problematic: namely, a quasi-exoneration of Heidegger's philosophically overdetermined commitment to National Socialism.

For in the interview under dispute, following his cursory dismissal of Farias (a dismissal one would be hard pressed to refute), Derrida proceeds in a classically deconstructionist mode. He attempts to "overturn" and "reinscribe" an inherited "binary opposition": in the case at hand, the binary opposition between Nazism and non-Nazism. There is, to be sure, nothing illegitimate about such a procedure. For example, we now realize that without a certain measure of complacency-cum-complicity on the part of the Western powers, Hitler would never have been able to bring off his stunning foreign policy successes of the years 1936–38—from the remilitarization of the Rhineland, to the *Anschluss* with Austria, to the invasion of Czechoslovakia. After this point, the European conflagration—which cost, according to some estimates, as many as 70,000,000 lives—became a foregone conclusion.

But what is especially troubling about Derrida's text (and one might make the same observations about his book on the subject, *Of Spirit: Heidegger and the Question*) is that the "foundational" deconstructive gesture of overturning and reinscription ends up by threatening to efface many of the essential differences between Nazism and non-Nazism. As a result, in the case at issue, the specificity and extent of Heidegger's commitment to National Socialism is severely relativized.

To take only one of the most egregious examples: Derrida seeks to compare and equate Heidegger's inaugural lecture as National Socialist rector of Freiburg University with kindred discourses on the crisis of the European spirit by Edmund Husserl and Paul Valéry. But whereas Heidegger perversely equates this recovery of spirit with "the will of the German Volk," "the forces of soil and blood," and, more generally, a Storm Trooper mentality of *Sturm und Kampf*, there is nothing remotely analogous in the texts by Valéry and Husserl.[4]

In *Of Spirit* Derrida points out that Husserl, in a 1935 lecture on "Philosophy and the Crisis of European Humanity," observes that certain peoples—Eskimos, Indians, and Gypsies—may well fall outside the spiritual orbit of Europe.[5] Husserl's remarks read as follows:

We pose the question: How is the spiritual shape of Europe to be characterized? Thus we refer to Europe not as it is understood geographically, as on a map, as if thereby the group of people who live together in this territory would define European humanity. In the spiritual sense the English Dominions, the United States, etc., clearly belong to Europe, whereas the Eskimos or Indians presented as curiosities at fairs, or the Gypsies, who constantly wander about Europe, do not. Here the title "Europe" clearly refers to the unity of a spiritual life, activity, creativity, with all its ends, interests, cares, and endeavors, with its products of purposeful activity, institutions, organizations.

In a post-colonial era, we have certainly become more sensitized to the potentials for exclusion contained in Husserl's remarks. Nevertheless, when taken at face value, they possess an incontestable descriptive-empirical cogency. To admit less, to refuse to acknowledge that peoples cannot be described geographically but that instead one must heed above all their various cultural orientations and specificities (as Husserl implies in the context at hand), would be equally one-sided and misleading. Derrida, conversely, seeks to interpret Husserl's characterization as exemplary of the discourse of Euro-imperialism *simpliciter.* Hence, after having first "overturned" the discourses of Husserl and Heidegger— both of which take as their point of departure the European spiritual crisis of the inter-war period—Derrida thereby seeks to "remark" or "reinscribe" them by alleging that, on the basis of their mutual preoccupations with "spirit," they possess an essential element of unsavory commonality. Both discourses are criticized for their logocentric fixation on "spirit." In both cases, Derrida alleges, it is the metaphysical, teleological excesses of this discourse that subtend the racist-imperialist political excesses that follow in practice.[6] But in the end this extremely narrow and arbitrary fixation on the figure of "spirit" in the discourses of the two thinkers—a move Derrida *is forced to make*; for as an "anti-logocentric" thinker, he must trace back the follies of humanity a priori to specific *metaphysical* failings and shortcomings—ends up confusing more than it clarifies.

In stark contrast to the case of Heidegger's Rectoral Address, Husserl ties his invocation of spirit to no specific political program. The dissimilarities in content, tenor, and vocabulary of the two discourses are so far at odds that they are in truth incommensurable. One is an unexceptionable (if in retrospect naive) plea for humanistic renewal. The only hope for a reinvigoration of a European culture, which is on the verge of being devoured by totalitarian "isms," argues Husserl in *The Crisis,* lies in a revitalization of the rational spirit of the Greek tradition. The other discourse, that of Heidegger, concludes with a cynical appeal to the German Volk to "fulfill its historical mission." Historically, we know where such appeals led. For his actions and words, Heidegger was tried and convicted after the war by a university denazification commission for political crimes committed in office; specifically, for having, "in the fateful year of 1933, consciously placed the great prestige of his scholarly reputation . . . in the service of the National Socialist Revolution, and thereby [making] an essential contribution to the legitimation of this revolution in the eyes of educated Germans."[7] His Rectoral Address, "The Self-Assertion of the German University," is one of the tracts that the commission found particularly objectionable (specifically, Heidegger's frequent allusions to the *Füherprinzip* and his appeals to the imperatives of military and labor service). Thus Derrida's comparison between the two men takes on an almost macabre aspect now that we know that Husserl—Heidegger's teacher and predecessor at Freiburg— is alleged to have endured persecution at the hands of his former student in his new capacity as university "Rector-Führer."[8] As one scholar has recently discussed the relative merits of their respective inter-war political positions: "Husserl's rejection of National Socialism, weak as it unfortunately was, shines like a beacon in comparison with the more typical philosophical effort to embrace, or at least to cooperate with, Hitler's movement, above all by Martin Heidegger."[9]

I have chosen to examine Derrida's highly selective reading of the "Heidegger controversy" at some length because I find it symptomatic of certain conceptual problems that may be characteristic of deconstruction in general.[10] And as I've already indicated, the problems raised by this interpretation—specifically, the risk of leveling important distinctions between Nazism and non-Nazism—might also account for Derrida's reluctance to see the text more widely "disseminated."[11]

In the interview under dispute, "Philosophers' Hell," Derrida's main interpretive strategy is to show that Heidegger's enthusiasm for Nazism is predicated on a discourse on spirit that he shares with a host of other contemporary European intellectuals. The typically Euro-American, "liberal" attempt to separate the philosophical rudiments of Nazism from anti-Nazism, therefore, will not wash, he wishes to suggest. Liberalism, too—or, more precisely, its philosophical underpinnings—is also fully implicated, according to this deconstructive reading, in the catastrophe that has transpired. Thus, alleges Derrida, Heidegger's commitment to National Socialism is specifically predicated on a "voluntarist" and "metaphysical" frame of reference. It is of a piece with the discourse of Western metaphysics and its logocentric reign. As Derrida observes, in the Rectoral Address, "[Heidegger] engages in a voluntarist and metaphysical discourse that he will subsequently view with suspicion. To this extent at least, by celebrating the freedom of spirit, its glorification resembles other European discourses (spiritualist, religious, humanist) that people generally consider opposed to Nazism. A complex and unstable skein that I try to unravel by recognizing the threads shared by Nazism and non-Nazism . . . " He goes on to summarize the essence of his interpretive demarche in the following passage:

> Nazism would never have been able to develop without the variegated yet decisive complicity of other countries, "democratic" states, universities, and religious institutions. Across this European network this hymn to the freedom of spirit—which is at least consonant with Heidegger's, precisely in the case of the Rectoral Address and in other analogous texts—always wells up and arises. I attempt [in *De l'esprit*] to recapture the law of commonality, terribly contaminating, of these exchanges, shared perspectives, reciprocal translations.

The comparison with Husserl's lecture on "The Crisis of the European Spirit," which we have already surveyed, is a classical instance of such "commonality."

But Derrida gets most of this wrong; in fact, terribly and horrendously wrong. The fateful submission to Hitler at Munich in 1938 (to take the most infamous moment of democratic capitulation) may have been an expression of weakness (more likely war-weariness) on the part of the Western democracies, but in no way may it be construed as a manifestation, however contorted, of covert pro-fascist sentiment by the governments in question. That is to say, such "complicity," if we can speak of it as such, was hardly a matter of a *shared metaphysical paradigm* (such as "voluntarism"), of "spiritual affinities," or even of a common political philosophy. It was instead a fatal miscalculation based on political expediency and hardly a matter of ideology, as Derrida implies. The fascist program, whose ideological origins date from the counter-revolutionary doctrines of the early nineteenth century (Bonald, de Maistre, etc.), was above all bent on forcibly extirpating the liberal-democratic heritage of the French Revolution.[12] As Joseph Goebbels stated triumphantly and unambiguously a few months after Hitler's 1933 seizure of power: "The year 1789 is hereby eradicated from history." What Derrida would have us believe about the fatal ideological entwinement of democracy and fascism serves mostly to blur and confuse historical distinctions that are crucial for all subsequent attempts to come to terms with the poisonous cultural legacy of political illiberalism, in Europe and elsewhere. As Karl Dietrich Bracher pointedly reminds us: "The intellectual forerunners on whom National Socialism drew in the development of its Weltanschauung were primarily ideologists fervently opposed to the ideas of democratic revolution, human rights, freedom, and equality."[13]

But where Derrida's reading really goes awry is in its interpretation of Heidegger. He contends that it is a combination of "metaphysics" and "voluntarism"—the twin sins of logocentrism, as it were—that seduces the Freiburg sage into sporting Nazi insignia and a brown uniform in 1933. I would like to claim that the *reverse* is true: insofar as Heidegger remained wedded to the discourse of humanism and to the heritage of Western metaphysics (or "first philosopohy") as he understood it, he was *prevented* from identifying wholesale with Nazi ideology as it was historically constituted—that is, in the first instance as a discourse of biology and race. One might even say that it was his conscience as a philosopher in the Socratic tradition that resulted in the frequent tensions that emerged between Heidegger and the party hierarchy, culminating in the charge (which, in retrospect, redounds to Heidegger's credit) that Heidegger was engaged in cultivating a type of "Privat-Nationalsozialismus"—a "private National Socialism," which, at key points, remained at odds with party orthodoxy.

To be sure, at the beginning, Heidegger tried to reconcile a philosophical "discourse on spirit" with the demands of the German Revolution, but the result was a miscarriage, a monstrosity, about whose failure neither side had many illusions. It was far less "spirit" or "metaphysics" that induced Heidegger's infamous political conversion of 1933 than the anti-modernist, conservative revolutionary worldview he had embraced as far back as *Being and Time* (the critique of "everydayness," the "They," "idle talk," and so forth; coupled with an exaltation of "destiny," "decisiveness," "authenticity," and—on at least one occasion —the "Volk"). It was that very discourse on spirit, therefore, that allowed him to preserve an element of philosophical autonomy vis-à-vis the brutish apostles of racial-biological thinking with whom he had entered into a temporary, ill-fated, ignominious alliance.

That we still read Heidegger today—and read him with profit—we may attribute to his singular contributions to a discourse on spirit that remains essentially and inalienably part of our tradition. To be sure, it is a far from uncontested tradition. But its strength may be found in that very capacity for self-contestation which is the hallmark of a living tradition—that is, a tradition that is inimical to dogmatic authority and rigid convention.

Inherited distinctions and so-called binary oppositions must be called into question, but not, one would hope, at the cost of blurring essential differences. In Derrida's desire to reconstruct the binary opposition between Nazism and non-Nazism, in his unwillingness to specify the essential differences between them, one is reminded of Heidegger's own astoundingly myopic conviction that, as far as the destiny of Europe was concerned, the outcome of World War II failed to change anything "essential." "Today," he observes, writing in 1945, "everything stands under this reality [of the will to power] whether it is called communism or fascism or world democracy."[14] "Essentially"—that is, when viewed from Heidegger's own ethereal philosophical standpoint of the "history of Being"—all contemporary political forms are sub-species of "European nihilism," as originally diagnosed by Nietzsche, Spengler, Ernst Jünger, and a host of other German "critics of civilization" who were in search of a "third way" (that is, non-Western in the sense of France and England, and non-Eastern in the sense of Bolshevist Russia). But we now know—and can state unequivocally—that the most important political event of post-war Europe has been the thoroughgoing de-legitimation of the twin forms of totalitarian rule, fascism and communism. It is only in the aftermath of their virtual elimination that one can go about building a democracy of substance.

These are some of the "essential" conclusions (in a non-Heideggerian sense) one might draw from reading the Heidegger controversy through the prism of recent European history and political theory. That Derrida has chosen to remain on the margins of this discussion—as one sees by his apologetic and relativizing treatment of Heidegger's ties to Nazism—is, I believe, far from accidental. It raises the question of deconstruction's adequacy as a heuristic for guiding our judgments in the ethico-political realm. For there are some binary oppositions that need to be strengthened, rather than "deconstructed" and, hence, relativized. The opposition between Nazism and non-Nazism is perhaps one of them.[15]

Notes

1. See Christian Jambet, "Préface" to Victor Farias, *Heidegger et le Nazisme* (Lagrasse: Editions Verdier, 1987), p. 14. My own criticisms of Farias' book are elaborated in the essay "French Heidegger Wars," with which this volume concludes.

2. De Man's collaborationist misdeeds were subsequently discussed by the historian Jon Wiener (following the researches of the Belgian scholar Ortwin de Graef) in the January 9, 1988, issue of *The Nation*. Wiener's articles on the affair have been reprinted in *Professors, Politics and Pop* (London: Verso, 1991). Many of de Man's collaborationist articles have been collected in Paul de Man, *Wartime Journalism, 1939–1943* (Lincoln: University of Nebraska, 1988). See also the anthology of commentaries on the De Man affair, *Responses: On Paul de Man's Wartime Journalism*, ed. W. Hamacher et al. (Lincoln: University of Nebraska, 1989), which contains Derrida's essay, "Like the Sound of the Sea Deep within a Shell: Paul de Man's War." See also Derrida's *Mémoires of Paul de Man* (New York: Columbia University Press, 1986). One may further consult David Lehman's, *Signs of the Times: Deconstruction and the Fall of Paul de Man* (New York: Poseidon Press, 1991). Although Lehman's book may be useful from a documentary standpoint, his understanding of deconstruction qua method is at times so woefully hackneyed and caricatural as to disqualify it as a reliable guide to the important theoretical issues that have surfaced in the dispute.

3. See Derrida, "The Politics of Friendship," *The Journal of Philosophy* 85 (1988): 632–644. Schmitt defined the capacity to distinguish between friend and enemy (*Freund-Feind*) as the basis of authentic politics in *The Concept of the Political* (1927); English translation by George Schwab, (New Brunswick: Rutgers, 1976). For more on Schmitt see Richard Wolin, "Carl Schmitt, Political Existentialism, and the Total State," in Wolin, *The Terms of Cultural Criticism: The Frankfurt School, Existentialism, Poststructuralism* (New York: Columbia, 1992). See also Wolin, "Carl Schmitt, the Conservative Revolutionary Habitus, and the Aesthetics of Horror," *Political Theory* (20) 3, (August 1992):424–447.

4. Heidegger's Rectoral Address, "The Self-Assertion of the German University," is reprinted on pages 29–39 of this book. I discuss this text at some length in *The Politics of Being: The Political Thought of Martin Heidegger* (New York: Columbia University Press, 1990), pp. 85–95. The texts discussed by Derrida are Edmund Husserl, *The Crisis of the European Sciences and Transcendental Phenomenology*, translated by David Carr (Evanston: Northwestern, 1970) and Paul Valéry, *Reflections on the World Today*, translated by Francis Scarfe (London: Thames and Hudson, 1951) (the original French text, "The Crisis of Spirit," was a lecture given by Valéry in 1919). See Derrida's discussion of both in *De l'esprit: Heidegger et la question* (Paris: Galilée, 1987), pp. 94–100 (English translation published by University of Chicago Press, 1990).

5. See Husserl, "Philosophy and the Crisis of European Humanity," appendix 1 to *The Crisis*, p. 273.

6. Derrida, *De l'esprit, passim*; especially pp. 85–95.

7. See the discussion of this text in Wolin, *The Politics of Being*, pp. 6–8.

8. See the discussion of the relationship between Husserl and Heidegger in Hugo Ott, *Martin Heidegger: Unterwegs zu seiner Biographie* (Frankfurt: Campus, 1988), especially pp. 167–179. (Why Ott's important work on Heidegger remains as yet untranslated into English remains a mystery.) See also Husserl's letter to Dietrich Mahnke of May 4, 1933, in which he complains of Heidegger's growing anti-Semitism. The letter is reproduced in Bernd Martin, *Martin Heidegger und das dritte Reich* (Darmstadt: Wissenschaftliche Buchgesellschaft, 1989), pp. 148–149.

9. Tom Rockmore, *Heidegger's Nazism and Philosophy* (Berkeley: University of California, 1992), p. 33.

10. I discuss these problems at greater length in "The House that Jacques Built: Deconstruction and Strong Evaluation," in *The Terms of Cultural Criticism*, pp. 194–217 (see note 3).

11. It may be of interest to note that the interview failed to appear in the overseas edition of the November 6–12 issue of *Le Nouvel Observateur*. It would therefore be unavailable in almost all North American libraries. There is, however, a German translation of the text. It appears in Jürg Altwegg, *Die Heidegger Kontroverse* (Frankfurt: Athenäum, 1988), pp. 83–93, under the subtitle "Die Hölle der Philosophie."

12. See Zeev Sternhell, *Antisemitism and the Right in France* (Jerusalem: Shahar Library, Institute of Contemporary Jewry, 1988) and Isaiah Berlin, "Joseph de Maistre and the Origins of Fascism," in *The Crooked Timber of Humanity* (New York: Knopf, 1991).

13. Karl Dietrich Bracher, *The German Dictatorship*, translated by Jean Steinberg, introduction by Peter Gay (Fort Worth: Holt, Rinehart, 1970), p. 10.

14. Heidegger, *Die Selbstbehauptung der deutschen Universität/Das Rektorat 1933–34* (Frankfurt: Klostermann, 1983), p. 25. See my discussion of this passage in *The Politics of Being*, pp. 143–147.

15. Here, I do not wish in the least to preclude the necessity of examining various pseudo-oppositions to National Socialism, which may parade under the banner of "non-Nazism." The German Communist Party conviction in the pre–Popular Front era that its main opponents were to be found on the *left* (hence, the characterization of the Social Democrats as "social fascists"), and the failure of so many powers in Europe and North America (both secular and ecclesiastical) to oppose Hitler's persecution of the Jews, are only two such instances. My specific concern about the methods of deconstruction in the instance at hand is that, while highlighting the elements of commonality between Nazism and non-Nazism, it tends—to an extreme—to elide the differences—as I think the comparison between Husserl and Heidegger well illustrates.

THE HEIDEGGER CONTROVERSY
A Critical Reader

INTRODUCTION

"OVER THE LINE":
Reflections on Heidegger and
National Socialism

Richard Wolin

Given the significant attachment of the philosopher to the mood and intellectual habitus of National Socialism, it would be inappropriate to criticize or exonerate his political decision in isolation from the very principles of Heideggerian philosophy itself. It is not Heidegger, who, in opting for Hitler, "misunderstood himself"; instead, those who cannot understand why he acted this way have failed to comprehend him. A Swiss lecturer regretted that Heidegger consented to compromise himself with daily affairs, as if a philosophy that explains Being from the standpoint of time and the everyday would not stand in relation to the daily affairs in which it makes its influence felt and originates. The possibility of a Heideggerian political philosophy was not born as a result of a regrettable miscue, but from the very conception of existence that simultaneously combats and absorbs the "spirit of the age."

Karl Löwith, "The Political Implications of
Heidegger's Existentialism"

I

In his marvelously thorough *New York Review of Books* essay on "Heidegger and the Nazis," Thomas Sheehan concludes by observing: "One would do well to read nothing of Heidegger's any more without raising political questions. . . . [One] must re-read his works—particularly but not exclusively those from 1933 on—with strict attention to the political movement with which Heidegger himself chose to link his ideas. To do less than that is, I believe, finally not to understand him at all."[1] Yet, ten years earlier, Sheehan had argued for a very different position: that the relationship between Heidegger's political commitment to Nazism and his philosophy itself was negligible; and that in any event, Heidegger's partisanship for National Socialism had been a short-lived affair, a regrettable, momentary *lapsus,* that was in no way a sincere expression of the philosopher's own innermost conviction. What was it that induced Sheehan to arrive at such a radical volte-face?

Above all, since the publication of the Heidegger biographies of Farias and Ott, the typical rationalizations that had been invoked in the past to minimize the extent of Heidegger's commitment to the Nazi cause have become wholly untenable. We now know that Heidegger's alliance with Nazism, far from being a temporary marriage of convenience, was grandiose and profound: at least for a short period of time, Heidegger labored under the delusion that he could play the role of "philosopher king" to Hitler's *Führerstaat*—which, to many, has suggested parallels with Plato's ill-fated venture with the tyrant Dionysius at Syracuse.[2] As the philosopher Otto Pöggeler has phrased it, Heidegger sought *"den Führer führen"*—"to lead the leader," Adolf Hitler, along the proper course so that the "National Revolution" might fulfill its appointed metaphysical destiny.[3] For Heidegger believed that in its early manifestations, National Socialism possessed the capacity to initiate a great spiritual renewal of German Dasein. In it, he saw a potential counter-movement to the fate of "European nihilism," of perpetual spiritual decline, as it had been diagnosed by the leading German "conservative revolutionary" critics of his generation—Oswald Spengler, Ludwig Klages, and Ernst Jünger; thinkers who in essence were merely following the powerful critique of Western modernity that had been outlined some forty years earlier by Friedrich Nietzsche.

To be sure, it appears that Heidegger's understanding of National Socialism had little in common with the ideology of genocidal imperialism via which the movement has left its gruesome imprint on twentieth-century history. But we know that he was sufficiently convinced of National Socialism's "inner truth and greatness"[4] to have acquired the reputation of a zealous propagandist on behalf of the new regime in its initial stages. And thus, following his acceptance of the rectorship at the University of Freiburg in May 1933, Heidegger traveled around Germany delivering speeches in favor of Hitler's policies. He also proved an enthusiastic supporter of *Gleichschaltung* legislation (the so-called "Law for Reconstituting the Civil Service"), which barred Jews and other undesirables from Germany's civil service, replacing them instead with Party members. Lastly, it should be kept in mind that Heidegger was not merely a Nazi sympathizer, but was in fact found guilty of political crimes by a (favorably disposed) university peer review committee immediately following the war. As a result, he was banned from university life for close to five years. These crimes included: denouncing political undesirables to the Nazi authorities, inciting students against "reactionary" (i.e., non-Nazi) professors, and enthusiastically transforming the university along the lines of the Nazi "leadership principle" or "*Führer-prinzip.*"[5]

In December 1945, the aforementioned peer review committee contacted the philosopher Karl Jaspers for an evaluation of Heidegger's activities and character. Among Jaspers' most telling observations, one finds the following remarks:

Heidegger is a significant potency, not through the content of a philosophical world-view, but in the manipulation of speculative tools. He has a philosophical aptitude whose perceptions are interesting; although, in my opinion, he is extraordinarily uncritical and stands at a remove from true science [*der eigentlichen Wissenschaft fern steht*]. He often proceeds as if he combined the seriousness of nihilism with the mystagogy of a magician. In the torrent of his language he is occasionally able, in a clandestine and remarkable way, to strike the core of philosophical thought. In this regard he is, as far as I can see, perhaps unique among contemporary German philosophers.

It is absolutely necessary that those who helped place National Socialism in the saddle be called to account. Heidegger is among the few professors to have done that. . . . In our situation [i.e., after the war] the education of youth must be handled with the greatest responsibility. . . . Heidegger's manner of thinking, which to me seems in its essence unfree, dictatorial, and incapable of communication [*communikationslos*], would today be disastrous in its pedagogical effects. . . . Heidegger certainly did not see through all the real powers and goals of the National Socialist leaders. . . . But his manner of speaking and his actions have a certain affinity with National Socialist characteristics, which makes his error comprehensible.[6]

And thus, in view of the extent and profundity of Heidegger's commitment to the National Socialist revolution, the question inevitably arises: to what extent is Heidegger's philosophy implicated in his ignominious life-choice of the early 1930s? It is presumably on the basis of such considerations that Jaspers, in the continuation of the remarks cited, recommends to university officials that Heidegger be suspended

3

from the faculty for a period of several years after the war; and that Thomas Sheehan urges a careful rereading of Heidegger's philosophical texts in light of his political beliefs. And it is undoubtedly as a result of a kindred set of concerns that Karl Löwith, in our opening citation, suggests that "it would be inappropriate to criticize or exonerate [Heidegger's] political decision in isolation from the very principles of Heideggerian philosophy itself."

Are, however, the preceding admonitions hermeneutically justifiable? For don't such interpretive practices risk imputing to Heidegger's philosophical doctrines a political content that only comes into view ex post? Isn't there, moreover, an even more serious risk at issue, one against which Heidegger's French defenders have stridently warned: the risk that we would judge the contributions of an undeniably great thinker exclusively on the basis of political motifs that are, strictly speaking, "extrinsic to thought"? We would thereby succumb to the practice of convicting the philosophy on the basis of a type of spurious "guilt by association."

It would be dishonest to deny the cogency of the foregoing caveats. And thus, it should be clearly acknowledged that to suggest that Heidegger's philosophy in its entirety would in some way be "disqualified" as a result of his political misdeeds—however egregious these might prove— would be an act of bad faith. For the requirements of intellectual honesty demand that we judge a philosopher in the first instance on the merits of his or her thought.

Yet it is precisely this comforting, artificial dichotomy between "work" and "world-view" that has been increasingly called into question of late in Heidegger's case.[7] For there is undeniable evidence to suggest that Heidegger himself viewed his political commitments in the early 1930s as of a piece with his philosophy; that he considered his "engagement" for National Socialism as a type of a "political actualization" of the "existentials" ("*Existenzialen*") of *Being and Time*: of categories such as "historicity," "destiny," "potentiality-for-Being-a-Self," and so forth. In the philosopher's own mind, his "existential decision" for National Socialism in 1933 signified a decision for authenticity. And thus, in a 1936 conversation with Löwith, Heidegger agrees "without reservation" with the suggestion that "his partisanship for National Socialism lay in the essence of his philosophy."[8] Of course, in keeping with the foregoing caveats, such conclusions should in no way be interpreted to suggest that Nazism would somehow constitute the necessary political corollary of a work like *Being and Time*. However, that in the mind of its author, its conceptual framework proved readily compatible with perhaps the greatest form of political despotism our century has known suggests the need for considerable critical reflection on the ethico-political substance of Heidegger's 1927 work.

It is in this vein that the philosopher Otto Pöggeler—in a manner that parallels Sheehan's cautionary remarks—has suggested, "Was it not through a definite orientation of his thought that Heidegger fell— and not merely accidentally—into the proximity of National Socialism, without ever truly emerging from this proximity?"[9] Pöggeler thereby implicitly seconds Sheehan's suggestion concerning the imperative necessity of reexamining Heidegger's corpus for those potential intellectual shortfalls that might have precipitated his engagement for Nazism in the early 1930s. However, Pöggeler's remarks also imply the possibility that in his later years Heidegger may have never completely emerged from that "proximity" to National Socialism. But this allegation must stand as an intellectual-philosophical rather than a political judgment. For we know that as of the mid-1930s Heidegger increasingly distanced himself from the realities of Nazism as a contemporary political movement. In his view, the "inner truth and greatness" of its historical potential (as an expression of "the encounter between planetary technology and modern man")[10] was perverted by usurpers and pretenders; for example, by those proponents of racial-biological National Socialism such as Ernst Krieck and Alfred Bäumler, who had, at Heidegger's expense, gained control of the "philosophical direction" of the movement. Heidegger explains the ideological basis for his support of National Socialism as follows:

I ... believed that the movement could be spiritually directed onto other paths and ... felt such an attempt could be combined with the social and overall political tendencies of the movement. I believed that Hitler, after he assumed responsibility for the *whole* Volk in 1933, would grow beyond the party and its doctrine and everything would come together, through a renovation and a rallying, in an assumption of Western responsibility. This belief proved erroneous, as I recognized from the events of June 30, 1934.[11]

Yet, although Heidegger was extremely critical of "historically exist-ing" National Socialism (his criticisms become quite explicit at times in his lectures of the late 1930s and early 1940s), he seems never to have abandoned his earlier conviction that the dawn of the movement itself— or the "National Awakening," as it was referred to among its supporters —contained seeds of true greatness. It is thus fairly clear that, to the end of his days, Heidegger never abandoned his faith in the movement's authentic historical potential, its "inner truth and greatness." Thus, in his 1945 apologia written for a university denazification commission, Heidegger, instead of critically distancing himself from his earlier beliefs, merely reaffirms his original pro-Nazi convictions: "I saw in the move-ment that had just come to power [in 1933] the possibility of a spiritual rallying and renewal of the Volk and a way of finding its western-historical destiny." And when questioned some twenty years later in *Der Spiegel* about the elegy to the "glory and greatness of the [National] Awakening" with which he concluded his 1933 Rectoral Address, Hei-degger can only reply—again, without a modicum of contrition—"Yes, I was convinced of that."[12] His refusal to come forth with an unambig-uous public disavowal of his earlier political ties, moreover, has been a source of great irritation and dismay, even among those seeking to defend his legacy.[13] A refusal which lends additional credence to Pögge-ler's suggestion that Heidegger may have "never fully emerged" from his fateful proximity to Germany's National Revolution.

II

Pöggeler's claim that it was through a "definite orientation of his thought that Heidegger fell into the proximity of National Socialism" may well prove an indispensable interpretive key for understanding the philosoph-ical bases of Heidegger's political involvement. His subsequent observa-tion that Heidegger may "have never truly emerged" from that proxim-ity suggests that there might be a much greater measure of continuity between the "early" and "later" Heidegger than is usually admitted. Wherein might this continuity lie? The critical issue may well hinge on a "historicization" of our understanding of Heidegger's philosophy. That is, on an appreciation of the extent to which his philosophy is implicated —almost despite itself—in a set of intellectual presuppositions shared by the German conservative intelligentsia of his era. Certainly the brilliant philosophical demarche that is *Being and Time* is in no way reducible to the aforementioned "historical" elements. And in this respect the contributions Heidegger has made toward recasting the traditional forms of philosophical questioning remain unimpugnable. Yet, if our earlier suggestion that, in the philosopher's own mind, there existed an essential relation between fundamental ontology and (a, to be sure, idealized version of) National Socialism remains cogent, it falls due to identify those aspects of his thinking that led him down the path of this fateful political partisanship.

The essential element of continuity linking the early and the later Heidegger—and that dimension of his thought that gives determinate content and meaning to Pöggeler's suggestive remarks concerning Heidegger's precarious political "proximity"—pertains to Heidegger's critique of modernity. In essence, Heidegger fully subscribes to the critical indictment of the totality of modern life-forms—which are associated with the traits of prosaic and materialistic, bourgeois *Zivilisation*—that has been a mainstay of German conservative *Kulturkritik* since the nineteenth century. This position received its consummate and most intellectually sophisticated articulation in Nietzsche's work. There, a far-reaching critique of modern philosophy, politics, and culture—which are viewed essentially as manifestations of decline—is combined with a nostalgic idealization of the pre-philosophical (i.e., pre-Socratic) Greek polis and the quasi-apocalyptical expectation that a nihilistic Western modernity will soon be supplanted by a new heroic ethos, in which the much vaunted "self-overcoming of nihilism" reaches a point of crystallization.

All three "spheres"—philosophy, politics, and art—suffer from the same affliction: a surfeit of subjectivity. Thus, modern philosophy, since Descartes, has become "epistemology," narrowing the scope and purview of philosophical questioning to *res cogitans* or "thinking substance": the new solipsistic *fundamentum inconcussum* that substitutes for the divine guarantees of scholasticism. Politics has become "liberalism," which means that the standpoint of the self-enclosed, monadic individual has emerged as its absolute point of reference. A greater antithesis to the classical polis, in which the individual good was always subordinated to the good of the whole, could scarcely be imagined.

Finally, modern art, from romanticism to art for art's sake, has assumed a predominantly effete, private, and self-referential character. It has thereby forfeited that monumental quality that once suffused Greek architecture and tragedy, and that was capable of spiritually uniting the polis and its citizens. Or, as Nietzsche himself formulates his indictment of aesthetic modernism with unabashed candor: "*L'art pour l'art*: the virtuoso croaking of shivering frogs, despairing in their swamp."[14]

Heidegger shares this resolutely anti-modernist world-view to an extreme. And if one is sincerely interested in understanding the political implications of his thought, it would be difficult to overemphasize the absolute centrality of this perspective, which served as the ideological prism, as it were, through which he interpreted the political events of the twentieth century. Despite the criticisms that are directed toward Nietzsche in the lectures of 1936–1941, Heidegger never breaks entirely with the fundamental terms of this—in essence, Nietzschean—"conservative revolutionary" critique of modernity. And thus, on one essential methodological point, Heidegger and Nietzsche show themselves to be in complete agreement: in the conviction that the decline of modernity has "progressed" so far that it can no longer be redeemed by the methods of immanent criticism; that is, in the manner of earlier critics of modernity qua "bourgeois society," such as Hegel, Tocqueville, and Marx, who still believed that the value-orientations of this society were capable of redemption from within. Instead, for both Nietzsche and Heidegger, only the categories of "total critique" will suffice to capture the essence of this Fichtean era of "absolute sinfulness."

Thus, Heidegger, while proceeding from a significantly different philosophical orientation, shares with Nietzsche a number of essential value-premises. Among them are the aforementioned glorification of the pre-Platonic polis (Heidegger's emphasis of course falls on pre-Socratic philosophy rather than, as with Nietzsche, on Attic tragedy); and, perhaps most importantly, the conviction that it is art rather than science that indicates the essential path along which an authentic "overcoming" ("*Überwindung*") of modern nihilism must proceed. This explains the seminal role played by the concepts of *poesis* and "poetic dwelling" in Heidegger's later philosophy.[15] Here, too, it would be fruitful to compare Nietzsche's youthful enthusiasm for Greek tragedy and the music of Wagner with Heidegger's parallel enthusiasm for Hölderlin in the *Erläuterungen zu Hölderlins Dichtung (Commentaries on Hölderlin's Poetry)*. According to Heidegger, as Sophocles was to ancient Greece, Hölderlin is to modern Germany. And thus, "the essential disposition [*Grundstimmung*], that is, the truth of the Dasein of a nation [*Volk*], is originally founded by the poet."[16] Or, as Heidegger remarks elsewhere, the poet is the "voice of the Volk."[17]

That Heidegger shares the *Zeitdiagnose* proffered by Nietzsche, according to which European culture is viewed as essentially moribund and nihilistic, accounts for the distinctive ideological tenor of the value judgments he sets forth concerning modern forms of life. Thus, for example, in the *Spiegel* interview, Heidegger summarily dismisses modern literature (*"heutige Literatur"*) as "predominantly destructive," insofar as, in contrast to the poetry of Hölderlin or the art of the Greeks, it lacks grounding in the historical life of a people.[18] Or, as Heidegger observes elsewhere, in a thinly veiled attack against the spirit of "cosmopolitanism": "Does not the flourishing of any genuine work depend upon its roots in a native soil?"[19] Similarly, in the Nietzsche lectures of the late 1930s, while flirting with the Wagnerian ideal of the *"Gesamtkunstwerk"* (the "collective work of art"), he reaffirms his conviction that art must serve as the foundation of the *Volksgemeinschaft*—the Nazi term for the German "National Community":

With reference to the historical position of art, the effort to produce the "collective artwork" [*"Gesamtkunstwerk"*] remains essential. The very name is demonstrative. For one thing, it means that the arts should no longer be realized apart from one another, but that they should be conjoined in *one* work. But beyond such sheer quantitative unification, the artwork should be a celebration of the *Volksgemeinschaft*: it should be *the* religion.[20]

Heidegger emphatically seconded the historian Jacob Burckhardt's opinion that the institution of democracy was responsible for the downfall of the ancient polis. Thus, in *What is Called Thinking* (1954), he approvingly cites Nietzsche's characterization of "modern democracy" as a "degenerate form of the state" (*"Verfallsform des Staats"*).[21] And further, Heidegger summarily dismisses political liberalism, which is "tyrannical insofar as it requires that everybody be left to his own opinion."[22]

His criticism of the inadequacies of modern "science" (in the German sense of *Wissenschaft*) dates from the 1929 Freiburg inaugural lecture, "What is Metaphysics?" and the celebrated debate with Cassirer in Davos, also in 1929, over the legacy of neo-Kantianism. In the former work, Heidegger laments the lack of existential rootedness and unity afflicting the various contemporary sciences: "The scientific fields are still far apart. Their subjects are treated in fundamentally different ways. Today this hodgepodge of disciplines is held together only by the technical organization of the universities and faculties and preserves what meaning it has only through the practical aims of the different branches. The sciences have lost their roots in their essential ground."[23] And in the debate with Cassirer, he risks, in two crucial respects, crossing "over the line" separating "scientific" from "non-scientific" statements; that is, the "line" separating falsifiable from non-falsifiable claims to truth. First, in his proclamation of the equiprimordiality of "truth" and "untruth." Or as Heidegger phrases it: "On the basis of finitude man's Being-in-the-truth is simultaneously a Being-in-the-untruth. *Untruth belongs to the innermost core of Dasein*." Second, in his attempt to link the "question of Being" itself to a specific ideological perspective or, as he calls it, a "determinate world-view": "In what way must a metaphysic of Dasein be initiated?," inquires Heidegger. "Does not a determinate world-view lie at its basis? It is not philosophy's task to provide a world-view; however, to do philosophy [*Philosophieren*] indeed *already presupposes such a world-view*."[24] Over the next few years, as the crisis of the Weimar Republic reached its point of no return, Heidegger will make few efforts to conceal the "determinate world-view" that subtends his own manner of doing philosophy.[25]

There is a direct conceptual lineage between the criticisms of "science" voiced in these "purely philosophical" writings of the late 1920s and the dubious political positions Heidegger will espouse four years hence in the 1933 Rectoral Address—where he openly mocks the existence of the "much-ballyhooed 'academic freedom'" and redefines the "will to science" (*"Wille zur Wissenschaft"*) as "a will to the historical-spiritual mission of the German *Volk* that knows itself in its State."[26] In dicta such as these, moreover, Heidegger is only a hair's breadth removed from the militant appeals for "politicized science" that swept Nazi Germany during these years. For Heidegger, "mere intelligence is a semblance of spirit, masking its absence."[27] And thus, the "sham-culture" ("*Scheinkultur*") of Western *Zivilisation* will be overcome only if the "spiritual world" of the Volk is grounded in "the deepest preservation of the forces of soil and blood."[28] Such conclusions derive from an all-too-familiar rejection of the spirit of modernity, which fosters values that are "cosmopolitan" and, as such, alien to the "forces of soil and blood" that Heidegger—anachronistically—views as a precondition for historical greatness.

It is this critique of "science" and "intelligence" as part of the "sham-culture" of modernity that provides the crucial moment of intellectual continuity between Heidegger's philosophical writings of the late 1920s and his pro-Nazi texts of the early 1930s. And, in retrospect, it is perhaps this dimension of his thought that strikes one as most problematic—yet highly symptomatic. For the critique of "science" is perfectly indicative of the way in which "philosophy" and "ideology" become inextricably commingled in Heidegger's post-1927 thinking. Moreover, a great danger haunts this immoderate rejection of all inherited "Wissenschaft"; one to which we have already alluded and that will beset the entirety of his subsequent philosophical oeuvre: the danger that Heidegger's own philosophizing will "cross the line" separating warranted philosophical assertion from unverifiable, ex cathedra pronouncements. More and more, especially in the later writings, Heidegger's philosophical comportment resembles that of a prophet who views himself as standing in a position of immediate access to Being. Increasingly, his discourse threatens to make its stand beyond the realm of philosophical statements that are capable of being discursively redeemed. In celebrating the ineffability of Being (or, according to Heidegger's quasi-theological answer to the *Seinsfrage* in the 1946 "Letter on Humanism": "Yet Being—what is Being? It is *It* itself"),[29] Heidegger risks promoting an intellectual method and style whose distinguishing feature is its "non-falsifiability." Nor is the credibility of his standpoint furthered by claims such as the following: "Thinking begins only when we have come to know that reason, glorified for centuries, is the most stiff-necked adversary of thought."[30] And thus, when faced with philosophical disquisitions that claim a privileged relation vis-à-vis the mysterious destinings of *Seinsgeschick,* the claims of critical philosophy—that is, of a post-Kantian thought that is capable of reflecting in earnest on its own foundations—must go by the board.

Heidegger's thinking, therefore, appears to be afflicted by a twofold debility: a disdain of traditional methods of philosophical argumentation, which emphasize the non-esoteric, generalizable character of philosophical contents and judgments; and an "empirical deficit," which follows from his rejection of the individual sciences. Inevitably, the question must arise: did not a certain metaphysical hubris, stemming in part from a philosophically conditioned neglect of empirical findings— for example, the disciplines of history and the social sciences—adversely affect the philosopher's capacity for political discernment? For when the trajectory of concrete historical life is restyled according to the logic of a self-positing "history of Being," whose ethereal "sendings" ("*Schickungen*") seem impervious to counterfactual instances and arguments, political judgment is potentially deprived of any intersubjectively verifiable basis or touchstone.

In this regard, Karl Löwith had contributed the following sober reflections on Heidegger's methodological afflictions:

Philosophical reflection on the whole of what exists in nature, which is the world . . . cannot merely "pass science by" without falling into the void. It is easily said, and it would be a relief, if philosophical thought were to dwell beyond what is provable and refutable; if, however, the realm of [Heideggerian] "essential thinking" were to surpass all proof and refutation, then philosophy would have to do neither with truth nor with probability, but rather with uncontrollable claims and allegations.[31]

III

It is clear that as of the early 1930s, Heidegger sought to immerse the "question of Being" in the vortex of contemporary political events. Thus, turning to the 1935 *Introduction to Metaphysics*—the same text in which we find the aforementioned eulogy to the "inner truth and greatness of National Socialism"—Heidegger proffers his own "metaphysical" ("*seinsgeschichtlich*") *Zeitdiagnose:*

The spiritual decline of the earth is so far advanced that the nations are in danger of losing the last bit of spiritual energy that makes it possible to see the decline (taken in relation to the history of "Being"), and to appraise it as such. This simple observation has nothing to do with *Kulturpessimismus,* and of course it has nothing to do with any sort of optimism either; for the darkening of the world, the flight of the gods, the destruction of the earth, the transformation of men into a mass, the hatred and suspicion of everything free and creative, have assumed such proportions throughout the earth that such childish categories as pessimism and optimism have long since become absurd.

We are caught in a pincers. Situated in the center, our *Volk* incurs the severest pressure. It is the *Volk* with the most neighbors and hence the most endangered. With all this, it is the most metaphysical of nations. . . . All this implies that this *Volk,* as a historical *Volk,* must move itself and thereby the history of the West beyond the center of their future "happening" and into the primordial realm of the powers of Being. If the great decision regarding Europe is not to bring annihilation, that decision must be made in terms of the new spiritual energies unfolding historically from out of the middle.[32]

The foregoing historical commentary in no way represents an extraneous, non-philosophical digression from the primary ontologico-metaphysical question at issue. In point of fact, Heidegger's lectures and texts of the 1930s and 1940s abound with kindred sweeping historico-philosophical judgments. For it is clear that, for Heidegger, our very capacity to pose the *Seinsfrage* itself is integrally tied to our ability to overcome the contemporary historical crisis—"the darkening of the world, the flight of the gods, the destruction of the earth, the transformation of men into a mass"; and in this overcoming, history and politics will undeniably play a primary role. For if the "clearing" ("*Lichtung*") that is a prerequisite for the emergence of Being is a *temporal* clearing, this means that the "presencing" of Being is essentially a historical presencing—a *Seinsgeschichte.* And in this sense, as Heidegger makes undeniably clear in the remarks just cited, the "question of Being" is, according to its essence, a historical question. This is a conviction that follows directly from one of the most central (anti-Platonic) insights of *Being and Time*: that Being's coming to presence is inexorably a temporal coming to presence. Yet this is only another way of saying that the emergence (or self-concealment) of Being is essentially a question of historicity. For Heidegger, too, "readiness is all"; that is, all depends on our readiness to heed the call of Being. However, our receptivity to Being is ineluctably tied to our current state of historical-ontological preparedness. When Heidegger, a few paragraphs after the preceding citation, observes: "That is why we have related the question of Being to the destiny of Europe, where the destiny of the earth is being decided— while our own [i.e., Germany's] historic Dasein proves to be the center for Europe itself"[33]—he betrays unambiguously the historical-ontological rationale behind his partisanship for what he will refer to as "Western-Germanic historical Dasein."[34]

Astonishingly, references to the "historical singularity of National Socialism" persist as late as 1942.[35] And that "singularity," moreover, is in no way viewed negatively, that is, as a "regression" vis-à-vis historically received principles of justice, morality, and truth. Instead, it points to National Socialism's "inner truth and greatness," which Germany and the Germans proved too weak to realize. To the bitter end, Heidegger holds out in his belief that the "overcoming of nihilism was announced in the poetic thinking and singing of the Germans."[36] Or as he opines in 1943: "The planet is in flames. The essence of man is out of joint. Only from the Germans can there come a world-historical reflection—if, that is, they find and preserve their 'Germanness' ['*das Deutsche*']."[37] Thus, according to Heidegger's contorted, neo-ontological reading of contemporary history, Germany still represents the "saving power" of Western humanity—instead of its scourge. In "Overcoming Metaphysics," Nazism, rather than signifying a "totalitarian deformation" of Western modernity, is merely its nihilistic "consummation."

But can't this astounding theoretical myopia—in truth, part of a grandiose and elaborate "strategy of denial"—at least in part be attributed to Heidegger's own efforts toward self-exculpation? For if it is, as we learn in "Overcoming Metaphysics," "Western metaphysics" that is in fact responsible for the devastating "events of world history in this century,"[38] then certainly Germany as a nation—which Heidegger persists on viewing as the vehicle of our salvation—need bear special responsibility neither for the European catastrophe nor for its "crimes against humanity." It is in this vein that his insensitive response to Herbert Marcuse's query as to why he never bothered to publicly condemn such "crimes" must be understood. Or as Heidegger observes, in a monumental instance of bad faith, with reference to the annihilation of millions of European Jews: "If instead of 'Jews' you had written 'East Germans,' then the same holds true for one of the allies, with the difference that everything that has occurred since 1945 has become public knowledge, while the bloody terror of the Nazis in point of fact had been kept a secret from the German people."³⁹

Given Heidegger's penchant for dogmatic historical judgments and the equation of incomparables, it is hardly surprising if, upon turning to the text of a 1949 lecture, we find the following observations: "Agriculture is today a motorized food industry, in essence the same as the manufacture of corpses in gas chambers and extermination camps, the same as the blockade and starvation of countries, the same as the manufacture of atomic bombs."⁴⁰ But here, too, the essential point is *philosophical,* not biographical: such travesties of historical reasoning in no way represent tangential asides; instead, they go to the essence of the judgmental incapacities of the doctrine of the "history of Being" as a framework for historical understanding.

IV

Few thinkers can claim as auspicious a philosophical debut as could Heidegger with *Being and Time.* But already in that work, one finds a characteristic disdain of traditional methods of philosophical argumentation. At crucial junctures, Heidegger's modus operandi tends to be "evocative" rather than "discursive." And thus, according to Ernst Tugendhat, "the procedure of explication through the sheer accumulation of words [*Worthäufung*] is frequent in *Being and Time;* it is connected with what I have called the *evocative method*"—a method that is characterized by the employment of neologisms whose conceptual self-evidence is merely assumed rather than argued for.⁴¹ It is this method that provoked Adorno's polemical ire in *The Jargon of Authenticity,* where it is alleged that Heideggerian *Existenzphilosophie* "sees to it that what it wants is on the whole felt and accepted through its mere delivery, without regard to the content of the words used." Thus, insofar as "the words of the jargon sound as if they said something higher than what they mean . . . whoever is versed in the jargon does not have to say what he thinks, does not even have to think it properly."⁴² All of which is to say that Heidegger's ambivalences about "Wissenschaft," or about traditional discursive methods of philosophical argumentation, are already fully apparent in his magnum opus of 1927. Moreover, as a number of critics have pointed out, Heidegger's imperious use of philosophical terminology—what Tugendhat has called "the procedure of explication through the sheer accumulation of words"—is far from unrelated to his distasteful political leanings. And thus, it falls due to inquire as to whether in Heidegger's case a certain "linguistic authoritarianism" does not in fact prove the harbinger of a distinctly authoritarian political disposition. Or, as the German political scientist Alfons Söllner has remarked, echoing Adorno's suspicions: "The authoritarian sense or non-sense of Heideggerian philosophy lies in its jargon and its linguistic gestures."[43]

In his post hoc attempts to account for his involvement with the politics of German fascism, Heidegger never made a secret of the fact that in 1933, he "expected from National Socialism a spiritual renewal of life in its entirety, a reconciliation of social antagonisms, and a deliverance of Western Dasein from the dangers of communism."[44] To be sure, Heidegger's expectations were ultimately disappointed. But our discussion thus far has sought to make clear that the aforementioned political desiderata derive directly from Heidegger's philosophical program itself; specifically, they result from that program's radicalization in the late 1920s, as Heidegger becomes increasingly convinced of the essentially nihilistic tenor of Western "science"—a term that for him becomes synonymous with the totality of inherited intellectual paradigms *simpliciter*. It is the radicality of this critique that convinces Heidegger of the necessity of "extreme solutions" and the need to make a total break with value-orientations of European modernity. He believed—erroneously, as it would turn out—that National Socialism offered the prospect of an awakening of Germany's "epochal" historical mission, which he incongruously equates with a "repetition" of the "Greek beginning." And even after the German collapse of 1945, he would perversely insist that if only the right pressures had been brought to bear on the movement in its early stages, everything might have turned out for the better: "[Who knows] what would have happened and what could have been averted if in 1933 all available powers had arisen, gradually and in secret unity, in order to purify and moderate the 'movement' that had to come to power?"[45]

With the advantages of some sixty years of historical hindsight, it is of course easy for us to condemn Heidegger's actions and beliefs. Yet pre-Nazi Germany was exposed in rapid succession to a demoralizing defeat in world war, an exacting peace treaty, catastrophic inflation, political chaos, and a severe economic depression. The historically available progressive political options were indeed few.

What cannot help give cause for dismay, however, is Heidegger's repeated insistence after the war that, if only the proper forces had been brought to bear on Germany's National Revolution, matters would have been entirely different. But such a claim is extremely difficult to uphold. As we indicated above, Heidegger dates his disillusionment with the National Socialist program from June 30, 1934. Yet one must be absolutely clear about the fact that as of the regime's first few months, the brutal characteristics of totalitarian rule were as plain as noonday: the Reichstag lay in flames, parliament had been dissolved, the Social Democratic Party had been banned, the trade unions had been forcibly disbanded, Jews had been dismissed from the civil service (university teaching included), civil liberties had been suspended, and as of the Enabling Act of March 24, 1933, Hitler was in essence governing by decree. That Heidegger felt sufficiently comfortable with the trappings of totalitarian rule to emerge as Germany's most prominent academic spokesman for the new regime helps place his political actions in the proper historical perspective. No doubt, he at least in part shared the sentiments of the German shopkeeper who, when questioned by an American researcher about Germany's devastating loss of freedom under Hitler, responded: "You don't understand. Before we had parties, elections, political campaigns and voting. Under Hitler, we don't have these anymore. Now we are free!"

As late as 1936—that is, two years after his putative withdrawal of support for the regime—Heidegger could remark in a lecture course: "These two men, Hitler and Mussolini, who have, each in essentially different ways, introduced a countermovement to nihilism, have both learned from Nietzsche. The authentic metaphysical realm of Nietzsche has, however, not yet been realized."[46] His later claims to have offered "spiritual resistance" to Nazism are surely exaggerated.

V

It would be facile to dismiss the Nietzschean-inspired, conservative revolutionary critique of modernity, that so influenced Heidegger's political views, as "reactionary" or "proto-fascistic"; even if it was precisely this intellectual paradigm that very much facilitated Germany's "spiritual preparation" for National Socialism.[47] Simplistic intellectual classifications always fall short of the demands of complex historical circumstances. Moreover, it could easily be shown how, *mutatis mutandis,* a surprisingly similar critique of modernity was shared by the radical left.[48] That Nietzsche's critique, as well as Heidegger's appropriation of it, is capable of sensitizing us to the "excrescences of modernity"—to the ways in which the rationality of "progress," as buttressed by categories of formal or technical reason, begins to take on an apparent life of its own, divorced from the needs of the historical actors who originally set it in motion—remains undeniable. Yet by highlighting the failings of modernity to the exclusion of its specific advances—which Hegel (to take merely one example), in the wake of the democratic revolutions of the eighteenth century, identifies with "progress in the consciousness of freedom"—this critique proves, in the last analysis, woefully imbalanced and myopic. It thereby seemingly invites the political extremism that it embraces in point of fact. For if the "present age" is indeed one of total perdition—"the collapse of the world," "the devastation of the earth," "the unconditional objectification of everything present," is how Heidegger describes it in "Overcoming Metaphysics"[49]—then "extreme solutions" alone would be warranted, even mandated, to combat the manifold failings of modernity. Even after the war, Heidegger steadfastly refuses to abandon the conviction that "democracy" (along with Christianity and the constitutional or *Rechtsstaat*) is a mere "half-measure" ("*Halbheit*"), from which no real solution might emerge.[50] Here, too, it behooves us to keep in mind Pöggeler's question as to whether Heidegger "ever truly emerged" from the ideological proximity in which he felt so at home during the early 1930s.

Germany's political dilemmas have often been described in terms of its status as a "belated nation"—that is, in terms of its delayed assimilation of the constituent features of political modernity: national unification, an autonomous civil society, and parliamentary government.[51] Earlier, we suggested the need for a historicization of Heidegger's philosophical project. Could it be that Heidegger's own philosophical shortcomings parallel those of his nation's own historical formation? That his thought, too, in significant respects fails to make the transition to modern standards of philosophical and political rationality? It is likely that the most significant long-term repercussions of the Heidegger controversy will be concerned with these and related themes.

Notes

1. Thomas Sheehan, "Heidegger and the Nazis," *New York Review of Books*, June 16, 1988, p. 47. For Sheehan's earlier defense of Heidegger (in response to Stephen Eric Bonner's "Martin Heidegger: The Consequences of Political Mystification," *Salmagundi* [Summer-Fall]:38–39, 1977), see *Salmagundi* (Winter):173–184, 1979.

2. See, for example, Hans-Georg Gadamer, "Back from Syracuse?" *Critical Inquiry* 15(2):427–430, 1989.

3. Otto Pöggeler, "Den Führer führen? Heidegger und kein Ende," *Philosophische Rundschau* 32:26–67, 1985.

4. The phrase Heidegger uses in *An Introduction to Metaphysics* (New Haven: Yale University Press, 1959), p. 199.

5. In his biography of Heidegger, *Martin Heidegger: Unterwegs zu seiner Biographie* (Frankfurt: Campus, 1988), Hugo Ott has reproduced the report of the Freiburg University denazification commission on pp. 305ff.

6. Cited in ibid., pp. 316–317.

7. See, for example, Jürgen Habermas' essay, "Work and Weltanschauung: The Heidegger Controversy from a German Perspective," in Jürgen Habermas, *The New Conservatism: Cultural Criticism and the Historians' Debate*, edited and translated by Shierry W. Nicholsen (Cambridge, Mass.: MIT Press, 1989).

8. Karl Löwith, "My Last Meeting with Heidegger in Rome, 1936," reprinted in this volume.

9. Otto Pöggeler, *Martin Heidegger's Path of Thinking*, translated by D. Magurshak and S. Barber (Atlantic Highlands, N.J.: Humanities Press, 1987), p. 272.

10. Heidegger, *An Introduction to Metaphysics*, p. 199 (translation slightly altered).

11. See Martin Heidegger, "Letter to the Rector of Freiburg University, November 4, 1945," reprinted in part I below. The allusion to June 30, 1934 is of course a reference to the so-called "night of the long knives," the Nazi purge of the Röhm faction (the S.A.) and the "socialist" wing of the National Socialist movement, centered around the brothers Gregor and Otto Strasser.

12. See Martin Heidegger, *Das Rektorat 1933–34: Tatsachen und Gedanken* (Frankfurt: Klostermann, 1983), p. 23; and *Der Spiegel* interview, "Only a God Can Save Us," reprinted in part I of this volume.

13. See, for example, the contributions by Emmanuel Levinas and Maurice

Introduction

Blanchot in the dossier entitled, "Heidegger et la pensée Nazie," *Le nouvel Observateur*, January 22–28, 1988, pp. 41–49.

14. Friedrich Nietzsche, *The Will to Power*, edited by Walter Kaufmann (New York: Vintage, 1967), no. 809.

15. See the excellent discussion of this theme in Michael Zimmerman, *Heidegger's Confrontation with Modernity* (Bloomington: Indiana University Press, 1990), p. 113: "Beginning in the mid-1930s . . . Heidegger concluded that the work of art could help to make possible the non-representational, non-calculative, meditative thinking which would usher in the post-metaphysical age."

16. Martin Heidegger, *Hölderlins Hymnen "Germanien" und "Der Rhein."* *Gesamtausgabe* 39 (Frankfurt: Klostermann, 1980).

17. Martin Heidegger, *Existence and Being* (Chicago: Regnery, Gateway, 1949), p. 287; emphasis added.

18. See below, p. 106.

19. Martin Heidegger, *Discourse on Thinking* (New York: Harper, 1966), p. 47.

20. Martin Heidegger, *Nietzsche: The Will to Power as Art*, translated by D. F. Krell (New York: Harper and Row, 1979), pp. 85–86.

21. See H. W. Petzet, *Auf einen Stern zugehen: Begegnungen und Gespräche mit Martin Heidegger, 1929–1976* (Frankfurt: Societät, 1983), p. 232; and Martin Heidegger, *Was heisst Denken?* (Tübingen: M. Niemeyer, 1954), p. 65.

22. Martin Heidegger, *Beiträge zu Philosophie* (Frankfurt: Klostermann, 1989), p. 38.

23. Martin Heidegger, *Basic Writings* (New York: Harper and Row, 1977), p. 96 (translation altered).

24. "Arbeitsgemeinschaft Cassirer-Heidegger," in Guido Schneeberger, *Ergänzungen zu einer Heidegger Bibliographie* (Bern: Suhr, 1960), pp. 20–21; emphasis added. English translation in N. Lagiulli, ed., *The Existentialist Tradition: Selected Writings* (Garden City, N.Y.: Doubleday, 1971).

25. For the best discussion of this theme in Heidegger, see Winfried Franzen, "Die Suche nach Härte und Schwere," in A. Gethmann-Siefert and O. Pöggeler, eds., *Heidegger und die praktische Philosophie* (Frankfurt: Suhrkamp, 1988), pp. 78–92.

26. Martin Heidegger, "The Self-Assertion of the German University," p. 22ff. below.

27. Heidegger, *An Introduction to Metaphysics*, p. 47.

28. Heidegger, "The Self-Assertion of the German University," p. 34.

29. Heidegger, *Basic Writings*, p. 210.

30. Martin Heidegger, "The Word of Nietzsche: 'God is Dead,'" in *The Question Concerning Technology and Other Essays*, edited and translated by William Lovitt (New York: Harper, 1977), p. 112.

31. Karl Löwith, *Heidegger: Denker in dürftiger Zeit* (Stuttgart: Metzler, 1984), pp. 173–174.

32. Heidegger, *An Introduction to Metaphysics*, pp. 38–39.

33. Ibid., p. 42.

34. Heidegger, *Hölderlins Hymnen "Germanien" und "Der Rhein,"* p. 134.

35. Martin Heidegger, *Hölderlins Hymne der "Ister." Gesamtausgabe* 53 (Frankfurt: Klostermann, 1984), p. 106.

36. Heidegger, *Das Rektorat 1933–34*, p. 39.

37. Martin Heidegger, *Heraklit. Gesamtausgabe* 55 (Frankfurt: Klostermann, 1979), p. 123.

38. Martin Heidegger, "Overcoming Metaphysics," in *The End of Philosophy* (New York: Harper and Row, 1973), p. 86.

39. See below, p. 163.

40. Martin Heidegger, "Insight into That Which Is," cited in Wolfgang Schirmacher, *Technik und Gelassenheit* (Freiburg and Munich: Albers, 1983), p. 25.

41. Cf. Ernst Tugendhat, *Self-Consciousness and Self-Determination* (Cambridge, Mass.: MIT Press, 1986), p. 187 (translation slightly altered). For more on this point, see his contribution to this volume, "Heidegger's Idea of Truth."

42. Theodor Adorno, *The Jargon of Authenticity* (New York: Seabury, 1973), p. 8.

43. Alfons Söllner, "Left Students of the Conservative Revolution," *Telos* 61:59, 1984.

44. Martin Heidegger, letter to Herbert Marcuse of January 20, 1948; see below, p. 162.

45. Heidegger, *Das Rektorat 1933–34*, p. 25.

46. An observation from Heidegger's 1936 Schelling lectures, cited by Pöggeler in "Den Führer führen," p. 56.

47. See Kurt Sontheimer, "Anti-Democratic Thought in the Weimar Republic," in Lawrence Wilson, ed., *The Road to Dictatorship* (London: Oswald Wolff, 1964), pp. 42ff.: "It is hardly a matter of controversy today that certain ideological predispositions in German thought generally, but particularly in the intellectual and political climate of the Weimar Republic . . . prepared the intellectual soil for the growth of National Socialism." For more on the intellectual origins of Nazism, see Fritz Stern, *The Politics of Cultural Despair: A Study in the Rise of the Germanic Ideology* (New York: Knopf, 1972) and George Mosse, *The Crisis of the German Ideology: The Intellectual Origins of the Third Reich* (New York: Grosset and Dunlap, 1964). For a thorough account of Heidegger's intellectual indebtedness to the paradigm of conservative revolutionary thought which attained prominence in Germany between the wars, see Pierre Bourdieu, *L'Ontologie politique de Martin Heidegger* (Paris: Editions de Minuit, 1988).

48. On this point see the two important books by Michael Löwy, *Georg Lukács: From Romanticism to Bolshevism* (London: New Left Books, 1978) and *Utopie et rédemption: le judaisme libertaire en Europe centrale* (Paris: PUF, 1988).

49. Heidegger, "Overcoming Metaphysics," pp. 85–86.

50. See his remarks to this effect in *Was heisst Denken* p. 65 and "Only a God Can Save Us," p. 105 below.

51. For the classical account, see Helmuth Plessner, *Die verspätete Nation* (Frankfurt: Suhrkamp, 1974). See also Ralf Dahrendorff, *Society and Democracy in Germany* (New York: Norton, 1979).

PART ONE

TEXTS BY MARTIN HEIDEGGER

INTRODUCTION

In the dossier that follows, we present texts that offer crucial insight into the motivations underlying Heidegger's partisanship for National Socialism in the 1930s.

At the same time, there is little that is "self-evident" about the materials contained in the ensuing documentation. Both Heidegger's detractors and apologists err in disseminating simplifying verdicts which tend to suppress the profound complexities of the all-important relationship between politics and philosophy in Heidegger's work. And thus, while Heidegger was far from being a "Nazi philosopher" (as some have recently claimed), neither can one make a neat and total separation between his philosophical and political beliefs. Only when one fully appreciates the intellectual complexities of Heidegger's political commitment—that is, the fact that his was by no means a National Socialism of the "rank and file" variety, but a highly "spiritualized" conception of the movement (the best account of this dimension of Heidegger's work remains Jacques Derrida's *Of Spirit*)—can one begin to do justice to the peculiar intricacies of Heidegger's case. Thus, in order to "judge"—or, better still, to "understand"—the bases of Heidegger's political involvements, it is essential to take into consideration the key philosophical works of the period, from *Being and Time* (1927) to *An Introduction to Metaphysics* (1935).

Of course, Heidegger's engagement for National Socialism was overdetermined circumstantially as well as philosophically. That a philosopher of his acumen and brilliance was so readily seduced by the Hitler-euphoria that swept Germany in the early 1930s should serve as a cautionary tale about the uncritical veneration of intellectual genius. It seems, moreover, to offer an excellent illustration of Kant's point, in *The Groundwork of the Metaphysics of Morals*, about a "good will" as the only capacity worth having for its own sake, since other intellectual talents and competences can always be perverted in the direction of ignoble ends.

And yet to claim that it was an intellectually "spiritualized" conception of National Socialism to which Heidegger swore allegiance cannot help but raise an entire series of troublesome hermeneutical questions about the elective affinities that Heidegger indeed perceived between the doctrines of fundamental ontology and German fascism. For as we see clearly in the political texts that follow—above all, in the 1933 Rectoral Address as well as in the political addresses from the same period—Heidegger's appeals in support of the "movement" strike a peculiar balance between the *Sturm und Kampf* idiom of National Socialism and the existential analytic of *Being and Time*. The virtues of the movement are enthusiastically portrayed via the discourse of "authentic decision" that is readily identifiable to all those familiar with Heidegger's 1927 magnum opus. Thus, as Karl Löwith convincingly demonstrates in his excellent essay on "The Political Implications of Heidegger's Existentialism," terms such as "Being-towards-death," "destiny," "authentic choice of oneself," and so forth, figure quite prominently in virtually all of Heidegger's political addresses of the period. In no uncertain terms, it seems that Heidegger himself viewed his Nazi engagement of the early 1930s as a type of authentic, "ontic" realization of the "Existentials" of *Being and Time.* Facts such as these cannot but lead one to conclude that *Being and Time,* in addition to being a pathbreaking work in existential phenomenology, is much more thoroughly rooted in the concerns and dilemmas of its age than may at first appear. That is, it is not only a work of *prima philosophia,* but is itself saturated with historicity. To do justice to Heidegger as a thinker, then, means to open oneself to both the historical as well as the intra-philosophical bases of his thought.

Chapters 3 and 5 reproduce two of the apologiae set forth by Heidegger over the years. In the debate that has been spawned in the aftermath of Victor Farias' book, *Heidegger and National Socialism,* the philosopher's attempts at self-exculpation have been viewed with increased skepticism.

First, Heidegger's account of the circumstances surrounding his accession to the rectorship in May 1933 have been vigorously contested by the historian Hugo Ott.[1] Though Heidegger has tried to portray himself as a champion of moderation, who, by virtue of his international renown, alone could forestall the rampant politicization of university life, the facts of the case are at odds with this characterization. Instead, we now know that Heidegger was quite active in the promulgation of *Gleichschaltung* legislation, which entailed the transformation of university life in line with the Nazi *Führerprinzip* or leadership principle. Since Heidegger thought of himself as a leader—indeed, according to the pro-rector, Joseph Sauer, as the greatest philosopher since Heraclitus—this move, which ended a longstanding tradition of university self-govern-ment, seemed quite natural for him. Further, he recommended that appointments be based on "political criteria" and was not averse to denouncing to Nazi higher-ups faculty members who could not be trusted to toe the new line. And thus, during his rectorship, the Baden university system was widely perceived as a "model instance" of National Socialist educational reform.

Heidegger insists that he opposed the propagation of anti-Jewish sentiment (such as the hanging of "Juden nicht erwünscht!" posters) during his tenure as rector. Yet a prerequisite for taking office was the enforcement of the anti-Jewish decrees of April 1, 1933 (the so-called "Law for the Reconstitution of the Civil Service"), as a result of which Jews were summarily dismissed from university positions. Moreover, during his rectorship, Heidegger refused to accept any Jewish dissertation students. He is alleged to have callously dashed the hopes of one of his own highly regarded Jewish doctoral candidates, who was on the verge of attaining her degree, with the words: "You understand, Frau Mintz, that because you are a Jew I cannot supervise your promotion."[2]

Finally, we have included one of Heidegger's key philosophical writings from the 1930s and 1940s, "Overcoming Metaphysics," a text that is indispensable for understanding the so-called "turn" in his thinking from "existential ontology" to the "history of Being." Written in note form, and contemporaneous with the 1936–1941 Nietzsche lectures, these theses offer privileged insight into Heidegger's ontological-histori-cal (*seinsgeschichtlich*) understanding of the contemporary European crisis—"the unconditional objectification of everything present," "the collapse of the world," "the desolation of the earth"—which Heidegger views as a direct result of the "consummation [*Vollendung*] of metaphys-ics"; that is, the consummation of the project of the metaphysical domi-nation of the earth, as foreshadowed by the philosophical "will to will" (e.g., in Descartes and Nietzsche) and as prophesied by Ernst Jünger's theory of planetary technology, which Heidegger finds so instructive.

But here one also finds clear traces of the philosopher's disillusionment with historically existing National Socialism, as it became increasingly clear to him that the movement had abandoned its putative metaphysical promise in favor of other ideologies and political goals. Thus, in thesis XXVI, for example, we find a pointed critique of the leadership principle and of actual leaders, who have been reduced to mere pawns and executors of a fate—a *Seinsgeschick*—that has been mysteriously preordained by Being itself.

But at the same time, one cannot help but raise doubts concerning the diagnostic capacities of the ontological-historical standpoint adopted by Heidegger (that of *Seinsgeschichte* or the history of Being) when it comes to proffering judgments about the immanent trajectory of contemporary historical life. Thus, for example, when Heidegger, also in thesis XXVI, attempts to account for the century's two world wars in terms of our purported "abandonment by Being" ("*Seinsverlassenheit*"), the palpable weaknesses of the "history of Being" as an explanatory device seem self-evident.

Notes

1. See Hugo Ott, "Wie Heidegger Rektor wurde," in *Martin Heidegger: Unterwegs zu seiner Biographie* (Frankfurt: Campus, 1988), pp. 138–145.
2. Leopoldine Weizmann, "Heidegger, était-il Nazi?" *Etudes* 368(5):638, 1988.

I

THE SELF-ASSERTION OF THE GERMAN UNIVERSITY

Assuming the rectorship means committing oneself to leading this university *spiritually and intellectually*. The teachers and students who constitute the rector's following [*Gefolgschaft der Lehrer und Schüler*] will awaken and gain strength only through being truly and collectively rooted in the essence of the German university. This essence will attain clarity, rank, and power, however, only when the leaders are, first and foremost and at all times, themselves led by the inexorability of that spiritual mission which impresses onto the fate of the German Volk the stamp of their history.

Do we know of this spiritual mission? Whether yes or no, the question remains unavoidable: are we, the teachers and students of this "high" school, truly and collectively rooted in the essence of the German university? Does this essence truly have the power to shape our existence? It does, but only if we *will* this essence fully. But who would wish to doubt that? The predominant, essential character of the university is generally considered to reside in its "self-governance"; this shall be preserved. But have we also fully considered what this claim to the right of self-governance demands of us?

Self-governance means: to set ourselves the task and to determine ourselves the way and means of realizing that task in order to be what we ourselves ought to be. But do we know *who we ourselves are,* this body of teachers and students at the highest school of the German Volk? *Can* we know that at all, without the most constant and most uncompromising and harshest *self-examination* [*Selbstbesinnung*]?

Neither knowledge of the conditions that prevail today at the university nor familiarity with its earlier history guarantees sufficient knowl-

"The Self-Assertion of the German University" ("Die Selbstbehauptung der deutschen Üniversität") by Martin Heidegger first appeared in 1933 with Korn Verlag in Breslau. It was republished in 1983 by Klostermann Verlag in Frankfurt.

edge of the essence of the university unless we first delimit, clearly and uncompromisingly, this essence for the future; in such self-limitation, *will* it; and, in this willing, *assert* ourselves.

Self-governance can exist only on the basis of self-examination. Self-examination, however, can only take place on the strength of the *self-assertion* of the German university. Will we carry this out, and how?

The self-assertion of the German university is the original, common will to its essence. We regard the German university as the "high" school which from science [*Wissenschaft*]* and through science, educates and disciplines the leaders and guardians of the fate of the German Volk. The will to the essence of the German university is the will to science as the will to the historical spiritual mission of the German Volk as a Volk that knows itself in its state. Science and German fate must come to power at *the same time* in the will to essence. And they will do this then and *only* then when we—the teachers and students—expose science to its innermost necessity, *on the one hand,* and, *on the other,* when we stand firm in the face of German fate extreme in its extreme distress [*Not*].

We will, to be sure, not experience the essence of science in its innermost necessity as long as we simply—talking about the "new concept of science"—provide for the independence and freedom from presuppositions of a science that is all too contemporary. This activity, which is simply negating and scarcely looks back beyond the last decades, has virtually taken on the appearance of a true effort to understand the essence of science.

If we wish to grasp the essence of science, then we must first ask ourselves the decisive question: should science still continue to *exist* for us in the future, or ought we to let it drift off to a quick end? That

* Translator's note: Though the German "Wissenschaft" is frequently translated as "science," it is slightly misleading in the context at hand to so render it. For Heidegger's employment of the word harks back to the "authentic" German philosophical meaning of the word as "true knowing," as is suggested by Fichte's *Wissenschaftslehre,* Hegel's *Wissenschaft der Logik,* as well as Husserl's "Philosophie als strenge Wissenschaft." Thus, the word not only has nothing to do with what we in English refer to as the "natural sciences." Heidegger's reliance on "Wissenschaft"—a central motif in his important texts from 1929 to 1935—also strives to differentiate rigorous philosophical thought, in which the *Seinsfrage* occupies its rightful pride of place, from the "inferior" versions of Wissenschaft that were prominent in his day, such as neo-Kantianism, positivism, empiricism, and so forth.

science should exist at all has never been unconditionally necessary. But if science should exist, and should exist *for* us and *through* us, then under what conditions can it truly exist?

Only when we submit to the power of the *beginning* of our spiritual-historical existence. This beginning is the beginning [*Aufbruch*] of Greek philosophy. That is when, from the culture of one Volk and by the power of that Volk's language, Western man rises up for the first time against *the totality of what is* and questions it and comprehends it as the being that it is. All science is philosophy, whether it knows it and wills it or not. All science remains bound to that beginning of philosophy and draws from it the strength of its essence, assuming that it still remains at all equal to this beginning.

Here we want to recover for *our* existence two distinguishing characteristics of the original Greek essence of science.

Among the Greeks there circulated an old report that Prometheus had been the first philosopher. It is this Prometheus into whose mouth Aeschylus puts an adage that expresses the essence of knowledge:

techne d'anangkes asthenestera makro

"But knowledge is far less powerful than necessity." That means: all knowledge of things remains beforehand at the mercy of overpowering fate and fails before it.

It is precisely for that reason that knowledge must develop its highest defiance, for which alone the entire might of the concealedness of what is will first rise up, in order really to fail. Thus what is reveals itself in its unfathomable inalterability and confers its truth on knowledge. This adage about the creative impotence of knowledge is a saying of the Greeks, in whom we all too easily see the model for knowledge that is purely self-reliant and thus lost to the world; this knowledge is presented to us as the "theoretical" attitude. But what is *theoria* for the Greeks? It is said that it is pure contemplation, which remains bound only to its object in its fullness and in its demands. The Greeks are invoked to support the claim that this contemplative behavior is supposed to occur for its own sake. But this claim is incorrect. For, on the one hand, "theory" does not happen for its own sake; it happens only as a result of the passion to remain close to what is as such and to be beset by it. On the other hand, however, the Greeks struggled to understand and carry out this contemplative questioning as a—indeed as *the*—highest mode of man's *energeia*, of man's "being at work." It was not their wish to bring practice into line with theory, but the other way around: to understand theory as the supreme realization of genuine practice. For the Greeks science is not a "cultural treasure," but the innermost determining center of their entire existence as a Volk and a state. Science is also not merely the means of making the unconscious conscious, but the force that keeps all of existence in focus and embraces it.

Science is the questioning standing firm in the midst of the totality of being as it continually conceals itself. This active perseverance knows of its impotence in the face of Fate.

That is the essence of science in its beginning. But have not two and a half millennia passed since this beginning? Has the progress that has occurred in human activity not changed science as well? Certainly! The Christian-theological interpretation of the world that followed, as well as the later mathematical-technical thinking of the modern age, have removed science from its beginnings both in time and in its objects [*zeitlich und sachlich*]. But that has by no means relegated the beginning itself to the past, let alone destroyed it. For, assuming that the original Greek science is something great, then the *beginning* of this great thing remains its *greatest* moment. The essence of science could not even be emptied and used up [*vernutzt*]—which it is today, all results and "international organizations" notwithstanding—if the greatness of the beginning did not *still* exist. The beginning *exists* still. It does not lie *behind* us as something long past, but it stands *before* us. The beginning has— as the greatest moment, which exists in advance—already passed indifferently over and beyond all that is to come and hence over and beyond us as well. The beginning has invaded our future; it stands there as the distant decree that orders us to recapture its greatness.

Only if we resolutely obey this decree to win back the greatness of the beginning, only then will science become the innermost necessity of our existence. Otherwise, science will remain something in which we become involved purely by chance or will remain a calm, pleasurable activity, an activity free of danger, which promotes the mere advancement of knowledge [*Kenntnisse*].

If, however, we obey the distant decree of the beginning, then science must become the fundamental event of our spiritual existence as a Volk [*geistig-volklichen Daseins*].

And if our ownmost existence itself stands on the threshold of a great transformation; if it is true what the last German philosopher to passionately seek God, Friedrich Nietzsche, said: "God is dead"; if we must take seriously the abandonment of man today in the midst of Being, what then does this imply for science?

Then the Greeks' perseverance in the face of what is, a stance that was initially one of wonder and admiration, will be transformed into being completely exposed to and at the mercy of what is concealed and uncertain, that is, what is worthy of question. Questioning will then no longer be simply the preliminary stage to the answer as knowledge, a stage that we can put behind us, but questioning will itself become the highest form of knowledge. Questioning will then unfold its ownmost power for disclosing the essence of all things. Then questioning will compel us to simplify our gaze to the extreme in order to focus on what is inescapable.

Such questioning will shatter the encapsulation of the various fields of knowledge into separate disciplines; it will return them from the isolated fields and corners into which they have been scattered, without bounds and goals; and it will ground science once again directly in the fruitfulness and blessing of all the world-shaping forces of man's historical existence, such as: nature, history, language; the Volk, custom, the state; poetry, thought, belief; sickness, madness, death; law, economy, technology.

If we will the essence of science in the sense of *the questioning, unsheltered standing firm in the midst of the uncertainty of the totality of being,* then *this* will to essence will create for our Volk a world of the innermost and most extreme danger, i.e., a truly *spiritual* world. For "spirit" is neither empty acumen nor the noncommittal play of wit nor the busy practice of never-ending rational analysis nor even world reason; rather, spirit is the determined resolve to the essence of Being, a resolve that is attuned to origins and knowing. And the *spiritual world* of a Volk is not its cultural superstructure, just as little as it is its arsenal of useful knowledge [*Kenntnisse*] and values; rather, it is the power that comes from preserving at the most profound level the forces that are rooted in the soil and blood of a Volk, the power to arouse most inwardly and to shake most extensively the Volk's existence. A spiritual world alone will guarantee our Volk greatness. For it will make the constant decision between the will to greatness and the toleration of decline the law that establishes the pace for the march upon which our Volk has embarked on the way to its future history.

If we will *this* essence of science, then the teachers of the university must really advance to the outermost positions where they will be exposed to the danger of the world's constant uncertainty. If they stand firm there, i.e., if from there—in essential proximity to and beset by all things—there arises for them a common questioning and saying pervaded with a sense of community, then they will become strong enough to lead. For what is decisive in leading is not merely going ahead, but the strength to go alone, not out of obstinacy and the desire to dominate, but by virtue of the most profound destiny and the broadest obligations. Such strength binds to what is essential; it effects the selection of the best, and it awakens the genuine following [*Gefolgschaft*] of those who are of new courage [*neuen Mutes*]. But we do not need to first awaken such a following. The German students are on the march. And *whom* they are seeking, that is those leaders through whom they intend to elevate their own destiny to a grounded, knowing truth and to place it in the clarity of the interpreting-effective word and deed [*deutend-wirkenden Wortes und Werkes*].

Out of the resolve of the German students to stand firm in the face of the extreme distress of German fate comes a will to the essence of the university. This will is a true will, provided that the German students, through the new Student Law,* place themselves under the law of their essence and thereby delimit this essence for the very first time. To give law to oneself is the highest freedom. The much praised "academic freedom" is being banished from the German university; for this freedom was false, because it was only negating. It meant predominantly lack of concern, arbitrariness in one's intentions and inclinations, lack of restraint in everything one does. The German student's notion of

*Translator's note: An example of *Gleichschaltung* legislation, the new Student Law of May 1, 1933 was intended to organize university students in accordance with the *Führerprinzip* in order thereby to ensure their integration within the National Socialist state.

freedom is now being returned to its truth. Out of this freedom will develop for German students certain bonds and forms of service.

The first bond is the one that binds to the ethnic and national community [*Volksgemeinschaft*].* It entails the obligation to share fully, both passively and actively, in the toil, the striving, and the abilities of all estates and members of the Volk. This bond will henceforth be secured and rooted in student existence [*Dasein*] through *labor service*.

The second bond is the one that binds to the honor and the destiny of the nation in the midst of the other peoples of the world. It demands the readiness, secured in knowledge and ability and firmed up through discipline, to give one's utmost. This bond will in the future embrace and pervade all of student existence in the form of *military service*.

The third bond is the one that binds the students to the spiritual mission of the German Volk. This Volk is playing an active role i n shaping its fate by placing its history into the openness of the overpowering might of all the world-shaping forces of human existence and by struggling ever anew to secure its spiritual world. Thus exposed to the extreme questionableness of its own existence, this Volk has the will to be a spiritual Volk. It demands of itself and for itself, and of its leaders and guardians, the hardest clarity that comes from the highest, broadest, and richest knowledge. Young students, who are venturing early into manhood and spreading their will over the destiny of the nation, are compelling themselves, thoroughly, to serve this knowledge. They will no longer permit *knowledge service* to be the dull, quick training for an "elegant" profession. Because the statesman and the teacher, the doctor and the judge, the pastor and the master builder lead the Volk in its existence as a Volk and a state and watch over this existence in its essential relations to the world-shaping forces of human Being and keep it focused, these professions and the education for them are entrusted to the knowledge service. Knowledge does not serve the professions, but the other way around: the professions realize and administer the Volk's highest and most essential knowledge, that of its entire existence. But for us this knowledge is not the calm taking note of essences and values in themselves; rather, it is the placing of one's existence in the most acute

* Translator's note: *Volksgemeinschaft* was the National Socialist expression for the "national community," that is, a new, organic, communal social order bereft of the divisions and antagonisms of modern "society."

danger in the midst of overpowering Being. The questionableness of Being in general compels the Volk to work and struggle and forces it into its state, to which the professions belong.

The three bonds—*through* the Volk to the destiny of the state *in its* spiritual mission—are *equally original* aspects of the German essence. The three forms of service that follow from them—labor service, military service, and knowledge service—are equally necessary and of equal rank.

Knowledge of the Volk that is actively involved with the Volk, knowledge of the destiny of the state that holds itself in readiness; it is these that, together with the knowledge of the spiritual mission, first create the original and full essence of science, the realization of which has been given to us as our task—assuming that we obey what the beginning of our spiritual-historical existence decreed in the distant past.

It is *this* science that is meant when the essence of the German university is defined as the high school that, from science and through science, educates and disciplines the leaders and guardians of the fate of the German Volk.

This primordial concept of knowledge commits one not just to "objectivity," but, first of all, to essential and simple questioning in the midst of the historical-spiritual world of the Volk. Indeed, it is only from here that objectivity can establish itself, i.e., find its character and limits.

Science in this sense must become the force that shapes the corporate body of the German university. This implies two things: first, the teachers and students must each in their own way be *seized* by the idea of science and *remain* seized by it. At the same time, however, this concept of science must penetrate into and transform the basic forms in which the teachers and students collectively pursue their respective scholarly activities: it must transform from within the *faculties* [*Fakultäten*] and the *disciplines* [*Fachschaften*].

The faculty will only be a faculty if it develops into a capacity for spiritual legislation, a capacity that is rooted in the essence of that faculty's particular science, so that it can give shape to the forces of existence that beset *it* and fit them into the *one* spiritual world of the Volk.

The discipline will only be a discipline if it places itself from the very outset within the realm of this spiritual legislation, thereby bringing down disciplinary barriers and overcoming the musty and false character of higher education as superficial professional training.

At the moment when the faculties and disciplines get the essential and simple questions of their science underway, the teachers and students will already be in the embrace of the *same* ultimate necessities and afflictions attendant to existence as a Volk and a state.

Giving form to the original essence of science, however, demands such a degree of rigorousness, responsibility, and superior patience that by comparison, for example, the conscientious observance or the zealous modification of fixed ways of doing things hardly matters.

If, however, the Greeks needed three centuries just to put the *question* of what knowledge is on the proper footing and on the secure path, then *we* certainly cannot think that the elucidation and unfolding of the essence of the German university can occur in the present or coming semester.

But there is, to be sure, *one thing* that we do know which follows from the essence of science as indicated above, and that is that the German university can only then attain form and power when the three forms of service—labor service, military service, and knowledge service—come together primordially into *one* formative force. That is to say:

The teachers' will to essence must awaken to the simplicity and breadth of the knowledge of the essence of science and grow strong. The students' will to essence must force itself into the highest clarity and discipline of knowledge and must shape, through its demands and determinations, the engaged knowledge of the Volk and its state and incorporate this knowledge into the essence of science. Both wills must ready themselves for mutual struggle. All capacities of will and thought, all strengths of the heart, and all capabilities of the body must be developed *through* struggle, must be intensified *in* struggle, and must remain preserved *as* struggle.

We choose the knowing struggle of those who question, and declare with Carl von Clausewitz: "I renounce the foolish hope in salvation by the hand of chance."

The community of teachers and students in struggle will, however, transform the German university into the site of spiritual legislation and realize in it a concentrated center [*die Mitte der straffsten Sammlung*] for the highest service to the Volk in its state only if the teachers and students arrange their existence to be simpler, tougher, and more modest in its needs than that of all other *Volksgenossen.** All leadership must allow following to have its own strength. In each instance, however, to follow carries resistance within it. This essential opposition between leading and following must neither be covered over nor, indeed, obliterated altogether.

Struggle alone will keep this opposition open and implant within the entire body of teachers and students that fundamental mood out of which self-limiting self-assertion will empower resolute self-examination to true self-governance.

Do we will the essence of the German university, or do we not will it? It is up to us whether and how extensively we endeavor, wholeheartedly and not just casually, to bring about self-examination and self-assertion; or whether we—with the best intentions—merely alter the old arrangements and add some new ones. No one will prevent us from doing this.

But neither will anyone ask us whether we will it or do not will it when the spiritual strength of the West fails and the West starts to come apart at the seams, when this moribund pseudocivilization collapses into itself, pulling all forces into confusion and allowing them to suffocate in madness.

Whether such a thing occurs or does not occur, this depends solely on whether we as a historical-spiritual Volk will ourselves, still and again, or whether we will ourselves no longer. Each individual *has a part* in deciding this, even if, and precisely if, he seeks to evade this decision.

But it is our will that our Volk fulfill its historical mission.

We will ourselves. For the young and youngest elements of the Volk, which are already reaching beyond us, *have* already *decided* this.

We can only fully understand the glory and greatness of this new beginning, however, if we carry within ourselves that deep and broad thoughtfulness upon which the ancient wisdom of the Greeks drew in uttering the words:

*Translator's note: *Volksgenossen* was the National Socialist term for a "comrade" or fellow Nazi.

ta . . . megala panta episphale . . .

"All that is great stands in the storm . . ."

(Plato, *Republic,* 497d, 9)

*Translated by William S. Lewis**

* The translator would like to acknowledge the fact that he consulted with profit Karsten Harries' translation of "The Self-Assertion of the German University" in *The Review of Metaphysics* 38:467–481, 1985.

POLITICAL TEXTS, 1933–1934

Schlageter
(May 26, 1933)

In the midst of our work, during a short break in our lectures, let us remember the Freiburg student Albert Leo Schlageter,* a young German hero who a decade ago died the most difficult and the greatest death of all.

Let us honor him by reflecting, for a moment, upon his death in order that this death may help us to understand our lives.

Schlageter died the *most difficult* of all deaths. Not in the front line as the leader of his field artillery battery, not in the tumult of an attack, and not in a grim defensive action—no, he stood *defenseless* before the French rifles.

But he stood and bore the most difficult thing a man can bear.

Yet even this could have been borne with a final rush of jubilation, had a victory been won and the greatness of the awakening nation shone forth.

Instead—darkness, humiliation, and betrayal.

And so, in his most difficult hour, he had also to achieve *the greatest thing of which man is capable*. Alone, drawing on his own inner strength,

Heidegger's "Political Texts: 1933–1934" can be found in Guido Schneeburger, *Nachlese zu Heidegger* (Bern: Suhr, 1962).

* Albert Leo Schlageter, a former student at Freiburg University, was shot for acts of sabotage against the French occupation army in the Ruhr on May 26, 1923. Subsequently, he was elevated to the status of a Nazi martyr and hero.

he had to place before his soul an image of the future awakening of the Volk to honor and greatness so that he could die believing in this future.

Whence this *clarity of heart,* which allowed him to envision what was greatest and most remote?

When this *clarity of heart,* which allowed him to envision what was greatest and most remote?

Student of Freiburg! German student! When on your hikes and outings you set foot in the mountains, forests, and valleys of this Black Forest, the home of this hero, experience this and know: the mountains among which the young farmer's son grew up are of primitive stone, of granite. They have long been at work hardening the will.

The autumn sun of the Black Forest bathes the mountain ranges and forests in the most glorious clear light. It has long nourished clarity of the heart.

As he stood defenseless facing the rifles, the hero's inner gaze soared above the muzzles to the daylight and mountains of his home that he might die for the German people and its Reich with the Alemannic countryside before his eyes.

With a hard will and a clear heart, Albert Leo Schlageter died his death, the most difficult and the greatest of all.

Student of Freiburg, let the strength of this hero's native mountains flow into your will!

Student of Freiburg, let the strength of the autumn sun of this hero's native valley shine into your heart!

Preserve both within you and carry them, hardness of will and clarity of heart, to your comrades at the German universities.

Schlageter walked these grounds as a student. But Freiburg could not hold him for long. He was compelled to go to the Baltic; he was compelled to go to Upper Silesia; he was compelled to go to the Ruhr.

He was not permitted to escape his destiny so that he could die the most difficult and greatest of all deaths with a hard will and a clear heart.

We honor the hero and raise our arms in silent greeting.

Labor Service and the University*
(June 20, 1933)

In the future, the *school* will no longer enjoy its exclusive position in education. With the *Labor Service*, there has arisen a new and decisive force for education [*Erziehungsmacht*]. The *work camp* is now taking its place alongside home, youth league, military service, and school.

A new institution for the direct revelation of the *Volksgemeinschaft* is being realized in the work camp. In the future, young Germans will be governed by the knowledge of *labor*, in which the Volk concentrates its strength in order to experience the hardness of its existence, to preserve the momentum of its will, and to learn anew the value of its manifold abilities. The work camp is at the same time a camp for training leaders in all social groups [*Stände*] and professions. For what counts in the camp is exemplary acting and working together, but not standing by and supervising. And least of all capable of grasping the new reality of the work camp are those who visit such a camp one time as "sightseers."

* Appeared in the *Freiburger Studentenzeitung*. This organ, in which many of Heidegger's political tracts and speeches from the early 1930s appeared, was published by the Freiburg Student Association, which had become the official Nazi student organization.

In his May 27, 1927 Rectoral Address, Heidegger refers to three types of "service" that should be rendered by students to the state: "labor service," "military service," and "service in knowledge." In order to understand the significance of Heidegger's repeated emphasis on the virtues of "labor service," it is important to realize that in the early stages of the Nazi regime, "labor camps" were deemed important vehicles of National Socialist indoctrination, in which the differences among various social classes would be leveled, resulting in the creation of a homogeneous and seamless *Volksgemeinschaft* (national community).

Not only does the work camp awaken and educate to the knowledge of the laboring community of all social groups [*die arbeitende Gemeinschaft aller Stände*], but in the future, this knowledge, rooted in the souls of young Germans, will also have a purifying effect on the *school* and will legislate what it can and cannot, and should and should not, do.

At the same time, the work camp is, as an educational institution in its own right, becoming a new source of those energies through which all other educational institutions—especially the school—are being forced to decide where they stand [*zur Entscheidung gezwungen*] and are being transformed.

Our university is surrounded in the immediate vicinity by work camps that are co-supervised by teachers from this school.

A new reality is present in the work camp. This reality serves as a symbol for the fact that our university is opening itself to the new force for education embodied in the Labor Service. Camp and school are resolved to bring together, in reciprocal give and take, the educational forces of our Volk into that new rooted unity from which the Volk in its State will commit itself to act in accordance with its destiny.

The University in the New Reich*
(June 30, 1933)

We have the new Reich and the university that is to receive its tasks from the Reich's will to existence. There is revolution in Germany, and

* A speech given by Heidegger as part of a series of political lectures organized by the Heidelberg Student Association, which appeared in the *Heidelberger Neuste Nachrichten*, July 1, 1933. It is of interest to note that In Heidegger's two post festum justifications of his activities as rector, *Das Rektorat 1933–34: Tatsachen und Gedanken* (Frankfurt: Klostermann, 1983) and *Der Spiegel*'s interview, "Only a God Can Save Us," Heidegger claims that he accepted the position only in order to prevent the rampant politicization of university life. Yet in "The University in the New Reich," as well as other speeches, it is clear that Heidegger set little store by "academic freedom" in the traditional sense. Instead, as we see, his program held that the university must be "integrated again into the *Volksgemeinschaft* and be joined together with the State . . . in the National Socialist spirit."

we must ask ourselves: *Is there revolution at the university as well?* No. The battle still consists of skirmishes. So far, only on one front has a breakthrough been achieved: because the education of young people is now occurring [*durch die Bildung neuen Lebens*] in the work camp and educational association [*Erziehungsverband*] as well as at the university, the latter *has been relieved of educational tasks* to which it *has till now believed it had an exclusive right.*

The possibility could exist that the university will suffer death through oblivion and forfeit the last vestige of its educational power. It must, however, be *integrated again into the Volksgemeinschaft* and *be joined together with the State.* The university must again become an educational force that draws on knowledge to educate the State's leaders to knowledge. This goal demands three things: 1) knowledge of today's university; 2) knowledge of the dangers today holds for the future; 3) new courage.

Up to now, *research* and *teaching* have been carried on at the universities as they were carried out for decades. Teaching was supposed to develop out of research, and one sought to find a pleasant balance between the two. It was always only the point of view of the teacher that spoke out of this notion. No one had concerned himself with the university as community. Research *got out of hand* and concealed its uncertainty behind the idea of international scientific and scholarly progress. Teaching that had become aimless hid behind examination requirements.

A fierce battle must be fought against this situation in the National Socialist spirit, and this spirit cannot be allowed to be suffocated by humanizing, Christian ideas that suppress its unconditionality. Nor is it enough if one wishes to take the new situation [*dem Neuen*] into account by painting everything with a touch of political color. Of great *danger* are *the noncommittal plans and slogans* that are turning up everywhere; and so, too, is the *"new" concept of Wissenschaft,* which is nothing more than the old one with a slight anthropological underpinning. All of the talk about "politics" is nonsense as well, for it does nothing to put an end to the old routine way of doing and thinking about things [*dem alten Schlendrian*]. What the real gravity of the new situation [*des Neuen*] calls for is the experience of affliction [*Not*], is the active engagement with real conditions [*die zugreifende Auseinandersetzung mit den wirklichen Zuständen*]. Only *that activity is justified* that *is performed with full inner commitment to the future.* The warning cry has already been sounded: "Wissenschaft is endangered by the amount of time lost in martial sports and other such activities." But what does that mean, to lose time, when it is a question of fighting for the State! *Danger* comes not from *work* for *the State.* It comes only from indifference and resistance. For that reason, only true strength should have access to the right path, but not halfheartedness.

New courage allows these dangers to be seen clearly. Only it alone opens our eyes to that which is to come and which is now emerging. It forces each teacher and pupil to *make up his mind about the fundamental questions of Wissenschaft,* and this decision is of epochal importance, for on it depends whether we Germans shall remain a people that is, in the highest sense of the word, knowing. The new teaching which is at issue here does not mean conveying knowledge, but allowing students to learn and inducing them to learn. This means allowing oneself to be beset by the unknown and then becoming master of it in comprehending knowing; it means becoming secure in one's sense for what is essential. It is from such teaching that true research emerges, interlocked with the whole through its rootedness in the Volk and its bond to the State. The student is forced out into the uncertainty of all things, in which the necessity of engagement [*Einsatz*] is grounded. *University study must again become a risk* [*Wagnis*], not a refuge for the cowardly. Whoever does not survive the battle, lies where he falls. The new courage must accustom itself to steadfastness, for the battle for the institutions where our leaders are educated will continue for a long time. It will be fought out of the strengths of the new Reich that Chancellor Hitler will bring to reality. A hard race [*Geschlecht*] with no thought of self must fight this battle, a race that lives from constant testing and that remains directed towards the goal to which it has committed itself. It is a battle to determine who shall be the *teachers* and *leaders* at the university [*ein Kampf um die Gestalt des Lehrers und des Führers an der Universität*].

Martin Heidegger

German Students*
(November 3, 1933)

The National Socialist revolution is bringing about the total transformation of our German existence [*Dasein*].

In these events, it is up to you to remain the ones who always urge on and who are always ready, the ones who never yield and who always grow.

Your will to know seeks to experience what is essential, simple, and great.

You crave to be exposed to that which besets you most directly and to that which imposes upon you the most wide-ranging obligations.

Be hard and genuine in your demands.

Remain clear and sure in your rejection.

Do not pervert the knowledge you have struggled for into a vain, selfish possession. Preserve it as the necessary primal possession of the leader [*führerischen Menschen*] in the *völkisch* professions of the State. You can no longer be those who merely attend lectures [*die nur "Hören-den"*]. You are obligated to know and act together in the creation of the

---

*An appeal launched by Heidegger on the occasion of the plebiscite of November 12, 1933 called by Hitler to sanction (ex post facto) Germany's withdrawal from the League of Nations. Joachim Fest has referred to this plebiscite as "one of [Hitler's] most effective chess moves in the process of consolidating his power within Germany" (see Joachim C. Fest, *Hitler*, translated by Richard and Clara Winston [New York: Harcourt, Brace, 1974], p. 439). Fest continues: "Since Hitler had intertwined his policies as a whole with the resolution to withdraw from the League by framing his plebiscite question in general terms, there was no way for the voter to express approval of his position on the League of Nations and at the same time condemn his domestic policies." That in his speech Heidegger accepted the Nazi Party line as suggested by Fest is illustrated by his remark in the following speech, "German Men and Women," that "there are not separate foreign and domestic policies." In other words, one should not quibble over individual aspects of the Nazi program. Either one accepts it as a whole, or one does not accept it at all. And thus, the November 12 plebiscite, though nominally concerned with a question of foreign policy, must be treated as a general confirmation of the National Revolution.

46

future university [*hohe Schule*] of the German spirit. Every one of you must first prove and justify each talent and privilege. That will occur through the force of your aggressive involvement [*Einsatz*] in the struggle of the entire Volk for itself.

Let your loyalty and your will to follow [*Gefolgschaftswille*] be daily and hourly strengthened. Let your courage grow without ceasing so that you will be able to make the sacrifices necessary to save the essence of our Volk and to elevate its innermost strength in the State.

Let not propositions and "ideas" be the rules of your Being [*Sein*].

The Führer alone *is* the present and future German reality and its law. Learn to know ever more deeply: from now on every single thing demands decision, and every action responsibility.

Heil Hitler!

Martin Heidegger, Rector

German Men and Women!*

(November 10, 1933)

The German people has been summoned by the Führer to vote; the Führer, however, is asking nothing from the people. Rather, he *is giving* the people the possibility of making, directly, the highest free decision of all: whether it—the entire people—wants its own existence [*Dasein*] or whether it does *not* want it.

This election simply cannot be compared to all other previous elections. What is unique about this election is the simple greatness of the decision that is to be executed. The inexorability of what is simple and ultimate [*des Einfachen und Letzten*], however, tolerates no vacillation and no hesitation. This ultimate decision reaches to the outermost limit of our people's existence. And what is this limit? It consists in the most basic demand of all Being [*Sein*], that it preserve and save its own essence. A barrier is thereby erected between what can be reasonably expected of a

---

* Another appeal to support the upcoming plebiscite, published by Heidegger in the *Freiburger Studentenzeitung*.

people and what cannot. It is by virtue of this basic law of honor that a people preserves the dignity and resoluteness of its essence.

It is not ambition, not desire for glory, not blind obstinacy, and not hunger for power that demands from the Führer that Germany withdraw from the League of Nations. It is only the clear will to unconditional self-responsibility in enduring and mastering the fate of our people.

That is *not* a turning away from the community of nations. On the contrary—with this step, our people is submitting to that essential law of human existence to which every people must first give allegiance if it is still to be a people. It is only out of the parallel observance by all peoples of this unconditional demand of self-responsibility that there emerges the possibility of taking one another seriously so that a community can be affirmed.

The will to a true community of nations [*Völkergemeinschaft*] is equally far removed both from an unrestrained, vague desire for world brotherhood and from blind tyranny. Existing beyond this opposition, this will allows peoples and states to stand by one another in an open and manly fashion as self-reliant entities [*das offene und mannhafte Aufsich- und Zueinanderstehen der Völker und Staaten*].

The choice that the German people will now make is—simply as an event in itself, and independent of the outcome—the strongest evidence of the new German reality embodied in the National Socialist State.

Our will to national [*völkisch*] self-responsibility desires that each people find and preserve the greatness and truth of its destiny [*Bestimmung*]. This will is the highest guarantee of security among peoples; for it binds itself to the basic law of manly respect and unconditional honor.

On November 12, the German people as a whole will choose *its* future. This future is bound to the Führer. In choosing this future, the people cannot, on the basis of so-called foreign policy considerations, vote *Yes* without also including in this Yes the Führer and the political movement that has pledged itself unconditionally to him. There are not separate foreign and domestic policies. There is only the one will to the full existence [*Dasein*] of the State.

The Führer has awakened this will in the entire people and has welded it into a single resolve.

No one can remain away from the polls on the day when this will is manifested.

Heidegger
Rector

Declaration of Support for Adolf Hitler and the National Socialist State*(November 11, 1933)

German teachers and comrades!
German Volksgenossen and Volksgenossinnen!

The German people has been summoned by the Führer to vote; the Führer, however, is asking nothing from the people. Rather, he is giving the people the possibility of making, directly, the highest free decision of all: whether the entire people wants its own existence [*Dasein*] or whether it does *not* want it.

Tomorrow the people will choose nothing less than its future.

This election remains absolutely incomparable with all previous elections. What is unique about this election is the simple greatness of the decision that is to be executed. The inexorability of what is simple and ultimate [*des Einfrachen und Letzten*] tolerates no vacillation and no hesitation. This ultimate decision reaches to the outermost limit of our people's existence. And what is this limit? It consists in the most basic demand of all Being [*Sein*], that it keep and save its own essence. A barrier is thereby erected between what can be reasonably expected of a people and what cannot. It is by virtue of this basic law of honor that

* Address presented by Heidegger at an election rally held by German university professors in Leipzig in support of the upcoming plebiscite.

the German people retains the dignity and resoluteness of its life. However, the will to self-responsibility is not only the basic law of the people's existence; it is also the fundamental event in the bringing about of the people's National Socialist State. From this will to self-responsibility, every effort, be it humble or grand, of each social and occupational group [*Stand*] assumes its necessary and predestined place in the social order [*in den Standort und Rang ihrer gleich notwendigen Bestimmung*]. The labor of the various groups [*Stände*] supports and strengthens the living framework of the State; labor reconquers for the people its rootedness; labor places the State, as the reality of the people, into the field of action of all essential forces of human Being.

It is not ambition, not desire for glory, not blind obstinacy, and not hunger for power that demands from the Führer that Germany withdraw from the League of Nations. It is only the clear will to unconditional self-responsibility in suffering and mastering the fate of our people. That is *not* a turning away from the community of peoples. On the contrary: with this step, our people is submitting to that essential law of human Being to which every people must first give allegiance if it is still to be a people.

It is only out of the parallel observance by all peoples of this unconditional demand of self-responsibility that there emerges the possibility of taking each other seriously so that a community can also be affirmed. The will to a true national community [*Volksgemeinschaft*] is equally far removed both from an unrestrained, vague desire for world brotherhood and from blind tyranny. Existing beyond this opposition, this will allows peoples and states to stand by one another in an open and manly fashion as self-reliant entities [*das offene und mannhafte Aufsich- und Zueinanderstehen der Völker und Staaten*]. What is it that such a will brings about? Is it reversion into barbarism? No! It is the averting of all empty negotiation and hidden deal-making through the simple, great demand of self-responsible action. Is it the irruption of lawlessness? No! It is the clear acknowledgment of each people's inviolable independence. Is it the denial of the creative genius of a spiritual [*geistig*] people and the smashing of its historical traditions? No! It is the awakening of the young who have been purified and are growing back to their roots. Their will to the

State will make this people hard towards itself and reverent towards each genuine deed.

What sort of event is this then? The nation is winning back the *truth* of its will to existence, for truth is the revelation of that which makes a people confident, lucid, and strong in its actions and knowledge. The genuine will to know arises from such truth. And this will to know circumscribes the right to know. And from there, finally, the limits are measured out within which genuine questioning and research must legitimize and prove themselves. Such is the origin of Wissenschaft, which is constrained by the necessity of self-responsible *völkisch* existence. Wissenschaft is thus the passion to educate that has been restrained by this necessity, the passion to want to know in order to make knowing. *To be* knowing, however, means to be master of things in clarity and to be resolved to action.

We have declared our independence from the idol of thought that is without foundation and power. We see the end of the philosophy that serves such thought. We are certain that the clear hardness and the sure, steady competency [*werkgerechte Sicherheit*] of unyielding, simple questioning about the essence of Being are returning. For a *völkische* Wissenschaft, the courage either to grow or to be destroyed in confrontation with Being [*dem Seienden*], which is the first form of courage, is the innermost motive for questioning. For courage lures one forward; courage frees itself from what has been up to now; courage risks the unaccustomed and the incalculable. For us, questioning is not the unconstrained play of curiosity. Nor is questioning the stubborn insistence on doubt at any price. For us, questioning means: exposing oneself to the sublimity of things and their laws; it means: not closing oneself off to the terror of the untamed and to the confusion of darkness. To be sure, it is for the sake of this questioning that we question, and *not* to serve those who have grown tired and their complacent yearning for comfortable answers. We know: the courage to question, to experience the abysses of existence and to endure the abysses of existence, is in itself already a *higher* answer than any of the all-too-cheap answers afforded by artificial systems of thought.

And so we, to whom the preservation of our people's will to know shall in the future be entrusted, declare: the National Socialist revolution is not merely the assumption of power as it exists presently in the State by another party, a party grown sufficiently large in numbers to be able to do so. Rather, this revolution is bringing about *the total transformation of our German existence [Dasein]*. From now on, each and every thing demands decision, and every deed demands responsibility. Of this we are certain: if the will to self-responsibility becomes the law that governs the coexistence of nations, then each people can and must be the master who instructs every other people in the richness and strength of all the great deeds and works of human Being [*Sein*].

The choice that the German people must now make is, *simply as an event in itself,* quite independently of the outcome, the strongest expression of the new German reality embodied in the National Socialist State. Our will to national [*völkisch*] self-responsibility desires that each people find and preserve the greatness and truth of its destiny [*Bestimmung*]. This will is the highest guarantee of peace among nations, for it binds itself to the basic law of manly respect and unconditional honor. The Führer has awakened this will in the entire people and has welded it into *one* single resolve. No one can remain away from the polls on the day when this will is manifested. Heil Hitler!

A Word from the University*
(January 6, 1934)

This retrospective look at its own history obligates the *Freiburger Zeitung* to commit itself to the future. The more directly the individual states that existed previously are absorbed by the new National Socialist State, the more resolutely the ethnic-cultural character [*das Volkstum*] of each Gau must be awakened and preserved in its original form; for only then will the entire Volk be able to develop its manifold strengths for creating a state. It was in order to realize this task that German education brought its work in line with the National Socialist political will [*Staatswille*]. The university is becoming the highest political school for the

---

*An article written by Heidegger on the occasion of the sesquicentennial of the *Freiburger Zeitung*.

people of the region where it is located. This newspaper, however, which is limited to and bound to the concerns and traditions of the Alemannic people, must not merely print the occasional report on school celebrations or faculty appointments. It must transform the educational work of the school into public state-mindedness in the village and, in the city, into a political existence that remains bound to the rural areas.

Heidegger

Rector of the University of Freiburg

The Call to the Labor Service*
(January 23, 1934)

The new path that is being followed by the education of our German young men [*Jungmannschaft*] leads through the Labor Service.

Such service provides the basic experience of hardness, of closeness to the soil and to the implements of labor, of the rigorous law that governs the simplest physical—and thus essential—labor in a group.

Such service provides the basic experience of daily existence in a camp community, an existence that is strictly ordered according to the requirements of the tasks that the group has undertaken.

Such service provides the basic experience of having put daily to the test [*auf die Probe und in die Entscheidung gestellt*], and thus clarified and reinforced, one's sense of social origin [*der ständischen Herkunft*] and of the responsibility that derives for the individual from the fact that all belong together in an ethnic-cultural [*volkhaft*] unity.

Such service provides the basic experience of the origin of true comradeship. True comradeship only arises under the pressure of a great common danger or from the ever-growing commitment to a clearly perceived task; it has nothing to do with the effusive exchange of psychological [*seelisch*] inhibitions by individuals who have agreed to sleep, eat, and sing under one roof.

* An article written by Heidegger for the *Freiburger Studentenzeitung*.

Such service provides the basic experience of those things which will allow the individual to be able to truly take stock of himself, and it takes the final decision in the choice of a profession out of the realm of the private bourgeois calculation of prospects according to the principle of "appropriateness to one's social standing."

We must think beyond the immediate effects of Labor Service, which are already apparent, and learn to comprehend the fact that here, with the German young people who are now taking their place in society, a complete transformation of German existence [*Dasein*] is being made ready. Within the German university, a new basic attitude towards scholarly and scientific *work* [*wissenschaftliche Arbeit*] will slowly develop. And as this happens, that notion of the "intellect" ["*Geist*"] and of "intellectual work" ["*geistige Arbeit*"] will completely disappear in terms of which the "educated" person has up to now defined his life and which even now his envoys want to salvage for a separate estate [*Stand*] of "intellectual producers." Only then will we learn that, *as work,* all work is *spiritual* [*geistig*]. Animals and all beings that merely exist cannot work. They lack the basic experience that work requires: the decisive commitment to a task, the capacity for resoluteness and steadfastness in an assignment they have accepted. In short, they lack *freedom,* that is: spirit [*Geist*].

So-called "intellectual work" ["*geistige Arbeit*"] is not spiritual [*geistig*] because it relates to "higher spiritual things" ["*höhere geistige Dinge*"]. It is spiritual [*geistig*] because, *as work,* it reaches back more deeply into the afflictions [*Not*] that are part of a people's historical existence [*Dasein*] and because it is more directly—because more knowingly—beset by the hardness and danger of human existence [*Dasein*].

There is only *one single* German "estate" ["*Lebensstand*"]. That is the *estate of labor* [*Arbeitsstand*] which is rooted in and borne by the Volk and which has freely submitted to the historical will of the State. The character of this estate is being pre-formed in the National Socialist *Workers' Party* movement.

A call to the Labor Service is being sounded.

Those who are lame, comfortable, and effete will "go" into the Labor Service because it will perhaps jeopardize their degree and employment prospects to stay away. Those who are strong and unbroken are proud that extreme demands are being made of them: for that is the moment when they rise up to the hardest tasks, those for which there is neither pay nor praise, but only the "reward" of sacrifice and service in the area of the innermost necessities of German Being [*deutschen Seins*].

National Socialist Education *
(January 22, 1934)

German Volksgenossen! German Workers!

As Rector of the University, I cordially welcome you to our institution. This welcome will at the same time be the beginning of our work together. Let us start by understanding clearly the significance of the fact that you, for whom the City of Freiburg has created jobs by emergency decree, are coming together with us in the largest lecture hall of the University.

What does this fact mean?

Because of novel and comprehensive measures on the part of the City of Freiburg you have been given work and bread has been put on your tables. You thereby enjoy a privileged position among the rest of the City's unemployed. But this preferential treatment means at the same time an obligation.

And your duty is to understand the creation of jobs, and to accept the work for which you are paid, in the way that the Führer of our new State demands. For the creation of jobs means not only the alleviation of external need, not only the elimination of inner discouragement or, indeed, despair; the creation of jobs means not only the *warding off* of that which burdens. The creation of jobs is at the same time, and in its

* An address given by Heidegger at Freiburg University to 600 beneficiaries of the National Socialist "labor service" (*Arbeitsdienst*) program (see note, p. 42). Published in *Der Alemann: Kampfblatt der Nationalsozialisten Oberbadens*, February 1, 1934.

essence, an act of *building up* and construction [*Aufbau und Bau*] in the new future of our Volk.

The creation of work must, first of all, make the unemployed and jobless *Volksgenosse* again *capable of existing* [*daseinsfähig*] in the State and for the State and thereby capable of existing for the Volk as a whole. The *Volksgenosse* who has found work should learn thereby that he has not been cast aside and abandoned, that he has an ordered place in the Volk, and that every service and every accomplishment possesses its own value that is fungible by other services and accomplishments. Having experienced this, he should win back proper dignity and self-confidence in his own eyes and acquire proper self-assurance and resoluteness in the eyes of his *Volksgenossen*.

The goal is: to become strong for a fully valid existence as a *Volksgenosse* in the German *Volksgemeinschaft*.

For this, however, it is necessary:
  to know where one's place in the Volk is,
  to know how the Volk is organized and how it renews itself in this organization,
  to know what is happening with the German Volk in the National Socialist State,
  to know in what a bitter struggle this new reality was won and created,
  to know what the future recovery of the body of the Volk [*Volkskörper*] means and what it demands of each individual,
  to know to what point urbanization has brought the Germans, how they would be returned to the soil and the country through resettlement,
  to know what is entailed in the fact that 18 million Germans belong to the Volk but, because they are living outside the borders of the Reich, do not yet belong to the Reich.

Everyone of our Volk who is employed must *know for what reason* and *to what purpose* he is where he is. It is only through this living and ever-present *knowledge* that his life will be rooted in the Volk as a whole, and in its destiny. *Providing this knowledge is thus a necessary part of the creation of work;* and it is your right, but therefore also your obligation, to demand this knowledge and to endeavor to acquire it.

And now, your younger comrades from the *university* stand ready to help you acquire this knowledge. They are resolved to help that knowledge to become alive in you, to help it develop and grow strong and never again to slumber. They stand ready, not as "intellekshuals" ["*Gschtudierten*"] from the class of your "betters," but as *Volksgenossen*' who have recognized their duty.

They stand ready, not as the "educated" vis-à-vis a class—indeed, a "lower class"—of *uneducated* individuals, but as comrades. They are prepared to listen to your questions, your problems, your difficulties, and your doubts, to think through them with you, and, in shared effort, to bring them to a clear and decisive resolution. What, therefore, is the significance of the fact that you are assembled here in the auditorium of the University with us?

This fact is a sign that a new, common will exists, the will to build *a living bridge* between the worker of the "hand" and the worker of the "head." Today, the will to bridge this gap is no longer a project that is doomed to failure. And why not? Because the whole of our German reality has been changed by the National Socialist State, with the result that our whole past way of understanding and thinking must also become different.

What we thought up to now when we used the words "knowledge" and "Wissenschaft" has taken on another significance.

What we meant up to now with the words "worker" and "work" has acquired another meaning.

"Wissenschaft" is not the possession of a privileged class of citizens, to be used as a weapon in the exploitation of the working people. Rather, Wissenschaft is merely the *more rigorous* and hence *more responsible* form of that knowledge which the entire German Volk must seek and

57

demand for its own historical existence as a state [*sein eigenes geschicht-lich-staatliches Dasein*] if it still wants to secure its continued existence and greatness and to preserve them in the future. *In its essence,* the knowledge of true Wissenschaft does *not* differ *at all* from the knowledge of the farmer, woodcutter, the miner, the artisan. For knowledge means: *to know one's way around* in the world into which we are placed, as a community and as individuals.

Knowledge means: in our decisions and actions *to be up to* the task that is assigned us, whether this task be to till the soil or to fell a tree or to dig a ditch or to inquire into the laws of Nature or to illumine the fate-like force of History.

Knowledge means: to be *master* of the situation into which we are placed.

What is decisive is not so much how varied our knowledge is and what quantity of things we know, but whether our knowledge has grown naturally out of and is directed towards our circle of existence [*ein ursprünglich gewachsenes und auf unseren Daseinskreis aussgerichtetes*] and whether, through our deeds and in our behavior, we take responsibility for what we know. We no longer distinguish between the "educated" and the "uneducated." And not because these are both the same, but because we no longer tie our estimation of a person to this distinction. We do, on the other hand, differentiate between *genuine knowledge* and *pseudo-knowledge.* Genuine knowledge is something that both the farmer and the manual laborer have, each in his own way and in his own field of work, just as the scholar has it in his field. And, on the other hand, for all his learning, the scholar can in fact simply be wasting his time in the idle pursuit of pseudo-knowledge.

If you are to become *ones who know* here, then that does not mean that you will be served up scraps of some "general education," as a charitable afterthought. Rather, *that knowledge* shall be awakened in you *by means of which you*—each in his respective class and work group—*can be clear and resolute Germans.*

Knowledge and the possession of knowledge, as National Socialism understands these words, does not divide into classes, but binds and unites *Volksgenossen* and social and occupational groups [*Stände*] in the one great will of the State.

Like these words "knowledge" and "Wissenschaft," the words "worker" and "work," too, have a transformed meaning and a new sound. The "worker" is not, as Marxism claimed, a mere object of exploitation. The workers [*Arbeiterstand*] are not the class of the disinherited who are rallying for the general class struggle. But labor is also not simply the production of goods for others. Nor is labor simply the occasion and the means to earn a living. Rather:

For us, "work" is the title of every well-ordered action that is borne by the responsibility of the individual, the group, and the State and which is thus of service to the Volk.

Work only exists where man's determination and perseverance are freely engaged in the assertion of will and the accomplishment of a task; *but there it exists everywhere.* Therefore, all work is, *as work,* something spiritual [*Geistiges*], for it is founded in the free exercise of expert knowledge and in the competent understanding of one's task; that is: it is founded in authentic knowledge [*eigentliches Wissen*]. The accomplishment of a miner is basically no less spiritual [*geistig*] than the activity of a scholar.

Worker and work, as National Socialism understands these words, does not divide into classes, but binds and unites *Volksgenossen* and the social and occupational groups into the one great will of the State.

The "workers" and "academics" [*die "wissenschaftlich Wissenden"*] are not opposites. Every worker is, in his own way, one who knows; and only as one who knows is he able to work at all. The privilege of work is denied the animal. And conversely: every person who acts knowingly and who makes decisions in and on the basis of Wissenschaft [*wissenschaftlich Entscheidender*] *is a worker.*

Martin Heidegger

For this reason, neither for you nor for us can the will to build a living bridge remain any longer an empty, hopeless wish. This will, *to consummate the creation of jobs by providing the right kind of knowledge,* this will must be our innermost certainty and never-faltering faith. For in what this will wills, we are only following the towering will of our Führer. To be his loyal followers means: to will that the German people shall again find, as a people of labor, its organic unity, its simple dignity, and its true strength; and that, as a state of labor, it shall secure for itself permanence and greatness.

To the man of this unprecedented will, to our Führer *Adolf Hitler*—a threefold "Sieg Heil!"

Translated by William S. Lewis

3

LETTER TO THE RECTOR OF FREIBURG UNIVERSITY, NOVEMBER 4, 1945

With reference to the Rector's letter of October 30, 1945, I request to be reinstated in my professorial duties (reintegration). I also remind you that on October 8, 1945 I submitted my request for emeritus status to the philosophy faculty. I ask that you convey this request to the proper authorities.

Regarding the reasons for and conditions of my entry into the Party on May 1, 1933, as well as my relations with the Party during the years 1933–1945, I wish to make the following observations:

I. The Rectorship, 1933–1934

In April 1933, I was unanimously elected Rector (with two abstentions) in a plenary session of the university and not, as rumor has it, appointed by the National Socialist minister. It was as a result of pressure from my circle of colleagues, and especially upon the urgent request of my predecessor [Wilhelm] von Möllendorff, that I consented to be a candidate for this election and agreed to serve. Previously I neither desired nor occupied an academic office. I never belonged to a political party nor maintained a relation, either personal or substantive, with the NSDAP or with governmental authorities. I accepted the rectorship reluctantly and in the interest of the university alone.

However, I was nevertheless absolutely convinced that an autonomous alliance of intellectuals [der Geistigen] could deepen and transform a number of essential elements of the "National Socialist movement"

Heidegger's Letter to the Rector of Freiburg University, November 4, 1945, may be found in Karl A. Moehling, "Martin Heidegger and the Nazi Party: An Examination." Ph.D. dissertation, Northern Illinois University, 1972.

and thereby contribute in its own way to overcoming Europe's disarray and the crisis of the Western spirit. Three [sic] addresses by a man of no lesser rank than Paul Valéry ("The Crisis of Spirit," "The Politics of Spirit," "Our Sovereign Good," "The Balance of Intelligence") constitute sufficient proof of the seriousness, concern, and profundity with which the destiny of the West became an object of reflection outside of Germany during these years. Also, insofar as the will manifested by the free choice of the preponderant majority of the German people affirmed the labor of reconstruction in a National Socialist direction, I viewed it as necessary and feasible to join in at the university level in order to remedy in a consistent and effective manner the general confusion and threat that weighed against the West. And it is precisely because in the realm of the sciences and of spirit so-called "impossible" persons strove to assert their power and influence on the "movement" that it seemed to me necessary to emphasize essentially spiritual goals and horizons and to try, on the basis of Western responsibility, to further their influence and reality. I explained my intentions with sufficient clarity in my rectoral address, "The Self-Assertion of the German University" (1933). If I may be permitted to explain the basic spiritual tenor of the address from a twofold perspective: on page 13, with reference to the essential task of spirit, it says: "And the spiritual world of a people is neither the superstructure of a culture, nor an attestation of practical knowledge and values. . . . The greatness of a Volk is guaranteed by its spiritual world alone." For those who know and think, these sentences express my opposition to [Alfred] Rosenberg's conception, according to which, conversely, spirit and the world of spirit are merely an "expression" and emanation of racial facts and of the physical constitution of man. According to the dogma of "politicized science," which was then propagated by the National Socialist student organizations, the sciences should serve as a model for vocational goals, and the value or the lack of value of knowledge should be measured according to the needs of "life." In response, the address clearly and unambiguously has this to say: "Knowledge does not stand in the service of the professions, but the reverse: the professions effectuate and administer this highest, essential knowledge of the Volk concerning its entire Dasein." "The university" is "the locus of spiritual legislation." All of those who are capable of substantive thought [*sachliche Denken*] will be able to judge whether the essence of the university can be thought in a more exalted manner than here. And whether the essence of the various fields of knowledge has, from a spiritual standpoint, been defined in a more clear or categorical fashion than in this formulation: "The departments are only departments if they are deployed in a power of spiritual legislation that is rooted in a capacity consistent with their essence, in order that they might transform the force of Dasein which besieges *them* into a *single* spiritual world of the Volk."

In the spirit of this address, I tried, following the irremediably disruptive summer semester of revolution [in 1933] and despite the many setbacks experienced thus far, in the initial months of the 1933–34 winter semester to keep the business of the university going. It was clear for me that to act in the middle of the frictions of real life was not possible without compromise and concessions in unessential matters. But I was equally convinced, especially following Hitler's May 1933 speech asking for peace, that my basic spiritual position and my conception of the task of the university could be reconciled with the political will of those in power.

The practical efforts of the winter semester failed. During the few days of Christmas vacation I realized that it was a mistake to believe that, from the basic spiritual position that was the result of my long years of philosophical work, I could immediately influence the transformation of the bases—spiritual or non-spiritual—of the National Socialist movement. At the beginning of 1934 I decided to abandon my duties at the end of the semester. The increasing hostility of the minister to my work as rector manifested itself in practice by the summons to replace the deans of the divisions of law and medicine (professors Wolf and von Möllendorff) because they were politically unacceptable. I refused to acquiesce in this demand and handed in my resignation. (I refused equally to assist in the traditional ceremony of the inauguration of my successor, who was installed by force and acclaimed as the first National Socialist rector. I gave as my explanation that there was nothing to "hand over" since the new rector was chosen and nominated by the government.)

II. My Entry into the Party

A short while after I took control of the rectorship the district head presented himself, accompanied by two functionaries in charge of university matters, to urge me, in accordance with the wishes of the minister, to join the Party. The minister insisted that in this way my official relations with the Party and the governing organs would be simplified, especially since up until then I had had no contact with these organs. After lengthy consideration, I declared myself ready to enter the Party in the interests of the university, but under the express condition of refusing to accept a position within the Party or working on behalf of the Party either during the rectorship or afterward. These conditions were accepted by the leader of the district, and I adhered to them strictly thereafter.

III. My Relation to the Party after 1933

My membership [in the Party] resulted in practically no advantages as far as the facilitation of my administrative duties was concerned. I was never invited to meetings of the district leadership. University personnel began to mistrust me. After my resignation from the rectorship it became clear that by continuing to teach, my opposition to the principles of the National Socialist world-view would only grow. There was little need for me to resort to specific attacks; it sufficed for me to express my fundamental philosophical positions against the dogmatism and primitivism of Rosenberg's biologism. I found myself in an essentially different situation from that of other representatives of scientific disciplines, where there was neither immediately nor in principle a need to formulate fundamental metaphysical positions; and this is precisely what I did during all of my hours in the classroom. Since National Socialist ideology became increasingly inflexible and increasingly less disposed to a purely philosophical interpretation, the fact that I was active as a philosopher was itself a sufficient expression of opposition. During the first semester that followed my resignation I conducted a course on logic and under the title, the doctrine of *logos,* treated the essence of language. I sought to show that language was not the biological-racial essence of man, but conversely, that the essence of man was based in language as a basic reality of *spirit.* All intelligent students understood this lecture as well as its basic intention. It was equally understood by the observers and informers who then gave reports of my activities to [Ernst] Krieck in Heidelberg, to [Alfred] Bäumler in Berlin, and to Rosenberg, the head of National Socialist scientific services. Thereafter there began a malicious polemic against my thought and person in *Volk im Werden,* a review edited by Krieck. During the journal's twelve years in print, there hardly appeared an issue that didn't contain some heinous and misleading point about my thought. All these declarations emanating from the Party press were made in the same tone whenever I lectured before scholarly organizations, in my lectures on "The Origins of the Work of Art," or on "The Metaphysical Foundations of the Modern Picture of the World." No member of the Freiburg University faculty was defamed to such a degree during the years 1933–34 in newspapers and journals, and, in addition, in the journal of the Hitler Youth, *Will and Power.*

Beginning in 1936 I embarked on a series of courses and lectures on Nietzsche, which lasted until 1945 and which represented in even clearer fashion a declaration of spiritual resistance. In truth, it is unjust to assimilate Nietzsche to National Socialism, an assimilation which— apart from what is essential—ignores his hostility to anti-Semitism and his positive attitude with respect to Russia. But on a higher plane, the debate with Nietzsche's metaphysics is a debate with *nihilism* as it manifests itself with increased clarity under the political form of fascism.

The Party functionaries also took note of the spiritual resistance of my courses on Nietzsche, which led to measures such as the following:

In 1934, I was excluded, at Rosenberg's urging, from the German delegation of the International Congress of Philosophy. I was also excluded in 1937 from the German delegation at the Descartes conference in Paris, which was also an international philosophical conference (although the French for their part twice expressly requested that I attend). The reedition of my work, *Kant and the Problem of Metaphysics,* which originally appeared in 1929 and which was out off print as of 1931, and which contained a refutation of philosophical anthropology, was also banned at the instigation of the same office. From 1938 on, one could no longer cite my name nor evaluate my works as a result of secret instructions given to journal editors. I cite one such directive dating from 1940, which was revealed to me in confidence by friends:

Z.D. 165/34. Edition No. 7154

Martin Heidegger's essay, "Plato's Concept of Truth," to appear soon in the Berlin journal, *Jahrbuch für geistige Überlieferung,* edited by Helmut Küper, may be neither reviewed nor cited. Heidegger's participation in this number of the journal, which otherwise may be reviewed, should not be mentioned.

The publication of this essay, which was accepted by the editor for a special edition to be sold in bookstores, was forbidden. The same thing occurred with my contribution to a volume commemorating Hölderlin, which had to appear in a separate edition.

Whereas my name and writings have been passed over in silence in Germany, where it has been impossible for me to publish individual works—in 1943 three small lectures appeared in secret, without ever being cited in any bibliography—during the war I was on many occasions invited for propagandistic ends to give lectures in Spain, Portugal, and Italy. I formally refused these strange invitations by making it known that I was not disposed to lend my name abroad for purposes of propaganda while I was not allowed to publish my writings in my own country.

The German Institute of Paris utilized the same methods as the Ministry of Foreign Affairs. In a collection entitled *Friedrich Hölderlin,* which was published in 1943 in Paris, it reproduced my lecture, "Hölderlin and the Essence of Poetry," which appeared in 1936 and was translated into French in 1938, in the same translation and *without my knowledge,* and without the permission of the French translator. This arbitrary publication occurred despite the fact that I had already declined the offer to participate in a review published by the same institute.

I also demonstrated publicly my attitude toward the Party by not participating in its gatherings, by not wearing its regalia, and, as of 1934, by refusing to begin my courses and lectures with the so-called German greeting [Heil Hitler!].

There was nothing special about my spiritual resistance during the last eleven years. However, if crude claims continue to be advanced that numerous students had been "enticed" toward "National Socialism" by my year as rector, justice requires that one at least recognize that between 1934 and 1944 thousands of students were trained to reflect on the metaphysical basis of our age and that I opened their eyes to the world of spirit and its great traditions in the history of the West.

Martin Heidegger

Translated by Richard Wolin

4

OVERCOMING METAPHYSICS

I

What does "overcoming metaphysics" mean? In the thinking of the history of Being, this rubric is used only as an aid for that thinking to be comprehensible at all. In truth, this rubric is the occasion for a great deal of misunderstanding because it doesn't allow experience to reach the ground in virtue of which the history of Being first reveals its essence. This essence is the Appropriating in which Being itself is overcome. Above all, overcoming does not mean thrusting aside a discipline from the field of philosophical "education." "Metaphysics" is already thought as the destiny of the truth of beings, that is, of beingness, *as* a still hidden but distinctive Appropriating, namely the oblivion of Being.

Since overcoming is meant as a product of philosophy, the more adequate rubric might be: the past of metaphysics. Of course this calls forth new erroneous opinions. The past means here: to perish and enter what has been. In that metaphysics perishes, it *is* past. The past does not exclude, but rather includes, the fact that metaphysics is now for the first time beginning its unconditional rule in beings themselves, and rules as beings in the form, devoid of truth, of what is real and of objects. Experienced in virtue of the dawning of the origin, metaphysics is, however, at the same time past in the sense that it has entered its ending. The ending lasts longer than the previous history of metaphysics.

II

Metaphysics cannot be abolished like an opinion. One can by no means leave it behind as a doctrine no longer believed and represented.

"Overcoming Metaphysics" ("Überwindung der Metaphysik") first appeared in Martin Heidegger, *Vorträge und Aufsätze* (Pfullingen: Neske, 1954). This English translation by Joan Stambaugh appeared in Martin Heidegger, *The End of Metaphysics* (New York: Harper and Row, 1973). Grateful acknowledgment is made to Harper and Row for permission to reprint.

The fact that man as *animal rationale,* here meant in the sense of the working being, must wander through the desert of the earth's desolation could be a sign that metaphysics occurs in virtue of Being, and the overcoming of metaphysics occurs as the incorporation of Being. For labor (cf. Ernst Jünger, *Der Arbeiter,* 1932) is now reaching the metaphysical rank of the unconditional objectification of everything present which is active in the will to will.

If this is so, we may not presume to stand outside of metaphysics because we surmise the ending of metaphysics. For metaphysics overcome in this way does not disappear. It returns transformed, and remains in dominance as the continuing difference of Being and beings.

The decline of the truth of beings means: the openness of beings and *only* beings loses the previous uniqueness of their authoritative claim.

III

The decline of the truth of beings occurs necessarily, and indeed as the completion of metaphysics.

The decline occurs through the collapse of the world characterized by metaphysics, and at the same time through the desolation of the earth stemming from metaphysics.

Collapse and desolation find their adequate occurrence in the fact that metaphysical man, the *animal rationale,* gets fixed as the laboring animal.

This rigidification confirms the most extreme blindness to the oblivion of Being. But man wills *himself* as the volunteer of the will to will, for which all truth becomes that error which it needs in order to be able to guarantee for itself the illusion that the will to will can will nothing other than empty nothingness, in the face of which it asserts itself without being able to know its own completed nullity.

Before Being can occur in its primal truth, Being as the will must be broken, the world must be forced to collapse and the earth must be driven to desolation, and man to mere labor. Only after this decline does the abrupt dwelling of the Origin take place for a long span of time. In the decline, everything, that is, beings in the whole of the truth of metaphysics, approaches its end.

The decline has already taken place. The consequences of this occurrence are the events of world history in this century. They are merely the course of what has already ended. Its course is ordered historico-technologically in the sense of the last stage of metaphysics. This order is the last arrangement of what has ended in the illusion of a reality whose effects work in an irresistible way, because they claim to be able to get along without an unconcealment of the *essence of Being*. They do this so decisively that they need suspect nothing of such an unconcealment.

The still hidden truth of Being is withheld from metaphysical humanity. The laboring animal is left to the giddy whirl of its products so that it may tear itself to pieces and annihilate itself in empty nothingness.

IV

How does metaphysics belong to man's nature? Metaphysically represented, man is constituted with faculties as a being among others. His essence constituted in such a way, his nature, the what and how of his Being, are in themselves metaphysical: *animal* (sensuousness) and *rationale* (nonsensuous). Thus confined to what is metaphysical, man is caught in the difference of beings and Being which he never experiences. The manner of human representation which is metaphysically characterized finds everywhere only the metaphysically constructed world. Metaphysics belongs to the nature of man. But what is this nature itself? What is metaphysics itself? Who is man himself within this natural metaphysics? Is he only an ego which first thoroughly fixates itself in its egoity through appealing to a thou in the I-thou relationship?

For Descartes the *ego cogito* is what is already represented and produced in all *cogitationes,* what is present without question, what is indubitable and always standing within knowledge, what is truly certain, what stands firm in advance of everything, namely as that which places everything in relation to *itself* and thus "over against" others.

To the object there belongs both the what-constituent of that which stands over against (*essentia-possibilitas*) and the actual standing of that which stands opposite (*existentia*). The object is the unity of the constancy of what persists. In its standing, persistence is essentially related to the presentation of re-presentation as the guarantee of having-something-in-front-of-oneself. The original object is objectively itself. Original objectivity is the "I think," in the sense of the "I perceive" which already presents and has presented itself in advance for everything perceivable. It is the *subiectum*. In the order of the transcendental genesis of the object, the subject is the first object of ontological representation.

Ego cogito is *cogito: me cogitare.*

V

The modern form of ontology is transcendental philosophy which becomes epistemology.

How does such a thing arise in modern metaphysics? In that the beingness of beings is thought as presence *for* the guarantee of representation. Beingness is now objectivity. The question about objectivity, about the possibility of standing over against (namely, over against guaranteeing, calculating representation) is the question about knowability.

But this question is not really meant as the question about the psychophysical mechanism of the procedure of knowing, but rather about the possibility of the presence of the object in and for knowledge.

"Epistemology" is viewing, *theoria,* in that the *on,* thought as object, is questioned with regard to objectivity and what makes objectivity possible (*be on*).

How does Kant guarantee the metaphysical element of modern metaphysics through the transcendental manner of questioning? In that truth becomes certainty and thus the beingness (*ousia*) of beings changes to the objectivity of *perceptio* and the *cogitatio* of consciousness, of knowledge; knowing and knowledge move to the foreground.

"Epistemology" and what goes under that name is at bottom metaphysics and ontology which is based on truth as the certainty of guaranteed representation.

On the other hand, the interpretation of "epistemology" as the explanation of "knowledge" and as the "theory" of the sciences errs, although this business of guaranteeing is only a consequence of the reinterpretation of Being as objectivity and representedness.

"Epistemology" is the title for the increasing, essential powerlessness of modern metaphysics to know its own essence and the ground of that essence. The talk about "metaphysics of knowledge" remains within the same misunderstanding. In truth, it is a matter of the metaphysics of the object, that is, of beings as object, of the object for a subject.

The mere reverse side of the empirical-positivistic misinterpretation of epistemology shows itself in the growing dominance of logistics.

VI

The completion of metaphysics begins with Hegel's metaphysics of absolute knowledge as the Spirit of will.

Why is this metaphysics only the beginning of the completion and not the completion itself? Hasn't unconditional certainty come to itself as absolute reality?

Is there still a possibility here of self-transcendence? Probably not. But the possibility of unconditional self-examination as the will of life is still not accomplished. The will has not yet appeared as the will to will in its reality which it has prepared. Hence metaphysics is not yet completed with the absolute metaphysics of the Spirit.

In spite of the superficial talk about the breakdown of Hegelian philosophy, one thing remains true: only this philosophy determined reality in the nineteenth century, although not in the external form of a doctrine followed, but rather as metaphysics, as the dominance of being-ness in the sense of certainty. The countermovements to this metaphysics belong *to* it. Ever since Hegel's death (1831), everything is merely a countermovement, not only in Germany, but also in Europe.

VII

It is characteristic for metaphysics that in it *existentia* is always consistently treated only briefly and as a matter of course, if it is treated at all (cf. the inadequate explanation of the postulates of reality in Kant's *Critique of Pure Reason*). The sole exception is Aristotle, who thinks out *energeia*, without this thinking ever being able to become essential in its originality in the future. The transformation of *energeia* to *actualitas* and reality buried everything which became apparent in *energeia*. The connection between *ousia* and *energeia* becomes obscure. Hegel first thinks out *existentia*, but in his "Logic." Schelling thinks it in the distinction of ground and existence. However, this distinction is rooted in subjectivity.

A later and confused echo of Being as *physis* shows itself in the narrowing down of Being to "Nature."

Reason and freedom are contrasted with nature. Because nature is what-is, freedom and the ought are not thought as Being. The opposition of Being and the ought, Being and value, remains. Finally Being itself, too, becomes a mere "value" when the will enters its most extreme deformation of essence. Value is thought as a condition of the will.

VIII

Metaphysics is in all its forms and historical stages a unique, but perhaps necessary, fate of the West and the presupposition of its planetary dominance. The will of that planetary dominance is now in turn affecting the center of the West. Again, only a will meets the will from this center.

The development of the unconditional dominance of metaphysics is only at its start. This beginning starts when metaphysics affirms its deformation of essence which is adequate to it, and surrenders its essence to that deformation and fixates it there.

Metaphysics is a fate in the strict sense, which is the only sense intended here, that it lets mankind be suspended in the middle of beings as a fundamental trait of Western European history, *without* the Being of beings ever being able to be experienced and questioned and structured in its truth *as the twofoldness* of both in terms of metaphysics and through metaphysics.

This fate, which is to be thought in the manner of the history of Being, is, however, necessary, because Being itself can open out in its truth the difference of Being and beings preserved in itself only when the difference explicitly takes place. But how can it do this if beings have not first entered the most extreme oblivion of Being, and if at the same time Being has not taken over its unconditional dominance, metaphysically incomprehensible, as the will to will which asserts itself at first and uniquely through the sole precedence of beings (of what is objectively real) over Being?

Thus what can be distinguished in the difference in a way presents itself, and yet keeps itself hidden in a strange incomprehensibility. Hence the difference itself remains veiled. A sign of this is the metaphysico-technological reaction to pain which at the same time predetermines the interpretation of the essence of pain.

Together with the beginning of the completion of metaphysics, the preparation begins, unrecognized and essentially inaccessible to metaphysics, for a first appearance of the twofoldness of Being and beings. In this appearance the first resonance of the truth of Being still conceals itself, taking back into itself the precedence of Being with regard to its dominance.

IX

Overcoming metaphysics is thought in the manner of the history of Being. It is the preliminary sign of the primal incorporation of the oblivion of Being. More prior, although also more concealed than the preliminary sign, is what shows itself in that sign. This is Appropriation itself. What looks to the metaphysical way of thinking like the preliminary sign of something else, is taken into account only as the last mere illusion of a more primal opening out.

Overcoming is worthy of thought only when we think about incorporation. This perduring thinking still thinks at the same time about overcoming. Such remembrance experiences the unique Appropriating of the expropriating of beings, in which the need of the truth of Being, and thus the origination of truth, opens up and radiates upon human being in the manner of a parting. Overcoming is the delivering over of metaphysics to its truth.

At first the overcoming of metaphysics can only be represented in terms of metaphysics itself, so to speak, in the manner of a heightening of itself through itself. In this case the talk about the metaphysics of metaphysics, which is touched upon in the book *Kant and the Problem of Metaphysics,* is justified in that it attempts to interpret the Kantian idea from this perspective, which still stems from the mere critique of rationalist metaphysics. However, more is thus attributed to Kant's thinking than he himself was able to think within the limits of his philosophy.

The talk of overcoming metaphysics can also mean that "metaphysics" is the name for the Platonism portrayed in the modern world by the interpretation of Schopenhauer and Nietzsche. The reversal of Platonism, according to which for Nietzsche the sensuous becomes the true world and the suprasensuous becomes the untrue world, is thoroughly caught in metaphysics. This kind of overcoming of metaphysics, which Nietzsche has in mind in the spirit of nineteenth-century positivism, is only the final entanglement in metaphysics, although in a higher form. It looks as if the "meta," the transcendence to the suprasensuous, were replaced by the persistence in the elemental world of sensuousness, whereas actually the oblivion of Being is only completed and the suprasensuous is let loose and furthered by the will to power.

X

Without being able to know it and without permitting a knowledge about it, the will to will wards off every destiny, whereby we understand by destiny the granting of an openness of the Being of beings. The will to will rigidifies everything in lack of destiny. The consequence of lack of destiny is the unhistorical. Its characteristic is the dominance of historiography. Historiography's being at a loss is historicism. If one wanted to construct the history of Being in accordance with the *historiographical* representational thinking common today, the dominance of the oblivion of Being's destiny would be confirmed by this mistake in the most blatant way. The epoch of completed metaphysics stands before its beginning.

The will to will forces the calculation and arrangement of everything for itself as the basic forms of appearance, only, however, for the unconditionally protractible guarantee of itself.

The basic form of appearance in which the will to will arranges and calculates itself in the unhistorical element of the world of completed metaphysics can be stringently called "technology." This name includes all the areas of beings which equip the whole of beings: objectified nature, the business of culture, manufactured politics, and the gloss of ideals overlying everything. Thus "technology" does not signify here the separate areas of the production and equipment of machines. The latter of course have a position of power, to be more closely defined, which is grounded in the precedence of matter as the supposedly elemental and primarily objective factor.

The name "technology" is understood here in such an essential way that its meaning coincides with the term "completed metaphysics." It contains the recollection of *techne,* which is a fundamental condition of the essential development of metaphysics in general. At the same time, the name makes it possible for the planetary factor of the completion of metaphysics and its dominance to be thought without reference to historiographically demonstrable changes in nations and continents.

XI

Nietzsche's metaphysics makes apparent the second to the last stage of the will's development of the beingness of beings as the will to will. The last stage's failure to appear is grounded in the predominance of "psychology," in the concept of power and force, in life-enthusiasm. For this reason this thinking lacks the strictness and carefulness of the concept and the peacefulness of historical reflection. Historiography rules and, thus, apologetics and polemics.

Why did Nietzsche's metaphysics lead to a scorn of thinking under the banner of "life"? Because no one realized how, according to Nietzsche's doctrine, the representational-calculative (empowering) guarantee of stability is just as essential for "life" as "increase" and escalation. Escalation itself has been taken only in the aspect of the intoxicating (psychologically), but not in the decisive aspect of at the same time giving to the guarantee of stability the true and ever new impulse and the justification for escalation. Hence it is the unconditional rule of calculating reason which belongs to the will to power, and not the fog and confusion of an opaque chaos of life. The misled Wagnerian cult imposed an artistic aura on Nietzsche's thinking and its presentation, which, after the process of the scorn of philosophy (that is, Hegel's and Schelling's) through Schopenhauer, and after Schopenhauer's superficial interpretation of Plato and Kant, prepared the last decades of the nineteenth century for an enthusiasm for which the superficial and foggy element of ahistoricality automatically serves as a characteristic of what is true.

Behind all this, however, lies the singular incapacity of thinking in terms of the being of metaphysics and recognizing the scope of truth's essential transformation and the historical sense of the awakening predominance of truth as certainty. Behind it, too, lies the incapacity of thinking Nietzsche's metaphysics in its relation to the simple paths of modern metaphysics in terms of this knowledge, instead of making a literary phenomenon out of it which rather overheats our brains than purifies, and makes us pause, and perhaps even frightens us. Finally, Nietzsche's passion for creators betrays the fact that he thinks of the genius and the geniuslike only in a modern way, and at the same time technologically from the viewpoint of accomplishment. The two constitutive "values" (truth and art) in the concept of the will to power are only circumscriptions for "technology," in the essential sense of a planning and calculating stabilization as accomplishment, and for the creating of the "creators" who bring a new stimulus to life over and above life as it is, and guarantee the business of culture.

All of this remains in the service of the will to power, but it also prevents the will to power's being from entering the clear light of the broad, essential knowing which can only have its origin in the thinking of the history of Being.

The being of the will to power can only be understood in terms of the will to will. The will to will, however, can only be experienced when metaphysics has already entered its transition.

XII

Nietzsche's metaphysics of the will to power is prefigured in the sentence: "The Greek knew and sensed the terrors and horrors of existence: in order to be able to live at all, he had to set up the radiant dream-creation of Olympus above them" (*Socrates and Greek Tragedy*, chapter 3, 1871; the original version of *Birth of Tragedy from the Spirit of Music*, Munich, 1933).

The opposition of the "titanic" and the "barbaric," of the "wild" and the "impulsive" is put here on *one* side, and beautiful, sublime appearance on the *other*.

Although it is not yet clearly thought out and differentiated and seen from a unified perspective, the idea is prefigured here that the "will" needs *at the same time* the guarantee of stability and escalation. But the fact that will is will to power still remains concealed. Schopenhauer's doctrine of the will dominates Nietzsche's thinking at first. The preface to the work is written "on Schopenhauer's birthday."

With Nietzsche's metaphysics, philosophy is completed. That means: it has gone through the sphere of prefigured possibilities. Completed metaphysics, which is the ground for the planetary manner of thinking, gives the scaffolding for an order of the earth which will supposedly last for a long time. The order no longer needs philosophy because philosophy is already its foundation. But with the end of philosophy, thinking is not also at its end, but in transition to another beginning.

XIII

In the notes to the fourth part of *Thus Spoke Zarathustra*, Nietzsche writes (1886): "*We are attempting a venture with truth!*" Perhaps humanity will perish by it! So be it!" (WW XII, p. 307).

An entry written at the time of *The Dawn of Day* (1880–81) reads: "What is new about our present position with regard to philosophy is the conviction which no age has ever yet had: *that we do not have the truth*. All men of earlier times 'had the truth'—even the skeptics" (WW XI, p. 268).

What does Nietzsche mean when he speaks now and then of "the truth"? Does he mean "what is true," and does he think this as what truly is, or as what is valid in all judgments, behavior, and life?

What does this mean: to attempt a venture with the truth? Does it mean: to bring the will to power into relation with the eternal recurrence of the same as what truly is?

Does this thinking ever get to the question as to *wherein* the *essential being* of truth consists and *whence* the truth of this *essential being* occurs?

XIV

How does objectivity come to have the character of constituting the essential being of beings as such?

One thinks "Being" as objectivity, and then tries to get to "what is in itself." But one only forgets to ask and to say what one means here by "what is" and by "in itself."

What "is" Being? May we inquire into "Being" as to *what* it *is*? Being remains unquestioned and a matter of course, and thus unthought. It holds itself in a truth which has long since been forgotten and is without ground.

XV

There can be an object in the sense of ob-ject only where man becomes a subject, where the subject becomes the ego and the ego becomes the *ego cogito,* only where this *cogitare* is conceived in its essence as the "original synthetic unity of transcendental apperception," only where the apex for "logic" is attained (in truth as the certainty of the "I think"). Here the being of the object first reveals itself in its objectivity. Here it first becomes possible and, as a consequence, unavoidable to understand objectivity itself as "the new true object" and to think it unconditionally.

XVI

Subjectivity, object, and reflection belong together. Only when reflection as such is experienced, namely, as the supporting relation to beings, only then can Being be determined as objectivity.

The experience of reflection as this relation, however, presupposes that the relation to beings *is* experienced as *repraesentatio* in general: as re-presentation.

But this can become a matter of destiny only when the *idea* has become *perceptio.* The transformation of truth as correspondence to truth as certainty, in which the *adaequatio* remains preserved, underlies this change. Certainty as self-guaranteeing (willing-oneself) is *iustititia* as the justification of the relation to beings and of their first cause, and thus of the belongingness to beings. *Iustificatio* in the sense of the Reformation and Nietzsche's concept of justice as truth are the same thing.

Essentially, *repraesentatio* is grounded in *reflexio.* For this reason, the being of objectivity as such first becomes evident where the being of thinking is recognized as explicitly brought about as "I think something," that is, as reflection.

XVII

Kant is on the way to thinking the being of reflection in the transcendental, that is, in the ontological sense. This occurs in the form of a hardly noticeable side remark in the *Critique of Pure Reason* under the title "On the Amphiboly of the Concepts of Reflection." The section is a supplement, but it is filled with essential insight and critical dialogue with Leibniz, and thus with all previous metaphysics, as Kant himself sees it and as it is grounded in its ontological constitution in egoity.

XVIII

Regarded from the outside, it looks as if egoity were only the retroactive generalization and abstraction of what is egolike from the individual "egos" of man. Descartes above all obviously thinks of his own "ego" as the individual person (*res cogitans* as *substantia finita*). Kant, on the other hand, thinks "consciousness in general." But Descartes also already thinks his own individual ego in the light of egoity which, however, is not yet explicitly represented. This egoity already appears in the form of the *certum,* the certainty which is nothing other than the guaranteeing of what is represented for representational thinking. The hidden relation to egoity as the certainty of itself and of what is represented is already dominant. The individual ego can be experienced as such only in terms of this relation. The human ego as the individual self completing itself can only will itself in the light of the *relation* of the will to will, as yet unknown, *to* this ego. No ego is there "in itself," but rather is "in itself" always only as appearing "within itself," that is, as egoity.

For this reason, egoity is also present where the individual ego by no means presses forward, where it rather retreats, and society and other communal forms rule. There, too, and precisely there, we find the pure dominance of "egoity" which must be thought metaphysically, and which has nothing to do with naively thought "solipsism."

Philosophy in the age of completed metaphysics is anthropology (cf. *Holzwege,* p. 91f.). Whether or not one says "philosophical" anthropology makes no difference. In the meantime philosophy has become anthropology and in this way a prey to the derivatives of metaphysics, that is, of physics in the broadest sense, which includes the physics of life and man, biology and psychology. Having become anthropology, philosophy itself perishes of metaphysics.

XIX

The will to will presupposes as the condition of its possibility the guarantee of stability (truth) and the possibility of exaggerating drives (art). Accordingly, the will to will arranges even beings as Being. In the will to will, technology (guarantee of stability) and the unconditional lack of reflection ("experience") first come to dominance.

Technology as the highest form of rational consciousness, technologically interpreted, and the lack of reflection as the arranged powerlessness, opaque to itself, to attain a relation to what is worthy of question, belong together: they are the same thing.

We are presupposing that why this is so and how it came to this has been experienced and understood.

We only want to consider the fact that anthropology is not exhausted by the study of man and by the will to explain everything in terms of man as his expression. Even where nothing is studied, where rather decisions are sought, this occurs in such a manner that one kind of humanity is previously pitted against another, humanity is acknowledged as the original force, just as if it were the first and last element in all beings, and beings and their actual interpretation were only the consequence.

Thus the solely decisive question comes to predominance: to what form does man belong? "Form" is thought here in an indefinite metaphysical way, that is, Platonically as what is and first determines all tradition and development, itself, however, remaining independent of this. This anticipatory acknowledgment of "man" leads to searching for Being first of all and only in man's environment, and to regarding man himself as human stability, as the actual *me on* to the *idea*.

XX

In that the will to power attains its most extreme, unconditional guarantee, it is the sole criterion that guarantees everything, and thus what is correct. The correctness of the will to will is the unconditional and complete guaranteeing of itself. What is in accordance with its will is correct and in order, because the will to will itself is the only order. In this self-guaranteeing of the will to will, the primal being of truth is lost. The correctness of the will to will is what is absolutely untrue. The correctness of the untrue has its own irresistibility in the scope of the will to will. But the correctness of the untrue which remains concealed *as such* is at the same time the most uncanny thing that can occur in the distortion of the being of truth. What is correct masters what is true and sets truth aside. The will to unconditional guaranteeing first causes ubiquitous uncertainty to appear.

XXI

The will is in itself already the accomplishment of striving as the realization of what is striven for. What is striven for is explicitly known and consciously posited in the concept, that is, as something represented in general. Consciousness belongs to the will. The will to will is the highest and unconditional consciousness of the calculating self-guaranteeing of calculation (cf. *The Will to Power*, no. 458).

Hence there belongs to it the ubiquitous, continual, unconditional investigation of means, grounds, hindrances, the miscalculating exchange and plotting of goals, deceptiveness and maneuvers, the inquisitorial, as a consequence of which the will to will is distrustful and devious toward itself, and thinks of nothing else than the guaranteeing of itself as power itself.

The aimlessness, indeed the essential aimlessness of the unconditional will to will, is the completion of the being of will which was incipient in Kant's concept of practical reason as pure will. Pure will wills itself, and as the will is Being. Viewed from the perspective of content, pure will and its law are thus formal. Pure will is the sole content for itself as form.

XXII

In virtue of the fact that the will is sometimes personified in individual "men of will," it looks as if the will to will were the radiation of these persons. The opinion arises that the human will is the origin of the will to will, whereas man is willed by the will to will without experiencing the essence of this willing.

In that man is what is thus willed and what is posited in the will to will, "the will" is also of necessity addressed in its essence and released as the instance of truth. The question is whether the individuals and communities are in virtue of this will, or whether they still deal and barter with this will or even against it without knowing that they are already outwitted by it. The uniqueness of Being shows itself in the will to will, too, which only admits one direction in which to will. The uniformity of the world of the will to will stems from this, a uniformity which is as far removed from the simplicity of what is original, as deformation of essence from essence, although the former belongs to the latter.

XXIII

Because the will to will absolutely denies every goal and only admits goals as means to outwit itself willfully and to make room for this game; because, however, the will to will nevertheless may not appear as the anarchy of catastrophes that it really is, if it wants to assert itself in beings; it still must legitimate itself. The will to will invents here the talk about "mission." Mission is not thought with regard to anything original and its preservation, but rather as the goal which is assigned from the standpoint of "fate," thus justifying the will to will.

XXIV

The struggle between those who are in power and those who want to come to power: on every side there is the struggle for power. Everywhere power itself is what is determinative. Through this struggle for power, the being of power is posited in the being of its unconditional dominance by both sides. At the same time, however, one thing is still covered up here: the fact that this struggle is in the service of power and is willed by it. Power has overpowered these struggles in advance. The will to will alone empowers these struggles. Power, however, overpowers various kinds of humanity in such a way that it expropriates from man the possibility of ever escaping from the oblivion of Being on such paths. This struggle is of necessity planetary and as such undecidable in its being because it has nothing to decide, since it remains excluded from all differentiation, from the difference (of Being from beings), and thus from truth. Through its own force it is driven out into what is without destiny: into the abandonment of Being.

XXV

The pain which must first be experienced and borne out to the end is the insight and the knowledge that lack of need is the highest and most hidden need which first necessitates in virtue of the most distant distance. Lack of need consists in believing that one has reality and what is real in one's grip and knows what truth is, without needing to know in what truth *presences*.

The essence of the history of Being of nihilism is the abandonment of Being in that in it there occurs the self-release of Being into machination. This release takes man into unconditional service. It is by no means a decline and something "negative" in any kind of sense.

Hence not just any kind of humanity is suited to bring about unconditional nihilism in a historical manner. Hence a struggle is even necessary about the decision as to which kind of humanity is capable of the unconditional completion of nihilism.

XXVI

The signs of the ultimate abandonment of Being are the cries about "ideas" and "values," the indiscriminate back and forth of the proclamation of "deeds," and the indispensability of "spirit." All of this is already hitched into the armament mechanism of the plan. The plan itself is determined by the vacuum of the abandonment of Being within which the consumption of beings for the manufacturing of technology, to which culture also belongs, is the only way out for man who is engrossed with still saving subjectivity in superhumanity. Subhumanity and superhumanity are the same thing. They belong together, just as the "below" of animality and the "above" of the *ratio* are indissolubly coupled in correspondence in the metaphysical *animal rationale*. Sub- and superhumanity are to be thought here metaphysically, not as moral value judgments.

The consumption of beings is such and in its course determined by armament in the metaphysical sense, through which man makes himself the "master" of what is "elemental." The consumption includes the ordered use of beings which become the opportunity and the material for feats and their escalation. This use is employed for the utility of armaments. In that in the unconditionality of escalation and of self-guaranteeing armament runs out and in truth has aimlessness as its aim, the using is a using up.

The "world wars" and their character of "totality" are already a consequence of the abandonment of Being. They press toward a guarantee of the stability of a constant form of using things up. Man, who no longer conceals his character of being the most important raw material, is also drawn into this process. Man is the "most important raw material" because he remains the subject of all consumption. He does this in such a way that he lets his will be unconditionally equated with this process, and thus at the same time become the "object" of the abandonment of Being. The world wars are the antecedent form of the removal of the difference between war and peace. This removal is necessary since the "world" has become an unworld as a consequence of the abandonment of beings by Being's truth. For "world" in the sense of the history of Being (cf. *Being and Time*) means the nonobjective presencing of the truth of Being for man in that man is essentially delivered over to Being. In the age of the exclusive power of power, that is, of the unconditional pressing of beings toward being used up in consumption, the world has become an unworld in that Being does presence, but without really reigning. As what is real, beings are real. There are effects everywhere, and nowhere is there a worlding of the world and yet, although forgotten, there is still Being. Beyond war and peace, there is the mere erring of the consumption of beings in the plan's self-guaranteeing in terms of the vacuum of the abandonment of Being. Changed into their deformation of essence, "war" and "peace" are taken up into erring, and disappear into the mere course of the escalating manufacture of what can be manufactured, because they have become unrecognizable with regard to any distinction. The question of when there will be peace cannot be answered not because the duration of war is unfathomable, but rather because the question already asks about something which no longer exists, since war is no longer anything which could terminate in peace. War has become a distortion of the consumption of beings which is continued in peace. Contending with a long war is only the already outdated form in which what is new about the age of consumption is acknowledged. This long war in its length slowly eventuated not in a peace of the traditional kind, but rather in a condition in which warlike characteristics are no longer experienced as such at all and peaceful characteristics have become meaningless and without content. Erring knows no truth of Being. Instead, it develops the completely equipped plan and certainty of all plans whatsoever in every area. In the encompassment (circle) of areas, the particular realms of human equipment necessarily become "sectors"; the "sector" of poetry, the "sector" of culture are also only the areas, guaranteed according to plan, of actual "leadership" along with others. The moral outrage of those who do not yet know what is going on is often aimed at the arbitrariness and the claim to dominance of the "leaders"—the most fatal form of continual valuation. The leader is the source of anger who cannot escape the persecution of anger which they only appear to enact, since they are not the acting ones. One believes that the leaders had presumed everything of their own accord in the blind rage of a selfish egotism and arranged everything in accordance with their own will. In truth, however, they are the necessary consequence of the fact that beings have entered the way of erring in which the vacuum expands which requires a single order and guarantee of beings. Herein the necessity of "leadership," that is, the planning calculation of the guarantee of the whole of beings, is required. For this purpose such men must be organized and equipped who serve leadership. The "leaders" are the decisive suppliers who oversee all the sectors of the consumption of beings because they understand the whole of those sectors and thus master erring in its calculability. The manner of understanding is the ability to calculate which has totally released itself in advance into the demands of the constantly increasing guarantee of plans in the service of the nearest possibilities of plans. The adjustment of all possible strivings to the whole of planning and guaranteeing is called "instinct." The word here designates the "intellect" which transcends the limited understanding that only calculates in terms of what lies closest. Nothing which must go into the calculation of the miscalculating of individual "sectors" as a "factor" escapes the "intellectualism" of this intellect. Instinct is the superescalation to the unconditional miscalculation of everything. It corresponds to superhumanity. Since this miscalculation absolutely dominates the will, there does not seem to be anything more besides the will than the safety of the mere drive for calculation, for which calculation is above all the first calculative rule. Until now, "instinct" was supposed to be a prerogative of the animal which seeks and follows what is useful and harmful to it in its life sphere, and strives for nothing beyond that. The assurance of animal instinct corresponds to the blind entanglement in its sphere of use. The complete release of subhumanity corresponds to the conditionless empowering of superhumanity. The drive of animality and the *ratio* of humanity become identical.

The fact that instinct is required for superhumanity as a characteristic means that, understood metaphysically, subhumanity belongs to superhumanity, but in such a way that precisely the animal element is thoroughly subjugated in each of its forms to calculation and planning (health plans, breeding). Since man is the most important raw material, one can reckon with the fact that some day factories will be built for the artificial breeding of human material, based on present-day chemical research. The research of the chemist Kuhn, who was awarded the Goethe prize of the city of Frankfurt, already opens up the possibility of directing the breeding of male and female organisms according to plan and need. The way in which artificial insemination is handled correspond with stark consistency to the way in which literature is handled in the sector of "culture." (Let us not flee because of antiquated prudery to distinctions that no longer exist. The need for human material underlies the same regulation of preparing for ordered mobilization as the need for entertaining books and poems, for whose production the poet is no more important than the bookbinder's apprentice, who helps bind the poems for the printer by, for example, bringing the covers for binding from the storage room.)

The consumption of all materials, including the raw material "man," for the unconditional possibility of the production of everything is determined in a concealed way by the complete emptiness in which beings, the materials of what is real, are suspended. This emptiness has to be filled up. But since the emptiness of Being can never be filled up by the fullness of beings, especially when this emptiness can never be experienced as such, the only way to escape it is incessantly to arrange beings in the constant possibility of being ordered as the form of guaranteeing aimless activity. Viewed in this way, technology is the organization of a lack, since it is related to the emptiness of Being contrary to its knowledge. Everywhere where there are not enough beings—and it is increasingly everywhere and always not enough for the will to will escalating itself—technology has to jump in, create a substitute, and consume the raw materials. But in truth the "substitute" and the mass production of ersatz things is not a temporary device, but the only possible form in which the will to will, the "all-inclusive" guarantee of the planning of order, keeps itself going and can thus be "itself" as the "subject" of everything. The increase in the number of masses of human beings is done explicitly by plan so that the opportunity will never run out for claiming more "room to live" for the large masses whose size then again requires correspondingly higher masses of human beings for their arrangement. This circularity of consumption for the sake of consumption is the sole procedure which distinctively characterizes the history of a world which has become an unworld. "Leader natures" are those who allow themselves to be put in the service of this procedure as its directive organs on account of their assured instinct. They are the first employees within the course of business of the unconditional consumption of beings in the service of the guarantee of the vacuum of the abandonment of Being. This course of business of the consumption of beings in virtue of the unknowing defense against unexperienced Being excludes in advance the distinctions between nations and countries as still being essential determinative factors. Just as the distinction between war and peace has become untenable, the distinction between "national" and "international" has also collapsed. Whoever thinks in "a European way" today, no longer allows himself to be exposed to the reproach of being an "internationalist." But he is also no longer a nationalist, since he thinks no less about the well-being of the other nations than about his own.

Nor does the uniformity of the course of history of our present age consist in a supplementary assimilation of older political systems to the latest ones. Uniformity is not the consequence, but the ground of the warlike disputes of individual intendants of the decisive leadership within the consumption of beings for the sake of securing order. The uniformity of beings arising from the emptiness of the abandonment of Being, in which it is only a matter of the calculable security of its order which it subjugates to the will to will, also conditions everywhere in advance of all national differences the uniformity of leadership, for which all forms of government are only one instrument of leadership among others. Since reality consists in the uniformity of calculable reckoning, man, too, must enter monotonous uniformity in order to keep up with what is real. A man without a uni-form today already gives the impression of being something unreal which no longer belongs. Beings, which alone are admitted to the will to will, expand in a lack of differentiation which is only masked by a procedure and arrangement which stands under the "principle of production." This seems to have as a consequence an order of rank; whereas in truth it has as its determining ground the lack of rank, since the goal of production is everywhere only the uniform vacuity of the consumption of all work in the security of order. The lack of differentiation, which erupts glaringly from this principle, is by no means the same as the mere leveling down, which is only the disintegration of previous orders of rank. The lack of differentiation of total consumption arises from a "positive" refusal of an order of rank in accordance with the guardianship of the emptiness of all goal-positing. This lack of differentiation bears witness to the already guaranteed constancy of the unworld of the abandonment of Being. The earth appears as the unworld of erring. It is the erring star in the manner of the history of Being.

XXVII

Shepherds live invisibly and outside of the desert of the desolated earth, which is only supposed to be of use for the guarantee of the dominance of man whose effects are limited to judging whether something is important or unimportant for life. As the will to will, this life demands in advance that all knowledge move in the manner of guaranteeing calculation and valuation.

The unnoticeable law of the earth preserves the earth in the sufficiency of the emerging and perishing of all things in the allotted sphere of the possible which everything follows, and yet nothing knows. The birch tree never oversteps its possibility. The colony of bees dwells in its possibility. It is first the will which arranges itself everywhere in technology that devours the earth in the exhaustion and consumption and change of what is artificial. Technology drives the earth beyond the developed sphere of its possibility into such things which are no longer a possibility and are thus the impossible. The fact that technological plans and measures succeed a great deal in inventions and novelties, piling upon each other, by no means yields the proof that the conquests of technology even make the impossible possible.

The realism and moralism of chronicle history are the last steps of the completed identification of nature and spirit with the being of technology. Nature and spirit are objects of self-consciousness. The unconditional dominance of self-consciousness forces both in advance into a uniformity out of which there is metaphysically no escape.

It is one thing just to use the earth, another to receive the blessing of the earth and to become at home in the law of this reception in order to shepherd the mystery of Being and watch over the inviolability of the possible.

XXVIII

No mere action will change the world, because Being as effectiveness and effecting closes all beings off in the face of Appropriation. Even the immense suffering which surrounds the earth is unable to waken a transformation, because it is only experienced as suffering, as passive, and thus as the opposite state of action, and thus experienced together with action in the same realm of being of the will to will.

But the earth remains preserved in the inconspicuous law of the possible which it is. The will has forced the impossible as a goal upon the possible. Machination, which orders this compulsion and holds it in dominance, arises from the being of technology, the word here made equivalent to the concept of metaphysics completing itself. The unconditional uniformity of all kinds of humanity of the earth under the rule of the will to will makes clear the meaninglessness of human action which has been posited absolutely.

The desolation of the earth begins as a process which is willed, but not known in its being, and also not knowable at the time when the being of truth defines itself as certainty in which human representational thinking and producing first become sure of themselves. Hegel conceives this moment of the history of metaphysics as the moment in which absolute self-consciousness becomes the principle of thinking.

It almost seems as if the being of pain were cut off from man under the dominance of the will, similarly the being of joy. Can the extreme measure of suffering still bring a transformation here?

No transformation comes without an anticipatory escort. But how does an escort draw near unless Appropriation opens out which, calling, needing, envisions human being, that is, sees and in this seeing brings mortals to the path of thinking, poetizing building.

Translated by Joan Stambaugh

5

"ONLY A GOD CAN SAVE US": Der Spiegel's Interview with Martin Heidegger

Introductory Note in Der Spiegel

Der Spiegel's interview with Martin Heidegger, which appears in this issue, was forbidden to be made known until after his death. This was the strict wish of the philosopher. Born in Messkirch on September 26, 1889, and without doubt one of the most important existentialists in Germany, indeed one of the most important existentialists internationally, Heidegger died this past Wednesday in Freiburg. By way of background, let us mention that in March 1966 Heidegger sent a letter to the editor of Der Spiegel in which he contradicted some of the statements which are found in the literature about his behavior during the Third Reich. After twenty years of silence on the subject, this was unique for him. This letter to the editor was at the same time a subtle hint to Der Spiegel that Heidegger was ready to address himself to these reproaches. In September 1966, Rudolph Augstein and Georg Folff conducted Der Spiegel's interview with Heidegger, the topic of which soon passed far beyond the year 1933. Heidegger resolutely resisted any suggestion to publish the interview before his death: "It is neither pride nor stubbornness, but rather sheer care for my work, whose task has become with the years more and more simple and in the field of thinking that means more and more difficult."

"Only a God Can Save Us" ("Nur ein Gott kann uns noch retten") first appeared in Der Spiegel, May 31, 1976. The present translation by Maria P. Alter and John D. Caputo appeared in Philosophy Today XX(4/4):267–285, 1976. The editor gratefully acknowledges permission from Philosophy Today to reprint.

Der Spiegel's Interview with Martin Heidegger on September 23, 1966

Spiegel: Professor Heidegger, we have stated time and again that your philosophical work has been somewhat overshadowed by some events in your life which, while they did not last very long, have still never been cleared up.

Heidegger: You mean 1933.

S: Yes, before and after. We would like to put this in a larger context and, from that vantage point, raise some questions which appear to be important, e.g., what are the possibilities that philosophy could have an effect on reality, in particular on political reality?

H: These are important questions. Who is to say that I can answer them? But first of all I must say that, before my rectorship, I was not in any way politically active. In the winter semester of 1932–33, I had a leave of absence, and I spent most of that time at my cabin.

S: Well, then how did it happen that you became rector of the University of Freiburg?

H: In December 1932, my neighbor, von Möllendorff, who was Professor of Anatomy, was elected rector. The term of office of the new rector at the University of Freiburg begins on April 15. During the winter semester of 1932–33, he and I often spoke of the situation, not only of the political situation, but especially of that of the universities, and of the situation of the students which appeared in part to be hopeless. My judgment was this: insofar as I could judge things, only one possibility was left, and that was to attempt to stem the coming development by means of constructive powers which were still viable.

S: So you saw a connection between the situation of the German university and the political situation in Germany as a whole?

H: I certainly followed political events between January and March 1933 and occasionally I spoke about them with my younger colleagues. But my work itself was concerned with a comprehensive interpretation of pre-Socratic thought. At the beginning of the summer semester I returned to Freiburg. In the meantime, on April 16, Professor von Möllendorff had begun his office as rector. Scarcely two weeks later he was relieved of his office by the then Badish Minister of Culture. The occasion for this decision by the minister, an occasion for which the minister was presumably looking, was the fact that the rector had forbidden posting the so-called Jewish proclamation.

S: Professor von Möllendorff was a Social Democrat. What did he do after his removal?

H: On the very day he was removed, von Möllendorff came to me and said: "Heidegger, now you must take over the rectorship." I said that I lacked experience in administration. The vice-rector at that time, Professor Sauer (Theology), likewise urged me to become a candidate for the rectorship. For otherwise the danger would be that a party functionary would be named rector. The younger faculty, with whom I had been discussing the structure of the University for many years, besieged me to take over the rectorship. For a long time I hesitated. Finally I said that I was ready to take over the office in the interest of the University, but only if I could be certain of a unanimous agreement of the Plenum. My doubts about my suitability for the rectorship persisted. On the morning of the day which had been set for the election, I went to the rector's office and explained to von Möllendorff (who though no longer rector was present there) and to Professor Sauer, that I just could not possibly take over the office. Both these colleagues told me that the election had been set up in such a way that I could no longer withdraw my candidacy.

S: And after this you declared yourself ready. How then was your relationship with the National Socialists formed?

H: On the second day after I had assumed office, the "student leader" with two companions visited me as rector and demanded again the posting of the Jewish proclamation. I declined. The three students left remarking that the prohibition would be reported to the National Student Leadership. After a few days a telephone call came from the Office of Higher Education [SA *Hochschulamt*], in the highest SA echelons, from the SA Leader Dr. Baumann.* He demanded the posting of the so-called proclamation, since it had already been posted in other universities. If I refused I would have to reckon with removal, if not, indeed, with the closing of the University. I attempted to win the support of the Badish Minister of Culture for my prohibition. The latter explained that he could do nothing in opposition to the SA. Nevertheless, I did not retract my prohibition.

S: Up to now that was not known.

H: The motive which moved me to take over the rectorship had

---

* Translators' note: *Sturm Abteilung,* or Storm Troop.

already appeared in my inaugural address at Freiburg in the year 1929, *What is Metaphysics?*: "The fields of the sciences lie far apart. The methods of treating their objects are fundamentally different. Today this fragmented multiplicity of discipline is held together only by the technical organization of the universities and the faculties and held together as a unit of meaning only through the practical orientation of the academic departments. The roots of the sciences in their essential ground have withered away."* What I attempted to do during my term of office with respect to this situation of the university (which has by today deteriorated to the extreme) is contained in my rectoral address.†

S: We attempted to find out how and whether this remark from 1929 coincided with what you said in your inaugural address as rector in 1933. We are taking a sentence out of context. "The much-sung 'academic freedom' is driven out of the German university. This freedom was false because it was only negative." We might suppose that this sentence expresses at least in part ideas which are even today not foreign to you.

H: Yes, I still stand behind that statement. For this academic "freedom" was all too often only a negative one: freedom *from* taking the trouble to reflect and meditate as scientific studies demand. But the sentence which you have picked out should not be isolated. It should, rather, be read in context. Then what I wanted understood by "negative freedom" will become clear.

S: Good. One can understand that. Still we believe that we perceive a new tone in your rector's address when you speak there, four months after Hitler was named Chancellor of the Reich, of the "greatness and glory of this new dawn."

H: Yes, I was convinced of that.

S: Could you explain that a bit more?

H: Gladly. At that time I saw no alternative. In the general confusion of opinions and of the political trends of 22 parties, it was necessary to

*Translators' note: Martin Heidegger, "Was ist Metaphysik?" 9. Aufl. (Frankfurt: Klostermann, 1965), pp. 24–25; English translation: "What is Metaphysics?" translated by R. F. C. Hull and A. Crick in *Existence and Being*, edited by W. Brock (London: Vision Press, 1956), p. 356. With the exception of this passage, we have used the existing English translations of the works of Heidegger referred to in the interview.

†Translators' note: Martin Heidegger, *Die Selbstbehauptung der deutschen Universität* (Breslau: Korn, 1933).

find a national, and above all a social, point of view, perhaps of the sort attempted by Friedrich Naumann. To give you one example, I can only refer you here to an essay by Eduard Spranger, which goes far beyond my rector's address.*

S: When did you begin to be concerned with political situations? The 22 parties had been there for a long time. And there were millions of unemployed people in 1930.

H: At that time I was completely taken up with the questions that are developed in *Being and Time* (1927) and in the writings and lectures of the following years. These are the fundamental questions of thinking which in an indirect way affect even national and social questions. The question which concerned me directly as a teacher in the university was the question of the meaning of the sciences and, in connection with this, the question of the determination of the task of the university. This concern is expressed in the title of my rectoral address: "The Self-Assertion of the German University." Such a title had not been risked in any rectoral address up to that time. And yet who among those who have engaged in polemics against this address has read it thoroughly, thought it through and interpreted it in terms of the situation of those times?

S: But to speak of the self-assertion of the German university in such a turbulent world, wasn't that a bit inappropriate?

H: Why so? The self-assertion of the university: that goes against the so-called "political science" which was demanded at that time in the Party and by the National Socialist Students. At that time the title had a completely different meaning: it did not mean the science of politics, as it does today; rather it meant: science as such in the meaning and worth, is devalued in favor of the practical needs of the people. The counterposition to such politicizing of science is rightly expressed in the rectoral address.

S: Do we understand you correctly? While you drew the university into something which you at that time felt to be a new dawn, still you wished to see the university assert itself against currents which were overpowering and which would have no longer allowed the university to keep its identity?

* Translators' note: This essay appeared in a periodical, *Die Erziehung*, edited by A. Fischer, W. Flitner, H. Nohl, and E. Spranger, 1933, p. 401.

H: Certainly. But self-assertion should simultaneously pose the task of retrieving from the merely technical organization of the university a new meaning which could come out of a reflection on the tradition of Western European thought.

S: Professor, are we to understand that you thought at that time that it was possible for the university to regain its health in alliance with the National Socialists?

H: That is not exactly correct. I did not say in alliance with the National Socialists. Rather, the university should renew itself by means of its own reflection and in this way secure a firm position against the danger of the politicization of science—in the aforementioned sense.

S: And that is why you proclaimed these three pillars in your rectoral address: the service of work, military service, and the service of knowledge. In this way you meant to say, the "service of knowledge" should be lifted up to a position of equal rank with the other two, something which the National Socialists surely would not have granted it?

H: There was no talk of "pillars." If you read it carefully, you will see that the "service of knowledge" does, to be sure, stand in the third place in the enumeration, but in terms of its meaning it is first. One ought to remember that work and the military, like every human activity, are grounded in knowledge and are enlightened by it.

S: But we must—and this will be the end of this miserable quoting —still mention one more remark, one which we cannot imagine that you would still subscribe to today. You said in the fall of 1933: "Do not let doctrines and ideas be the rules of your Being. The Führer himself and he alone *is* the present and future German reality and its rule."

H: These sentences are not found in the rectoral address, but only in the local *Freiburg Students Newspaper,* at the beginning of the 1933–34 winter semester. When I took over the rectorship it was clear to me that I would not see it through without some compromises. I would today no longer write the sentences which you cite. Even by 1934 I no longer said such things.

S: May we ask you once more a related question? It has become clear up to this point in this conversation that your position in the year 1933 fluctuated between two poles. You had to say many things *ad usum delphini* [for the use of the Dauphin, i.e., for public consumption]; that is one pole. But the other pole was more positive, and this you express by saying: I had the feeling that here is something new, here is a new dawn.

H: That is right. It's not that I had spoken only for the sake of appearances; I also saw such a possibility.

S: You know that some reproaches have been made against you in this connection concerning your collaboration with the NSDAP* and its units and which are still not contradicted. Thus you have been accused of having taken part in the book burnings by the student body or by the Hitler Youth.

H: I had forbidden the planned book burning which was to take place in front of the University buildings.

S: Then you were also accused of having had the books of Jewish authors removed from the library or from the Philosophical Seminar.

H: As Director of the Seminar I had authority only over its library. I did not comply with the repeated demands to remove the books of Jewish authors. Former participants in my seminars could testify today that not only were no books of Jewish authors removed, but that these authors, and above all Husserl, were cited and discussed just as before 1933.

S: Well, then how do you explain the origin of such rumors? Is it just maliciousness?

H: According to my knowledge of the sources, I am inclined to believe that. But the motives of the defamation lie deeper. Taking over the rectorship was probably only the occasion, but not the determining cause. Probably the polemics will flare up again and again, whenever the occasion presents itself.

S: You had Jewish students also after 1933. Your relationship to some of these students is supposed to have been quite warm.

H: My attitude after 1933 remained unchanged. One of my oldest and most gifted students, Helene Weiss, who later emigrated to Scotland, was awarded her doctorate from Basel—for this was no longer possible at Freiburg—with a dissertation, "Causality and Chance in the Philosophy of Aristotle," printed in Basel in 1942. At the conclusion of the foreword, the author writes: "The attempt at a phenomenological interpretation, which we here submit in its preliminary stage, was made

*Translators' note: *Nationalsozialistische Deutsche Arbeiterpartei* (the National Socialists or "Nazis").

possible by M. Heidegger's unpublished interpretations of Greek philosophy." I have here a copy of the book with a dedication by the author in her own handwriting. I visited Dr. Weiss several times in Brussels before her death.

S: You and Jaspers were friends for a long time. Then after 1933 this relationship became clouded. The story goes that the problem was that Jaspers had a Jewish wife. Would you comment on that?

H: Karl Jaspers and I had been friends since 1919. I visited him and his wife in Heidelberg during the summer semester of 1933. Karl Jaspers sent me all his publications between 1934 and 1938, "with warm regards."

S: You were a student of Edmund Husserl, your Jewish predecessor in the Chair of Philosophy at Freiburg University. He had recommended you to the faculty to be his successor as professor. Your relationship with him must have included some gratitude.

H: To be sure. You know the dedication of *Being and Time*.

S: Of course. But later on this relationship too became clouded. Can you and are you willing to tell us what caused this?

H: Our differences with respect to philosophical matters had been accentuated. In the beginning of the 1930s, Husserl settled accounts with Max Scheler and me in public, the clarity of which left nothing to be desired. I could not discover what had moved Husserl to cut himself off from my thought in such a public way.

S: On what occasion was this?

H: Husserl spoke in the Berlin Sports Palace before the student body. Erich Mühsam reported it in one of the large Berlin newspapers.

S: In our context, the actual controversy itself is not of interest. All that is interesting is that there was no controversy which had anything to do with 1933.

H: None in the least.

S: Reproaches were made against you that, in 1941, the year of the publication of the fifth edition of *Being and Time*, you left out the original dedication to Husserl.

H: That's right. I explained this in my book, *On the Way to Language*. I wrote there, "To counter widely circulated allegations, let it be stated here explicitly that the dedication of *Being and Time* mentioned on p. 16 [p. 92 in the German edition of *Unterwegs zur Sprache*] of the

Dialogue remained in *Being and Time* until its fourth edition of 1935. In 1941, when my publishers felt that the fifth edition might be endangered and that, indeed, the book might be suppressed, I finally agreed, at the suggestion and wish of Niemeyer, that the dedication be omitted from the edition on the condition imposed by me that the note to page 38 [of the German edition of *Being and Time*] be retained—a note which in fact states the reason for that dedication, and which runs: 'If the following investigation has taken any steps forward in disclosing the "things themselves," the author must first of all thank E. Husserl, who, by providing his own incisive personal guidance and by freely turning over his unpublished investigations, familiarized the author with the most diverse areas of phenomenological research during his student years at Freiburg.' "*

S: Then we hardly need to ask whether it is correct that you, as rector of the University of Freiburg, had forbidden Professor Emeritus Husserl to enter or to use the University Library or the library of the Philosophical Seminar.

H: That is a slander.

S: And there is no letter which contains this prohibition against Husserl? Then how did this rumor get started?

H: I don't know that either. I cannot find an explanation for it. I can show you the impossibility of this whole affair by means of something else which is not known. When I was rector I was able, in a meeting I had with the Minister, to retain the then Director of the Medical Clinic, Professor Thannhauser and also Professor von Hevesy, Professor of Physics, who was later to be a Nobel Prize winner. Both of these men were Jews, whom the Ministry had demanded be removed. Now it is absurd that I would have retained both these men and at the same time have taken the alleged steps against Husserl, who was an emeritus and my own teacher. Moreover, I kept the students and lecturers from organizing a demonstration against Professor Thannhauser. At that time, there were unsalaried lecturers who were stuck without students and who thought: now is the time to be promoted. When they met with me about this, I turned them all down.

*Translators' note: Martin Heidegger, *Unterwegs zur Sprache* (Pfullingen: Neske, 1959), p. 269; English translation: *On the Way to Language,* translated by Peter Hertz (New York: Harper and Row, 1971), pp. 199–200.

S: You did not attend Husserl's funeral in 1938.

H: Let me say the following about that. The reproach that I broke off my relations with Husserl is unfounded. In May 1933, my wife wrote a letter in both our names to Frau Husserl in which we expressed our unaltered gratitude. We sent this letter to Husserl with a bouquet of flowers. Frau Husserl answered tersely in a formal thank you note and wrote that relations between our families were broken off. It was a human failing that [at Husserl's sickbed or at the time of his death] I did not express once more my gratitude and my admiration. And for that I asked Frau Husserl's forgiveness in writing.

S: Husserl died in 1938. By February 1934, you had already resigned the rectorship. How did that come about?

H: I should expand upon that somewhat. I had the intention of doing something about the technical organization of the University, that is, of reforming the faculties from the inside and on the basis of the tasks imposed upon them by their various fields. With this in mind, I proposed to nominate as deans of the individual faculties for the winter semester of 1933–34 younger and, above all, outstanding men, without regard for their position in the Party. Thus deans were appointed as follows: in the Law School, Professor Erich Wolff; in Philosophy, Professor Schadewaldt; in Natural Sciences, Professor Soergel; in Medicine, Professor von Möllendorff, who had been removed as rector in the spring. But by Christmas 1933 it became clear to me that the innovations for the University which I had in mind could not be carried out because of opposition both within the faculty and from the Party. The faculty, for example, took it amiss that I included students in responsible positions in the administration of the University, much as is the case today. One day I was called to Karlsruhe. There the Minister, through his assistant and in the presence of the Nazi student leader, demanded that I replace the deans of the Law School and Medical School by other members of the faculty who would be acceptable to the Party. I refused to do this and tendered my resignation from the rectorship, should the Minister persist in his demands. That is what happened. That was in February 1934. I stepped down after ten months in office, even though rectors at that time remained in office two or more years. While both the foreign and domestic press commented in the most divergent ways about the appointment of the new rector, they were silent about my resignation.

S: Did you have the opportunity at that time to present your thoughts about university reform to the Reichs Minister?

H: At what time?

S: One still hears of a trip which Rust made to Freiburg in 1933.

H: We are dealing here with two different episodes. I gave a brief formal greeting to the Minister on the occasion of the Schlageter* celebration in Schönau i.W. Secondly, I spoke with the Minister in November 1933 in Berlin. I presented my views to him on the sciences and the possible structure of the faculties. He listened to everything so attentively, that I had the hope that my presentation would have an effect. But nothing happened. It is beyond me why I should be reproached for this conversation with the then Reichs Minister of Education, while at that very time all foreign governments hastened to recognize Hitler and to show him the customary international courtesies.

S: Did your relationship with the NSDAP change after you resigned as rector?

H: After I stepped down as rector I limited myself to teaching. In the summer semester of 1934 I lectured on "Logic." In the following semester I gave the first Hölderlin lecture. In 1936, I began the Nietzsche lectures. Anyone with ears to hear heard in these lectures a confrontation with National Socialism.

S: How did the transfer of offices take place? You did not participate in the celebration.

H: Right, I did indeed decline to participate in the ceremony of the change of rectors.

S: Was your successor a committed Party member?

H: He was a member of the Law Faculty. The Party newspaper, *Der Alemanne,* announced his appointment as rector with a banner headline: "The First National Socialist Rector of the University."

S: How did the Party act toward you?

H: I was constantly under surveillance.

S: Were you aware of that?

* Translators' note: Albert Leo Schlageter (1894–1923), shot by the French for his role in the resistance to the French occupation in the Ruhr.

H: Yes—the case with Dr. Hanke [sic].

S: How did you find that out?

H: He came to me himself. He had already received his doctorate [*promoviert*] in the winter semester of 1936–37 and he was a member of my advanced seminar in the summer semester of 1937. He had been sent by the SD* to keep me under surveillance.

S: Why did he suddenly come to you?

H: Because of my Nietzsche seminar in the summer semester of 1937 and because of the way in which the work proceeded in the seminar, he told to me that he could no longer maintain the surveillance which he was assigned to do. And he wanted to make me aware of this situation in view of my future teaching activity.

S: So the Party kept a watchful eye over you?

H: I only knew that my writings were not allowed to be discussed, for example the essay, "Plato's Theory of Truth." My Hölderlin lecture, which was given in the spring of 1936 in Rome at the Germanic Institute, was attacked in an insidious way in the Hitler Youth magazine *Wille und Macht* [*Will and Power*]. Those who are interested should read the polemics against me which start in the summer of 1934 in Krieck's magazine, *Volk im Werden* [*People in Process*]. I was not a delegate from Germany at the International Congress of Philosophy in Prague in 1934. I was also supposed to be excluded from the Descartes Congress in Paris in 1937. This seemed so odd in Paris that the leadership of the Congress there—Professor Bréhier of the Sorbonne—asked me on his own why I was not a part of the German delegation. I answered that the leadership of the Congress could inquire about this at the Reichs Ministry of Education. After some time a request came from Berlin that I should belatedly join the delegation. But I declined. My lectures, *What is Metaphysics?* and *On the Essence of Truth*, were sold there under the counter with a plain dust wrapper. Soon after 1934 the rectoral address was withdrawn from circulation at the instigation of the Party.

S: Did things get worse later on?

H: In the last year of the war, 500 of the most important scholars [*Wissenschaftler*] and artists of every kind were exempted from war

* Translators' note: *Sicherheitsdients,* the Security Service.

service. I was not among the exempted. On the contrary, in the summer of 1944 I was ordered to work on the fortifications over on the Rhine.

S: Karl Barth worked on the fortifications on the Swiss side.

H: It is interesting how this took place. The rector called together all the faculty [Dozentenschaft]. Then he gave a speech to the effect that what he was saying at that time was in agreement with the regional Nazi leaders [NS-Kreisleiter and NS-Gauleiter]. The entire faculty was to be divided into three groups. First, those who could be dispensed with completely; second, those who could only be partially dispensed with; third, those who were indispensable. The category of completely dispensable people included Heidegger and also G. Ritter.* In the winter semester of 1944–45, after finishing my work on the fortifications on the Rhine, I gave a lecture course with the title "Poetizing and Thinking." This was in a certain sense a continuation of my Nietzsche lectures, that is to say, a confrontation with National Socialism. After the second lecture I was drafted into the Volkssturm—the oldest member of the faculty to be called up.†

S: Perhaps we might summarize: in 1933 you were, as an unpolitical man in the strict sense, not in the wider sense, caught up in the politics of this supposed new dawn . . .

H: By way of the university . . .

S: . . . caught up by way of the university in this supposed new dawn. After about a year you gave up the function you had assumed. But in a lecture in 1935, which was published in 1953 as An Introduction to Metaphysics, you said, "The works that are being peddled (about) nowadays as the philosophy of National Socialism, but have nothing whatever to do with the inner truth and greatness of this movement (namely, the encounter between global technology and contemporary man), have

---

* Translators' note: Der Spiegel provides the following note: Professor Gerhard Ritter, at that time full Professor of Modern History in the University of Freiburg, was imprisoned on November 1, 1944 in connection with the assassination attempt on Hitler on July 20, 1944 and was freed by the allied troops only on April 25, 1945. The historian became professor emeritus in 1956 and died in 1967 (from Carl Goerdeler und die deutsche Widerstandsbewegung).

† Translators' note: "It was in order to utilize the last reserves of his manpower that Hitler had created a new fighting force of hurriedly-trained civilians—the Volkssturm— into which all able-bodied males between 16 and 60 were compulsorily drafted" (Richard Grundberger, Germany 1918–1945 [New York: Harper and Row, 1964], p. 181).

all been written by men fishing the troubled waters of values and totalities."* Did you only add the words in parentheses in 1953, that is, with the book's publication—perhaps in order to explain to the reader of 1953 how you in 1935 saw the inner truth and greatness of this movement, that is, of National Socialism? Or was this parenthetical remark explaining your viewpoint already there in 1935?

H: It was present in my manuscript from the beginning and agreed completely with my conception of technology at that time, though not as yet with the later interpretation of the essence of technology as the "frame" ["*das Ge-Stell*"].† The reason I did not read this passage aloud was that I was convinced that my audience were understanding me correctly. The dumb ones, the spies, and the snoopers wanted to understand me otherwise, and would, no matter what.

S: Certainly you would also have classified the Communist movement that way too?

H: Yes, definitely—as determined by global technology.

S: And also "Americanism"?

H: Yes, I would say that too. Meanwhile, in the past thirty years it should have become clearer that the global movement of modern technology is a force whose scope in determining history can scarcely be overestimated. A decisive question for me today is: how can a political system accommodate itself to the technological age, and which political system would this be? I have no answer to this question. I am not convinced that it is democracy.

S: "Democracy" is a catch-all word under which quite different ideas can be brought together. The question is whether a transformation of this political structure is still possible. After 1945, you addressed yourself to the political aspirations of the Western world and then you spoke also of democracy, of the political expression of the Christian worldview, and even of the idea of a constitutional state—and you have labeled all these aspirations "half truths."

H: First of all, would you please tell me where I spoke about democ-

*Translators' note: Martin Heidegger, *Einführung in die Metaphysik*, 2. Aufl. (Tübingen: Max Niemeyer, 1958), p. 152; English translation: *An Introduction to Metaphysics*, translated by Ralph Manheim (Garden City, N.Y.: Doubleday, 1961), p. 166.

†Translators' note: For Joan Stambaugh's translation of "*Ge-Stell*" as "frame," see her introduction to Martin Heidegger, *Identity and Difference* (New York: Harper and Row, 1959), p. 14, n. 1.

racy and all the other things you refer to? I would characterize them as half truths because I do not see in them a genuine confrontation with the technological world, because behind them there is in my view a notion that technology is in its essence something over which man has control. In my opinion, that is not possible. Technology is in its essence something which man cannot master by himself.

S: In your view, which of all these things you have just sketched out is the most timely?

H: That I don't see. But I do see a decisive question here. We must first of all clarify what you mean by "timely," that is, what "time" means. And still more, we must ask whether timeliness is the measure of the "inner truth" of human action, or rather, whether thinking and poetizing are not the activity which gives us the measure, despite the heretical meaning we have given to that term.

S: It is striking that man at no time has been able to master his own tools; I am thinking of "The Magician's Apprentice."* Isn't it then a bit too pessimistic to say that we will not be able to manage this much greater tool of modern technology?

H: Pessimism, no. Pessimism and optimism are attitudes which we are trying to consider, and they do not go far enough. Above all, modern technology is not a tool and it has nothing to do with tools anymore.

S: Why should we be so thoroughly overpowered by technology?

H: I did not say overpowered. I am saying that we still have no way to respond to the essence of technology.

S: One could make the following quite naive rejoinder: what is to be overcome here? Everything is functioning. More and more power plants are being built. We have peak production. Men in the highly technological parts of the world are well provided for. We live in prosperity. What is really missing here?

H: Everything is functioning. This is exactly what is so uncanny, that everything is functioning and that the functioning drives us more and more to even further functioning, and that technology tears men loose from the earth and uproots them. I do not know whether you were frightened, but I at any rate was frightened when I saw pictures coming from the moon to the earth. We don't need any atom bomb. The

---

* Translators' note: A poem by Goethe.

uprooting of man has already taken place. The only thing we have left is purely technological relationships. This is no longer the earth on which man lives. As you know, I recently had a long conversation with René Char of the Provence, the poet and resistance fighter. Rocket bases are being built in the Provence and the country is being devastated in an incredible way. This poet, who certainly cannot be suspected of sentimentality and of glorification of the idyllic, tells me that the uprooting of man which is taking place there will be the end, if poetry and thought do not once more succeed to a position of might without force.

S: We say now that we would rather be here, and of course in our lifetime we will not have to leave. But who knows whether it is the destiny of man to remain on this earth. It is conceivable that man has no destiny at all. But at any rate, one could envisage the possibility that man would reach out from this earth to other planets. That will certainly not be for a long time. But where is it written that man's place is here?

H: According to our human experience and history, at least as far as I see it, I know that everything essential and everything great originated from the fact that man had a home and was rooted in a tradition. Present-day literature, for example, is predominantly destructive.

S: The word "destructive" bothers us, especially since the word "nihilistic," thanks to you and your philosophy, has received an all-encompassing breadth of meaning. It is shocking to hear the word "destructive" in regard to literature, which you could and ought after all to see as completely part and parcel of this nihilism.

H: I would like to say that the literature I have in mind is not nihilistic in the way that I think of nihilism.

S: You obviously envisage, and this is what you have already said, a world movement which either leads up to or has already led up to the absolute technological state.

H: Yes.

S: Good. Now the question naturally comes up: can the individual in any way influence this network of inevitabilities, or could philosophy influence it, or could both together influence it inasmuch as philosophy could guide the individual or several individuals toward a specific action?

H: Let me respond briefly and somewhat ponderously, but from long reflection: philosophy will not be able to effect an immediate transformation of the present condition of the world. This is not only true of philosophy, but of all merely human thought and endeavor. Only a god can save us. The sole possibility that is left for us is to prepare a sort of readiness, through thinking and poetizing, for the appearance of the god or for the absence of the god in the time of foundering [*Untergang*]; for in the face of the god who is absent, we founder.

S: Is there a connection between your thinking and the emergence of this god? Is there in your view a causal connection? Do you think that we can think god into being here with us?

H: We can not think him into being here; we can at most awaken the readiness of expectation.

S: But are we able to help?

H: The preparation of a readiness may be the first step. The world cannot be what it is or the way that it is through man, but neither can it be without man. According to my view, this is connected with the fact that what I name with the word Being, a word which is of long standing, traditional, multifaceted, and worn out, needs man for its revelation, preservation, and formation. I see the essence of technology in what I call the frame [*das Ge-stell*], an expression which has often been laughed at and is perhaps somewhat clumsy. The frame holding sway means: the essence of man is framed, claimed, and challenged by a power which manifests itself in the essence of technology, a power which man himself does not control. To help with this realization is all that one can expect of thought. Philosophy is at an end.

S: In earlier times—and not only in earlier times—it was thought that philosophy effected a great deal indirectly—seldom in a direct way —and that indirectly it could effect a great deal, that it could help new currents to break through. If one only thinks of the Germans, of the great names of Kant, Hegel, up to Nietzsche, not to mention Marx, then it can be shown that philosophy has had, in a roundabout way, a tremendous effect. Do you really think the effectiveness of philosophy has come to an end? And if you say that the old philosophy is dead, no longer exists, does this not include the idea that this effectiveness of philosophy (if indeed there ever were such) today, at least, no longer exists?

H: If one thinks in different terms a mediated effect is possible, but not a direct one. Hence thinking, as it were, can causally change the situation of the world.

S: Excuse me, we do not want to philosophize. We are not up to that. But we have here touched upon the boundaries between politics and philosophy. So please overlook the fact that we are drawing you into such a conversation. You have just said that philosophy and the individual are capable of nothing other than . . .

H: . . . this preparation of the readiness, of keeping oneself open for the arrival of or the absence of the god. Moreover, the experience of this absence is not nothing, but rather a liberation of man from what I called "fallenness amidst beings" in *Being and Time*. A meditation on what is today belongs to the preparation of the readiness we referred to.

S: But then as a matter of fact the celebrated impetus would have to come from the outside, from a god or whomever. Thus thinking could today no longer be effective of itself and autonomous. But this was the case formerly in the opinion of the people of earlier days and, I believe, in ours too.

H: But not immediately.

S: We have already mentioned Kant, Hegel, and Marx as men who caused a great stir. But there have also been impulses coming from Leibniz—for the development of modern physics and therefore for the origin of the modern world in general. We believe that you have just said that you no longer take such an effect into account today?

H: No longer in the sense of philosophy. The role which philosophy has played up to now has been taken over by the sciences. In order to give an adequate explanation of the "effect" of thought, we must discuss more thoroughly what "effect" and "effecting" can mean. If we have discussed the Principle of Sufficient Reason sufficiently, one ought to make here fundamental distinctions among occasion, impetus, furthering, assistance, obstacle, and cooperation. Philosophy dissolves into the individual sciences: psychology, logic, and political science.

S: And now what or who takes the place of philosophy?

H: Cybernetics.

S: Or the pious one who keeps himself open.

H: But that is no longer philosophy.

S: What is it then?

H: I call it the "other thinking."

S: You call it the "other thinking." Would you like to formulate that a bit more clearly?

H: Did you have in mind the concluding sentence in my lecture, "The Question of Technology": "Questioning is the piety of thought"?*

S: We found a sentence in your Nietzsche lectures which is enlightening. You said there: "It is because the highest possible bond prevails in philosophical thought that all great thinkers think the same. This sameness, however, is so essential and rich that one individual can never exhaust it, so each only binds himself to the other all the more strictly." But it appears that, in your opinion, just this philosophical edifice has led us to a very definite end.

H: It has come to an end, but it has not become for us null and void; rather it has turned up anew in this conversation. My whole work in lectures and exercises in the past 30 years has been in the main only an interpretation of Western philosophy. The regress into the historical foundations of thought, the thinking through of the questions which are still unasked since the time of Greek philosophy—that is not a cutting loose from the tradition. I am saying: the traditional metaphysical mode of thinking, which terminated with Nietzsche, no longer offers any possibility for experiencing in a thoughtful way the fundamental traits of the technological age, an age which is just beginning.

S: Approximately two years ago, in a conversation with a Buddhist monk, you spoke of "a completely new way of thinking" and you said that "only a few people are capable of" this new way of thought. Did you want to say that only a very few people can have the insights which in your view are possible and necessary?

H: To "have" them in the utterly primordial sense, so that they can, in a certain way, "say" them.

S: But you did not make clear in this conversation with the Buddhist just how this passing over into reality [*Verwirklichung*] takes place.

H: I cannot make this clear. I know nothing about how this thinking "has an effect" ["*wirkt*"]. It may be that the path of thinking has today reached the point where silence is required to preserve thinking from

* Translators' note: Martin Heidegger, *Vorträge und Aufsätze* (Pfullingen: Neske, 1954), p. 44.

being all jammed up just within a year. It may also be that it will take 300 years for it "to have an effect."

S: We understand that very well. But since we don't live 300 years from now, but here and now, silence is denied to us. We politicians, semi-politicians, citizens, journalists, etc., we constantly have to make decisions of one kind or another. We must try to adapt to the system we live in, we must attempt to change it, we must look for the small opportunity of reform and the still smaller one of revolution. We expect help from the philosopher, if only indirect help, help in a roundabout way. And now we hear: I cannot help you.

H: And I cannot.

S: That surely discourages the non-philosopher.

H: I cannot, because the questions are so difficult that it would be contrary to the meaning of the task of thought to step up publicly, as it were, to preach and to impose moral judgment. Perhaps one might risk the following: to the mystery of the superior global power of the unthought essence of technology there corresponds the tentativeness and inconspicuousness of thought, which attempts to meditate this still unthought essence.

S: You do not number yourself among those who could show a way, if people would only listen to them?

H: No. I know of no paths to the immediate transformation of the present situation of the world, assuming that such a thing is humanly possible at all. But it seems to me that the thinking which I attempt would awaken, clarify, and fortify the readiness which we have mentioned.

S: A clear answer. But can and may a thinker say: just wait and within the next 300 years something will occur to us?

H: It is not a matter simply of waiting until something occurs to man within the next 300 years, but of thinking ahead (without prophetic proclamations) into the time which is to come, of thinking from the standpoint of the fundamental traits of the present age, which have scarcely been thought through. Thinking is not inactivity but is in itself the action which stands in dialogue with the world mission [*Weltgeschick*]. It seems to me that the distinction, which stems from metaphysics, between theory and praxis, and the representation of some kind of transmission between the two, blocks the way to an insight into what I understand by thinking. Perhaps I may refer here to my lectures which appeared in 1954 with the title *What is Called Thinking?** Perhaps it is also a sign of the times that this book of all my publications has been read the least.

S: Let us go back to our beginning. Would it not be conceivable to regard National Socialism, on the one hand, as the realization of that "global encounter" and, on the other, as the last, worst, strongest, and at the same time most impotent protest against this encounter "of global technology" and contemporary man? Evidently you experience an opposition in your own person which is such that many by-products of your activity can really only be explained by the fact that, with various parts of your being, which are not concerned with your philosophical core, you cleave to many things which you as a philosopher know have no substance—concepts, for example, like "homeland," "roots," or the like. How do global technology and the homeland fit together?

H: I would not say that. It seems to me that you are taking technology too absolutely. I do not see the situation of man in the world of global technology as a fate which cannot be escaped or unraveled. On the contrary, I see the task of thought to consist in helping man in general, within the limits allotted to thought, to achieve an adequate relationship to the essence of technology. National Socialism, to be sure, moved in this direction. But those people were far too limited in their thinking to acquire an explicit relationship to what is really happening today and has been underway for three centuries.

S: Perhaps present-day Americans have this explicit relationship?

H: They do not have it either. They are still caught up in a thought (Pragmatism) which favors functions and manipulations but which, at the same time, blocks the way to a meditation on what properly belongs to modern technology. Meanwhile there are in the U.S.A. some stirrings of efforts to get away from pragmatic-positivistic thought. And who of us can say whether or not one day in Russia and China the ancient traditions of a "thought" will awaken which will help make possible for man a free relationship to the technical world?

* Translators' note: Martin Heidegger, *Was Heisst Denken?* 2. Aufl. (Tübingen: Niemeyer, 1961); English translation: *What is Called Thinking?*, translated by F. Wieck and J. Glenn Gray (New York: Harper, 1968).

S: But if no one has it and the philosopher cannot give it to anyone
. . .

H: It is not for me to decide how far I will get with my attempt to
think and in what way it will be accepted in the future and transformed
in a fruitful way. In 1957 I gave a lecture on the anniversary of the
University of Freiburg, called "The Principle of Identity."* That lecture
tried to show, in a few steps, just how far a thoughtful experience of
what is most proper to modern technology can go. It showed that the
possibility arises for man in the technological world to experience a
relationship to a claim which he not only can hear but to which he
himself belongs. My thinking stands in a definitive relationship to the
poetry of Hölderlin. I do not take Hölderlin to be just any poet whose
work, among many others, has been taken as a subject by literary
historians. For me Hölderlin is the poet who points to the future, who
expects god and who therefore may not remain merely an object of
Hölderlin research and of the kind of presentations offered by literary
historians.

S: A propos of Hölderlin, we ask your indulgence to quote your own
writings. In your Nietzsche lectures you said that the "widely known
opposition between the Dionysian and the Apollonian, between the
sacred passion and sober presentation, is a hidden stylistic law of the
historical destiny of the Germans and we must be prepared and ready
one day to be formed by it. This opposition is not a formula with whose
help we describe 'culture.' With this opposition, Hölderlin and Nietzsche
have put a question mark before the Germans' task to find their being
historically. Will we understand this sign, this question mark? One thing
is sure. History will take revenge upon us if we don't understand it." We
do not know in what year you wrote that. We would guess it was in
1935.

H: The quote probably belongs to the Nietzsche lecture, "The Will
to Power as Art," 1936–37. It could also have been written in the
following years.†

S: So, would you clarify this a bit? It leads us from generalities to the
concrete destiny of the Germans.

---

* Translators' note: See n. 11.

†Translators' note: Heidegger's guess is right; cf. Martin Heidegger, *Nietzsche* (Pfullingen: Neske, 1961), B. I, p. 124.

H: I could explain what was said in the quotation in the following way: it is my conviction that a reversal can be prepared only in the same place in the world where the modern technological world originated, and that it cannot happen because of any takeover by Zen Buddhism or any other Eastern experiences of the world. There is need for a rethinking which is to be carried out with the help of the European tradition and of a new appropriation of that tradition. Thinking itself can be transformed only by a thinking which has the same origin and calling.

S: It is exactly at the same place where the technological world originated, that it must, as you think . . .

H: . . . be transcended [*aufgehoben*] in the Hegelian sense, not pushed aside, but transcended, but not through man alone.

S: You assign in particular a special task to the Germans?

H: Yes, in the sense of the dialogue with Hölderlin.

S: Do you believe that the Germans have a special qualification for this reversal?

H: I have in mind especially the inner relationship of the German language with the language of the Greeks and with their thought. This has been confirmed for me today again by the French. When they begin to think, they speak German, being sure that they could not make it with their own language.

S: Are you trying to tell us that that is why you have had such a strong influence on the Romance countries, in particular the French?

H: Because they see that they can no longer get by in the contemporary world with all their great rationality when it comes right down to understanding the world in the origin of its being. One can translate thinking no more satisfactorily than one can translate poetry. At best one can circumscribe it. As soon as one makes a literal translation everything is changed.

S: A discomforting thought.

H: We would do well to take this discomfort seriously and on a large scale, and to finally consider the grave consequences of the transformation which Greek thought experienced when it was translated into Roman Latin. Indeed this today, even this, blocks the way to an adequate reflection on the fundamental words of Greek thought.

S: Professor, we must always start with the optimistic assumption that something which can be communicated can also be translated. For if we cease to be optimistic about the contents of thought being communicated beyond linguistic barriers, then we are threatened by provincialism.

H: Would you characterize Greek thought as it differs from the mode of representation in the Roman Empire as "provincial"? Business letters can be translated into all languages. The sciences (today, the natural sciences with mathematical physics as the fundamental science) are translatable into all world languages. Or put more accurately: they are not translated but the same mathematical language is spoken. We are touching here on a field which is broad and difficult to survey.

S: Perhaps this is also part of the problem. It is no exaggeration to say that we have at the moment a crisis of the democratic-parliamentary system. We have had it for a long time! We have it especially in Germany, but not only in Germany. We have it also in the classical democratic countries, England and America. In France it is not even a crisis anymore. Now for the question. Could not the "thinker" provide us with indications—as far as I am concerned as by-products—which would show that either this system must be replaced by a new one (and, if so, how this new system is supposed to look) or else that a reform ought to be possible (and if so, how this reform could come about)? Otherwise, we are left with this situation: the person normally in charge of things (even though he might not determine them and even though things are usually in charge of him) is not a person trained in philosophy and is going to reach faulty conclusions, perhaps with disastrous results. So shouldn't the philosopher be prepared to give thought to how human beings can get along with their fellow men in a world which they themselves have made so thoroughly technological, and which has perhaps overpowered them? Isn't one justified in expecting a philosopher to give us some indications as to how he perceives the possibility for life? And does the philosopher not miss a part (if you want, a small part) of his profession and his calling if he has nothing to say about that?

H: So far as I can see, an individual is not, because of thought, in a position to grasp the world as a whole so that he could give practical instructions, particularly in the face of the problem of finding a basis for thinking itself. So long as it takes itself seriously vis-à-vis the great tradition, it would be asking too much of thinking to have it set about giving instructions. By what authority could this take place? In the realm of thinking there are no authoritative assertions. The only measure for thinking is the matter which is itself to be thought. But this is above everything else questionable. In order to make this state of affairs clear we would need above a discussion of the relationship between philosophy and the sciences, for the technical and practical successes of the sciences make thinking in the sense of philosophy appear today to be more and more superfluous. Thinking has by reason of its own task put itself in a difficult situation. And along with this difficulty, there is also an alienation from thinking, an alienation which is nourished by the position of power occupied by the sciences, so that thinking must give up answering questions of a practical and world-wide character, the very answers that are demanded by daily necessities.

S: Professor, in the realm of thinking there are no authoritative assertions. So it can really not be surprising that modern art finds it difficult to make authoritative assertions. Nevertheless, you call it destructive. Modern art often considers itself experimental art. Its works are attempts . . .

H: I don't mind being taught.

S: . . . attempts [which arise] out of the isolated situation of contemporary man and of the artist. And out of 100 attempts now and again one will chance to hit the mark.

H: This is exactly the great question. Where does art stand? What place does it occupy?

S: Good enough. But then you are asking of art what you no long demand of thought.

H: I ask nothing of art. I am only saying that there is a question about what place art occupies.

S: If art does not know its place, is it therefore destructive?

H: All right, cross that out! However, I would like to say that I do not see how modern art shows the way, especially since we are left in the dark as to how modern art perceives or tries to perceive what is most proper to art.

S: The artist, too, lacks a sense of being bound to that which has been handed down. He can find something to be beautiful, and he can say: one could have painted that 600 years ago or 300 years or even 30. But he can no longer do it. Even if he wanted to, he could not do it. For otherwise the greatest artist would be the ingenious forger, Hans van Meergeren, who would then paint "better" than all the others. But that just isn't true anymore. So the artist, writer, and poet are in a situation similar to the thinker. How often must we say: close your eyes?

H: If one takes the "culture industry" as a framework for relating art and poetry and philosophy, then the comparison is justified. However, if not only the idea of an "industry" is questionable, but also what "culture" means, then the meditation on what is questionable here belongs to the realm of those tasks which are assigned to thought, whose distressing situation can hardly be comprehended. But the greatest distress of thought consists in the fact that today, as far as I can see, no thinker speaks who is "great" enough to bring thinking immediately, and in a formative way, before its subject matter, and thereby to get it underway. For us contemporaries the greatness of what is to be thought is too great. Perhaps we might bring ourselves to build a narrow and not far-reaching footpath as a passageway.

S: Professor Heidegger, thank you for this interview.

Translated by Maria P. Alter and John D. Caputo

PART TWO

CONTEXT AND TESTIMONY

6

TOTAL MOBILIZATION

Ernst Jünger

Introduction

Ernst Jünger (b. 1895) came to prominence during the 1920s as the foremost chronicler of the "front experience" ("*Fronterlebnis*") of World War I. His well-nigh lyrical descriptions of trench warfare and the great "battles of materiel" ("*Materialschlachten*")—that is, of those aspects which made this war unique in human history—in works such as *In the Storm of Steel* (1920) and *War as Inner Experience* (1922) earned him the reputation of a type of "aesthetician of carnage." In this way, Jünger, who was, like Heidegger, deeply influenced by Nietzsche's critique of "European Nihilism," viewed the energies unleashed by the Great War as a heroic countermovement to European world-weariness: as a proving ground for an entire series of masculinist warrior-virtues that seemed in danger of eclipse at the hands of an effete, decadent, and materialistic bourgeois *Zivilisation*. Yet, the war of 1914–1918 had proved that in the modern age warfare was more dependent on the amassing of technological capacities rather than acts of individual heroism, and this realization left a deep imprint on all of Jünger's writing in the form of a profound *amor fati*. Thus, as the following passage from *War as Inner Experience* demonstrates, in the last analysis the war did not so much present opportunities for acts of individual prowess as it offered the possibility of a metaphysical confrontation with certain primordial, chthonic elements: forces of annihilation, death, and horror: "The enthusiasm of manliness bursts beyond itself to such an extent that the blood boils as it surges through the veins and glows as it foams through the heart. . . . [War] is an intoxication beyond all intoxication, an un-

Ernst Jünger, "Total Mobilization" ("Totale Mobilmachung") first appeared in *Krieg und Krieger,* edited by Ernst Jünger (Berlin: Junker und Dünnhaupt, 1930).

leashing that breaks all bonds. It is a frenzy without caution and limits, comparable only to the forces of nature. There the individual is like a raging storm, the tossing sea, and the roaring thunder. He has melted into everything. He rests at the dark door of death like a bullet that has reached its goal. And the purple waves dash over him. For a long time he has no awareness of transition. It is as if a wave slipped back into the flowing sea."[1]

In the late twenties Jünger published over 100 essays in leading organs of Germany's conservative revolutionary movement (*Arminius, Deutsches Volkstum, Vormarsch,* and *Widerstand*), thus establishing himself, along with figures such as Moeller van den Bruck and Oswald Spengler, as one of the movement's most celebrated and influential figures. "Total Mobilization" appeared in the 1930 anthology *Krieg und Krieger* (*War and Warrior,* which was edited by Jünger himself). It represents a distillation of the argument of his book-length study of two years hence, *Der Arbeiter*—a work which enjoyed a tremendous commercial success and which, along with "Total Mobilization," represents a remarkable prefiguration of totalitarian rule.

It is important to understand the paramount strategic role played by works such as "Total Mobilization" and *The Worker* among the German conservative intelligentsia in the postwar period. For thereupon hinges the all-important difference between the "traditional German conservatism" and the new generation of "conservative revolutionaries." (For this generational split, moreover, the "front experience" of 1914–1918 represents, as it were, the great divide.) For whereas traditional German conservatives often rejected the utilitarian mind-set of Western modernity in the name of an idealized, pre-capitalist *Gemeinschaft,* the conservative revolutionaries—Jünger foremost among them—understood that if Germany were to be victorious in the *next* European war, a modus vivendi would have to be found with the forces of modern technology, on which the future balance of power depended. Certain of these thinkers, therefore, began to flirt with the idea of a "modern community"—a restoration of the integralist values of *Gemeinschaft* in a manner nevertheless consistent with the new demands of the industrial era. In this way Enlightenment progressivism would undergo a transformation from quantity to quality: for the very forces of science, reason, and technological progress that had been the animating values of the bourgeois epoch had seemingly reached a point where the inordinate degree of technological concentration itself threatened to undermine the survival of bourgeois liberalism. Or as Jünger argues forcefully in "Total Mobilization," in an age of total warfare, the difference between "war" and "peace" is effaced, and no sector of society can remain "uninte-grated" when the summons to "mobilization" is announced.

The two works by Jünger, "Total Mobilization" and *The Worker,* had an indelible impact on Heidegger's understanding of modern politics. In fact, it would not be much of an exaggeration to say that his "option" for National Socialism in the early 1930s was based on the supposition that Nazism was the legitimate embodiment of the *Arbeiter-gesellschaft* (society of workers) that had been prophesied by Jünger and which, as such, represented the heroic overcoming of Western nihilism as called for by Nietzsche and Spengler. In "The Rectorship 1933–34: Facts and Thoughts" (1945), Heidegger readily admits the enormity of Jünger's influence on his comprehension of contemporary history:

The way I already viewed the historical situation at that time [i.e., in the early 1930s] may be indicated with a reference. In 1930, Ernst Jünger's essay on "Total Mobilization" appeared; in this essay the fundamental outlines of his 1932 book *The Worker* are articulated. In a small group, I discussed these writings at this time, along with my assistant [Werner] Brock, and attempted to show how in them an essential comprehension of Nietzsche's metaphysics is expressed, insofar as the history and the contemporary situation of the West is seen and foreseen in the horizon of this metaphysics. On the basis of these writings, and even more essentially on the basis of their foundations, we reflected on what was to come, i.e., we sought thereby to confront the later in discussions.[2]

In his lectures of the late 1930s, Heidegger would critically distance himself from Nietzsche's metaphysics. In the early 1930s, however, his relation to Nietzsche was far from critical. Instead, at this time, he clearly viewed the historical potentials of the Nazi movement—its "inner truth and greatness," as he would remark in *An Introduction to Metaphysics* (1935)—in a manner consistent with the doctrines of Nietzsche and Jünger; that is, as a resurgence of a new heroic ethos, a "will to power," that would place Germany in the forefront of a movement directed toward the "self-overcoming" of bourgeois nihilism. Thus, following the argument set forth by Jünger in *The Worker,* in which "the soldier-worker" is viewed as a new social "type" ("*Gestalt*") who is infatuated with risk, danger, heroism, and, as such, represents the antithesis to the timorous "bourgeois," Heidegger views Nazism as a Nietzschean-Jüngerian *Arbeitergesellschaft in statu nascendi*.

One of the most prescient contemporary reviews of *War and Warriors* was written by Walter Benjamin. The essence of Benjamin's views was conveyed unambiguously by the title he chose for his commentary, "Theories of German Fascism." One of his central insights concerns the peculiarly "aestheticist" tenor of Jünger's appreciation of modern warfare. Or as Benjamin expresses it, "This new theory of war . . . is nothing other than an unrestrained transposition of the theses of *l'art pour l'art* to war."[3] For Benjamin the salient feature of Jünger's glorification of war lies in the fact that it is not so much a question of the *ends* for which one is fighting, but of the intrinsic value of war as an end in itself. And thus, war becomes a type of aesthetic spectacle to be enjoyed for its own sake. Or as Jünger himself, speaking of the unprecedented carnage of the First World War, observes: "Whenever we confront efforts of such proportions, possessing the special quality of 'uselessness' ['*Zwecklosigkeit*']—say, the erection of mighty constructions like pyramids and cathedrals, or wars that call into play the ultimate mainsprings of life—economic explanations, no matter how illuminating, are not sufficient."

Notes

1. Ernst Jünger, *Kampf als inneres Erlebnis* (Berlin, 1922), p. 57.
2. Martin Heidegger, *Die Selbstbehauptung der deutschen Universität/Das Rektorat 1933–34* (Frankfurt: Klostermann, 1985), p. 24; translated in this volume as "The Self-Assertion of the German University."
3. Walter Benjamin, *Gesammelte Schriften* III (Frankfurt: Suhrkamp, 1972), p. 240.

I

It goes against the grain of the heroic spirit to seek out the image of war in a source that can be determined by human action. Still, the multitudinous transformations and disguises which the pure form [*Gestalt*] of war endures amid the vicissitudes of human time and space offers this spirit a gripping spectacle to behold.

This spectacle reminds us of volcanoes which, although they are at work in very different regions, constantly spew forth the same earthly fire. To have participated in a war means something similar: to have been in the vicinity of such a fire-spitting mountain; but there is a great difference between Hekla in Iceland and Vesuvius in the Gulf of Naples. One might say that the difference in the landscapes vanishes the closer one approaches the crater's glowing jaws; also at the point where authentic passion breaks through—above all, in the naked and immediate struggle for life and death—it becomes a matter of secondary importance in which century, for what ideas, and with what weapons the battle is being fought. But that is not the subject of our essay.

Instead, we will try to assemble a number of facts that distinguish the last war—our war, the greatest and most influential event of our age—from other wars whose history has been handed down to us.

2

Perhaps we can best identify the special nature of this great catastrophe by the assertion that in it, the genius of war was penetrated by the spirit of progress. This was not only the case for the fighting among the different countries; it was also true for the civil war that gathered a rich second harvest in many of them. These two phenomena, world war and world revolution, are much more closely interrelated than a first glance would indicate. They are two sides of an event of cosmic significance, whose outbreak and origins are interdependent in numerous respects.

It is likely that many unusual discoveries await our thinking regarding the reality hidden behind the concept "progress"—an ambiguous concept glittering in many colors. Undoubtedly the way we are inclined these days to make fun of it comes too cheap. To be sure, we could cite every truly significant nineteenth-century thinker in support of our aversion; still, by all our disgust at the dullness and uniformity of the life-forms at issue, the suspicion arises that their *source* is of much greater significance. Ultimately, even the process of digestion depends on the powers of a wondrous and inexplicable Life. Certainly, it can today be demonstrated convincingly that progress is, in fact, not really *progress*. But more important than this conviction, perhaps, is the question of whether the concept's real significance is not of a more mysterious and different sort: one which uses the apparently undisguised mask of reason as a superb place of hiding.

It is precisely the certainty with which progressive movements produce results contradicting their own innermost tendencies which suggests that here, as everywhere in life, what prevails are not so much these tendencies but other, more hidden impulsions. "Spirit" ["*Geist*"] has often justifiably reveled in contempt for the wooden marionettes of progress; but the fine threads that produce their movements are invisible.

If we wish to learn something about the structure of marionettes, there is no more pleasant guide than Flaubert's novel *Bouvard and Pécuchet*. But if we wish to consider the possibilities of this more secret movement—a movement always easier to sense than prove—both Pascal and Hamann offer a wealth of revealing passages.

"Meanwhile, our phantasies, illusions, *fallaciae opticae*, and fallacies stand under God's realm." We find statements of this sort frequently in Hamann; they reflect a sensibility that strives to incorporate the labors of chemistry into the realm of alchemy. Let us leave aside the question of which spirit's realm rules over the optical illusion of progress: this study is no demonology, but is intended for twentieth-century readers. Nevertheless, one thing is certain: only a power of cultic origin, only a *belief*, could conceive of something as audacious as extending the perspective of utility [*Zweckmässigkeit*] into the infinite.

And who, then, would doubt that progress is the nineteenth century's great popular church—the only one enjoying real authority and uncritical faith?

3

With a war breaking out in such an atmosphere, the relation of each individual contestant to progress was bound to play a decisive role. And precisely therein lies the authentic, moral factor of our age: even the strongest armies, equipped with the industrial era's latest weapons of annihilation, are no match for its fine, imponderable emanations; for this era can even recruit its troops from the enemy's camp.

In order to clarify this situation, let us here introduce the concept of *total mobilization*: the times are long gone when it sufficed to send a hundred thousand enlisted subjects under reliable leadership into battle —as we find, say, in Voltaire's *Candide;* and when, if His Majesty lost a battle, the citizen's first duty was to stay quiet. Nonetheless, even in the second half of the nineteenth century, conservative cabinets could still prepare, wage, and win wars which the people's representatives were indifferent towards or even against. To be sure, this presupposed a close relation between crown and army; a relation that had only undergone a superficial change through the new system of universal conscription and which still essentially belonged to the patriarchal world. It was also based on a fixed calculation of armaments and costs, which made war seem like an exceptional, but in no sense limitless, expenditure of available forces and supplies. In this respect, even general mobilization had the character of a *partial* measure.

These restrictions not only reflect the limited degree of means, but also a specific raison d'état. The monarch possesses a natural instinct warning him not to trespass the bounds of dynastic power. The melting down of his treasure seems less objectionable than credits approved by an assembly; and for the decisive moment of battle, he would rather reserve his guards than a quota of volunteers. We find this instinct remaining healthy in Prussia deep into the nineteenth century. One example among many is the bitter fight for a three years' conscription: whereas a brief period of service is characteristic for a volunteer army, when dynastic power is at stake, tried and tested troops are more reliable. Frequently, we even come upon—what by today's standards is almost unthinkable—a renunciation of progress and any consummate equipping of the army; but such scruples also have their reasons. Hence hidden in every improvement of firearms—especially the increase in range—is an indirect assault on the conditions of absolute monarchy. Each such improvement promotes firing at individual targets, while the salvo incarnates the force of fixed command. Enthusiasm was still unpleasant to Wilhelm I. It springs from a source that, like Aeolus' windsack, hides not only storms of applause. Authority's true touchstone is not the extent of jubilation it receives, but the wars that have been lost.

Partial mobilization thus corresponds to the essence of monarchy. The latter oversteps its bounds to the extent that it is forced to make the abstract forms of spirit, money, "folk"—in short, the forces of growing national democracy—a part of the preparation for war. Looking back we can now say that complete renunciation of such participation was quite impossible. The manner in which it was incorporated [into political life] represents the real essence of nineteenth-century statecraft. These particular circumstances explain Bismarck's maxim that politics is the "art of the possible."

We can now pursue the process by which the growing conversion of life into energy, the increasingly fleeting content of all binding ties in deference to mobility, gives an ever-more radical character to the act of mobilization—which in many states was the exclusive right of the crown, needing no counter-signature. The events causing this are numerous: with the dissolution of the estates and the curtailing of the nobility's privileges, the concept of a warrior caste also vanishes; the armed defense of the state is no longer exclusively the duty and prerogative of the professional soldier, but the responsibility of everyone who can bear arms. Likewise, because of the huge increase in expenses, it is impossible to cover the costs of waging war on the basis of a fixed war budget; instead, a stretching of all possible credit, even a taxation of the last pfennig saved, is necessary to keep the machinery in motion. In the same way, the image of war as armed combat merges into the more extended image of a gigantic labor process [*Arbeitsprozesses*]. In addition to the armies that meet on the battlefields, originate the modern armies of commerce and transport, foodstuffs, the manufacture of armaments— the army of labor in general. In the final phase, which was already hinted at toward the end of the last war, there is no longer any movement whatsoever—be it that of the homeworker at her sewing machine— without at least indirect use for the battlefield. In this unlimited marshaling of potential energies, which transforms the warring industrial countries into volcanic forges, we perhaps find the most striking sign of the dawn of the age of labor [*Arbeitszeitalter*]. It makes the World War a historical event superior in significance to the French Revolution. In order to deploy energies of such proportion, fitting one's sword-arm no longer suffices; for this is a mobilization [*Rüstung*] that requires extension to the deepest marrow, life's finest nerve. Its realization is the task of total mobilization: an act which, as if through a single grasp of the control panel, conveys the extensively branched and densely veined power supply of modern life towards the great current of martial energy.

At the beginning of the World War, the human intellect had not yet anticipated a mobilization of such proportions. Still, its signs were manifest in isolated instances—for example, the large employment of volunteers and reservists at the war's start, the ban on exports, the censor's regulations, the changes of currency rates. In the course of the war this process intensified: as examples, we can cite the planned management of raw materials and foodstuffs, the transposition of industrial conditions [*Arbeitsverhältnisses*] to military circumstances, civil-guard duty, the arming of trade vessels, the unexpected extension of the general staff's authority, the "Hindenburg program," Ludendorff's struggle for the fusion of military and political command.

Nevertheless, despite the spectacle, both grandiose and frightful, of the later "battles of materiel" ["*Materialschlachten*"], in which the human talent for organization celebrates its bloody triumph, its fullest possibilities have not yet been reached. Even limiting our scope to the technical side of the process, this can only occur when the image of martial operations is prescribed for conditions of peace. We thus see that in the postwar period, many countries tailor new methods of armament to the pattern of total mobilization.

In this regard, we can introduce examples such as the increasing curtailment of "individual liberty," a privilege that, to be sure, has always been questionable. Such an assault takes place in Russia and Italy and then here in Germany; its aim is to deny the existence of anything that is *not* a function of the state. We can predict a time when all countries with global aspirations must take up the process, in order to sustain the release of new forms of power. France's evaluation of the balance of power from the perspective of *énergie potentielle* belongs in this context, as does the model America has offered—already in peacetime—for cooperation between industry and the army. German war literature raised issues touching on the very essence of armament, forcing the general public to make judgments about matters of war (if somewhat belatedly and in reality anticipating the future). For the first time, the Russian "five-year plan" presented the world with an attempt to channel the collective energies of a great empire into a *single* current. Seeing how economic theory turns volte-face is here instructive. The "planned economy," as one of the final results of democracy, grows beyond itself into a general unfolding of power. We can observe this shift in many events of our age. The great surging forth of the masses thereby reaches a point of crystallization.

Still, not only attack but also defense demands extraordinary efforts, and here the world's compulsions perhaps become even clearer. Just as every life already bears the seeds of its own death, so the emergence of the great masses contains within itself a democracy of death. The era of the well-aimed shot is already behind us. Giving out the night-flight bombing order, the squadron leader no longer sees a difference between combatants and civilians, and the deadly gas cloud hovers like an elementary power over everything that lives. But the possibility of such menace is based neither on a partial nor general, but rather a *total* mobilization. It extends to the child in the cradle, who is threatened like everyone else—even more so.

We could cite many such examples. It suffices simply to consider our daily life, with its inexorability and merciless discipline, its smoking, glowing districts, the physics and metaphysics of its commerce, its motors, airplanes, and burgeoning cities. With a pleasure-tinged horror, we sense that here, not a single atom is not in motion—that we are profoundly inscribed in this raging process. Total Mobilization is far less consummated than it consummates itself; in war and peace, it expresses the secret and inexorable claim to which our life in the age of masses and machines subjects us. It thus turns out that each individual life becomes, ever more unambiguously, the life of a worker; and that, following the wars of knights, kings, and citizens, we now have wars of *workers*. The first great twentieth-century conflict has offered us a presentiment of both their rational structure and their mercilessness.

4

We have touched on the technical aspects of Total Mobilization; their perfection can be traced from the first conscriptions of the Convention government during the French Revolution and Scharnhorst's army reorganization* to the dynamic armament program of the World War's last

*Translators' note: Gerhard Johann David von Scharnhorst (1755–1813), Prussian

years—when states transformed themselves into gigantic factories, producing armies on the assembly line that they sent to the battlefield both day and night, where an equally mechanical bloody maw took over the role of consumer. The monotony of such a spectacle—evoking the precise labor of a turbine fueled with blood—is indeed painful to the heroic temperament; still, there can be no doubt regarding its symbolic meaning. Here a severe necessity reveals itself: the hard stamp of an age in a martial medium.

In any event, Total Mobilization's technical side is not decisive. Its basis—like that of all technology—lies deeper. We shall address it here as the *readiness* for mobilization. Such readiness was present everywhere: the World War was one of the most popular wars known to history. This was because it took place in an age that excluded a priori all but popular wars. Also, aside from minor wars of colonialism and plunder, the involved nations had enjoyed a relatively long period of peace. At the beginning of our investigation, however, we promised emphatically not to focus on the elementary stratum of human nature—that mix of wild and noble passions resting within it, rendering it always open to the battle cry. Rather, we will now try to disentangle the multiple signals announcing and accompanying this particular conflict.

Whenever we confront efforts of such proportions, possessing the special quality of "uselessness" ["*Zwecklosigkeit*"]—say the erection of mighty constructions like pyramids and cathedrals, or wars that call into play the ultimate mainsprings of life—economic explanations, no matter how illuminating, are not sufficient. This is the reason that the school of historical materialism can only touch the surface of the process. To explain efforts of this sort, we ought rather focus our first suspicions on phenomena of a cultic variety.

In defining progress as the nineteenth century's popular church, we have already suggested the source of the last war's effective appeal to the great masses, whose participation was so indispensable. This appeal alone accounts for the decisive aspect of their Total Mobilization: that aspect with the force of faith. Shirking the war was all the less possible

---

general and creator of the modern Prussian military system. Following Prussia's losses in the Napoleonic wars, he reformed the Prussian military by abolishing its predominantly mercenary character and opting instead for a national force based on universal conscription.

in proportion to the degree of their conviction—hence in proportion to the purity with which the resounding words moving them to action had a progressive content. Granted, these words often had a harsh and lurid color; their effectiveness cannot be doubted. They resemble the bright rags steering the battue prey towards the rifle's scope.

Even a superficial glance, geographically separating the warring parties into victors and vanquished, must acknowledge the advantage of the "progressive" nations. This advantage seems to evoke a deterministic process such as Darwin's theory of survival of the "fittest." Its deterministic quality is particularly apparent in the inability of victorious countries like Russia and Italy to avoid a complete destruction of their political systems. In this light, the war seems to be a sure-fire touchstone, basing its value judgments on rigorous, intrinsic laws: like an earthquake testing the foundations of every building.

Furthermore, it turns out that, in the late hour of belief in universal rights of man, monarchical systems are particularly vulnerable to war's destruction. Along with innumerable petty crowns, those of Germany, Prussia, Russia, Austria, and Turkey turn into dust. Austro-Hungary, a state that, similar to an island preserving an extinct epoch, schematically cast itself in a medieval mold, collapses like an exploding house. Czardom, Europe's last traditional absolute sovereignty, falls victim to a civil war, devouring it with horrific symptoms—as would a long suppressed epidemic.

On the other hand, the progressive system's unexpected powers of resistance, even in a situation of great physical weakness, are striking. Hence, in the midst of the French army's suppression of that highly dangerous 1917 mutiny, a second, moral "miracle of the Marne" unfolds, more symptomatic for this war than purely military factors. Likewise, in the United States with its democratic constitution, mobilization could be executed with a rigor that was impossible in Prussia, where the right to vote was based on class. And who can doubt that America, the country lacking "dilapidated castles, basalt columns, and tales of knights, ghosts and brigands," emerged the obvious victor of this war? Its course was already decided not by the degree to which a state was a "military state," but by the degree to which it was capable of Total Mobilization.

Germany, however, was destined to lose the war, even if it had won the battle of the Marne and submarine warfare. For despite all the care with which it undertook partial mobilization, large areas of its strength escaped Total Mobilization; for the same reason, corresponding to the inner nature of its armament, it was certainly capable of obtaining, sustaining, and above all exploiting partial success—but never a total success. To affix *such* success to our weapons would have required preparing for another Cannae, one no less significant than that to which Schlieffen devoted his life's work.*

But before carrying this argument forward, let us consider some disparate points, in the hope of further showing the link between progress and Total Mobilization.

5

One fact is clearly illuminating for those seeking to understand the word progress in its gaudy timbre: in an age that publicly executed, under horrific torture, a Ravaillac or even a Damiens† as progeny of hell, the assassination of royalty would damage a more powerful social stratum —one more deeply etched in belief—than in the century following Louis XVI's execution. It turns out that in the hierarchy of progress, the prince belongs to a not especially favored species.

Let us imagine, for a moment, the grotesque situation in which a major advertising executive had to prepare the propaganda for a modern war. With two possibilities available for sparking the first wave of excitement—namely, the Sarajevo assassination or the violation of Belgian neutrality—there can be no doubt which would promise the greater impact. The superficial cause of the World War—no matter how adventitious it might seem—is inhabited by a symbolic meaning: in the case of the Sarajevo culprits and their victim, the heir to the Habsburg crown,

---

* Translators' note: It was at the battle of Cannae in 216 B.C. that Hannibal defeated the Romans. In the history of warfare, the battle stands as the most perfect example of the double envelopment of an opposing army. It took Rome nearly a decade to recover from the loss.

General Alfred von Schlieffen (1833–1913) was head of the German general staff from 1891 to 1906. He was responsible for the "Schlieffen plan" employed in World War I, which concerned the problem of waging war on two fronts.

† Translators' note: François Ravaillac (1578–1610), regicide who assassinated King Henry IV.

Robert-François Damiens (1714–1757), who was tortured and executed for his attempt on the life of Louis XV.

national and dynastic principles collided—the modern "right of national self-determination" with the principle of legitimacy painstakingly restored at the Congress of Vienna [1815] through statecraft of the old style.

Now certainly, being untimely in the right sense—setting in motion a powerful effect in a spirit that desires to preserve a legacy—is praiseworthy. But this requires faith. It is clear, however, that the Central Powers' ideology was neither timely, nor untimely, nor beyond time. Rather, the mood was simultaneously timely and untimely, resulting in nothing but a mixture of false romanticism and inadequate liberalism. Hence the observer could not help but notice a predilection for outmoded trappings, for a late romantic style, for Wagner's operas in particular. Words evoking the fidelity of the Nibelungs, hopes pinned on the success of Islam's call to holy war, are examples. Obviously, technical questions and questions of government were involved here—the mobilization of substance but not the substance itself. But the ruling classes' inadequate relationship both to the masses and to profounder forces revealed itself precisely in blunders of this sort.

Hence even the famous, unintentionally brilliant reference to a "scrap of paper" suffers from having been uttered 150 years too late—and then from principles that might have suited Prussian Romanticism, but at heart were not Prussian. Frederick the Great might have spoken thus, poking fun at yellowed, musty parchment in the manner of an enlightened despotism. But Bethmann-Hollweg must have known that in our time a piece of paper, say one with a constitution written on it, has a meaning similar to that of a consecrated wafer for the Catholic Church —and that tearing up treaties certainly suits absolutism, but liberalism's strength lies in their exegesis. Study the exchange of notes preceding America's entry into the war and you will come upon a principle of "freedom of the seas"; this offers a good example of the extent to which, in such an age, one's own interests are given the rank of a humanitarian postulate—of an issue with universal implications for humanity. German social democracy, one of the bulwarks of German progress, grasped the dialectical aspect of its mission when it equated the war's meaning with the destruction of the czar's anti-progressive regime.

But what does that signify as compared to the possibilities for mobilizing the masses at the West's disposal? Who would deny that *"civilisation"* is more profoundly attached to progress than is *"Kultur"*; that its language is spoken in the large cities, and that it has means and concepts at its command to which *Kultur* is either hostile or indifferent? *Kultur* cannot be used for propaganda. An approach that tries exploiting it in this way is itself estranged from it—just as we find the serving up of great German spirits' heads on millions of paper stamps and bills to be pointless, or even sad.

We have, however, no desire to complain about the inevitable. We wish only to establish that Germany was incapable of convincingly taking on the spirit of the age, whatever its nature. Germany was also incapable of proposing, to itself or to the world, a valid principle superior to that spirit. Rather, we find it searching—sometimes in romantic-idealistic, sometimes in rational-materialistic spheres—for those signs and images that the fighting individual strives to affix to his standards. But the validity lying within these spheres belongs partly to the past and partly to a milieu alien to German genius; it is not sufficient to assure utmost devotion to the advance of men and machines—something that a fearful battle against a world demands.

In this light we must struggle all the more to recognize how our elemental substance, the deep, primordial strength of the Volk, remains untouched by such a search. With admiration, we watch how German youth, at the beginning of this crusade of reason to which the world's nations are called under the spell of such an obvious, transparent dogma, raise the battle cry: glowing, enraptured, hungering after death in a way virtually unique in our history.

If one of these youths had been asked his motive for taking the field, the answer, certainly, would have been less clear. He would hardly have spoken of the struggle against barbarism and reaction or for civilization, the freeing of Belgium or freedom of the seas; but perhaps he would have offered the response, "for Germany"—that phrase, with which the volunteer regiments went on the attack.

And yet, this smoldering fire, burning for an enigmatic and invisible Germany, was sufficient for an effort that left nations trembling to the marrow. What if it had possessed direction, awareness, and *form [Gestalt]*?

6

As a mode of organizational thinking, Total Mobilization is merely an intimation of that higher mobilization that the age is discharging upon us. Characteristic of this *latter* type of mobilization is an inner lawfulness, to which human laws must correspond in order to be effective.

Nothing illustrates this claim better than the fact that during war forces can emerge that are directed against war itself. Nonetheless, these forces are more closely related to the powers at work in the war than it might seem. Total Mobilization shifts its sphere of operations, but not its meaning, when it begins to set in motion, instead of the armies of war, the masses in a civil war. The conflict now invades spheres that are off limits to the commands of military mobilization. It is as if the forces that could not be marshaled for the war now demanded their role in the bloody engagement. Hence the more unified and profound the war's capacity to summon, from the outset, all possible forces for its cause, the surer and more imperturbable will be its course.

We have seen that in Germany, the spirit of progress could only be mobilized incompletely. To take just one among thousands of examples, the case of Barbusse shows us that in France, for instance, the situation was far more propitious.* In reality an outspoken opponent of war, Barbusse could only stay true to his ideas by readily affirming *this* one: to his mind, it reflected a struggle of progress, *civilisation*, humanity, and even peace, against a principle opposed to all these factors. "War must be killed off in Germany's belly."

No matter how complicated this dialectic appears, its outcome is inexorable. A person with the least apparent inclination for military conflict still finds himself incapable of refusing the rifle offered by the state, since the possibility of an alternative is not present to his consciousness. Let us observe him as he racks his brains, standing guard in the wasteland of endless trenches, abandoning the trenches as well as anyone when the time comes, in order to advance through the horrific curtain of fire of the war of materiel. But what, in fact, is amazing about this? Barbusse is a warrior like any other: a warrior for humanity, able

* Translators' note: Henri Barbusse (1873–1935), French writer whose experiences in World War I led him to pacifism. In 1916 he wrote the powerful anti-war novel, *Le feu* (*Under Fire*).

to forgo machine-gun fire and gas attacks, and even the guillotine, as little as the Christian church can forgo its worldly sword. To be sure, in order to achieve such a degree of mobilization, a Barbusse would need to live in France.

The German Barbusses found themselves in a more difficult position. Only isolated intellects moved early to neutral territory, deciding to wage open sabotage against the war effort. The great majority tried cooperating with the deployment. We have already touched on the case of German social democracy. Let us disregard the fact that, despite its internationalist dogma, the movement's ranks were filled with German workers, hence could be moved to heroism. No—in its very ideology, it shifted towards a revision that later led to the charge of "the betrayal of Marxism." We can get a rough idea of the procedure's details in the speeches delivered during this critical period by Ludwig Frank, the Social Democratic leader and Reichstag deputy, who, as a forty-year-old volunteer, fell from a shot to the head at Noissoncourt in September 1914. "We comrades without a fatherland still know that, even as stepchildren, we are children of Germany, and that we must fight for our fatherland against reaction. If a war breaks out, the Social Democratic soldiers will also conscientiously fulfill their duty" (August 29, 1914). This extremely informative passage contains in a nutshell the forms of war and revolution that fate holds in readiness.

For those who wish to study this dialectic in detail, the practices of the newspapers and journals during the war years offer a wealth of examples. Hence Maximilian Harden—the editor of *Die Zukunft* and perhaps the best-known journalist of the Wilhelminian period—began adjusting his public activity to the goals of the central command. We note, only insofar as it is symptomatic, that he knew how to play upon the war's radicalism as well as he would later play upon that of the Revolution. And thus, *Simplicissimus,** an organ that had directed its weapons of nihilistic wit against all social ties, and thus also against the army, now took on a chauvinistic tone. It is clear, moreover, that the journal's quality diminishes as its patriotic tenor rises—that is, as it abandons the field of its strength.

Perhaps the inner conflict at issue here is most apparent in the case of

*Translators' note: A late nineteenth-, early twentieth-century popular satirical quarterly based in Munich.

Rathenau;* it endows this figure—for anyone struggling to do him justice—with the force of tragedy. To a considerable extent, Rathenau had mobilized for the war, playing a role in organizing the great armament and focusing—even close to the German collapse—on the possibility of a "mass insurrection." How is it possible that soon after, he could offer the well-known observation that world history would have lost its meaning had the Reich's representatives entered the capital as victors through the Brandenburg Gate? Here we see very clearly how the spirit of mobilization can dominate an individual's technical capacities, yet fail to penetrate his essence.

7

With our last fighters still lying before the enemy, the secret army and secret general staff commanding German progress greeted the collapse with exultation. It resembled the exultation at a victorious battle. It was the closest ally of the Western armies soon to cross the Rhine, their Trojan horse. The reigning authorities acknowledged the new spirit by the low level of protest with which they hastily vacated their posts. Between player and opponent, there was no essential difference.

This is also the reason that in Germany, the political transformation [following the military collapse] took on relatively harmless form. Thus, even during the crucial days of decision, the Empire's Social Democratic minister could play with the idea of leaving the crown intact. And what would that have signified, other than maintaining a facade? For a long time, the building had been so encumbered with "progressive" mortgages, that no more doubt was possible as to the true owner's nature.

But there is another reason why the change could take place less violently in Germany than, say, Russia—besides the fact that the authorities themselves prepared the way for it. We have seen that a large portion of the "progressive forces" had already been occupied with directing the war. The energy squandered during the war was then no longer available for the internal conflict. To express it in more personal

*Translators' note: Walter Rathenau (1867–1922), leading German industrialist who played a key role in organizing the supply of raw materials for Germany's war effort during World War I. Served as minister of reconstruction and foreign minister during the Weimar Republic and negotiated the Treaty of Rapallo with the Soviet Union. Rathenau, who was Jewish, was assassinated by right-wing extremists on June 24, 1922.

terms: it makes a difference if former ministers take the helm or a revolutionary aristocracy, educated in Siberian exile.

Germany lost the war by winning a stronger place in the Western sphere—civilization, peace, and freedom in Barbusse's sense. But how could we expect anything different, since we ourselves had sworn allegiance to such values; at no price would we have dared extend the war beyond that "wall wrapped around Europe." This would have required different ideas and different allies, a deeper disclosure of one's own values. An incitement of substance could have even taken place with and through progressivist optimism—as Russia's case suggests.

8

When we contemplate the world that has emerged from the catastrophe —what unity of effect, what incredibly rigorous historical consistency! Really, if all the spiritual and physical structures of a non-civilizational variety extending from the nineteenth century's end to our own age had been assembled in a small space and fired on with all the world's weapons—the success could not have been more resounding.

The Kremlin's old chimes now play the Internationale. In Constantinople, schoolchildren use the Latin script instead of the Koran's old arabesques. In Naples and Palermo, Fascist police regulate the pace of southern life as if directing modern traffic. In the world's remotest, even legendary lands, houses of parliament are being ceremoniously dedicated. The abstractness, hence the horror, of all human circumstances is increasing inexorably. Patriotism is being diluted through a new nationalism, strongly fused with elements of conscious awareness. In Fascism, Bolshevism, Americanism, Zionism, in the movements of colored peoples, progress has made advances that until recently would have seemed unthinkable; it proceeds, as it were, head over heels, following the circular course of an artificial dialectic in order to continue its movement on a very simple plane. Disregarding its much diminished allowances for freedom and sociability, it is starting to rule nations in ways not very different from those of an absolute regime. In many cases the humanitarian mask has almost been stripped away, replaced by a half-grotesque, half-barbaric fetishism of the machine, a naive cult of technique; this occurs particularly where there is no direct, productive relation to those dynamic energies for whose destructive, triumphal course long-range artillery and bomb-loaded fighter squadrons represent only the martial expression. Simultaneously, esteem for quantity [*Massen*] is increasing: quantity of assent, quantity of public opinion has become the decisive factor in politics. Socialism and nationalism in particular are the two great millstones between which progress pulverizes what is left of the old world, and eventually itself. For a period of more than a hundred years, the masses, blinded by the optical illusion of the franchise, were tossed around like a ball by the "right" and "left." It always seemed that one side offered refuge from the other's claims. Today everywhere the reality of each side's identity is becoming more and more apparent; even the dream of freedom is disappearing as if under a pincers' iron grasp. The movements of the uniformly molded masses, trapped in the snare set by the world-spirit, comprise a great and fearful spectacle. Each of these movements leads to a sharper, more merciless grasp: forms of compulsion stronger than torture are at work here; they are so strong, that human beings welcome them joyfully. Behind every exit, marked with the symbols of happiness, lurk pain and death. Happy is he alone who steps armed into these spaces.

9

Today, through the cracks and seams of Babel's tower, we can already see a glacier-world; this sight makes the bravest spirits tremble. Before long, the age of progress will seem as puzzling as the mysteries of an Egyptian dynasty. In that era, however, the world celebrated one of those triumphs that endow victory, for a moment, with the aura of eternity. More menacing than Hannibal, with all too mighty fists, somber armies had knocked on the gates of its great cities and fortified channels.

In the crater's depths, the last war possessed a meaning no arithmetic can master. The volunteer sensed it in his exultation, the German demon's voice bursting forth mightily, the exhaustion of the old values being united with an unconscious longing for a new life. Who would have imagined that these sons of a materialistic generation could have greeted death with such ardor? In this way a life rich in excess and ignorant of the beggar's thrift declares itself. And just as the actual result of an upright life is nothing but the gain of one's own deeper character, for us the results of this war can be nothing but the gain of a deeper Germany. This is confirmed by the agitation around us which is the mark of the new race: one that cannot be satisfied by any of this world's ideas nor any image of the past. A fruitful anarchy reigns here, which is born from the elements of earth and fire, and which hides within itself the seeds of a new form of domination. Here a new form of armament stands revealed, one which strives to forge its weapons from purer and harder metals that prove impervious to all resistance.

The German conducted the war with a, for him, all too reasonable ambition of being a good European. Since Europe thus made war on Europe—who else but Europe could be the victor? Nevertheless, this Europe, whose area extends in planetary proportions, has become extremely thin, extremely varnished: its spatial gains correspond to a loss in the force of conviction. New powers will emerge from it.

Deep beneath the regions in which the dialectic of war aims is still meaningful, the German encounters a stronger force: he encounters himself. In this way, the war was at the same time about him: above all, the means of his own self-realization. And for this reason, the new form of armament, in which we have already for some time been implicated, must be a mobilization of the German—nothing else.

Translated by Joel Golb and Richard Wolin

7

MY LAST MEETING WITH HEIDEGGER IN ROME, 1936

Karl Löwith

Introduction

It would be difficult to discover more compelling testimony on the theme of the philosophical bases of Heidegger's political involvements than that of the German philosopher Karl Löwith (1897–1973)—a former student and intimate of Martin Heidegger, heretofore best known in the English-speaking world for his studies of modern historical consciousness (*Meaning in History, Max Weber and Karl Marx*), as well as his classical study of post-Hegelian German thought, *From Hegel to Nietzsche*. Löwith's 1928 *Habilitationsschrift, Der Individuum in der Rolle des Mitmenschen* was directed by Heidegger. He was a "dozent" or lecturer at Marburg University until Hitler's accession to power in 1933. Thereafter, he was forced to embark on a long and circuitous course of emigration: first in Italy, followed by four years in Japan, finally arriving in the United States in 1941, where he took up a position at the Hartford Theological Seminary. After teaching at the New School for Social Research for two years (1949–1951), he accepted a position in philosophy at Heidelberg University.

Löwith's account of his last meeting with Heidegger was originally written in Japan in 1939 as part of a competition for German emigrés sponsored by Harvard University for the best essay on the theme of "My Life in Germany Before and After 1933." Given his precarious life circumstances at the time, the $500 first prize (then the equivalent of nearly half a year's salary) undoubtedly seemed attractive.

Of course, Löwith did not receive the prize. His fascinating autobio-

Karl Löwith, "My Last Meeting with Heidegger in Rome, 1936" first appeared in *Mein Leben in Deutschland vor und nach 1933* (Stuttgart: Metzler, 1986), pp. 56–59.

graphical-philosophical jottings (which were undoubtedly too substantial for the tastes of the committee, which had already made it clear that "it had no interest in philosophical reflections about the past") were rediscovered by his widow and only published in 1986 under the same title as that of the essay competition—*Mein Leben in Deutschland vor und nach 1933.*

The following depiction of Löwith's last meeting with Heidegger outside of Rome in 1936 proves to be of much more than anecdotal import. And thus, his account of Heidegger's own unabashed insistence (upon being confronted with the theologian Hans Barth's opinion to the contrary) on the integral relation between his own thought and National Socialist doctrines reinforces a conclusion that is now widely accepted: that Heidegger understood his political "decision" of the early 1930s as an *"existentiell"* (or "ontic") realization of the existential analytic of *Being and Time.* Or, as Löwith shows in "The Political Implications of Heidegger's Existentialism" (included here in part III), one need only transpose the existential solipsism of Heidegger's 1927 work (e.g., the emphasis on *"Jemeinigkeit,"* "Potentiality-for-Being-a-Self," etc.) from an "individual" to a "collectivist" frame of reference, and it is now *German Dasein* that must choose its "destiny," stake a claim toward "authenticity," and so forth.

. . .

In 1936, during my stay in Rome, Heidegger gave a lecture on Hölderlin at the German-Italian Culture Institute. Later, he accompanied me to our apartment and was visibly taken aback by the poverty of our furnishings. . . .

The next day, my wife and I made an excursion to Frascati and Tusculum with Heidegger, his wife, and his two small sons, whom I often cared for when they were little. It was a radiant afternoon, and I was happy about this final get-together, despite undeniable reservations. Even on this occasion, Heidegger did not remove the Party insignia from his lapel. He wore it during his entire stay in Rome, and it had obviously not occurred to him that the swastika was out of place while he was spending the day with me.

We talked about Italy, Freiburg, and Marburg, and also about philosophical topics. He was friendly and attentive, yet avoided, as did his wife, every allusion to the situation in Germany and his views of it.

On the way back, I wanted to spur him to an unguarded opinion about the situation in Germany. I turned the conversation to the controversy in the *Neue Zuricher Zeitung* and explained to him that I agreed neither with [Hans] Barth's political attack [on Heidegger] nor with [Emil] Staiger's defense, insofar as I was of the opinion that his partisanship for National Socialism lay in the essence of his philosophy. Heidegger agreed with me without reservation, and added that his concept of "historicity" was the basis of his political "engagement." He also left no doubt concerning his belief in Hitler. He had underestimated only two things: the vitality of the Christian churches and the obstacles to the *Anschluss* with Austria. He was convinced now as before that National Socialism was the right course for Germany; one had only to "hold out" long enough. The only aspect that troubled him was the ceaseless "organization" at the expense of "vital forces." He failed to notice the destructive radicalism of the whole movement and the petty bourgeois character of all its "power-through-joy" institutions, because he himself was a radical petty bourgeois.

In response to my remark that there were many things about his attitude I could understand, with one exception, viz., how he could sit at the same table (at the Academy of German Law) with someone like J. Streicher,* he remained silent at first. Then, somewhat uncomfortably, followed the justification . . . that things would have been "much worse" if at least a few intelligent persons [*Wissenden*] hadn't become involved. And with bitter resentment against the intelligentsia, he concluded his explanation: "If these gentlemen hadn't been too refined to get involved, then everything would be different; but, instead, now I'm entirely alone." To my response that one didn't have to be especially "refined" in order to renounce working with someone like Streicher, he answered: one need not waste words over Streicher, *Der Stürmer* was nothing more than pornography. He couldn't understand why Hitler didn't get rid of this guy—he must be afraid of him.

These responses were typical, for nothing was easier for the Germans than to be radical when it came to ideas and indifferent in practical fact. They manage to ignore *all individual Fakta*, in order to be able to cling all the more decisively to their *concept of the whole* and to separate "matters of fact" from "persons." In truth, the program of "pornogra-

* Translator's note: A Nazi propagandist and editor of the popular anti-Semitic publication, *Der Stürmer* (see below).

phy" [e.g., embodied in anti-Semitic publications such as *Der Stürmer*] was fulfilled and became a German reality in 1938;* and no one can deny that Streicher and Hitler were in agreement on this matter.

In 1938, Husserl died in Freiburg. Heidegger proved the "Admiration and Friendship" (the terms in which he dedicated his 1927 work [*Sein und Zeit*] to Husserl) by wasting no words of remembrance or sympathy, either public or private, oral or written.

Translated by Richard Wolin

* Translator's note: One must recall that Löwith's reflections date from the year 1939. The allusion to 1938 is undoubtedly a reference to *Kristallnacht,* when the anti-Semitic propaganda of the Nazis turned into a bloody and horrifying reality.

LETTER TO THE FREIBURG UNIVERSITY DENAZIFICATION COMMITTEE
(December 22, 1945)

Karl Jaspers

Introduction

As of 1920, Heidegger and Jaspers (1883–1969) became friends. Jaspers felt that in Heidegger he had found a true kindred philosophical spirit. Or as he describes his initial contact with Heidegger in his *Philosophical Autobiography* (Munich: Piper, 1977, pp. 92ff.): "One can scarcely imagine the satisfaction I felt to be able to speak seriously with at least one member of the philosophical community." The two were united in their common scorn of traditional academic philosophy ("Both of us felt it as our task [to bring about] a renewal not of philosophy per se, but of the type of philosophy then dominant at the universities"); and in their deep appreciation of the philosophy of Kierkegaard, whose work had become a rite of passage for almost all of twentieth-century *Existenzphilosophie*—Sartre's included.[1]

Although Jaspers was initially attracted to Heidegger's unmistakable genius, their relations from the outset were not untroubled. In their dealings, Heidegger seemed temperamental and by nature inclined to silence. Their first real misunderstanding was provoked by a harsh and lengthy 1921 critique Heidegger wrote of Jaspers' 1919 work, *The Psychology of World-Views*, which Heidegger would only publish some

Reprinted with the kind permission of Dr. Hugo Ott, Professor of Economic and Social History at Freiburg University, from his *Martin Heidegger: Unterwegs zu seiner Biographie* (Frankfurt: Campus Verlag, 1988).

45 years later in *Wegmarken*. Jaspers found the criticisms both "unjustified" and unfruitful. According to Jaspers, it is likely that Heidegger was disappointed by Jaspers' failure to pursue the philosophical course outlined by his junior colleague.

Jaspers, for his part, admits to having reacted somewhat coolly to Heidegger's great work of 1927, *Being and Time*. In 1922, Heidegger gave Jaspers a few pages to read of a work-in-progress. Jaspers found them "incomprehensible"—largely, it seems, as a result of Heidegger's inordinate reliance on neologisms. When the book itself finally appeared in 1927, catapulting Heidegger to international renown, Jaspers displayed little interest. He found it "unproductive" (*"unergiebig"*), despite the "luster of powerful analysis" (*Philosophical Autobiography*, p. 98).

However, as one might suspect, their true falling-out occurred in 1933, as a result of Heidegger's political activism. Shortly after his accession to the rectorship at Freiburg in May 1933, Heidegger traveled to Heidelberg, where Jaspers taught, to give a public lecture. According to Jaspers, while the "form" of the address was "masterful," its content consisted of a typical appeal for a renewal of the German university system along National Socialist lines. Moreover, Heidegger went on to announce that the majority of professors currently in office were not up to the mission before them; and that in ten years' time, they would be replaced by a new generation of politically more capable docents.

During these crucial transitional months in which Germany's transformation from democracy to dictatorship took place, contact between the two men was awkward and brief. Jaspers recounts one such meeting in which he brought up the Jewish question to Heidegger; at which point the latter affirmed his belief in "a dangerous international alliance of Jews." In a tone of rage, Heidegger complained that there were too many philosophy professors in Germany, and that only two or three should be retained. To Jaspers' question, "Which ones, then?," Heidegger offered no response. Finally, when Heidegger was asked by his host how one could expect someone as uneducated (*ungebildet*) as Hitler to rule Germany, Heidegger responded: "It's not a question of education; just look at his marvelous hands!" (*Philosophical Autobiography*, p. 101).

Despite the intense strain on their relationship as a result of Heidegger's Nazi involvements, in the 1950s Jaspers would characterize his feelings about Heidegger in the following terms: "Among contemporary professional philosophers Heidegger was the only one who concerned me in an essential way. I feel the same way today. I have good relations with many others, I learn from them and respect their accomplishments, yet without their saying or doing anything as philosophers that belongs in the adytum of philosophy. Heidegger gained access to problem-complexes that appear to be the most hidden" (*Philosophical Autobiography*, p. 92).

Jaspers' deep ambivalences toward Heidegger—his equally strong admiration and reservations—come through clearly in the following letter, which was composed at the request of one of the members of the university denazification commission, the botanist Friedrich Oehlkers. Jaspers must have sensed what would indeed prove to be the case: that his recommendation would be the one that would tip the scales concerning the major dilemma confronting the highly conflicted university commission: whether to grant Heidegger "emeritus" status, by virtue of which he would have still been permitted to participate in university activities; or whether to ban him summarily from university life for an unspecified amount of time (while providing him with a pension that would enable him to continue to write). Given his longtime association with Heidegger, it must have certainly been painful for Jaspers to have recommended the second option, although it is a testament to his honesty that he explicitly grants permission for Heidegger to be apprised of the contents of his appraisal.

Finally, it is perhaps worth noting that one of Heidegger's only expressions of contrition over his ruthless behavior during the Nazi years comes in a letter to Jaspers of March 20, 1950. There he confides that he did not disdain visiting Jaspers because of the latter's Jewish wife, but instead, because he was "simply ashamed."[2]

Notes

1. See, for example, Sartre's important discussion of Kierkegaard, "Kierkegaard: The Singular Universal," in Jean-Paul Sartre, *Between Existentialism and Marxism* (New York: William Morrow, 1976), pp. 141–169.

2. Cited in Hugo Ott, *Martin Heidegger: Unterwegs zu seiner Biographie* (Frankfurt: Campus, 1988), p. 32.

Heidelberg, December 22, 1945

Dear esteemed Herr Oehlkers!

Your letter of December 15 reached me today. I am glad that the matter concerning Herr Gentner has worked out.* In the meantime he has perhaps even paid you the visit he was planning en route from a trip to Paris, whence we expect him to return shortly.

I want to answer the main question of your letter straight away. Owing to my earlier friendship with Heidegger, it is unavoidable that I touch on personal matters; nor will I be able to conceal a certain partiality in my judgments. You are correct in referring to the affair as complicated. As with everything complicated, here, too, one must strive to reduce things to what is simple and decisive, so as not to get trapped in the maze of complications. I hope you don't mind if I articulate separately some of the main points:

1) Aside from the case of intimate friends, I had hoped to be able to keep silent. This has been my thinking since 1933, as I resolved after my terrible disillusionment to remain silent out of loyalty to good memories. This became easy for me, since on the occasion of our last conversation in 1933, Heidegger was silent or imprecise about delicate questions—especially the Jewish question; and since we never saw each other again, insofar as he no longer continued his regular visits that had been going on for a decade. To the end he sent me his publications; after 1937–1938, he no longer confirmed receipt of the materials I sent him. Now I hoped more than ever to be able to remain silent. But now you ask me to voice my opinion not only officially in the name of Herr von Dietze,† but also at the request of Heidegger. This forces my hand.

2) In addition to what is publicly known, I am aware of a number of facts, two of which I find important enough to pass on.

On the orders of the National Socialist regime Heidegger provided a

---

*Translator's note: Wolfgang Gentner, a Heidelberg physicist who had recently accepted an appointment in Freiburg replacing a National Socialist functionary who had previously occupied the position.

†Translator's note: Constantin von Dietze, chairman of the university denazification commission.

letter of evaluation concerning [Eduard] Baumgarten* to the [Nazi] Docents Association in Göttingen, a copy of which came my way many years ago. In it one finds the following sentences: "During his stay here [at Freiburg] Baumgarten was anything but a National Socialist. By family background and intellectual orientation Dr. Baumgarten comes from the Heidelberg circle of liberal-democratic intellectuals around Max Weber. After failing with me he frequented, very actively, the Jew Fraenkel, who used to teach at Göttingen and just recently was fired from here [due to Nazi racial legislation banning Jews from the civil service]. Through Fraenkel he arranged for accommodations in Göttingen. . . . The judgment concerning [Baumgarten] naturally can not yet be final. There is still room for development on his part. There must be a suitable probation period before one can allow him entry into the National Socialist party." These days we have become accustomed to abominations; measured against these, it is perhaps difficult to understand the horror that seized me back then upon reading these lines.

Heidegger's assistant in the philosophy department, Dr. [Werner] Brock, was a Jew, a fact that was unknown to Heidegger at the time of his appointment. Brock was forced to give up his position as a result of National Socialist ordinances. According to information provided to me by Brock verbally at the time, Heidegger's behavior toward him was unobjectionable. Heidegger facilitated his resettlement in England through favorable recommendations.

In the 1920s Heidegger was not an anti-Semite. The completely unnecessary remarks about "the Jew Fraenkel" prove that in 1933 he became an anti-Semite, at least in certain contexts. With respect to this question he did not always exercise discretion. This doesn't rule out the possibility that, as I must assume, in other cases anti-Semitism went against his conscience and his sense of propriety.

3) Heidegger is a significant potency, not through the content of a philosophical world-view, but in the manipulation of speculative tools. He has a philosophical aptitude whose perceptions are interesting; although, in my opinion, he is extraordinarily uncritical and stands at a remove from true science [*der eigentlichen Wissenschaft fern steht*]. He

---

*Translator's note: For the details of Heidegger's denunciation of Baumgarten, see Ott, *Martin Heidegger*, pp. 183ff.; and Victor Farias, *Heidegger et le nazisme* (Paris: Verdier, 1987), pp. 243ff.

often proceeds as if he combined the seriousness of nihilism with the mystagogy of a magician. In the torrent of his language he is occasionally able, in a clandestine and remarkable way, to strike the core of philo- sophical thought. In this regard he is, as far as I can see, perhaps unique among contemporary German philosophers.

Therefore, it is urgently to be hoped and requested that he remain in the position to work and to write.

4) Today, one must unavoidably keep our general situation in mind in handling the cases of individual persons.

Hence, it is absolutely necessary that those who helped place National Socialism in the saddle be called to account. Heidegger belongs among the few professors to have so acted.

The severity of excluding from their positions numerous men who deep down were not National Socialists is widespread today. Were Heidegger to be kept on without restrictions, what would his colleagues say who were forced out, fell upon hard times, and who never acted on behalf of the National Socialists! Exceptional intellectual achievement can serve as a justifiable basis for facilitating the continuation of such work; not, however, for the resumption of office and teaching duties.

In our situation, the education of youth must be handled with the greatest responsibility. Complete freedom to teach is a desirable goal, but it cannot be realized immediately. Heidegger's manner of thinking, which to me seems in its essence unfree, dictatorial, and incapable of communication [*communikationslos*], would today in its pedagogical effects be disastrous. To me the manner of thinking seems more impor- tant than the content of political judgments, the aggressive character of which can easily change directions. As long as in his case an authentic rebirth does not come to pass, one that would be evident in his work, such a teacher cannot in my opinion be placed before the youth of today, which, from a spiritual standpoint, is almost defenseless. The youth must first reach a point where they can think for themselves.

5) To a certain extent I acknowledge the personal excuse that Heideg- ger was according to his nature unpolitical; the National Socialism which he embraced had little in common with existing National Social- ism. In this connection I would first of all call attention to Max Weber's 1919 remark: children who grab hold of the wheel of history are crushed. My second qualification: Heidegger certainly did not see through all the

real powers and goals of the National Socialist leaders. That he believed he could preserve an independence of will proves this. But his manner of speaking and his actions have a certain affinity with National Socialist characteristics which makes his error comprehensible. He and [Alfred] Bäumler and Carl Schmitt are the—among themselves very different—professors who attempted to reach a position of intellectual leadership under National Socialism. In vain. They made use of real intellectual capacities and thereby ruined the reputation of German philosophy. An aspect of the tragic nature of evil arises therefrom; here, I am in agreement with what you perceive.

A change of conviction as a result of directional shifts in the National Socialist camp can be judged according to the motivations which are in part revealed at the specific point in time. [The years] 1934, 1938, 1941 signify fundamentally different stages. In my opinion, for purposes of reaching a judgment a change of conviction is almost meaningless if it resulted only after 1941, and it is of trifling value if it did not occur radically after June 30, 1934.

6) In unusual cases unusual rules come into play, precisely insofar as the case is truly important. Therefore, my proposal is:

a) The allocation of a personal pension for Heidegger for the purposes of the continuation of his philosophical labors and the publication of his work, based on his recognized achievements and the expectation that writings of importance are still to come.

b) Suspension from teaching duties for several years. Thereafter a reassessment to be based on subsequent publications and the current academic situation. At that time the question should be raised whether a complete restoration of the earlier freedom of instruction can be risked; in which case convictions that are antagonistic and dangerous to the idea of the university may gain acceptance if they are represented by those who are intellectually esteemed. Whether we reach this point depends on the course of political events and on the development of our public spirit.

In the event that such a specific ruling in Heidegger's case is denied, I would hold preferential treatment within the framework of the general ordinances to be unjust.

I have expressed my opinion with a concision that is full of possible misunderstandings. In the event that you would like to bring this letter to Heidegger's attention, I give you permission to convey points 1, 2, 6, and also from point 3 the paragraph, "Therefore it is . . . to work and to write."

Please excuse the succinctness and brevity. I would have rather discussed the matter with you in conversation and then further clarified things upon hearing your ideas. But that is not possible at this point in time.

You write of the winter temperatures. These are certainly considerably greater in Freiburg than they are here, although we too are suffering. But until now it's been ok. As long as no serious frost comes.

My warmest greetings to you and your dear wife from my wife and myself,

Yours,

Karl Jaspers

Translated by Richard Wolin

9

AN EXCHANGE OF LETTERS

Herbert Marcuse and Martin Heidegger

Introduction

Existentialism collapses in the moment when its political theory is realized. The total-authoritarian state which it yearned for gives the lie to all its truths. Existentialism accompanies its collapse with a self-abasement that is unique in intellectual history; it carries out its own history as a satyr-play to the end. It began philosophically as a great debate with Western rationalism and idealism, in order to redeem the historical concretion of individual existence for this intellectual heritage. And it ends philosophically with the radical denial of its own origins; the struggle against reason drives it blindly into the arms of the reigning powers. In their service and protection it betrays that great philosophy which it once celebrated as the pinnacle of Western thinking.

Herbert Marcuse, "The Struggle Against Liberalism in the Totalitarian State"

(1934)

The full story of Marcuse's relation to Heidegger has yet to be written.

We know that during the four years Marcuse was in Freiburg studying with Heidegger, his enthusiasm for Heidegger's philosophy was unreserved. Or as Marcuse himself would observe in retrospect, "I must say frankly that during this time, let's say from 1928 to 1932, there were relatively few reservations and relatively few criticisms on my part."[1] From this period stem Marcuse's first essays—"Contributions to a Phenomenology of Historical Materialism," "On Concrete Philosophy," "The Foundations of Historical Materialism," "On the Philosophical

Herbert Marcuse's letters to Martin Heidegger were published by *Pflasterstrand* 279/ 280: 465–480, 1988. Heidegger's letter to Marcuse is in the Herbert Marcuse Archive, Stadtsbibliothek, Frankfurt am Main.

Foundations of the Concept of Labor in Economics," and "On the Problem of Dialectic"—which attempt to effectuate a synthesis between Marxism and existentialism.[2] Of course, the synthesis Marcuse was seeking is suggestive of the analogous philosophical enterprise undertaken by the late Sartre in *Critique of Dialectical Reason* and other works. Yet, whereas Marcuse was moving from Marxism to existentialism, Sartre's intellectual development followed the obverse trajectory. However, via the integration of Marxism and existentialism, both thinkers were pursuing a common end: they recognized that the crisis of Marxist thought—and practice—was in no small measure precipitated by its incapacity to conceptualize the problem of the "individual." And thus, in the doctrines of orthodox Marxism, the standpoint of the individual threatened to be crushed amid the weight of objective historical determinants and conditions. For Sartre, writing in the wake of Stalinism and the Soviet invasion of Hungary, a "critique of dialectical reason"—in the Kantian sense of establishing transcendental limits or boundaries—had become an urgent historical task. Marcuse's attempts to integrate these two traditions—which he would ultimately judge as failed—seemed to anticipate many of the historical problems of Marxism that would motivate Sartre's later philosophical explorations of these themes.

In Marx's 1846 "Theses on Feuerbach" he remarks that "the chief defect of all hitherto existing materialism (that of Feuerbach included) is that the thing, reality, sensuousness, is conceived only in the form of the *object or of contemplation,* but not as *sensuous human activity, practice,* not subjectively." In contradistinction to materialism, Marx continues, it fell to "idealism" to develop the "*active* side" of dialectics, i.e., that side that points in the direction of praxis: "revolutionary, 'practical-critical,' activity."[3] It is not hard to see that what Marcuse valorized above all about Heidegger's early philosophy was its potential contribution to the "active side" of dialectics in a way that paralleled the contribution made by German idealism to historical materialism in the previous century. If the "crisis of historical materialism" (in "Contributions to a Phenomenology of Historical Materialism," Marcuse alludes to "the bungled revolutionary situations" of which recent history had provided ample evidence) had been caused by the triumph of Marxism's "objectivistic" self-understanding, would not a new infusion of historically adequate idealist categories aid greatly in the resuscitation of a senescent Marxist theory?

In *History and Class Consciousness* Lukács observes that "[German] classical philosophy is able to think the deepest and most fundamental problems of the development of bourgeois society through to the very end—on the plane of philosophy. It is able—in thought—to complete the evolution of class. And—in thought—it is able to take all the paradoxes of its position to the point where the necessity of going beyond this historical stage in mankind's development can at least be seen as a problem."[4] In similar fashion, Marcuse perceives Heideggerian *Existenzphilosophie* to be the most advanced expression of contemporary bourgeois philosophy. However, its value is greater than being simply a "privileged" object of "ideology criticism." Instead, it has something specific and positive to contribute to materialist dialectics, in a way that parallels Lukács' own praise of idealism for having provided dialectical thought with the category of "mediation." And thus, in his "Contribution to a Phenomenology of Historical Materialism," Marcuse lauds Heidegger's *Being and Time* "as a turning point in the history of philosophy—the point where bourgeois philosophy transcends itself from within and opens the way to a new, 'concrete' science."[5]

A more detailed account of what it was about Heidegger's existentialism that Marcuse viewed as so promising has been provided elsewhere.[6] In the context at hand, it will hopefully suffice to highlight the two essential "moments" of Marcuse's appreciation of Heidegger's thought.

First, Marcuse emphasizes what might be referred to as the "hermeneutical point of departure" ("*Ansatz*") of *Being and Time;* i.e., the fact that human Being or Dasein occupies center stage in Heidegger's "existential analytic" (conversely, Marcuse shows very little interest in the strictly "metaphysical" or "ontological" dimension of *Being and Time,* i.e., Heidegger's posing of the *Seinsfrage*). He reveres this philosophical approach as an *Aufhebung* of the static, quasi-positivistic aspects of bourgeois philosophy and social science, whereby humanity is viewed predominantly as an object of scientific scrutiny and control, rather than as an active and conscious agent of change and historical becoming. By identifying Dasein as "care," as an "embodied subjectivity"—as "that Being for which its very Being is an issue for it"—Heidegger's thought displays a potential for the constructive transcendence of the traditional (bourgeois) philosophical antinomy between thought and being, *res cog-*

itans and *res extensa,* and—ultimately—theory and practice. By reject-
ing the objectivistic framework of previous philosophical thought, Heideggerian "Dasein encounters the objective world as a world of meaning
oriented toward existence. It does not encounter it as a rigid *res exten-
sae,* as independent, abstract physical things. Rather, they are related to
an *Existenz* that uses them, orients itself towards them, and deals with
them; thus ascribing to them meaning, time, and place."[7] By employing
a practically situated Dasein as its philosophical point of departure,
Heidegger's standpoint in effect emphasizes *the primacy of practical
reason;* and in this respect, his discussions of the problems of "Selfhood"
and "my ownmost capacity-for-Being" present a micro-philosophical
complement to the socio-historical analyses of Marxism.

But of equal importance in Marcuse's youthful appreciation of Heidegger is the category of *historicity;* i.e., Heidegger's contention in Division II of *Being and Time* that not only does all "life" exist *in history*
(this is the claim, e.g., of Dilthey's "historicism"), but that "existence"
itself is *historical*: that is, Dasein is engaged in a constant and active re-
appropriation and shaping of the pre-given semantic potentials of historical life. Dasein is thereby always surpassing itself in the direction of the
future. Or as Heidegger expresses it, *"The primary meaning of existen-
tiality is in the future."*[8] It is clear that in this "active," "future-oriented"
disposition of existential historicity, Marcuse perceives a crucial herme-
neutical-methodological tool whereby the problems of historical struggle
and contestation might be thematized; problems that Marxism in its
current, "objectivistic," "diamat" guise remained incapable of addressing. Or as Marcuse himself observes, "Past, present, and future are
existential characteristics, and thus render possible fundamental phenomena such as understanding, concern, and determination. This opens
the way for the demonstration of historicity as a fundamental existential
determination—which we regard as the decisive point in Heidegger's
phenomenology."[9] Moreover, by virtue of the centrality of the category
of "historicity" in *Being and Time,* there seemed to exist a necessary and
essential basis for the marriage of Marxism and phenomenology that
Marcuse was preoccupied with during these years.[10]

Marcuse's efforts to merge Marxism and existentialism would be
repeated by many others in the course of the twentieth century. Here, in
addition to Sartre, the names of Merleau-Ponty, Enzo Paci, Karel Kosik,
Pierre Aldo Rovatti, and Tran Duc Thao also come to mind.[11] Yet,

according to Marcuse's own retrospective appraisal, such attempts to combine Marxism and existentialism were predestined to failure. This was true insofar as existentialist categories such as "Dasein," "historicity," and "authenticity" were, in Marcuse's view, a priori capable of attaining only a "pseudo-concreteness." Marcuse describes his reasons for breaking with the paradigm of phenomenological Marxism in a 1974 interview in the following terms: "I soon realized that Heidegger's concreteness was to a great extent a phony, a false concreteness, and that in fact his philosophy was just as abstract and just as removed from reality, even avoiding reality, as the philosophies which at that time had dominated German universities, namely a rather dry brand of neo-Kantianism, neo-Hegelianism, neo-Idealism, but also positivism." He continues, "If you look at [Heidegger's] principle concepts . . . *Dasein, Das Man, Sein, Seiendes, Existenz,* they are 'bad' abstracts in the sense that they are not conceptual vehicles to comprehend the real concreteness in the apparent one. They lead away."[12]

In his essay, "Existential Ontology and Historical Materialism in the Work of Herbert Marcuse," Alfred Schmidt, echoing Marcuse's own sentiments, similarly emphasizes the inner conceptual grounds on which the marriage between Marxism and existentialism foundered. Schmidt seconds the verdict of the philosopher and former Heidegger student Karl Löwith concerning the inadequacies of the category of "historicity": viz., that Heidegger's "reduction of history to historicity is miles away from concrete historical thought"; and in this way, Heidegger in point of fact "falls behind Dilthey's treatment of the problem: for 'insofar as he radicalizes it, [he] thereby eliminates.' "[13]

The "pseudo-concreteness" of Heidegger's *Existenzphilosophie*—and thus the betrayal of its original phenomenological promise—to which Schmidt and Löwith allude, may be explained in the following terms. *Being and Time* operates with a conceptual distinction between "ontological" ("existential") and "ontic" ("existentiell") planes of analysis. The former level refers to fundamental structures of human Being-in-the-world whose specification seems to be the main goal of Heidegger's 1927 work. The latter dimension refers to the concrete, "factical" actualization of the "existential" categories on the plane of everyday life-practice. It is this level that exists beyond the purview of "existential analysis" or "fundamental ontology" properly so-called. Yet, if this is the case, then the dimension of ontic life or everyday concretion would seem to fall beneath the threshold of Heidegger's ontological vision. And consequently, his category of "historicity" would never be capable of accounting for the events of "real history." The dilemma is further compounded by the fact that Heidegger's existential analytic treats "everydayness" as such—and thus the sphere of "ontic life" in its entirety—as a manifestation of "inauthenticity." For to all intents and purposes, it has been "colonized" by the "They" (*"das Man"*).

But whatever the inner, conceptual grounds may have been for the breakdown of Marcuse's project of an "existential Marxism," the immediate cause for its dissolution seemed to owe more to the force of objective historical circumstances: Hitler's accession to power on January 30, 1933, followed by Heidegger's enthusiastic proclamation of support for the regime four months later.[14] In retrospect, Marcuse insists that during his stay in Freiburg, he never remotely suspected Heidegger of even covertly harboring pro-Nazi sentiments. Thus, the philosopher's "conversion" to the National Socialist cause in the spring of 1933 took him—as well as many others—by complete surprise. Nevertheless, Marcuse goes on to insist that had he at the time been slightly more attentive to the latent political semantics of *Being and Time* and other works, he might have been spared this later shock. As he explains:

> Now, from personal experience I can tell you that neither in his lectures, nor in his seminars, nor personally, was there ever any hint of [Heidegger's] sympathies for Nazism. . . . So his openly declared Nazism came as a complete surprise to us. From that point on, of course, we asked ourselves the question: did we overlook indications and anticipations in *Being and Time* and the related writings? And we made one interesting observation, *ex-post* (and I want to stress that, *ex-post,* it is easy to make this observation). If you look at his view of human existence, of Being-in-the-world, you will find a highly repressive, highly oppressive interpretation. I have just today gone again through the table of contents of *Being and Time* and had a look at the main categories in which he sees the essential characteristics of existence or Dasein. I can just read them to you and you will see what I mean: "Idle talk, curiosity, ambiguity, falling and Being-thrown, concern, Being-toward-death, anxiety, dread, boredom," and so on. Now this gives a picture which plays well on the fears and frustrations of men and women in a repressive society—a joyless existence: overshadowed by death and anxiety; human material for the authoritarian personality.[15]

Yet, in our opening citation from the 1934 essay, "The Struggle Against Liberalism in the Totalitarian State," Marcuse expresses a slightly different sentiment: viz., that in its partisanship for Nazism, *Existenzphilosophie* does not so much realize its "inner truth"; rather, it engages in a "radical denial of its own origins": i.e., its claim to being the legitimate heir of the Western philosophical tradition.

The 1947–48 exchange of letters between Marcuse and Heidegger shows Marcuse grappling with a seemingly inexplicable dilemma: how could Heidegger, who claimed to be the philosophical inheritor of the legacy of Western philosophy, place his thinking in the service of a political movement that embodied the *absolute negation* of everything that legacy stood for? Moreover, as becomes clear from the letters themselves, Marcuse's ties to Heidegger were not only intellectual, but also personal: he revered Heidegger not only as a thinker, but also as the teacher who had had the most significant impact on Marcuse's own intellectual development. His attachments remained strong enough to motivate the visit to Heidegger's Todtnauberg ski hut earlier in 1947. Moreover, we see that against the advice of his fellow German-Jewish emigrés (presumably, the other members of the Institute for Social Research), he continued, even after the disappointing discussion with Heidegger in Todtnauberg—like the poet Paul Celan (see his poem "Todtnauberg"), Marcuse, too, journeyed to Heidegger's Black Forest retreat in search of a "single word" of repentance, which the philosopher refused to grant—to send a "care package" to Heidegger at a time when the conditions of life in Germany remained tenuous; for this much he still owed "the man from whom I learned philosophy from 1928–1932."

As Marcuse explains in the 1974 interview, after this exchange of letters, all communication between the two men was broken off. And yet, if one turns to *One-Dimensional Man,* one finds Marcuse citing Heidegger's arguments from "The Question Concerning Technology" in support of Marcuse's own critique of instrumental reason ("Modern man takes the entirety of Being as raw material for production and subjects the entirety of the object-world to the sweep and order of production [*Herstellen*]").[16]

Turning now to Heidegger's letter of January 20, 1948: one finds there the familiar series of rationalizations, half-truths, and untruths that have recently been exposed in the books by Victor Farias and Hugo Ott.[17] But one also finds recourse to a strategy of denial and relativization that would become a commonplace in the Federal Republic during the "latency period" of the Adenauer years: the claim that the world operates with a double standard in its condemnation of *German* war crimes, since those of the Allies were equally horrible (Dresden, the expulsion of the Germans residing in the "eastern territories," etc.). To his credit, here Marcuse refuses to allow the "philosopher of Being" to have the last word.

Notes

1. "Heidegger's Politics: An Interview with Herbert Marcuse," in Robert Pippin et al., eds., *Herbert Marcuse: Critical Theory and the Promise of Utopia* (South Hadley, Mass.: Bergin and Garvey, 1988).

2. English translations of these essays are as follows: "Contributions to a Phenomenology of Historical Materialism," *Telos* 4:3–34, 1969 (caveat emptor: this is an extremely poor translation); "The Foundations of Historical Materialism," in Herbert Marcuse, *Studies in Critical Philosophy* (Boston: Beacon Press, 1973); "On the Philosophical Foundations of the Concept of Labor in Economics," *Telos* 16:9–37, Summer 1973; "On the Problem of Dialectic," *Telos* 27:12–39, Spring 1976. See also "Über konkrete Philosophie," *Archiv fur Sozialwissenschaft und Sozialpolitik* 62:111–128, 1929.

3. Karl Marx, *The German Ideology* (New York: International Publishers, 1970), p. 121.

4. Georg Lukács, *History and Class Consciousness* (Cambridge, Mass.: MIT Press, 1971), p. 121.

5. Marcuse, "Contribution to a Phenomenology of Historical Materialism," p. 12.

6. Cf. Douglas Kellner, *Herbert Marcuse and the Crisis of Marxism* (Berkeley: University of California Press, 1984), pp. 38ff.; Barry Katz, *Herbert Marcuse and the Art of Liberation* (London: New Left Books, 1982), pp. 58ff.

7. Marcuse, "Contribution to a Phenomenology of Historical Materialism," p. 13.

8. Martin Heidegger, *Being and Time* (New York: Harper and Row, 1962), p. 374.

9. Marcuse, "Contribution to a Phenomenology of Historical Materialism," p. 15.

10. In Marcuse's failed *Habilitationsschrift, Hegel's Ontology and the Theory of Historicity,* the Heideggerian category of historicity also occupies center stage. There is some dispute in the secondary literature as to whether Heidegger ever read (let alone rejected) the work, or whether Marcuse—aware of the difficulties he would be faced with pursuing a teaching career amid the changing political climate in Germany—ever bothered to submit the work to his mentor. For a discussion of this issue, see Seyla Benhabib, "Translator's Introduction" to *Hegel's Ontology and the Theory of Historicity* (Cambridge, Mass.: MIT Press, 1987), pp. x-xii. For another discussion of the relation of Marcuse to Heidegger

as it emerges in this 1932 work, see Robert Pippin, "Marcuse on Hegel and Historicity," *The Philosophical Forum* XVI(3):180–206, 1985. As opposed to other commentators who argue for a distinct break between the 1932 *Habilitationsschrift* and his next book on Hegel—the 1941 *Reason and Revolution*—Pippin seeks to emphasize the elements of continuity between the two works.

11. For a survey of these tendencies, see Paul Piccone, "Phenomenological Marxism," *Telos* 9:3–31, Fall 1971.

12. Marcuse, "Heidegger's Politics: An Interview," pp. 96–97.

13. Alfred Schmidt, "Existential Ontology and Historical Materialism in the Work of Herbert Marcuse," in Pippin et al., eds., *Herbert Marcuse*, pp. 49–50.

14. See Heidegger's Rectoral Address of May 27, 1933, *Die Selbstbehauptung der deutschen Universität/Das Rektorat 1933–34: Tatsachen und Gedanken* (Frankfurt: Klostermann, 1983); reprinted in this volume as "The Self-Assertion of the German University."

15. Marcuse, "Heidegger's Politics: An Interview," p. 99.

16. Herbert Marcuse, *One-Dimensional Man* (Boston: Beacon Press, 1964), pp. 153–154.

17. Victor Farias, *Heidegger et la nazisme* (Lagrasse: Editions Verdier, 1987) (an English translation of Farias' book has recently been published by Temple University Press); Hugo Ott, *Martin Heidegger: Unterwegs zu seiner Biographie* (Frankfurt: Campus, 1988).

Letter from Marcuse to Heidegger of August 28, 1947

4609 Chevy Chase Blvd.
Washington 15, D.C.

Lieber Herr Heidegger,

I have thought for a long time about what you told me during my visit to Todtnauberg, and I would like to write to you about it quite openly.

You told me that you fully dissociated yourself from the Nazi regime as of 1934, and that you were observed by the Gestapo. I will not doubt your word. But the fact remains that in 1933 you identified yourself so strongly with the regime that today in the eyes of many you are considered as one of its strongest intellectual proponents. Your own speeches, writings, and treatises from this period are proof thereof. You have never publicly retracted them—not even after 1945. You have never publicly explained that you have arrived at judgments other than those which you expressed in 1933–34 and articulated in your writings. You remained in Germany after 1934, although you could have found a position abroad practically anywhere. You never publicly denounced any of the actions or ideologies of the regime. Because of these circumstances you are still today identified with the Nazi regime. Many of us have long awaited a statement from you, a statement that would clearly and finally free you from such identification, a statement that honestly expresses your current attitude about the events that have occurred. But you have never uttered such a statement—at least it has never emerged from the private sphere. I—and very many others—have admired you as a philosopher; from you we have learned an infinite amount. But we cannot make the separation between Heidegger the philosopher and Heidegger the man, for it contradicts your own philosophy. A philosopher can be deceived regarding political matters; in which case he will openly acknowledge his error. But he cannot be deceived about a regime that has killed millions of Jews—merely because they were Jews—that made terror into an everyday phenomenon, and that turned everything that pertains to the ideas of spirit, freedom, and truth into its bloody opposite. A regime that in every respect imaginable was the deadly caricature of the Western tradition that you yourself so forcefully explicated and justified. And if that regime was not the caricature of that tradition but its actual culmination—in this case, too, there could be no deception, for then you would have to indict and disavow this entire tradition.

Is this really the way you would like to be remembered in the history of ideas? Every attempt to combat this cosmic misunderstanding founders on the generally shared resistance to taking seriously a Nazi ideologue. Common sense (also among intellectuals), which bears witness to such resistance, refuses to view you as a philosopher, because philosophy and Nazism are irreconcilable. In this conviction common sense is justified. Once again: you (and we) can only combat the identification of your person and your work with Nazism (and thereby the dissolution of your philosophy) if you make a public avowal of your changed views.

This week I will send off a package to you. My friends have recommended strongly against it and have accused me of helping a man who identified with a regime that sent millions of my co-religionists to the gas chambers (in order to forestall misunderstandings, I would like to observe that I was not only an anti-Nazi because I was a Jew, but also would have been one from the very beginning on political, social, and intellectual grounds, even had I been "100 percent Aryan"). Nothing can counter this argument. I excuse myself in the eyes of my own conscience, by saying that I am sending a package to a man from whom I learned philosophy from 1928 to 1932. I am myself aware that that is a poor excuse. The philosopher of 1933–34 cannot be completely different than the one prior to 1933; all the less so, insofar as you expressed and grounded your enthusiastic justification of the Nazi state in philosophical terms.

Letter from Heidegger to Marcuse of January 20, 1948

Lieber Herr Marcuse,

I received the package mentioned in your letter of August 28. I believe that I am acting in accordance with your wishes and in a way that will reassure your friends if I allow its entire contents to be distributed among former students who were neither in the Party nor had any association whatsoever with National Socialism. I thank you for your help also on their behalf.

If I may infer from your letter that you are seriously concerned with [reaching] a correct judgment about my work and person, then your letter shows me precisely how difficult it is to converse with persons who have not been living in Germany since 1933 and who judge the beginning of the National Socialist movement from its end.

Regarding the main points of your letter, I would like to say the following:

1. Concerning 1933: I expected from National Socialism a spiritual renewal of life in its entirety, a reconciliation of social antagonisms and a deliverance of Western Dasein from the dangers of communism. These convictions were expressed in my Rectoral Address (have you read this *in its entirety?*), in a lecture on "The Essence of Science" and in two speeches to students of [Freiburg] University. There was also an election appeal of approximately 25–30 lines, published in the [Freiburg] student newspaper. Today I regard a few of the sentences as misleading [*Entgleisung*].

2. In 1934 I recognized my political error and resigned my rectorship in protest against the state and party. That no. 1 [i.e., Heidegger's Party activities] was exploited for propaganda purposes both here and abroad, no. 2 [his resignation] hushed up for equally propagandistic reasons, failed to come to my attention and cannot be held against me.

3. You are entirely correct that I failed to provide a public, readily

comprehensible counter-declaration; it would have been the end of both me and my family. On this point, Jaspers said: that we remain alive is our guilt.

4. In my lectures and courses from 1933–44 I incorporated a standpoint that was so unequivocal that among those who were my students, none fell victim to Nazi ideology. My works from this period, if they ever appear, will testify to this fact.

5. An avowal after 1945 was for me impossible: the Nazi supporters announced their change of allegiance in the most loathsome way; I, however, had nothing in common with them.

6. To the serious legitimate charges that you express "about a regime that murdered millions of Jews, that made terror into an everyday phenomenon, and that turned everything that pertains to the ideas of spirit, freedom, and truth into its bloody opposite," I can merely add that if instead of "Jews" you had written "East Germans" [i.e., Germans of the eastern territories], then the same holds true for one of the allies, with the difference that everything that has occurred since 1945 has become public knowledge, while the bloody terror of the Nazis in point of fact had been kept a secret from the German people.

Letter from Marcuse to Heidegger of May 12, 1948

4609 Chevy Chase Blvd.
Washington 15, D.C.

Lieber Herr Heidegger,

For a long time I wasn't sure as to whether I should answer your letter of January 20. You are right: a conversation with persons who have not been in Germany since 1933 is obviously very difficult. But I believe that the reason for this is not to be found in our lack of familiarity with the German situation under Nazism. We were very well aware of this situation—perhaps even better aware than people who were in Germany. The direct contact that I had with many of these people in 1947 convinced me of this. Nor can it be explained by the fact that we "judge the beginning of the National Socialist movement from its end." We knew, and I myself saw it too, that the beginning already contained the end. The difficulty of the conversation seems to me rather to be explained by the fact that people in Germany were exposed to a total perversion of all concepts and feelings, something which very many accepted only too readily. Otherwise, it would be impossible to explain the fact that a man like yourself, who was capable of understanding Western philosophy like no other, was able to see in Nazism "a spiritual renewal of life in its entirety," a "redemption of occidental Dasein from the dangers of communism" (which, however, is itself an essential component of that Dasein!). This is not a political but instead an intellectual problem—I am tempted to say: a problem of cognition, of truth. You, the philosopher, have confused the liquidation of occidental Dasein with its renewal? Was this liquidation not already evident in every word of the "leaders," in every gesture and deed of the SA, long before 1933?

However, I would like to treat only one portion of your letter; otherwise my silence could be interpreted as complicity.

You write that everything that I say about the extermination of the Jews applies just as much to the Allies, if instead of "Jews" one were to insert "East Germans." With this sentence don't you stand outside of the dimension in which a conversation between men is even possible— outside of Logos? For only outside of the dimension of logic is it possible to explain, to relativize [*auszugleichen*], to "comprehend" a crime by saying that others would have done the same thing. Even further: how is it possible to equate the torture, the maiming, and the annihilation of millions of men with the forcible relocation of population groups who suffered none of these outrages (apart perhaps from several exceptional instances)? From a contemporary perspective, there seems already to be a night and day difference in humanity and inhumanity in the difference between Nazi concentration camps and the deportations and internments of the postwar years. On the basis of your argument, if the Allies had reserved Auschwitz and Buchenwald—and everything that transpired there—for the "East Germans" and the Nazis, then the account would be in order! If, however, the difference between inhumanity and humanity is reduced to this erroneous calculus, then this becomes the world historical guilt of the Nazi system, which has demonstrated to the world what, after more than 2,000 years of Western Dasein, men can do to their fellow men. It looks as though the seed has fallen upon fertile ground: perhaps we are still experiencing the continuation of what began in 1933. Whether you would still consider it to be a "renewal" I am not sure.

Translated by Richard Wolin

PART THREE

INTERPRETATIONS

10

THE POLITICAL IMPLICATIONS OF HEIDEGGER'S EXISTENTIALISM

Karl Löwith

Introduction

"The Political Implications of Heidegger's Existentialism" appeared as part of Löwith's study, "Europäische Nihilismus," under the subheading "Der politische Horizont von Heideggers Existenzialontologie." This text is now available in volume 2 of his collected works, *Weltgeschichte und Heilsgeschehen* (Stuttgart: Metzler, 1983). But the transmission of the essay itself has a curious history, resulting in the fact that there exist no fewer than three German versions (the other two are contained in volume 8 of his collected works, *Heidegger: Denker in dürftiger Ziet* [Stuttgart: Metzler, 1984], pp. 61–68; and the autobiographical study, *Mein Leben in Deutschland vor und nach 1933* [Stuttgart: Metzler, 1986], pp. 27–42). Moreover, the first published version was a French translation that appeared in a 1946 issue of *Les Temps Modernes* under the title "Les implications politiques de la philosophie de l'existence chez Heidegger."

It is worth noting that the appearance of the essay in 1946 occasioned what proved to be the first Heidegger controversy. Thus, Löwith's meditations on the philosophical bases of Heidegger's politics inspired spirited rebuttals by Eric Weil and Alphons de Waehlens in subsequent issues of *Les Temps Modernes,* with both contending in effect that Heidegger's Nazism had nothing to do with his philosophy.

Karl Löwith, "The Political Implications of Heidegger's Existentialism," ("Les implications politiques de la philosophie de l'existence chez Heidegger") first appeared in *Les Temps Modernes* 14 (1946–47). German variants of the text may be found in Löwith, *Sämtliche Schriften* 8 (Stuttgart: Metzler, 1984), pp. 61–68, and *Mein Leben in Deutschland vor und nach 1933* (Stuttgart: Metzler, 1986), pp. 27–42.

The uniqueness of Löwith's reflections on "The Political Implications of Heidegger's Existentialism" derives not only from the fact that he was thoroughly familiar with Heidegger's thought, but also a witness to the political events—the various stages of Germany's "National Revolution" —he describes. As such, he offers, as it were, a firsthand account of the transmogrification of Heidegger's seemingly apolitical fundamental ontology of *Being and Time* into a philosophical justification for the National Socialist Revolution—Heidegger's "private National Socialism."

But Löwith is in no way out to settle scores. His own intellectual indebtedness to Heidegger's philosophical tutelage is fully acknowledged from the outset. Nor is he interested in a facile dismissal of Heidegger's greatness as a thinker on the basis of the philosopher's conviction that there existed profound elective affinities between his own "analytic of Dasein" and the "National Awakening" of 1933. Instead, with admirable forthrightness and clarity, he seeks to account for a perplexing, if seminal, issue in the intellectual history of the twentieth century: the bases internal to Heidegger's philosophy that led the philosopher to become a diehard spokesman and advocate of Nazi policies during the years 1933–34.

. . .

The essay that follows was written outside of Germany in 1939 with the sole aim of clarifying my own ideas and without any intention of being published. Today [1946], I am publishing it in French translation, since I am convinced that the immediate political—i.e., National Socialist— implications of Heidegger's concept of existence—though they might seem outstripped by contemporary events—possess a historical significance that reaches well beyond the figure of Heidegger as well as the German situation of the interwar period. The fact that Heidegger found during the last war a wide audience among French intellectuals, in contrast to the situation of Germany at that time, is a symptom that merits renewed attention.

His *Being and Time,* which appeared in 1927, is still one of the rare, truly important contemporary philosophical publications, and when an author succeeds so rapidly in an era such as ours to develop a following and to increase his influence continually over the course of 25 years, he must certainly contain something of substance. One should not forget either that this same man, whose thought was so relevant, also assimilated Greek philosophy and scholastic theology into his work. His knowledge, which is of the firsthand variety, derives from the sources themselves.

The following study treats the implications and historico-philosophical consequences of Heidegger's philosophy almost exclusively in relation to his speeches and lectures, rather than in terms of his philosophical oeuvre properly speaking. This may appear unjust insofar as the influence of Heidegger's thought has been spurred much more by his work than his speeches, which aim explicitly at a practical effect. This appearance of injustice disappears, however, as soon as one realizes that *Being and Time* also represents—and in a far from inessential manner —a theory of historical existence; whereas, on the other hand, the practical application of this project to an actual historical situation is only possible insofar as *Being and Time* already contains a relation to contemporary reality. It is this practical-political application in terms of an actual commitment to a determinate decision that in truth justifies or condemns the philosophical theory that serves as the basis of this commitment. What is true or false in theory is also so in practice, above all when the theory itself originates in conscious fashion from a supreme fact—historical existence—and when its path leads it toward the latter.

The author, for many years a student of Heidegger, indebted to his master for certain essential intellectual impulses, will undoubtedly have to justify the employment of passages taken from private letters in face of the currently dominant conception of the separation of public from private life. My sole justification is that the personal and spontaneous thoughts of a thinker who was so discrete and guarded about his powerful dialectical capacities clarifies the fundamental traits of his philosophical aim better than a sagacious discussion of the existential categories, whose aspects have already been fully elaborated.

The reader of the essay at hand will find, at his own choosing, a significant defense of Heidegger's philosophy or a condemnation of his political attitudes. In the author's eyes, these alternatives lack real meaning, insofar as the historical importance of Heideggerianism rests to a large extent on the fact that he took on political responsibilities and involvements in a manner consistent with the fundamental thesis of *Being and Time*: "Only an essentially futural being . . . that is free for its death and can let itself be thrown back upon its factical 'there' by shattering itself against death ... can, by handing down to itself the possibility it has inherited, take over its own thrownness and be in the *moment of vision* for 'its time'" (*Being and Time,* no. 74).

In order to understand the historical background of Heidegger's philosophy, it will be useful to relate it to remarks by Rilke and van Gogh. Certain sentences from Rilke's letters (cf. *Briefe,* 1914–1921, pp. 89ff.) could easily serve as guiding threads to the intellectual achievement of Heidegger's oeuvre. By dint of belief in progress and humanity, observes Rilke, the bourgeois world has forgotten the "ultimate instances" of human life, i.e., "that it has been once and for all surpassed by death and by God." In *Being and Time,* death has no other meaning than that of an "unsurpassable last instance" of our Being and capacities. In Heidegger, God is no longer at issue; he had been too much of a theologian to be able, like Rilke, to once again tell "Stories of the Dear Lord." For Heidegger, death is the nothingness that reveals the finitude of our temporal existence; or, as he put it in one of his first courses in Freiburg, death is historical "facticity."

Van Gogh is the painter whose influence was the greatest in Germany after World War I. "For years," Heidegger wrote me in 1923, "a saying of van Gogh's has obsessed me: 'I feel with all my power that the history of man is like that of wheat: if one is not planted in the earth to flourish, come what may, one will be ground up for bread.' Woe to him who is not pulverized." Instead of devoting oneself to the general need for cultivation, as one would upon receiving the command to "save culture," one must—in a [time of] radical disintegration and regression, a *Destruktion*—convince oneself firmly of "the one thing that matters"* without bothering with the chatter and bustle of clever and enterprising men.

In this search for the "one thing that matters," Heidegger turns above all toward Kierkegaard, though he does not permit himself to be consumed by him. The goal and theme of his existentialist philosophy is not "to attract attention to Christianity, but to formally thematize this-worldly existence."

"My will, fundamentally, aspires to something else, and that is not much: living in an actual revolutionary situation, I pursue what I feel to

---

* As Rilke says in 1927: "It seems to me that at present, one thing alone, the sole thing that is valid and that matters, accords me the right to express myself."

be 'necessary,' without caring to know whether it emerges from 'culture' or whether my search will lead to ruin" (letter from Heidegger, 1920). He had a horror of all "philosophies of culture," as well as of philosophy conferences; the vast number of journals that appeared after World War I aroused his emotional wrath. With bitter severity, he wrote to Scheler that he "renewed" E. von Hartmann, while other scholars published an *Ethos* and a *Kairos,* in addition to an already antiquated *Logos.* "What will be next week's joke? I believe that a lunatic asylum viewed from within would offer a more reasonable and clear perspective than this epoch." Following this *negation in principle of all that existed,* as well as all programs aiming at reform, Heidegger at the same time made us guard against a false interpretation and overestimation of his own work —against the idea that he would have something "positive" to say or "new results" to show.

"The idea has emerged that our critique must be opposed to something that corresponds in content to that which has just been denied, or that our work would find its destiny in a school or trend, that it could be continued and complemented." This work, he continued, is nothing of this nature. It is limited to a critical and rational destruction of philosophical and theological traditions; it thereby remains "something apart from and perhaps out of reach of the bustle of the day" (letter from Heidegger, 1924). On the whole, by viewing himself as beyond what is in and out of fashion, the philosopher must derive satisfaction, for where things age rapidly, there is not necessarily much depth to be found. The later attempt at a "fundamental ontology" was born of this attitude: i.e., an analysis of Being that is based on temporal existence— our Dasein, which is at the same time historical and tied to particular moments—and the attempt to "destroy," beginning from this position, the history of the reflection on Being, from the Greeks to Nietzsche, in order thereby to concentrate this reflection completely on the unique question of the meaning of Being—the question that is, at the same time, the simplest, the most essential, and the most original.

It was only against his original expectations that the enormous success of his courses and the extraordinary influence of his work—despite its difficulty—would push him beyond the desired limits and make his thought fashionable. The primary attraction of his philosophical doctrine was not that it led his disciples to await a new system, but instead, its thematic indeterminacy and pureness; more generally, his concentration on "the one thing that mattered." It was only later that many of his students understood that this "one thing" was nothingness, a pure Resolve, whose "aim" was undefined. One day a student invented the far from innocent joke: "I am resolve, only toward what I don't know."

The inner nihilism, the "national socialism," of this pure Resolve in face of nothingness, remained at first hidden beneath certain traits that suggested a religious devotion; in effect, at this time [the early twenties], Heidegger had not yet definitively broken with his theological origins. I remember having seen on his desk in Freiburg portraits of Pascal and Dostoyevsky, and on the wall in a corner of the room—which resembled a cell—hung a magnificent expressionist crucifixion scene. He gave me *The Imitation* by Thomas à Kempis as a Christmas present in 1920. Again in 1925, he saw spiritual substance in theology alone, and even here, only in Karl Barth, whose *Commentary on the Epistle to the Romans* had appeared in 1918 (at the same time as Spengler's *Decline of the West*).

The extraordinary fascination that Spengler, Barth, and Heidegger— despite their various divergences—exerted upon a generation of young Germans following the First World War derives from a common source. Their shared position can be seen in the clear awareness of being situated in a crisis—a turning point between epochs; and thus being obliged to confront questions whose nature was too radical to find an answer in the enfeebled, nineteenth-century belief in progress, culture, and education. The questions that agitated this young generation, devoid of illusions, yet sincere, were fundamentally questions of faith. One read Nietzsche, Dostoyevsky, and Kierkegaard; and here one rediscovered the internal nexus between radical negation and radical affirmation, between skepticism and faith. In this period, Heidegger still counted himself explicitly among the ranks of the "theological Christians"; just as, ten years later, he affirmed that Nietzsche, the great destroyer, had been the "sole true believer" of the nineteenth century. The power of this spiritual stance is in direct relation to its power of negation, for a new faith is possible and necessary as soon as one has recognized the decrepitude of what one formerly believed. It was above all the young Luther —the Protestant whose rigorous faith considered the "natural reason" of the Scholastics to be a form of prostitution—to whom Heidegger was attracted. He knew Luther's works better than many a professional theologian.

The hidden motto of *Being and Time*—"*Unus quisque robustus sit in existentia sua*"—also comes from Luther. Heidegger, abandoning faith in God, translates it by ceaselessly insisting on that which alone, in his opinion, is important: "that each individual do what his capacities permit"—i.e., the "authentic potentiality-for-Being always specific to each individual"—or the "existential limit of our ownmost particular historical facticity."

He referred to this "potentiality-for-Being" both as a duty and as a "destiny." "I do only what I must do and what I believe to be necessary, and I do it as my powers permit. I do not embellish my philosophical labors with cultural requirements suitable for a vague historical present. I no longer subscribe to a Kierkegaardian outlook. I work from my own 'I am' and from my entirely particular spiritual origin. From this facticity surges the fury of 'Existence'" (letter, 1920).

Whoever, on the basis of these remarks, reflects on Heidegger's later partisanship for Hitler, will find in this first formulation of the idea of historical "existence" the constituents of his political decision of several years hence. One need only abandon the still quasi-religious isolation and apply [the concept of] authentic "existence"—"always particular to each individual"—and the "duty" ["*Müssen*"] that follows therefrom to "specifically German existence" and its historical destiny in order thereby to introduce into the general course of German existence the energetic but empty movement of existential categories ("to decide for oneself"; "to take stock of oneself in face of nothingness"; "wanting one's ownmost destiny"; "to take responsibility for oneself") and to proceed from there to "destruction" now on the terrain of politics. It is not by chance if one finds in Carl Schmitt a political "decisionism"* that corresponds to Heidegger's existentialist philosophy, in which the "potentiality-for-Being-a-whole" of individual authentic existence is transposed to the "totality" of the authentic state, which is itself always

---

*Translator's note: Cf. *Der Begriff des Politischen* (Berlin, 1927); English translation: *The Concept of the Political*, translated by G. Schwab (New Brunswick, N.J.: Rutgers University Press, 1976). On this theme see Löwith's essay "Der okkasionale Dezisionismus von Carl Schmitt," reprinted in *Sämtliche Schriften*, vol. 8 (Stuttgart: Metzler, 1984), pp. 32–60.

particular. Corresponding to the preservation and affirmation of this authentic "Dasein" [in Heidegger] is the affirmation of political existence [in Schmitt]; to "freedom for death" [in Heidegger], the "sacrifice of life" in the politically paramount case of war [in Schmitt]. The principle is the same in both cases: naked "facticity," *which is all that remains of life when one has suppressed all traditional living contents.*

The term in *Being and Time* that expresses the concept of facticity is "Existenz." It does not mean "the Being of a thing" ["*Was-Sein*"] (essentia), but the fact that a being *is* (existentia)—i.e., the pure fact of existing. This existence, stripped of all security and standing in relation to nothing other than itself, constitutes the essence of Dasein in Heideggerian philosophy; and Dasein itself is the foundation of all awareness of Being. Pure Dasein, the fundamental thesis of existential philosophy, presupposes that all traditional truths and contents of life have lost their substance. If one compares the modern conception of naked, resolute existence with the parallel notion in the Christian tradition, the revolutionary radicalism of Heidegger's central thesis emerges clearly. Medieval philosophy believed that all created being was differentiated into essence and existence; whereas God alone exists *essentially*, insofar as perfection pertains to his essence and perfection requires existence. The creator of Being alone unites essence and existence. But Heidegger's fundamental ontology no longer acknowledges an eternal creator outside of time with respect to this unity of essence and existence (formerly, the ontological prerogative of God). Instead, one is left with a "temporal" Dasein, abandoned to itself, whose essence derives alone from the fact "that it is" and that it "must be."

Certainly, Heidegger has not furnished an answer to the question of why this having-to-be is, and by not answering it, he avoids posing the question of suicide. In the Heideggerian analytic of Dasein, "freedom-for-death" merely signifies the possibility of consciously anticipating the temporal "end" and integrating the latter in "everyday Dasein." In this projection toward the imminence of death, the supreme freedom of Dasein as such is affirmed. But when one thinks of the thousands of actual suicides committed in Germany after 1933, first, by the adversaries and victims of the Third Reich, and later by its defeated representatives, one cannot deny that the attitude toward there-being and not-being [Dasein and *Nicht-Sein*] expressed in Heideggerian philosophy has an importance concerning practical consequences for life that cedes nothing to the belief in God and immortality. Without recourse to the idea of an eternal creator of Being, it would undoubtedly be very difficult to refute Heidegger's fundamental thesis concerning death as the "ultimate instance" of human Dasein, or to refute it from a moral standpoint. It is true that, from another perspective, the experience of the naked and insecure state of human Dasein constitutes a negative condition of the possibility of a religious vision of life. When one refuses to draw a religious conclusion from this fact, nothingness represents in effect the ultimate horizon before which the "meaning of Being" manifests itself. From this perspective, the nihilism of Heidegger's existential ontology possesses foundations that are much more solid and profound than his adversaries—who cling to the ideas of progress and culture—are willing to concede. The fact that Heidegger, by virtue of an irreverent radicalism that can often repel, constantly attracted new disciples, that he was offered a chair in 1930 (during Weimar, and not only during Nazi rule) at the most prestigious German university [Berlin], an offer which he refused, should give his adversaries cause for reflection. However, though Heidegger resisted the call to Berlin, he succumbed to the temptation of directing Freiburg University.

Heidegger's accession to the rectorship of Freiburg University was an event. It came at a decisive time during the "German Revolution," insofar as all the other universities at this critical juncture lacked a leader capable of filling his role—not merely by virtue of his Party membership, but by virtue of his intellectual stature. As a result, his decision took on a more than local significance. It was felt everywhere, for Heidegger was then at the zenith of his fame. The students in Berlin demanded that all the other universities follow the example of "*Gleichschaltung*" practiced in Freiburg. Heidegger's disciples were surprised by his decision. He had almost never expressed his opinion about political matters, and it didn't seem that he had a firm opinion concerning such issues.

Heidegger, however, inaugurated his rectorship with a speech on "The Self-Assertion of the German University." Compared to the numerous pamphlets and speeches published by professors who were the beneficiaries of "*Gleichschaltung*" after the fall of the Weimar government,

Heidegger's speech is philosophically demanding, a minor stylistic masterpiece. From a strictly philosophical standpoint, the speech is strangely ambiguous from beginning to end. It succeeds in positing existential and ontological categories at a specific historical "moment," in a way that suggests that their philosophical intentions go hand in hand a priori with the political situation, and that academic freedom jibes with political coercion. "Labor service" and "military service" are on a par with "service in knowledge" such that at the end of the speech, the listener was in doubt as to whether he should start reading the pre-Socratics or enlist in the SA. This is why the speech should not be judged according to one point of view alone, be it purely politically or purely philosophically. It would be equally weak considered as a political speech or a philosophical essay. It transposes Heideggerian historical existentialism to contemporary German reality; and thus for the first time the master's will to action finds suitable terrain and the formal outline of the existential categories receives decisive content.

The speech begins with a strange contradiction. In opposition to the subordination of university autonomy to the state, it advocates the "self-assertion" [of the university], while denying academic freedom in its "liberal" form as well as [academic] "self-administration," in order *to integrate the universities seamlessly* into the National Socialist schema of "leaders" and "followers." The duty of the rector consists in the spiritual leadership of the professors and students. But he too—the leader—must in his turn be led, by the "spiritual mission of the Volk." The content and direction of this historical mission remain indeterminate. The mission is in the last analysis decreed by "fate." Corresponding to the indeterminacy of the mission is an emphasis on its inexorability. The fate of the Volk is related to that of the university by unarguable decree; the mission with which the universities are charged is "the same" as that of the Volk. German science and German fate affirm their power in a *single* "essential will to power" ["*Wesenswillen zur Macht*"]. The will to essence is tacitly identified with the will to power, insofar as, from the National Socialist perspective, what is essential is the will as such. Prometheus, symbol of the Western "will," is the "first philosopher" deserving of a following. As characterized by this Promethean will,* European man is alleged "to have risen up against 'beings' " to

---

*In the same way, Karl Marx, in his dissertation on Epicurus and Democritus, claims Prometheus as the greatest of all philosophers.

inquire concerning their Being,* and this revolutionary "uprising" characterizes "Geist"—the latter surrenders before the superiority of fate,
but becomes creative by virtue of this very impotence. Spirit is neither
"universal reason" nor [the faculty of] understanding, but rather "knowing Resolve" ["*wissende Entschlossenheit*"] toward the essence of Being.
Thus the true world of spirit would be a "world of extreme outer and
inner danger." With military rigor, the student, animated by the will to
knowledge, is commanded to "advance" to "the outpost of the most
extreme danger," to march, to engage himself and to expose himself, to
persevere resolutely in the acceptance of German destiny "there" in the
Führer. The relation to Führer and Volk, to honor and the fate of the
Volk, is part and parcel of "service in knowledge." In response to the
Nietzschean question as to whether or not Europe wants to be itself,
Heidegger says: "We want ourselves." The youthful power of the German Volk has already decided in favor of the will to self-assertion, not
only in the university, but also with respect to German "Dasein" in its
totality. In order to fully appreciate "the splendor and greatness of this
awakening," one must recall the wisdom of Plato's saying that Heidegger translates (in a willful distortion) as *Alles Grosse steht im Sturm*"
—"Everything great stands in the storm."† So aggressively did Heidegger speak, that what young SS officer would not have felt moved or have
been able to see through the Greek nimbus of this highly German
"Stürmen." The community of teachers and students would also be a
"community of struggle," for only struggle [*Kampf*] furthers and preserves knowledge. In a lecture from the same period, Heidegger says:
"essence" discloses itself to courage alone, not to contemplation, truth
allows itself to be recognized only to the extent that one requires it of
oneself. The German "*Gemut*" (or temperament) itself is related to such
courage (*Mut*). Even the enemy is not only "*vorhanden*," but Dasein
must *create* its enemy, in order not to become deadened. In general, all
that "is" is "governed by struggle," and where there is neither struggle
nor authority, decadence reigns. Essence "essences" in struggle.

Heidegger was leader for only a year. After much disillusionment and
many vexations, he resigned his "commission" in order to oppose in his
usual way the new "they," risking bitter remarks in his lectures, which

---

*Here it is the Being of beings that is at issue, not the Being of man.
†In truth, this statement reads: "That which is great is most exposed to risk."

in no way contradicted his substantive attachment to National Socialism as a protestational movement of faith. For the "spirit" of National Socialism pertained less to the national or social dimension than to its Resolve [*Entschlossenheit*] and dynamics, which, trusting in itself alone —i.e., in its ownmost (German) "*Seinskönnen*" ["potentiality-for-Being"]— renounced all discussion and agreement. Expressions of violence and Resolve thoroughly determine both the vocabulary of National Socialist speeches as well as Heidegger's speeches. The *apodeictic* character of Heidegger's emotive formulations corresponds to the dictatorial style of the politics in question. It is the level of discourse, not the method, which defines the internal differences among a "community of followers"; and in the end it is "fate" which justifies all willing and confers its ontological-historical [*seinsgeschichtlichen*] mantle on the latter.

One month after Heidegger's speech, Karl Barth wrote his theological appeal against accommodation with the reigning powers, "Theological Existence Today." To be capable of an analogous act, philosophy, instead of treating "Being and *Time*," would have to treat "the Being of *Eternity*." But the important point about Heideggerian philosophy consisted precisely in its "resolute temporal understanding of time"; as a philosopher, Heidegger remained on this point a theologian, insofar as eternity seemed identical with God concerning whom the philosopher "could know nothing."

From this historical-political background, the specifically German aspects of Heidegger's conception of Dasein become clear: Existence and Resolve, Being and Potentiality-for-Being, the explanation of this capacity as duty and destiny, the stubborn insistence that this Potentiality-for-Being is "my particular" (German) Capacity; the terms which ceaselessly recur: discipline and coercion (even to attain "intellectual clarity," one must "coerce oneself"), hard, inexorable and severe, taut and sharp ("existence must be maintained at its peak"); to persevere and stand on one's own, to encounter and expose oneself to danger; revolution, awakening, and disruption. All these terms reflect the *disastrous intellectual mind-set* of the German generation following World War I. The minutiae of their thought was concerned with "origins" or "ultimates" or "boundary-situations." At base, all these terms and concepts are expressions of the bitter and hard Resolve that affirms itself in face of nothingness, proud of its contempt of happiness, reason, and compassion.

With the appearance of *Being and Time* it is likely that none of Heidegger's students would have imagined that "my ownmost" death, radically individualized, and a central category of *Being and Time*, would be travestied six years later in a celebration of a National Socialist "hero." But the leap in the existential analytic from death to Heidegger's Schlageter speech (*Freiburg Studentenzeitung*, June 1, 1933)* is merely a passage from a particular and individual Dasein to one that is general, no less particular by virtue of its generality insofar as it is a question of German Dasein. In this memorial speech, composed in bombastic style, it is said that Schlageter died "the hardest and greatest death," shot in cold blood while his humiliated nation lay on its knees. "Alone, he had to look to himself and to die in the faith of this vision, present to his soul, of the new future, the upsurge of his Volk toward honor and greatness." Heidegger inquires after the origin of this "firmness of will" and of this "clearness of heart." He cites in response "the native cliffs of the Black Forest" (Schlageter's home) and their autumnal limpidity. These earthy, natural forces are said to have been transposed into the heart of the young hero. In truth, Schlageter had been one of numerous young Germans left without recourse during the postwar years. Some became communists, some followed an opposite course. They are superbly described in E. von Salamon's novel, *The City*. Disenfranchised by the war, they returned from military service unable to find a place in civilian life and joined one of the numerous Freikorps units, living their lives in antisocial aimlessness, adhering to whatever unruly cause presented itself. This is what the existential philosopher calls a "duty." "He *had to* go to the Baltic countries, he *had to* go to upper Silesia, he *had to* go to the Ruhr"; he had to fulfill the destiny chosen by himself! Here is the *fatum* of classical tragedy become German verbosity—that of a philosopher, no less!

A few months after this speech Germany, with much fuss, left the League of Nations. The Führer decreed elections after the fact in order to demonstrate to world opinion that Germany and Hitler stood united. Heidegger made the Freiburg students march in formation to the local polling place so that they could give their assent to Hitler's decision en

* Translator's note: Schlageter, a student at Freiburg University, participated following the First World War in acts of sabotage against the French occupation army; he was executed by the French and then canonized by the National Socialists.

bloc. A "yes" to Hitler's decision seemed to him to signify an affirmation of "authentic existence." The electoral appeal he published in his capacity as rector conforms entirely with the National Socialist idiom and at the same time represents a popularized version of Heidegger's philosophy:

German Men and Women! The German people has been summoned by the Führer to vote; the Führer is asking nothing from the people. Rather, he *is giving* the people the possibility of making, directly, the highest free decision of all: whether it—the entire people—wants its own existence [Dasein] or whether it does *not* want it. The election simply cannot be compared to all other previous elections. What is unique about this election is the simple greatness of the decision that is to be executed. The inexorability of what is simple and ultimate [*des Einfachen und Letzten*], however, tolerates no vacillation and no hesitation. This ultimate decision reaches to the outermost limit of our people's existence. And what is this limit? It consists in the most basic demand of all Being, that it preserve and save its own essence. A barrier is thereby erected between what can be reasonably expected of a people and what cannot. It is by virtue of this basic law of honor that a people preserves the dignity and resoluteness of its essence. It is not ambition, not desire for glory, not blind obstinacy, and not hunger for power that demands from the Führer that Germany withdraw from the League of Nations. It is only the clear will to unconditional self-responsibility in enduring and mastering the fate of our people. That is *not* a turning away from the community of nations. On the contrary, with this step, our people is submitting to that essential law of human existence to which every people must first give allegiance if it is still to be a people. It is only out of the parallel observance by all peoples of this unconditional demand of self-responsibility that there emerges the possibility of taking one another seriously so that a community can be affirmed. The will to a true community of nations is equally far removed both from an unrestrained, vague desire for world brotherhood and from blind tyranny. Existing beyond this opposition, this will allows peoples and states to stand by one another in an open and manly fashion as self-reliant entities. The choice that the German Volk will now make is—simply as an event in itself, and independent of the outcome—the strongest evidence of the new German reality embodied in the National Socialist State. Our will to national [*völkisch*] self-responsibility desires that each people find and preserve the greatness and truth of its destiny. This will is the highest guarantee of security among peoples; for it binds itself to the basic law of manly respect and unconditional honor. On November 12, the German Volk as a whole will choose *its* future. This future is bound to the Führer. In choosing this future, the people cannot, on the basis of so-called foreign policy considerations, vote "yes" without also including in the "yes" the Führer and the political movement that has pledged itself unconditionally to him. There are not separate foreign and domestic policies. There is only the one will to the full existence [Dasein] of the State. The Führer has awakened this will in the entire people and has welded it into a single Resolve. No one can remain away from the polls on the day when this will is manifested. (*Freiburger Studentenzeitung*, November 10, 1933)

It was in his Freiburg inaugural address ("What is Metaphysics?") that Heidegger spoke for the first time of "the ultimate greatness" of Dasein, which consisted in the latter's "daring" willingness to expend itself without regard to consequences. Now he made greater usage of the idea of heroic grandeur. The latter applies to Schlageter's death no less than Hitler's daring decision to undertake an audacious and surprise move that rendered meaningless all contractual relations and juridical principles. This act, moreover, was allegedly not an abandonment of the community of European nations, but it alone, "on the contrary," established the possibility of a true community, where each nation exists on its own, discovering in this stance the true basis of mutuality!

One week before this electoral appeal, Heidegger published a speech intended for the student body composed in very general terms (*Freiburger Studentenzeitung*, November 13, 1933) where he states that the National Socialist Revolution represents a "total transformation of German Dasein." It is up to the students, in their will to knowledge, to remain faithful to what is essential, simple, and great, to be disciplined and authentic in their demands, clear and sure in their refusals; to be engaged fighters and to fortify their courage in being ready to sacrifice in order to save what is essential and to enhance the strength of the Volk. It is not ideas that should guide the existence of the students. Hitler alone should be their only law: "The Führer alone *is* the German present and future reality and its law."

The philosophical definition of Dasein as an existing *factum brutum* which "is and must be" (*Being and Time*, #29)—this sinister, active Dasein, stripped of all content, all beauty, all human kindness—is a mirror image of the "heroic realism" of those Nazi-bred, German faces that stared out at us from every magazine. In his lectures, Heidegger "philosophized with a hammer," as Nietzsche had done in *Twilight of the Idols*, yet without the latter's brilliant psychological acumen. And while Nietzsche maintained an oppositional stance versus Bismarck's Reich, the "highest free" decision of Heidegger's *Rektoratsrede* philosophy gave the sublime name of "fate" to the *factum brutum* of contemporary German events.

The petty-bourgeois orthodoxy of the Party was suspicious of Heidegger's National Socialism insofar as Jewish and racial considerations played no role. *Being and Time* was dedicated to the Jew, Husserl, his Kant book to the half-Jew, Scheler, and in his courses at Freiburg, Bergson and Simmel were taught. His spiritual concerns did not seem to conform to those of the "Nordic race," which cared little about Angst in face of nothingness.* Conversely, Professor H. Naumann† did not hesitate to explain German mythology with the help of concepts from *Being and Time,* discovering "care" in Odin and the "they" in Baldur. Yet, neither the aforementioned disdain or approval of his National Socialist credentials counts for much in itself. Heidegger's decision for Hitler went far beyond simple agreement with the ideology and program of the Party. He was and remained a National Socialist, just as Ernst Jünger, who was certainly on the margins and isolated, but nevertheless far from being without influence. Heidegger's influence came through the *radicalism* with which he based the freedom of one's ownmost individual as well as German Dasein on the manifestness of the naught [*das Nichts*]. Even today [1939],‡ Hitler's daring decision to risk a war for the sake of Danzig serves as a good illustration of Heidegger's philosophical concept of *"courage for* Angst" before nothingness [*"Mut zur Angst" vor dem Nichts*]—a paradox in which the entire German situation is captured in a nutshell.

Given the significant attachment of the philosopher to the climate and intellectual habitus of National Socialism, it would be inappropriate to criticize or exonerate his political decision in isolation from *the very principles* of Heideggerian philosophy itself. It is not Heidegger, who, in opting for Hitler, "misunderstood himself"; instead, those who cannot understand why he acted this way have failed to understand him. A Swiss professor regretted that Heidegger consented to compromise himself with the "everyday," as if a philosophy that explains Being from the

---

* Cf. A. Hoberg, *Dasein des Menschen* (1937).

† Hans Naumann, *Germanischer Schicksalsglaube* (Jena: E. Diedrichs, 1934).

‡ Translator's note: This sentence was inserted from the original 1939 version of Löwith's essay and does not appear in the version published in 1946.

standpoint of time and the everyday would not stand in relation to the daily historical realities that govern its origins and effects. The possibility of a Heideggerian political philosophy was not born as a result of a regrettable "miscue," but from the very conception of existence that simultaneously combats and absorbs the "spirit of the age."

The ultimate motivation of this will to rupture, revolution, and awakening, of this newly politicized Youth Movement from prior to World War I, is to be found in the awareness of *ruination* and *decline,* in European nihilism. It is significant that this "European" nihilism had been elevated in Germany, by Nietzsche, to the rank of the principal philosophical theme, and that it was in Germany that it was able to take on a political form. "The German, first and foremost, bears witness to the universal historical mission of radicalism. . . . No one else is so inexorable and ruthless, for he does not merely limit himself to turning upside down a world that is already upright in order to remain upright himself, he turns himself upside down. Where the German demolishes, a god must fall and a world must perish. For the German, to destroy is to create, and the crushing of the temporal is his eternity" (Max Stirner). The Germans have no aptitude for the rational application of freedom within the bounds of human experience [*in den Grenzen des Menschlichen*]. One cannot understand the influence which Heidegger's philosophical corpus has exerted upon us apart from this will to destruction. Its internal justification is always based on the radical character of the historical situation: on the fact that "old Europe" is finished. Heidegger's fundamental idea is in effect free of all concern for the alternative: "whether from this destruction a new 'culture' will emerge or an acceleration of decline" (letter of 1920). Similarly, the conclusion of the rectoral address of 1933 says that it is too late to transform the old institutions, let alone to add new ones, one should instead return to the "original beginnings" of the Greeks in order to begin again in Europe. The danger according to him is that the spiritual power of the West will dry up, that the West will come apart at the seams before we can decide in favor of this renewal, and that as a result, "this exhausted pseudoculture" will collapse, encompassing in the disorder all that is still living. At this time, Heidegger still thought that whether we could survive the collapse or not depended entirely on us, "whether we want ourselves, ourselves again and anew, or whether we do not want ourselves." He believed that the decision had already been reached in a positive way in the collective decision to follow the Führer. Three years later, in 1936, in a lecture on Hölderlin, Heidegger concluded on a much more resigned note. He shows us, with Hölderlin, "the era in which the gods have fled and of the god to come." The present, hemmed in by this double negative, the "being-no-longer of the gods that have fled" and the "not-yet" of the god to come, is essentially an impoverished and indigent era; no longer is it a question of the "glorious" beginning of 1933.

In such an era the poet resists and perseveres in the nothingness of this night, an image that recalls the somber conclusion of Max Weber in "Science as a Vocation" (1919). "Of what use are poets in an age of affliction?" Heidegger, too, posed this question on many an occasion. To find an answer would undoubtedly be more difficult for him than for the poet himself.

The fascination exerted by Heidegger since 1920, as a result of his Resolve devoid of content and by his ruthless critique, has endured. The influence of his teachings can be felt almost everywhere—in France no less than elsewhere. The extraordinary success of his teachings is independent of the various relations, good or bad, that Heidegger maintained with the National Socialist Party over the course of the last 12 years. In reality what is demonstrated by the somewhat naive apology of the author of "A Visit with M. Heidegger" [Jean Beaufret] (*Les Temps Modernes*, January 1946) is not that Heidegger was not a distinguished representative of the German Revolution, but that he was so in a manner more radical than [Ernst] Krieck or [Alfred] Rosenberg.

Whether he merely put up with Hitler's rule or whether he regretted his involvement as an error, the very possibility of his support for the "revolution of nihilism" must be explained from his basic philosophical principle. This principle—existence reduced to itself and resting on itself alone in face of nothingness—is by no means a gratuitous invention. It corresponds, on the contrary, to the radical character of the real historical situation with which Heideggerian existentialism, understood temporally and historically, explicitly identified. This historical situation cannot be dated from the contemporary period, nor is it specifically German. For a century already it has been felt and expressed by perspicuous Europeans of all countries as a relentlessly approaching catastrophe. "European nihilism" which "prefers to will nothingness than to will nothing at all," as the later Nietzsche acknowledged and defined it, has had its nervous prophets since the beginnings of the nineteenth century: Niebuhr and Goethe; toward the middle of the century with Burckhardt and Bruno Bauer, in Danilevsky and Kirojevsky, in Marx and Kierkegaard, in Proudhon and Donoso Cortes, in Flaubert and Baudelaire; and at the end of the century with Tolstoy and Dostoyevsky. And *if* the truth of Dasein is really temporal and historical, it must be admitted—at the possible risk of self-contradiction—that the truth of contemporary German existence must be found more than ever in Heidegger as far as philosophy is concerned, in Karl Barth with respect to theology, and with Spengler in the case of the philosophy of history; and not with those who try to resurrect the tradition of German idealism for the benefit of German youth. Radical events require radical decisions and modes of thought. The German situation, for which Heidegger was the principal philosophical spokesman, has not become less radical since 1945; it has become, on the contrary, all the more so, and it is difficult to say where it will lead.

Translated by Richard Wolin

MARTIN HEIDEGGER: ON THE PUBLICATION OF THE LECTURES OF 1935[1]

Jürgen Habermas

Introduction

Habermas' 1953 review essay of Heidegger's *An Introduction to Metaphysics* is both an incisive commentary by a promising 24 year-old scholar and a prescient anticipation of themes that would only come to the fore in debates of several decades hence over Heidegger's political involvements.

It is also noteworthy for at least two other reasons. First, the article (originally published in the July 25, 1953 issue of the *Frankfurter Allgemeine Zeitung*) represents an important way station in the course of Habermas' own intellectual development. For up until that point, Heidegger's philosophy had been perhaps the foremost intellectual influence on Habermas. Or, as he remarks in a 1984 interview, during his student years (1949–1954), "The most powerful systematic impulses came from the early Heidegger."[1] "Then I saw that Heidegger, in whose philosophy I had been living, had given this lecture in 1935 and published it without a word of explanation—that's what really disturbed me."[2] For what Habermas came to realize at this time was that, in the Federal Republic, the intellectual continuity with the National Socialist period had in no way been broken. His own two philosophy teachers and dissertation supervisors, Ernst Rothacker and Oskar Becker, both avid supporters of

Jürgen Habermas, "On the Publication of Lectures of 1935" ("Zur Veröffentlichung von Vorlesungen vom Jahre 1935") appeared in the *Frankfurter Allgemeine Zeitung*, July 25, 1953 and has been reprinted in Habermas, *Philosophisch-politische Profile* (Frankfurt: Suhrkamp, 1971), pp. 67–75.

Germany's National Revolution, were a typical case in point. As Habermas remarks: "Nobody told us about their past. We had to find out step by step for ourselves. It took me four years of studies, mostly just accidentally looking into books in libraries, to discover what they had been thinking only a decade or a decade and a half ago. Think what that meant!"[3]

What shocked Habermas about Heidegger's 1935 lecture course was the fact that, in this text, the "question of Being" was ineluctably tied to the success of Germany's National Revolution. Habermas, moreover, took exception to the fact that Heidegger had allowed the text of the lecture to be republished (apparently) unchanged—which suggested that the philosopher's own political views had remained unrevised. Specifically, Habermas called attention to one passage toward the end of the lecture, in which Heidegger, speaking of National Socialism, sings the praises of the "inner truth and greatness of this movement"; a characterization which is then parenthetically defined in terms of "the encounter between planetary technology and modern man."[4] Habermas' review in essence set off the first German "Heidegger controversy," with Heidegger himself deigning to reply in a September 24, 1953 letter to *Die Zeit*.

The reply to Habermas' critique was written by Christian Lewalter (*Die Zeit*, August 13, 1953), who read Heidegger's remarks about National Socialism's "inner truth and greatness" as suggesting that the philosopher harbored a less favorable view of Nazism than might appear on first view. Instead, Lewalter argued, the parenthetical remarks concerning "the encounter between planetary technology and modern man" meant that Heidegger viewed the regime not as an "indication of new well-being," but as a "further symptom of decline" amid the *Verfallsgeschichte* of the decline of metaphysics in general.[5] Thus, Lewalter continued, "the Nazi movement is a symptom for the tragic collision of man and technology, and as such a symptom it has its 'greatness,' because it affects the entirety of the West and threatens to pull it into destruction."

For his part, Heidegger, in his September 1953 letter to the editor of *Die Zeit*, showed himself to be in full agreement with Lewalter's interpretation: "Christian E. Lewalter's interpretation of the sentence taken from my lecture is accurate in every respect. . . . It would have been easy to remove that sentence, along with the others you have mentioned, from the printed version. I have not done this, and will not do it in the future. On the one hand, the sentence historically belongs to the lecture; on the other, I am convinced that the lecture itself can clarify it to a reader who has learned the craft of thinking."

Heidegger would reaffirm in the 1966 *Der Spiegel* interview that the phrase in parentheses was not a later addition, but stood in the original version (although, he would add, it was not read at the time). But it is at this point that dishonesty and deception set in. For we now know, from a variety of sources, that the parenthetical remarks at issue were in fact a later addition which Heidegger inserted when going over the proofs of the soon-to-be-published lecture course. Pöggeler testifies to this effect in his afterword to the 1983 edition of *Heidegger's Path of Thinking*. But of equal importance, he indicates that the original manuscript referred to "the inner truth and greatness of *National Socialism,*" instead of the less explicit "this movement" which appears in the edition published in 1953.[6] This is also the conclusion that has been reached by the editors of the Heidegger *Gesamtausgabe* in their afterword to the reedition of the lecture. Adding to the aura of scandal surrounding the philological dispute is the fact that the manuscript page in question is, according to Pöggeler, now "missing," leading to speculation that the ultimate "proof" concerning the affair has been "suppressed" by untrustworthy administrators of Heidegger's estate. Finally, former Heidegger intimate Rainer Marten has recently stepped forth to explain the incident as follows: Heidegger added the parenthetical remarks as a type of compromise, after refusing the advice of his editorial assistants to the effect that the provocative reference to "the inner truth and greatness of National Socialism" should be struck entirely.[7]

The upshot of the controversy is that by adding the parentheses in 1953, Heidegger disingenuously misrepresented his later *critical* interpretation of National Socialism (one that would emerge from his Nietzsche lectures of the late 1930s) as a view he already held in 1935.

With his recently published essay, "Work and Weltanschauung: The Heidegger Controversy from a German Perspective,"[8] Habermas has gone far toward clarifying the way in which Heidegger's disappointment with National Socialism served as a major stimulus for the *seinsgeschichtliche* "Turn" his philosophy took in the late 1930s. But already in a 1984 interview, Habermas presented the following lapidary remarks on the fateful confluence of politics and philosophy in Heidegger's work:

My thesis is that the whole Heideggerian notion of a history of Being cannot be derived from the internal development of his philosophy prior to 1934 or 1935. There is no real problem in his thought up to that date which would have made him rethink his whole project. The transition to his later philosophy—a process which took exactly ten years, from 1935 to 1945, between *An Introduction to Metaphysics* and the "Letter on Humanism"—was thus largely determined by external events. Heidegger had treated the whole framework of *Being and Time* without any obvious change up to 1933. Then he suddenly gave it a collectivist turn: Dasein was no longer this poor Kierkegaardian-Sartrean individual hanging in the air, in *Sorge*. But now Dasein was the Dasein of the people, of the *Volk*. I can show that line by line. All his election speeches—and he made lots of them he wrote for a local paper; he made a speech in Leipzig where there was a rally of scientists for the Führer, on a platform bedecked with Nazi flags (we have pictures of it); he made speeches at the University (all of them for the November elections) and also, of course, his Inaugural Address as Rector at Freiburg, although that is the least revealing—all of these publications and utterances show that he gave to *Being and Time* a national-revolutionary reading. In fact, he reinterpreted one substantive point in his theory, without touching any single category of the whole framework. Now, after a year or two—and I suppose it was only two years after and not just three months or so—he started to become hesitant about the whole cause with which he had been identifying. You must understand that he had really been fighting at the front. He had the nutty idea that he, as a spiritual leader, could set himself at the head of the whole movement. You have to be brought up in a German Gymnasium to have such notions. But now he became disillusioned. What was he to do? What if the whole philosophical project of *Being and Time*—identified with the movement from which he now retreated—were to be affected and discredited by it? Given Heidegger's personality structure, one solution was to interpret what had happened as an objective, fatal mistake, one for which he was no longer responsible as a person—an error which revealed itself like fate in a Sophoclean tragedy. You can trace the lines where he took this way out. But also, of course, changed his interpretation of the role of fascism itself. As late as 1935, he had still seen it as a movement which accomplished the destiny of the national revolution, including the use of technology as Ernst Jünger had extolled it in *Der Arbeiter*. Later he turned this interpretation upside down: and by the later thirties and early forties fascism had become the epiphenomenon of a fate which had turned out to be not the salvation from, but the last act of, nihilism. It is these external reasons that lie significantly behind the emergence of the later idea of the history of Being.[9]

Notes

1. Jürgen Habermas, "A Philosophical-Political Profile," in Peter Dews, ed., *Habermas: Autonomy and Solidarity* (London: Verso, 1986), pp. 149–150.
2. Jürgen Habermas, "Political Experience and the Renewal of Marxist Theory," in Dews, *Habermas*, p. 77.
3. Jürgen Habermas, "Life-Forms, Morality and the Task of the Philosopher," in Dews, *Habermas*, p. 196.
4. Martin Heidegger, *An Introduction to Metaphysics* (New Haven: Yale University Press, 1959), p. 199.
5. See Habermas' own recent account of this debate in Jürgen Habermas, *The New Conservatism: Cultural Criticism and the Historians' Debate*, edited by Shierry W. Nicholsen (Cambridge, Mass.: MIT Press, 1989), p. 162.
6. For a discussion of the controversy surrounding this passage, see Hugo Ott, *Martin Heidegger: Unterwegs zu seiner Biographie* (Frankfurt: Campus, 1988), pp. 277–278; and Otto Pöggeler, *Martin Heidegger's Path of Thinking* (Atlantic Heights, N.J.: Humanities Press, 1987), p. 278.
7. Rainer Marten, "Ein rassistisches Konzept von Humanität," *Badisches Zeitung,* December 19–20, 1987.
8. This essay, which appeared as the foreword to the German edition of Victor Farias' book, *Heidegger and the Nazis,* has been published in English in Habermas, *The New Conservatism.*
9. Habermas, "Life-Forms, Morality and the Task of the Philosopher," pp. 195–196.

. . .

We are not concerned here with the philosopher Martin Heidegger as philosopher but with the political influence that emanated from him, his influence not on discussions within the community of scholars but on the formation of the wills of easily excited and enthusiastic students. Genius has an equivocal, shady character; perhaps Hegel is right when he claims that world-historical individuals cannot be measured by moral standards. But there, where this moral half-light grants or even nurtures an interpretation of genius that results in political destruction, there public criticism assumes its rights as watchman. However, it is not the task of this criticism to dispute what remains inaccessible to it: those things that occur within the intimate field of the decisions of private existence; it must simply clarify the conditions under which public disturbances took place, conditions, that is, that must be changed in order to avoid such disturbances in the future. Since 1945, Heidegger's fascism has been discussed from various points of view. At the center of this discussion has been, for the most part, the rectoral address of 1933, in which Heidegger celebrates the "transformation of German existence." To develop the critique from that point is to simplify. What is worthy of consideration is rather the question how the author of *Sein und Zeit* (the most significant philosophical event since Hegel's *Phänomenologie*), how, that is, a thinker of this rank could fall into so obvious a primitivism as manifests itself, to a sober observer, in the hectic tastelessness of that call for the self-assertion of the German university.

The problem of the fascist intelligentsia that is concealed in this event becomes all the more focused and challenging if one bears in mind that the only reason there was no fascist intelligentsia as such was because the mediocrity of the upper-echelon fascist leadership was unable to accept what the intellectuals had to offer. Thinkers whose motives and mentality matched the trend of the fascist models were certainly there. To name names today would lead to misunderstandings. These elements were there. It was only the inferior quality of the political functionaries that drove them into the opposition. As a result, without accountable representatives of Germany's cultural heritage, the "movement" could create the impression that National Socialism was flotsam and jetsam from the general currents of the century, something unrooted, alien to the German tradition and grafted on to it. That National Socialism was not a necessary developmental consequence of the German tradition is certainly beyond question. But it does not follow from that that all attempts are false and reprehensible that seek, in the sense of Thomas Mann's Faustus novel, to probe the rootedness of fascist motives in the core of the German tradition and to uncover the dispositions that in a period of decline could lead to fascism. The problem of the fascist intelligentsia presents itself as the problem of the prehistory of fascism.

Since 1945 the German situation has been characterized by the constant evasion of this problem. For both, for the legitimacy of the problem and the evasion of it, there has recently appeared a significant piece of literary evidence: Heidegger has published lectures from the year 1935 under the title *Einführung in die Metaphysik*. As one learns from the foreword, the additions in parentheses were written at that same time. On page 152, Heidegger is concerned with National Socialism, "with the inner truth and greatness of this movement (that is, with the encounter between planetary technology and modern man)." Since these sentences were first published in 1953, without annotation, it may be supposed that they reproduce unchanged Heidegger's view today.

It would be pointless to quote the phrase about the inner truth and greatness of National Socialism if it did not follow from the context of the lecture. Heidegger expressly brings the question of all questions, the question of Being, together with the historical movement of those days.

It is well known that, for Heidegger, the fate of the present is forgetfulness of Being [*Seinsvergessenheit*]. To be sure, the various peoples have, in their vast activities and their products, a relationship to objects; but they have long ago fallen out of Being itself. Thus, we are "staggering," from a metaphysical point of view. This staggering manifests itself concretely in technological phenomena, whereby technology has not developed equally extensively everywhere. Rather, Europe lies in a great pair of pincers between Russia and America, which are, in their essence, the same: "the same hopeless frenzy of technology unbound and the unparalleled organization of the normalized man," for whom time means nothing more than speed. From both sides there is spreading over Europe the darkening of the world, the flight of the gods, the destruction of the earth, the massification of man, and hatred, suspicion toward all that is creative and free. For this reason, the fate of the earth will be decided in Europe; more precisely, in the heart of the people that forms its center and that is experiencing "the sharpest squeeze of the pincers": "the people that is richest in neighbors and thus the people that is most at risk and, in every respect, the metaphysical people." But this people will forge a great destiny out of its situation only if it creatively appropriates its tradition. Let us make sure we understand correctly: in the political situation of 1935, in which Germany's creation of a double front against East and West is becoming evident, Heidegger sees a reflection of an ontological-historical [*seinsgeschichtlich*] situation that has been in the making for over 2,000 years and that now places in the hands of the German people a world-historical mission. In order to understand properly the physiognomy and the intense eschatological aura of the lecture, it is necessary to grasp the dialectic of Heidegger's exhortation to his listeners of 1935 and his readers of 1953. He is calling for a heroic existence in opposition to the insipid, deteriorated condition of ordinary life. Three aspects of the peculiar coloring of this postulate can be sketched.

It is "strength" that elevates the aristocratic individual above the ordinary Many. The noble individual, who chooses fame, will be ennobled by the rank and mastery that belong to Being itself, while the Many —who, according to Heraclitus, whom Heidegger approvingly cites, are like well-fed cattle—the Many are the dogs and the asses. What is worthy of rank is that which is stronger, for which reason Being eludes whoever is concerned about evening out, reducing tension, leveling off: "The true is not for everyone, but only for the strong." Moreover, it is "spirit" ["*Geist*"] that distinguishes the thinker vis-à-vis the intellectual. Intelligent calculation is oriented towards objects and places them at man's disposal. Its leveling grasp brings all things down to one level: extension and number are its predominant dimensions. For this thinking, "ability" no longer means extravagant expenditure out of lofty abundance, but the sweaty performance of a routine. This thinking, which follows the laws of traditional logic, cannot understand the question about Being [*nach dem Sein*], let alone develop it, because logic is itself grounded in an answer to the question about what is [*nach dem Seienden*], an answer that closes off Being from the very outset. Students learn that reflecting on, calculating, and contemplating pregiven objects is a matter of mere talent and practice and mass distribution. Superficial and deep, empty and full of content, noncommittal and bearing witness, playful and serious are the antithetical attributes of intelligence and spirit, a spirit, by the way, that Heidegger, it cannot be denied, emphatically defends against all romantic effusiveness. It is only intelligence, not spirit, that Heidegger, with an eye to the Party's official eugenics policy, says ought to be subordinated to healthy physical fitness and character; for the degeneration of thinking to intelligence can only be overcome by thinking that is more primordial. Finally, "courage" must be added to strength and spirit, an ambiguous form of courage that does not even shrink back from violence and error. Appearance, deception, illusion, errancy are all powers that are appropriated by Being itself; it is only everyday reason [*Verstand*] that no longer experiences their numinous force and degrades them to mere error. The courageous individual repeats the beginning, in pre-Platonic Greece, of our intellectual-historical existence, saying Yes to all the disconcerting strangeness, the darkness, the uncertainty and insecurity of the true beginning. In the final analysis, the heroic individual develops his full essence [*Wesen*] as one who dares: he is the violent individual, the creative individual, who masters Being by placing the unsaid under the spell of his speech, the unseen under the spell of his gaze, and the unoccurred [*das Ungeschehene*] under the spell of his deed. In this context, violence is not to be taken to mean the banality of a "brute, arbitrary act." On the other hand, it is the faint-hearted man who is concerned with agreement, compromise, and mutual care and who is accordingly only able to experience violence as a disturbance of his life. "Thus the violence-doer [*der Gewalt-Tätige*] does not know kindness and appeasement (in the ordinary sense), nor is he soothed and quieted as a result of his successes or prestige." He despises the appearance of completion. The violent individual counterposes to the concerns of ordinary life the projection of his thought, the act that forms and builds, the state-creating action. The violent man is the towering individual, the uncanny solitary; he is, in the final analysis, the man with no way out, for whom non-existence represents the highest victory over Being, whose existence finds its tragic fulfillment "in the most profound and far-reaching Yes to his own destruction," who, in willing what is extraordinary, casts aside all help.

We ask of Heidegger's lecture the question what the object of its appeal is, what it calls upon its audience to do, and against what it takes its stand. And we recognize without difficulty that Heidegger—drawing on his experience of Hölderlin and Nietzsche, with the excessive pathos of the twenties, and with the immoderate self-confidence that comes from a sense of having a personal and a national mission—plays off the strong Chosen One against the bourgeois; primordial thinking against commonsense; and against the ordinariness of a life free of danger, the courage unto death of the extraordinary individual, elevating the one, condemning the other. It is superfluous to note that such a man, who, under the conditions of the twentieth century, would have come across as an ideological party whip [*Einpeitscher*], was, under the exalted conditions of 1935, inevitably perceived as a prophet.

Our way of looking at this question is non-objective in the sense that it is directed not at the objective context but at the physiognomy of the lecture. It is legitimate so long as we are concerned with the act of molding and forming political will. The physiognomy of a statement changes situations directly; it is the focus of the infection. For style is lived stance or attitude; it is the spark that causes certain behavior to form spontaneously; it is the perennial birth of existential motives; it causes the appeal [*Appell*] to catch fire. It is characteristic of the self-conscious historicity of Heidegger's philosophy that the appeal changes, while the structures of meaning preserve their continuity over the decades of his development. It is not our task to demonstrate the stability of the fundamental categories of Heidegger's thought from *Sein und Zeit* to the "Letter on Humanism." On the other hand, the variability in the quality of the appeal forces itself to our attention. Thus, today protection, remembrance, guardianship, graciousness, love, apprehension, surrender are spoken of wherever, in 1935, the violent deed was called for, while only eight years before Heidegger praised the quasi-religious decision to lead a private, isolated existence as the final act of autonomy within the nothingness of a world without gods. The appeal changed colors at least twice, according to the political situation, while the conceptual pattern of the summons to authenticity and of the polemic against decline remained stable. The lecture of 1935 mercilessly unmasks the fascist coloring of that time. The motives for that coloring are, however, not just extrinsic ones, but also ones that follow from the objective context.

According to the conception of the history of Being, a progressive forgetfulness of Being [*Seinsvergessenheit*] runs through Western philosophy from Plato to Nietzsche. This development is marked by three great phases: the transformation of pre-Socratic into Platonic-Aristotelian thought; of Greek into Roman-Christian thought; and finally of medieval into modern thought. Heidegger questions radically, and what he uncovers is primordial; the connections that he discovers are fascinating. Nonetheless, the conception is, on the whole, one-sided. This one-sidedness is grounded in a double flaw. Heidegger does not take into account the fact that the specific formulation of his questions is by no means original but has its origins in that peculiarly German way of thinking that goes back, via Schelling, Hölderlin, and Hegel, to Böhme. Furthermore, he no longer wishes to acknowledge his theological origins, nor admit that the historical existence of *Sein und Zeit* stakes out a realm of specifically Christian experience that extends back over Kierkegaard to Augustine. For our context it is important that with the suppression of these two circumstances two important controls fall away. When Christianity, with its reinforcement of the view that there are two worlds, is categorized as a mere stage in the degeneration of the West, then the idea of the equality of all before God and of the freedom of each individual—an idea that was still central for Hegel—can no longer offer an effective counterweight: neither the counterweight of individualistic egalitarianism against the notion of the natural privilege of the stronger, nor the counterweight of cosmopolitanism against the motif of the German people as history's chosen people. And secondly, when it is not acknowledged that since Descartes, alongside the line of thinking that calculates and makes disposable, there runs the other line of the interpretive apprehension of meaning [*des sinnverstehenden Vernehmenden*], then the dialectical plasticity of modern development does not emerge clearly; it is this dialectic that gives creative legitimacy to that form of thinking which aims at mastery through objectification and thus preserves it from being one-sidedly identified with ordinary opinion [*Meinen*]. Thus, from this side is lacking the corrective of pragmatic rationalism.

The nurturing of anti-Christian and anti-Western effects alone would have sufficed to promote the psychosis of irrationalism, an irrationalism that Heidegger did not want. Added to this, however, is an elementary self-deception on Heidegger's part. He presented his insights, which were supposed to lead to the encounter between planetary technology and modern man, he lectured on these insights in 1935, under conditions that were established by this technologically determined situation and that were still very much in effect. It was thereby virtually inevitable that he would initiate that automatism of misunderstanding that falsified his intention of overcoming technologized life when this intention was actually carried out. After all, this philosophical appeal to the students seemed at first to converge with what would later be required of them as officers. Certainly, that this convergence was only an apparent one is not altered one bit even by the fact that its initiator, Heidegger himself, succumbed to the belief in it for years. In any event, there are still two questions that remain in the end: in what is this, even if only apparent, convergence grounded? Does fascism perhaps have more to do with the German tradition than one would ordinarily like to admit? And secondly: why is Heidegger publishing his lecture today, in 1953, without qualification? That is consistent, to be sure, only for a stance that does not, as Heidegger after all requires, question the past again and again, as something that still lies ahead, but rather remains stuck in repetition. That is consistent for an assessment that seeks to explain in terms of the history of Being not only its own error but, in the place of moral clarification, also the "error" of the National Socialist leadership.

In view of the fact that students are today again exposed to misunderstanding that lecture, we are writing this essay reluctantly and, for our part, susceptible to being misunderstood ourselves. It serves only one question: can the planned murder of millions of human beings, which we all know about today, also be made understandable in terms of the history of Being as a fateful going astray? Is this murder not the actual crime of those who, with full accountability, committed it? Have we not had eight years since then to take the risk of confronting what was, what we were? Is it not the foremost duty of thoughtful people to clarify the accountable deeds of the past and keep the knowledge of them awake? Instead, the mass of the population practices continued rehabilitation, and in the vanguard are the responsible ones from then and now. Instead, Heidegger publishes his words, in the meantime eighteen years old, about the greatness and inner truth of National Socialism, words that have become too old and that certainly do not belong to those whose understanding still awaits us. It appears to be time to think with Heidegger against Heidegger.

Translated by William S. Lewis *

* Translator's note: In preparing this new translation of Habermas' review of Heidegger's *Einführung in die Metaphysik*, I have consulted, with profit, the earlier Habermas translation by Dale Ponikvar (*Graduate Faculty Philosophy Journal*, 6[2]:155–164, Fall 1977), as well as Ralph Manheim's excellent translation of the *Einführung* (*An Introduction to Metaphysics*, New Haven: Yale University Press, 1959).

12

HEIDEGGER'S POLITICAL SELF-UNDERSTANDING

Otto Pöggeler

Introduction

It would not be too much of an exaggeration to refer to Otto Pöggeler as Germany's leading Heidegger scholar. His 1963 book, *Martin Heidegger's Path of Thinking*—one of the first rigorous attempts to systematically account for the developmental trajectory of Heidegger's thought —remains an interpretive landmark among Heidegger studies. But Pöggeler is also a philosopher with broad intellectual interests. In addition to his writings on Heidegger, he has published a study of the poetry of Paul Celan (*Spur des Worts: Zur Lyrik Paul Celans*), a book on aesthetics (*Die Frage nach der Kunst: Von Hegel zu Heidegger*), and is director of the Hegel Archive at the Ruhr University in Bochum.

His probing efforts to reevaluate Heidegger's intellectual legacy in light of the philosopher's commitment to Nazism also distinguish him among Heidegger interpreters. When criticism of the philosopher's convictions and practices is called for, Pöggeler refuses to shy away from harsh judgments. Thus, for example, in the afterword to the 1983 reedition of *Heidegger's Path of Thinking*, he suggests: "Was it not through a definite orientation of his thought that Heidegger fell—and not merely accidentally—into the proximity of National Socialism, without ever truly emerging from this proximity?" For Pöggeler, the fact that Heidegger's philosophy and politics are necessarily interwoven becomes the point of departure for a series of fascinating meditations on the complex historical situatedness of ideas.

Otto Pöggeler, "Heidegger's Political Self-Understanding" ("Heideggers politisches Selbstverständnis") appeared in Annamarie Gethmann-Siefert and Otto Pöggeler, eds., *Heidegger und die praktische Philosophie* (Frankfurt: Suhrkamp, 1988).

And thus, in his many recent contributions on the theme of Heidegger and politics, Pöggeler has frequently argued for what might be called a "historicization" of Heidegger's political involvement. This approach—which is the methodological basis for the essay that follows—emphasizes the complexities and confusions of that desperate historical hour in German history when the nation embarked on its path to catastrophe—dragging much of Europe along with it. Victor Farias' simplistic equation of Heideggerianism with Nazism is in many respects the unspoken antagonist of Pöggeler's argument. In this vein, Pöggeler seeks to show how little Heidegger's own "political self-understanding" at the time had to do with the version of National Socialism that triumphed in Germany during these years; to the point where the philosopher himself was mocked for trying to institute his own "private" version of National Socialism, based on his understanding of the "Greek beginning" and on the need for a more primordial understanding of Being.

Pöggeler suggests that unless we proceed from a "historicized" understanding of Heidegger's Nazism, we run the risk of succumbing to the simplifications of "victor's justice." Or as Pöggeler observes at the outset of his essay, "Whoever once opted for Hitler or Stalin and thus did not stand on the side of the victors is subject to a curse which calls him to share in the guilt of others." In this connection, he invokes (on several occasions) the example of the murder during World War II of some 4,000 Polish officers at Katyn by the Red Army; an event for which, until quite recently, the Nazis have been held responsible.

But here one must proceed with caution. The appeal for a "historicization" of the German past was a key theme among those in the "revisionist" camp during the German "Historians' Debate" (*"Historikerstreit"*) of recent years. Fortunately, the main arguments of the revisionists—that the 1933–1945 period was an unessential "aberration" in the overall course of Germany history; that the crimes of the Bolshevik era were more "original" (a word which the historian Ernst Nolte explicitly borrows from Heidegger) than those of the Nazis at Auschwitz and elsewhere—were not accepted by a majority of the German public.[1]

Pöggeler is, however, fully aware of the complexities—and dangers—involved in "historicizing" Heidegger's questionable political allegiances. His is, therefore, a nuanced appeal for "historical understanding"—in keeping with the constructive sense in which the hermeneutical tradition has employed this term—rather than a simplistic apology or exoneration. Like many others, Pöggeler is disturbed by the fact that Heidegger can mourn the deaths of those German soldiers "sacrificed before their time through two World Wars," yet cannot bring himself to utter a word of contrition concerning the millions who died in Nazi concentration camps. He, too, is dismayed that Heidegger, when questioned in the 1966 *Der Spiegel* interview about future political prospects, "formulated a consistent renunciation of all hopes that were placed in democracy." He cites Heidegger's infamous observation from *What is Called Thinking?* (1951–52) to the effect that the outcome of the Second World War "has decided nothing" as far as "the essence of humanity" is concerned. But, here, Heidegger was misguided—incredibly so. For if ever there was a war that resulted in an outcome that was decisive for the "essence of humanity," it was World War II, where fascism was laid to rest in Europe as a viable political option. And it is because of political judgments of this nature that seem so out of touch with the realities of twentieth-century historical life, that, at a crucial juncture in his argument, Pöggeler feels compelled to observe: "Of course, one must always ask oneself whether Heidegger doesn't speak a language that has become impossible."

Notes

1. For an excellent commentary on the question of the "historicization" of the German past as it relates to the Historians' Debate, see Saul Friedländer, "Some Reflections on the Historicization of National Socialism," *German Politics and Society* 13:9–21, February 1988.

. . .

It is difficult to judge the political implications of a philosophy like Heidegger's, which was so blind to specific political questions but which felt challenged by politics and got deeply entangled in it. The famous author of *Being and Time* resolutely leaves behind as a mere academic affair the hermeneutic phenomenology he had developed from Husserl and Dilthey in order to join his more original questioning, unprotected, to the "awakening" which in 1933 finally seemed to prevail. After the Second World War the same philosopher, surprisingly enough, could demand an epochal "turn" for his age. More indirectly (indeed posthumously) and inextricably amalgamated with Nietzsche, of whom he had been sharply critical, Heidegger stamped that self-critique of European reason which emanated from Paris in the previous decade and found strong resonance in a deeply disquieted America. Are not the political indictments to which Heidegger was exposed in fact attempts to avoid the questions Heidegger put to the age in such powerfully effective ways? That is how Heidegger saw it. (The legends which were circulated about his relations with Husserl or Edith Stein generally just continued, in the battle of philosophical schools, that sort of propaganda at which Goebbels was a master.) In this situation it may be helpful to ask how Heidegger himself saw his political place.

Whoever once opted for Hitler or Stalin and thus did not stand on the side of the victors is subject to a curse which calls him to share in the guilt of others. Forty years after the war a memorial for the victims of Katyn was erected in Warsaw. It was to display what the Soviet prosecutors at the Nuremberg trials already wanted to have accepted as "truth," viz., that Polish officers had been murdered by the Germans. Outside of a few individuals, who would have shown any interest in clarifying the matter? The newspapers did report demonstrations in front of the memorial, including a banner: "Truth will prevail." A glance at history, however, leaves doubts whether such hopes are justified. Time and again the victors have enforced their "truth" and have taken from the vanquished even their great historical moments and appropriated them (as for example the Romans did with the Etruscans). A philosopher of history like Hegel even went so far as to memorialize the defeated with the claim that they must have had no world-historical right. On the other hand, it is no wonder if it sounds like "involved in a crime" when in America one is asked, "So, you are involved in Heidegger too?"

In Heidegger's lecture course of summer 1935 one reads the indifferent statement that "in spite of some house-cleaning [*Säuberung*]" the condition of the University remains unchanged (meaning it is still bad). In the summer 1942 lecture course Heidegger comments on America's "entry" into the planetary war as the "last American act of American historilessness and self-devastation." Heidegger speaks of America's entry into the war as though Japan had not attacked Pearl Harbor and as though Italy and Germany had not then declared war on America. He appeals to the "hidden spirit of the originary [*Anfänglichen*] in the West," which does not bother "even to look in disdain at this self-devastation of those without origins," but waits "in the stilling releasement [*Gelassenheit*] of the originary for its sterling hour." Hölderlin and the Sophocles of *Antigone* are said to indicate what is originary. One can imagine how these utterances are read by someone who was a victim of the aforementioned "house-cleaning" or who, when at last allowed to emigrate, could take only ten marks and had to be glad if some American aid organization together with his or her own labor—including scrub work for women, newspaper delivery for children—helped keep body and soul together. Virtually none of those to whom the statue at the entry to the port of Manhattan was genuinely a greeting of freedom repatriated to the country of Hölderlin, the country which had claimed Sophocles as its own. Is there any kind of bridge from these experiences to the words of Heidegger?[1]

To go on living human beings must also forget, and so they will always be touching up the image of the past. Still, it is striking that after 1945 no one seemed to have done and said all the things which nevertheless had been done and said. Thus it could be dismissed as an innocent error that Heidegger, like so many others, had seen the possibility of an awakening in the 1933 seizure of power which had finally broken through the crippling curse of mere tactical crisis management during the party-carousel charade of the Weimar Republic. Nor was it any longer supposed to be true that Hitler's so-called peace address of May 17, 1933, in which Heidegger saw himself confirmed in his choice, had been something new designed for English and American ears: a turn toward the line Wilson once advocated, the voicings of a humane Austrian in detested Prussian Berlin. Such things could no longer be discussed, for the Red Army had captured extermination camps such as Maidanek and Auschwitz and had exposed their machinery to the world. By the end of the war the residents of Goethe's Weimar had been led to Buchenwald to see with their own eyes what had taken place. No one could or would identify himself with the monstrous and terrifying things which now lay open to the light of day.

Of course it could be argued that Hitler had openly set forth even this "goal" of his politics in his programmatic book, *Mein Kampf,* but hardly anyone had read this book. References to its theses in 1933 were often defused by taking them as verbal power plays which would now have to give way to a realistic politics. But didn't depriving Jewish citizens of their rights show that the goals had remained the same? Yet even after the "Law for Reconstituting the Civil Service," Thomas Mann wrote in his diary "that the exclusion of Kerr's arrogant and poisonous yiddish Nietzscheanizing" is "in the end no misfortune; nor in the last analysis is the de-jewification of the legal system." Heidegger could send his rectoral address to a colleague like Richard Kroner—that Kroner was a Jew obviously did not hinder the attempt to win him over to the new way. In the first Hölderlin lecture course Heidegger already attacked what appeared to him disastrous in the new political ideas: the racism and biologism that had deep roots in cultural history, and not only in German cultural history. At the Evian Conference in July 1938 a group of European states identified the "Jewish question" as an international problem. Since by that time Hitler had begun his struggle for world domination, he intensified his measures against the Jews into a politics of emigration, that is to say, a politics of expulsion. With the invasion of the Soviet Union the extension toward the premeditated basis for the sought-after continental world domination began, and with it also the last step: the "final solution." What Hitler was still saying on the Jewish question during the days of his Nibelungen-decline is pure madness—in contrast to the tactical skill of the May 1933 peace address, which of course could already be said to be a demonic skill [*Geschick*]. Nevertheless, the "final solution," which Hitler considered part of his enduring legacy, together with the euthanasia programs, exhibits the core of National Socialist politics: "biological" revolution, breeding a pure racial elite for the sought-after world domination.

If Heidegger protested after the war that he had had nothing to do with such National Socialism, he was in a certain sense right. He had even positioned the province of Baden against Berlin centralization and had viewed Germany as a people among other European peoples. The mobilization of all energies toward the struggle for world domination had always been for him a disastrous perversion of the task at hand. He opposed the biologism which stood behind the racism. He had developed such an allergy to it that in the lecture course of winter 1934–35 he professed no surprise that though the "psychoanalytic foundations" of literary studies had been replaced overnight such that now "everywhere there is sniveling about the people [*Volkstum*] and blood and soil," nevertheless "everything remained the same." The lecture course of winter 1942–43, for example, rather enthematically forced Rilke's eighth Duino Elegy wholly under the shadow of this Nietzscheanizing biologism. But was it not already far too late to hope to prevent aberrations by such measures?[2]

In any case, throughout it all Heidegger's concern remained the attempt to respond with philosophizing to the European crisis that had become manifest through the First World War. For Heidegger this was the senseless self-destruction of Europe, arising because the European peoples did not individually seek creative solutions to their own problems, but instead plunged into an outward struggle for world domination. In retrospect, Heidegger cited the verses Stefan George wrote in the midst of the First World War: "these are the fiery signs—not the tidings." In his Inaugural Address before the Heidelberg Academy he alluded to the fact that that which pointed to the roots of the European crisis had emerged in the years between 1910 and 1914: the translation of Kierkegaard's writings and Dostoyevsky's novels, Nietzsche's late notes and the start of the edition of Dilthey's *Gesammelte Schriften,* the new view of Hölderlin and the poetry of Trakl. It had taken Heidegger a long time to see the full significance of what had already emerged: Dilthey's analyses initially led the way, accompanied by hints from Dostoyevsky and Kierkegaard; from 1929 Nietzsche and Hölderlin "called for decision," and after 1945 Trakl's path to decline became the focus of reflection. Thus, in looking back it is necessary to view Heidegger's thinking as an answer to a historical crisis whose outward signs lie in the First and Second World Wars as well as in the ostensible preparation for the Third.

At least in its present condition, the *Gesamtausgabe,* which is supposed to document Heidegger's "paths, not works," obstructs this view of things. Heidegger's publication history, compelled by University examinations, led to granting juvenilia like his dissertation and *Habilitation* thesis the undeserved distinction of marking Heidegger's beginnings. If one is to talk of genuine beginnings, however, these are not to be found in medieval Aristotelianism, in the Hegelianizing theology of the Tübingen school, or indeed in Rickert's neo-Kantianism, but rather in that non-metaphysical phenomenology and hermeneutics of factichistorical life Heidegger began developing around 1917. After the First World War, when Heidegger could once again teach undisturbed, he immediately linked these beginnings of his thinking to a reflection on the task of the University. In the summer semester of 1919 he lectured "On the Essence of the University and Academic Study." Seven years later, when Heidegger began to publish *Being and Time* prematurely for the sake of his career, the fragment stopped short of the genuine questions (namely, short of the third Division and the connection between [phenomenological] construction and destruction). The published portions only partially exhibit Heidegger's tendencies; thus, for example, it is not evident why historicality is more narrowly determined by words like "fate" and "destiny" (determinations which therefore remained outside the horizon of the Bultmannian reception as well). Of course one can claim a privilege for those works which already have a great effective history; yet this all too easily becomes a matter for those who have never really learned and above all want to learn nothing more.

In the winter of 1929–30, when the early signs of the global economic crisis and its domestic political reflection coincided with a crisis in Heidegger's religious and metaphysical convictions, he once again linked the question about the possibility of philosophy to the question of the role of the University, viz., in his Freiburg Inaugural Address and in the lecture-course "Introduction to Academic Study." These lines of questioning flow into the Rectoral Address, and thus it is not at all accidental that in 1933 Heidegger, in the circle of younger colleagues like Wolfgang Schadewaldt and Erik Wolf, grabbed for the rectorate and took pains to revolutionize his domain through a new Führer-Constitution. In the winter of 1933–34 Carl Friedrich von Weizsäcker could hear from a Freiburg student: "In the circle around Heidegger they have invented Freiburg National Socialism. Under their breath they say that the true Third Reich has not yet begun at all, that it is yet to arrive." This "arrival" was supposed to be prepared first through the reform of the University and then through reflection on Hölderlin. After the failure of his political engagement Heidegger saw himself driven into isolation: at the time he showed none of his students the material that, in the Sils-Maria breeze of Nietzsche, he worked out as his magnum opus—the *Beiträge zur Philosophie*.[3]

In the lecture course on Heraclitus from the summer of 1943, "Der

Anfang des abendländischen Denkens," Heidegger claims that Nietzsche's doctrine of the will to power is no "invention" of Nietzsche's or the Germans, but names the distinguishing mark of the age. Through a knowing which questions, a reflection on origins, the Germans—"and they alone"—could "save the West in its history." "The planet is in flames. The essence of humanity is out of joint. World historical reflection can come only from the Germans, assuming that they find and preserve 'what is German [*das Deutsche*].' That is not arrogance, rather it is the knowledge of the necessary arrangement [*Austragens*] of an originary need." Thus Heidegger wants to educate the thirty- and forty-year-olds of the coming decades "to think essentially," so that one day the Germans "in and through the readiness for death are strong enough to save the originary in its homely grace from the petty-mindedness of the modern world." The danger threatening the "holy heart of the peoples" is "not that of decline, but rather that we ourselves, in confusion, yield to the will to modernity and foster it."

The Heraclitus lecture course from summer 1944, "Logik," starts from the premise that the destiny which belonged to the Greeks is "a still undecided arrival" which "initially we Germans, and probably for a long time we alone, can and must come to face in thought." What Heraclitus said about the Logos, however, has been obscured by "logic" (i.e., by the dominant mode of classical philosophical thinking), so that even the Christian effort to secure salvation was able to combine with this self-securing logic. This development extends to Hegel's dialectic, to Nietzsche's will to power, and to modern technology. Christianity is powerless against this development since it essentially participates in it with the *techne*-oriented idea of creation. "From where else derives the historical bankruptcy of Christianity and its church in modern world history? Must there be a Third World War to prove it?" Today, in a "turning point of Western history, if not indeed of the occidentally determined world history of the planet as such," *techne* in the form of modern machine technology "is becoming the admitted or not yet admitted basic form of knowing." Thus Heidegger insinuates that the Third World War is to be a struggle for world domination with the help of technology—even if it is no longer war in the customary sense, made obsolete by technology.

When world history had long since entered into the "cold war"

Heidegger, in his new lecture course on logic of winter 1951–52, "What is Called Thinking?," said: "What did the Second World War really decide, not to speak of the terrible consequences for our Fatherland, in particular the tear through its center? This World War has decided nothing, if we use 'decision' here in so high and broad a sense that it pertains solely to the destiny of the essence of humanity upon the earth." To the restoration currently under way Heidegger then objected: "The European world of ideas between 1920 and 1930 was not even adequate to what had already come about. What shall become of a Europe which wants to assemble a montage with things confiscated from those decades after the First World War? A plaything for the powers, and for the immense native strength of the Eastern peoples." Heidegger recalled that in *Twilight of the Idols* Nietzsche had referred to old Russia as the "concept which suggests the opposite of the wretched European nervousness and system of small states." Seeing in "democratism" the decadent form of organizing power, Nietzsche still found in Russia "institutions," and a will to tradition and authority, which were "antiliberal to the point of malice." He means old Russia with its autocratic czars, the power of its nobility, its lack of bourgeois spirit (and its pogroms). Heidegger then further recalled that in unpublished notes to *Zarathustra*, Nietzsche came into proximity with Hölderlin when he demanded a "Caesar with the soul of Christ." Mistrustful of the English-speaking world, Nietzsche even on occasion countered the division of the world between Anglo-Saxons and Slavs by suggesting a worldwide German-Slavic regime.

Thus one does not do justice to Heidegger, a reader of Dostoyevsky, unless one sees that for him Russia had very little to do with ("West European") Soviet Marxism—just as little as Hölderlin or Heidegger's *Beiträge zur Philosophie* has to do with the externalized totalitarianism of National Socialism. In any case, Heidegger insisted that the mentality of the twenties (in which *Being and Time* also must be located) could provide no perspective for overcoming the crisis into which the world had fallen under the leadership of Europe. Only those new philosophical and political ventures could do so in pursuit of which the author of *Being and Time* had stood for a while in proximity to the National Socialist revolution. The Second World War had decided nothing (apart from the rending of Germany) because it had antagonistically brought to dominance that which, on Heidegger's interpretation, only conceals the root of the crisis. Having led the planet into the age of technology, Europe had not been able to bring about a turn on the basis of its own origins. After Austria-Hungary had collapsed in the First World War as a Central European bulwark of order, the catastrophe which was Prusso-Germany managed to remove even a victorious power like England from the circle of world powers and to turn Europe into an object of politics. The question remains: what sort of political conception guided Heidegger in this view of things and what conception finally remained for him?

I

To one of his Heidelberg auditors, the traveling Estonian nobleman von Uexküll, Hegel wrote that Europe had become a kind of cage where one [state] played the role of jailer while the other had to arrange things behind bars. European states had more or less reached the goal of their development. "Russia, on the other hand, already perhaps the strongest power among the rest, carries in its womb a tremendous possibility for developing its intensive nature." Hegel saw a similar plentitude of possibilities for development in the United States of America, but on his view of things the paths of the two powers currently flanking Europe with their tremendous resources were different. America had a society based on civic freedom, and once the way west had been exhausted it would finally have to raise itself to the level of a State. Russia was an authoritarian State with ancient agrarian foundations, but it had yet to develop a civil society with its constitutional forms. Strangely, Hegel never doubted that the transformation of the world which he clearly had in view could bring forth any forms of organization other than those which he sought to portray as the goal of development in Europe (namely forms combining those elements furnished through the original forms of human settlement with the results of the bourgeois movement in the cities of northern Europe especially, i.e., a constitutional monarchy with a bicameral system which integrated civil society into the State).

A few years after Hegel's death Tocqueville, who had traveled in America, saw things entirely differently. He opined that in 150 years America and Russia would divide the world among themselves. The danger from Russia lay in an authoritarian dictatorship together with a

Byzantine fusion of the governmental and religious or pseudo-religious spheres; while America threatened with a dictatorship of the majority which could suppress any deviating opinion and any creative risk through a consensus of the many. Through imperialism, open or concealed, Russia and America had acquired a huge and continuous territory (unlike the fragile, because discontinuous, English Imperium). Concerning the manner in which the North American Indians had been as good as obliterated, Tocqueville wrote that the result had been attained "with wonderful ease, quietly, legally, and philanthropically, without spilling blood and without violating a single one of the great principles of morality in the eyes of the world. It is impossible to destroy men with more respect to the laws of humanity." What such prognoses could mean for Central Europe, where the peoples pushed confusedly against one another in an unprotected geographical situation, was captured by Bismarck in a much quoted sentence: "If the power of Prussia is ever broken it will be difficult for Germany to avoid the fate of Poland," that is, "the destiny of a divided land, to be claimed by the great powers as glacis and perimeter of battle." Marx desired other things than did Bismarck but saw the dangers of Russian expansion in the same way.[4]

According to the report of E. Baumgarten, early in 1932 Jaspers clearly expressed the view that America and Russia would divide the world and that for Germany there remained only the vocation of a spiritual power. In this changing world Jaspers brought attention to the limit-situations of human life and to the possibility of communication between individuals. Heidegger's extremely influential book, *Being and Time,* also seemed to find its point of departure entirely within this "philosophy of existence." In his early Freiburg lecture courses Heidegger had referred repeatedly to Spengler's *Decline of the West.* Did he also have a political conception which justified his linking the individual and his fate to the destiny of a "Volk" in *Being and Time?* The first of the little texts now collected under the title *Denkerfahrungen* is an article the young theology student wrote for the unveiling of a monument to Abraham of Santa Clara in Kreenheinstetten on August 15, 1910. All of the Capuchin preaching against the "age of hurried living and the culture of exteriority" which Heidegger later wove into his lectures and writings appear to be anticipated here: "The ground-destroying rage for the new, the crazed leaping over the deeper spiritual content of life and art, the sense of modern life oriented toward continually self-canceling momentary stimulations, the closeness—sometimes to the point of suffocation—in which contemporary art of every sort moves, are moments which point toward a decadence, toward a pathetic revolt against the health and the transcendent value of life." The effect that Heidegger's fellow provincial Abraham had had in Vienna led to a recollection of the "unforgettable Lueger"—i.e., to that politician who, from social motives and from sympathy for the uprooted petty bourgeoisie, renounced both conservatism and high bourgeois liberalism and for a time created a counterpoise to social democratic tendencies.[5]

In *Der Spiegel*'s interview Heidegger claimed that his national and social orientation should be understood "somewhat in the sense of Friedrich Naumann's attempt." In a famous book from the middle of the First World War Naumann had posed the problem of "Central Europe." He took up Christian themes with an eye toward social questions, thinking that in this way he could still be effective from within the parties and the Church. When Heidegger pointed out the multiple afflictions of the age in his lecture course of winter 1929–30, this opportunity seemed to have passed; Heidegger now sought an ultimate radicality of thinking together with creative poetry and so a recollection of that terror which is bound up with every orientation toward a final "mystery." Thus Heidegger invoked "those able to instill our Dasein with a terror [*Schrecken*]," even if "contemporary everyman and Biedermann" sometimes becomes alarmed and sees red "so that he clings all the more desperately to his idols." Heidegger saw the mood of the age in that Nietzscheanism which, variously in Spengler, Klages, Scheler, and also Leopold Ziegler, problematized the relation between life and spirit. That which had deluged Europe in the 1920s—global economy, technology, the new media—was traced back to the alienated civilization of the big cities in which the West was dying. For Heidegger, Nietzsche himself had addressed the problematic more originally in his talk of the antagonism between the Dionysian and the Apollonian; even the playing off of Dionysus against that curse on life, the Crucified, also belonged to this antagonism. When Heidegger began to lecture on Hölderlin and Nietzsche a good five years later, he argued in the very first lecture that Hölderlin's letters to Böhlendorff and his late hymns had placed the meaning of this antagonism more purely into relief. In this Heidegger adopted an interpretation of the historical situation that had been advocated in the

George Circle since [Friedrich] Gundolf's Heidelberg Inaugural Lecture on Hölderlin's elegy *Archipelagus*, but also beyond this circle and in connection with expressionism, e.g., by Wilhelm Michel. This new question of the historical law of Greece and of the West, which went far beyond the older forms of the *querelle des anciens et des modernes*, became linked with the philosophical question of how an experience of Being and its truth could as such provide binding force.

In his Freiburg Inaugural Address Heidegger brusquely brought up the break with Husserl as inevitable; the Dilthey school's overture to discussion left him cold. Even fellow travelers Jaspers and Bultmann were soon given the cold shoulder. His departure from every merely academic philosophy was indicated publicly at Davos in the discussion with Cassirer. Repeatedly Heidegger called attention to the fact that he now conceived the "historical situation" in terms of Jünger's works: the essay "Die totale Mobilmachung" from the 1930 volume *Krieg und Krieger* and the 1932 book *Der Arbeiter* based upon it. He discussed these works in a small circle with his assistant, Brock (who subsequently had to emigrate), and tried to grasp the idea that from now on within the context of planetary history everything stands in the light of the universal rule of the will to power—whether "it is called communism or fascism or world democracy."

Jünger's essay "Die totale Mobilmachung" sees a decisive historical turning point in the First World War, but at the same time he sees it as a civil war, world war as world revolution. In the concept of total mobilization Jünger wants to show that "wars of workers" are now succeeding the wars of knights, kings, and citizens. No longer is it monarchs who, after consultation with their ministers, bring about a tactically calculated confrontation of armies. In those days the City Magistrate of Berlin could announce after the battle of Jena and Auerstädt that now, where the king has a lost "a bataille," peace is the first duty of the citizen. But Carl von Clausewitz tried to conceive the "God of War" itself as standing opposed to the monarchs of Europe after the *levée en masse* in the French Revolution and then Napoleon. Clausewitz concluded from the new character assumed by war, however, that the important thing was to return even such war to the service of politics. Against this, Jünger's war of workers is total in that it places all of life in its service— commerce and foodstuffs as well as armament. On Jünger's interpretation it was precisely the presence of retarding moments in Prussian politics that hindered the kind of mobilization necessary for Germany to win the First World War. America, not a military state but nevertheless a country without a past, had been to a greater extent capable of a total mobilization and thus had emerged from the war as the "clear victor."

The revolution in Soviet Russia also showed a thoroughgoing mobilization, for example, in the five-year plan. Progress—i.e., the world revolution—and total mobilization (by means of which the difference between war and peace was said to be eliminated) have many variants according to Jünger: "In fascism, in Bolshevism, in Americanism, in Zionism, and in the movement of the colored peoples progress initiates advances which hitherto one would have held unthinkable." The book *Der Arbeiter* opposes the workers who carry out the total mobilization to the security-seeking bourgeoisie, but not to the spirit of the warrior. On the contrary, in the annihilating slaughters of the World War the soldier is said to have experienced in death a higher reality, namely that "Gestalt" of the worker which now gives meaning to life. Escapist romanticism is rejected, yet this life of work and total mobilization itself once more becomes a "cult" and a "myth." In the *Stahlgewittern* Jünger had described his feeling of impending death after being seriously wounded as a joyous experience in which he—"as though illuminated by a flash of lightning"—grasped his life in its "innermost Gestalt."[6]

If in his Rectoral Address Heidegger imposes upon the University the duty of knowledge service which educates one to armed service and labor service, he is emphasizing the significance of a third factor over and against Jünger's talk of "war front" and "labor front." If after the failure of his Rectorship he reflects on Heraclitus and Hölderlin, he is thinking decisively beyond the horizon in which Jünger's attempt to conceptualize the age moved. Thus, too, in the following decade Heidegger interspersed his lecture courses with critical remarks about Jünger, e.g., that adventurism is not the same as daring, that for Jünger even language is nothing but armament, etc. A sharp criticism is inserted into the second Hölderlin lecture course of winter 1941–42: "The adventurous man can conceive care only as weakness and annoyance since he only thinks subjectively, i.e., metaphysically, and ostensibly loves severity. If this fails he takes flight into some kind of intoxication, be it only the intoxication of blood." Heidegger may be thinking of those passages in the 1922 essay *Der Kampf als inneres Erlebnis* which see a kind of pleasure even in the horror of annihilating slaughters—battle for the sake of battle: "The appearance of the foe brings, in addition to ultimate horror, also redemption from heavy, unendurable pressure. That is the voluptuousness of blood which hangs over war like a red warning flag over a black galley, comparable only to love in its limitless ardor." The conclusion to the Nietzsche lecture course of summer 1939, which could not be delivered because of the impending outbreak of war, termed "total mobilization" the "organization of unconditional meaninglessness by and for the will to power." In the winter of 1939–40 Heidegger again turns to discuss *Der Arbeiter* in a small circle and notes that in the book "Nietzsche's metaphysics is in no way grasped in thought; not even the paths toward comprehension are hinted at. On the contrary, instead of becoming questionable in a genuine sense this metaphysics becomes self-evident and seemingly superfluous."

In his autobiography Jaspers reported that in 1933 he said to Heidegger that everything is just as it was in 1914, by which he meant: the same illusions. Yet Heidegger, "beaming," is said to have taken the comparison as entirely positive. Without doubt Heidegger believed that Germany must finally, through an awakening, exorcise the highest danger and thus reclaim its place among the European peoples. For this reason, too, he referred to Albert Leo Schlageter in the addresses during his time as rector. A fellow provincial whom Heidegger had long held in esteem, Schlageter had fought in desperate nationalism against the French occupation of the Ruhr and was executed for it. The National Socialists took Schlageter as a resistance fighter and martyr and in this had Heidegger's full support. The "awakening" to which Heidegger attached himself in 1933 was a national one that was supposed to re-establish Germany's dignity and—according to Heidegger's conviction as well as the letter of Hitler's address—adapt itself to Wilson's program for the self-determination of peoples. That Heidegger as rector strove (naturally without the least success) to establish personal contact with Hitler, but also declined the call to Berlin for a second time, shows that he did not want to see Berlin centralization imposed on Germany. Heidegger's national concern included a social one: to overcome the unemployment of workers and the deracination of the peasants and petty bourgeoisie by means of the common work of everyone, indeed with spade in hand

Otto Pöggeler

(as Heidegger specified in his addresses). The new politics should not
come about by means of parliamentary debate and agreement among
groups and factions, but through adherence to the Führer who, in solitary resolve, takes upon himself the risk of decision for another future.
Not only had officers of the First World War like Ernst Jünger or the
great agriculturalists of eastern Germany embraced one form or another
of the *Führerprinzip*, but also a circle like that around Stefan George. In
the years around 1930 a large number of intellectuals, and especially
students, turned away from "Western" democracy. Moreover, the democratic parties of the period, during which a fascist awakening prevailed
in Italy, also embraced the necessity of some temporary, tempered form
of dictatorship, or else they set no decisive resistance against it. Thus
Heidegger (whose opting for Hitler predated 1933) could hope for widespread concurrence when, at the beginning of the winter semester of
1933–34, he said to his students ("only in the local Freiburg student
newspaper," as he protested in the *Spiegel* interview): "Precepts and
'ideas' are not the rules of your Being. The Führer *is* the one and only
present and future German reality and its law."[7]

This sentence renders Heidegger's basic conviction that the political,
thoughtful, or poetical setting into work of the truth of Being requires a
decision and a daring in which the exposed individual opens himself for
the greatness of the future. In particular this sentence renders quite
exactly Heidegger's concrete political conviction: what matters is not
precepts or ideas, and so also neither the program of the National
Socialist Party nor theories of race, but rather that the Chancellor of a
national coalition raise himself above his party and in this way finally
become Leader of the awakening. In his reflections on his 1933–34
rectorship Heidegger reported, certainly accurately, that immediately
following the Rectoral Address the National Socialist Minister registered
his objections: Heidegger advocates a "private National Socialism" since
he does not acknowledge the idea of race and rejects the idea of a
politicized science. In fact, Heidegger did immediately fight against the
transformation of the University into a politicized *Fachhochschule,* as
well as against "biologism." But his Rectoral Address itself occasioned
no substantive discussion. Werner Jaeger did want to publish the address
in the journal *Die Antike* as testimony to the continuation of the spirit

214

of the ancients; and on September 23, 1933, Karl Jaspers wrote to his friend Heidegger that the address was "up to now the only document of the contemporary academic Will ... that will endure." The address "endured" in the sense that after the Second World War Heidegger's fame insured that it was referred to precisely by those who knew almost nothing else about the addresses, testimonies, and deeds of those times.

What was astonishing at the time and alarming today, however, is that in the address someone stepped forward as spiritual Führer at an institution in which the rector had been and was supposed to be one among equals, an institution where corporative ballot and self-government had a long tradition. It may be that Bavaria put through a modified Führer-Constitution for the University during the same period; with Heidegger's vigorous help Baden led the way on this path. Thus, for example, the Führer Heidegger could appoint his deans as Assistant Führer by decree; he thus became implicated in the house-cleaning [*Säuberung*] and expulsions. Perhaps he intended to hinder the worst (such as book burnings and the posting of the "Jew notices"); nevertheless, at the Todtnauberg "camp" of student youths he fell into the new forms of controversy and so finally came into conflict with those who— like Baeumler—at first appeared to be kindred spirits. Heidegger failed utterly, precisely as "Führer."

Heidegger's break with his political engagement was total in 1934; and yet this break was at first only a continuation of "Freiburg National Socialism" by other means, viz., through the long path of revolutionary [*grundstürzenden*] reflection. In the summer of 1934 Heidegger did not hold the announced lecture course, which was supposed to be devoted to the problem of the State, but instead lectured on logic to an overflowing auditorium maximum. This logic, however, referred to the Heraclitean Logos, thus to the problem of language and so of spirit. Heidegger began with Fragment 53. The Rectoral Address had appealed to Nietzsche's saying, "God is dead," about which in his 1945–46 defense Heidegger says: "If this were not so, would the First World War have been possible? And even more, if this were not so would the Second World War have become possible?"[8] In an age when European history and planetary history in general had lost its direction Heidegger intended to quest once more, with Nietzsche, after an endangered and perishable "tragic" greatness—by way of an originary thinking and by way of an art which again provided a home for human beings in a world transformed by myths.

Jünger's Nietzscheanism pointed to the problem: if humanity rises up so as to mobilize all resources in a total armory and to bring them into its own service, is it still possible for the artist to give shape to the divine —as previously in the Parthenon standing above Athens? Nietzsche's hermeneutics of suspicion surmised that precisely what had counted as the greatest (the orientation toward Ideas and Ideals in Platonism and in Christianity) was already nihilism. This suspicion combines with that genealogy which locates greatness in the originary, subsequently covered up in the rebellion of the slaves against masters and free men. In Heraclitus Heidegger explored the origin of thinking. Heraclitus' discourse about war [*Kampf*], which according to Fragment 53 sorts out masters and slaves, and about Aion, which (at least according to Nietzsche's interpretation) puts both gods and men into play, is said to be a purer rendering of what Nietzsche had only touched upon. The Hölderlin lecture course of winter 1934–35 investigates the language of the poet and takes Heraclitus as representative of a "primordial power of occidental-germanic historical Dasein" within the tradition of thinking.

Portentous motives stand behind this blurring of history. If Parmenides envisions the whole of Being, Heraclitus listens to the *logos;* and thus he can be associated with the word arising in the heart as Meister Eckhart knew it and with Hölderlin's relation to the word. (Philo, who still provided the key to appropriating neo-Platonism for Hegel, is excluded.) Unhistorically, Heidegger sees a link between *physis, aletheia,* and *logos* in Heraclitus. This is because his reading of the sixth book of the *Nichomachean Ethics* attributed to the Situation and its *kairos* a peculiar *aletheuein* and a *logos,* related to Being, which in forms like *"bin"* was supposed to indicate emergence and becoming and thus the originary *physis.* If truth is unconcealedness, then it requires those authentic ones, those exposed ones, who are open for its depths and thus also for the struggle between masters and slaves. Already in May of 1933 Walter Eucken wrote that Heidegger feels himself to be "the sole and surpassing thinker since Heraclitus" and so "the born philosopher and spiritual leader of the new movement." In 1945–46 Heidegger found it necessary to justify his appeal to Heraclitus' Fragment 53, claiming that it neither glorified war nor a master race. But even a friend like Ochsner wrote in a note of November 9, 1933: "In Heidegger's interpretation of the 53rd Frgm of Heraclitus [there is] the experience and the sense of being conditioned by the historical situation. What is 'compelling' in the interpretation is provided by the contemporary situation, down to the very tone of voice in which he interprets. But if this situation were experienced otherwise or were an entirely different one, then the interpretation would also be otherwise."

If in his [announced but not held 1934] seminar Heidegger had intended to refer to Hegel regarding the problem of the State, then perhaps it was in the sense that thereby the specifically German historical path could be introduced (that is, Hegel's resistance to the idea of national representatives in Sieyes' parliamentary sense). Following the myth of the German relation to the Greeks which had arisen in the time of Goethe, Heidegger assumed a direct connection between Germanness [*das Deutsche*] and things Greek. Thus the Hölderlin lecture course of winter 1934–35 explores Hölderlin's poetry for the future essence of the Germans and speaks in this regard of a "Greek-German mission [*Sendung*]." Reflection on this mission is " 'politics' in the highest and most authentic sense," an awakening in which something other "than the mere variation of political conditions" takes place. The lecture course proceeds from Hölderlin's hymn "Germanien" in order to devote itself on that basis to the doctrine of the "demigods" in the Rhein hymn. Heidegger alludes to the fact that currently even Christ was being portrayed from the pulpit as Führer, and he finds it just as untrue as that Church apologetics which speak the language of Nietzsche. It is blasphemy, since according to Church dogmatics Christ is not simply essentially similar to the Father, but identical in essence. Thus, since the time of Boethius the concept of providence could be played off against that concept of fate which Hölderlin claimed for the demigods and Nietzsche for the great creators. Heidegger appeals to just this tradition which speaks out of orthodox church dogmatics: "The Being of the true and always unique Führer, on the contrary, points to the realm of the demigods. To be a Führer is a fate and thus finite Being." Yet the question now remains open as to whether there are such Führer even in the political realm, or the unique Führer, and whether there is that work which brings truth as *energeia* (but not as *entelecheia*) to display. Heidegger's hopes cling at first only to the realm of poetry and thinking.[9]

The *Introduction to Metaphysics* from the summer of 1935 explores the background of originary poetry and thinking in Heraclitus and Parmenides as well as in tragedy, especially Sophocles' *Antigone*. In translating its first Chorus Heidegger follows Hölderlin when he collapses the characterization of the heroes as *hypsipolis* and *apolis* into an oxymoron and so preserves the tragic greatness which must single itself out, expose itself, and fall. Rudolf Bultmann also wrote about *Antigone* at the time (in the Festschrift for Karl Barth). But in the sayings of the Chorus he heard, on the contrary, the acclamation given Hitler and (referring to *Being and Time!*) opposed to it that personal Being, in love and in relation to the dead, which may not be violated by the State. If Heidegger did not want to stand aloof in this way (like Dostoyevsky's Prince Myshkin), he nevertheless does not opt for Creon but for Antigone (and for foundered ones like Nietzsche, van Gogh, and Hölderlin).

With Hölderlin, Heidegger sees Germany as the (defenseless) "heart" of the European peoples. The *Introduction to Metaphysics* comprehends the "darkening of the world" from the perspective of Europe's fall: "This Europe, in its ruinous blindness forever on the point of cutting its own throat, lies today in a great pincers, squeezed between Russia on one side and America on the other. From the metaphysical point of view, America and Russia are the same; the same dreary technological frenzy, the same unrestricted organization of the average man." The situation is all the more ominous in that the disempowering of the Spirit arises from Europe itself. Since the so-called collapse of German Idealism, i.e., the inability of the age to live up to the spiritual world of such idealism, this disempowering of the Spirit has in various thrusts perfected itself as a reduction of Spirit to the mere instrument of intelligence. Heidegger distinguishes three instrumentalizations of the Spirit which easily divide up geographically: in "Marxism" intelligence as impotent superstructure is the arranging and controlling of material relations of production; in "Positivism" it is the ordering and explanation of whatever is presently on hand; and in National Socialism (which Heidegger dares not mention by name) it is the organizational management of the vital resources and race of a people. Heidegger had sufficient taste not to deliver a previous version of his lecture in which Carnap's emigration to America was put forth as confirmation of the convergence between Russian communism and the "type of thinking in America." The metaphysics which Carnap wanted to overcome through the positivism of his "logical analysis of language" is proposed as a problem. In this way the fate of Europe becomes linked to the question of Being which, following Nietzsche, is to be traced to the tragic world experience of the Greek archaic period. In this lecture, as in the Rectoral Address, Heidegger still demands a revolutionizing which is supposed to proceed from a transformed University but which cannot be achieved merely by introducing primordial and early German history into the school.[10]

By the lecture course of winter 1937–38 Heidegger can only mock the University as whose rector he came to grief only a few years before. Heidegger quotes the rector's Matriculation Address of December 1937 where it is claimed that the idle chatter about a crisis of the sciences has finally grown silent. To be sure, Heidegger does not refer to his predecessor, teacher, and opponent, Husserl, who could have said a thing or two about this crisis—at least in foreign countries. But he maintains that the crisis does not consist in the "Professoriat's" failure to teach "primordial history, folklore and racelore"; further, the sciences are already too in touch with life. The crisis does not originate in 1933 or in 1918 but is there "from the beginning of the modern period." In the Matriculation Address by the Dean of the Faculty of Medicine, Heidegger perceives the "merry and indeed clammy optimism which resurrects the *Gaudeamus igitur* and the *Ergo bibamus* as the crowning achievement of academic life." He sees the University slipping into "the most barren Americanism, according to whose fundamental principle that is true which succeeds" while everything else is seen as speculation and reveries foreign to life. As though he suspected how science, e.g., atomic physics, would be placed in the service of politics, Heidegger says (after the expulsion of thousands of German scientists): "Never before has it gone better for the 'sciences' than today, and it will go even better for them in the future. But no knowledgeable one [*Wissender*] will envy the 'scientists' —the most pitiable slaves of the current age."

In the lecture course on Schelling from summer 1936 Heidegger refers to Nietzsche's diagnosis of nihilism. He sees nihilism in the fact that though there is still culture and cultural institutions, church, and society, there is no creative work; "inner neglect and lostness" mount "into the immeasurable." A passage left out of the published text reads: "The two men who in different ways introduced a countercurrent to nihilism— Mussolini and Hitler—learned, in essentially different ways, from Nietzsche. But in these efforts the authentic realm of Nietzsche's metaphysics still did not come into play." The nihilism against which Mussolini, Hitler, and Heidegger do battle here is primarily the decadence of the Western world. Yet Heidegger also says that the politicians had not understood Nietzsche's diagnosis. Since by that time Heidegger had begun to argue that Nietzsche's diagnosis of nihilism did not bring genuine nihilism into view, the apparent praise of the politicians is actually a blunt gesture of dismissal. Still, the "Führer" are not yet taken as the embodiment of nihilism itself (as they will be in 1938 by Rauschning and then finally in Heidegger's own utterances).[11] In a famous formulation from the lecture course of summer 1935 Heidegger had written that that which is peddled about as the philosophy of National Socialism has "nothing whatever to do" with the "inner truth and greatness of National Socialism." Instead of "National Socialism," the published text reads "this movement" and includes the elucidation (which was not yet present even in the page proofs): "namely the encounter between global technology and modern man." With this elucidation the "greatness" of National Socialism is defined in a thoroughly negative way.

Already the lecture course from the summer of 1940, "Der europäische Nihilismus," does the same. In more nuanced fashion than in the wholesale and global theses from the summer of 1935, it lays out the path of modern man from the securing of certainty and the certifying of salvation to the domination of the entire earth and the instrumentalization of Spirit as mere intellect. For the historical moment Heidegger demands a humanity which lets itself be ruled entirely by the "essence" of technology in order thereby "to guide and to utilize the individual technical procedures and possibilities" (and to recover from [*verwinden*] technology, one of the modes of the openness of beings, in the full truth of Being). Heidegger takes the subjugation of France by German troops during this summer as testimony for the "mysterious law of history, that one day a people is no longer equal to the metaphysics originating from its own history, and this precisely at the moment when that metaphysics has transformed itself into something unconditioned." Heidegger does not hold French politics in the 1920s and 1930s responsible for the collapse, but rather France's inability to place itself creatively on the metaphysical path from Descartes to Nietzsche. Heidegger interprets the history of metaphysics with slogans from the contemporary propaganda wars; for example, Nietzsche's talk of "justice" in which the will to power lurks is illustrated by the differing judgments of the French, Germans, and English concerning the shelling of the French fleet by the British at Oran.

The Hölderlin lecture course from summer 1942 again emphasizes the "historical uniqueness" or "historical singularity" of National Socialism. This singularity is not understood, particularly by those academic partisans and fellow travelers who find in the Greek polis "politics" as it is proclaimed in the twentieth century and required by National Socialism. For Heidegger the Greek polis is the place of what is questionable, where even masters and slaves must come to differentiate themselves. On the other hand, "[t]he 'political' is the accomplishment of history. Because the political is thus the technical-historical certainty at the basis of all action, the 'political' is distinguished by the unconditional unquestionability of itself. The unquestionability of the 'political' and its totality belong together."[12] When with the collapse of the Sixth German Army at Stalingrad it finally became obvious to everyone that the German grab at continentally based world domination had failed, Heidegger once again claimed in his Parmenides lecture course of winter 1942–43: "Technology *is* our history." Heidegger said—still within Jünger's opposition between bourgeois and worker—that the "bourgeois world" does not understand "contemporary Russia's metaphysical passion for technology" which brings everything into "laboring accomplishment." "Whoever has ears to hear, i.e., whoever can see the metaphysical grounds and abysses of history and can take them seriously *as* metaphysical, could have heard what Lenin was saying already two decades ago: Bolshevism is Soviet power + electrification. That means: Bolshevism is the 'organic,' i.e., the organized and calculative (as +), merger of the unconditional power of the party with complete technologization."

For Heidegger, the alienation of what is genuinely Russian in favor of a thoroughly West European "Bolshevism" is a threat; but the starting point of his fear is rather the alienated "bourgeois" spirit in America as a land without origins. (Jünger spoke of "Americanism"; talk of "Americanization" seems to have taken on its virulence only after the Second World War.) If Heidegger also sees alienation in National Socialism, it is of course not because he follows the Marxist thesis that capitalism must lead to imperialism and finally seek its salvation in fascism. The "total politics" of which Heidegger speaks is not the "totalitarianism" which, after the Second World War, was introduced from a liberal and democratic perspective to cover both fascism and communism (by Hannah Arendt, responding to the shock of the experience of terror and the liquidation of millions in Siberia and Auschwitz, and by others in a more formalistic way). It is characteristic of Heidegger that he did not anchor unquestionability, in which every totalitarianism seeks to stabilize itself, in the concept of ideology, but in the concept of world-view (which, e.g., governs every posing of questions as Dilthey, still within the spirit of the age of Goethe, developed it). One must not overlook the fact that with the question of who man will in the future be, and in what forms of life, Heidegger renounces as mere stabilization through world-view not only the great totalitarianisms but also neo-Scholastic philosophy as support for theology and the de-scientification of theology by recourse to an existential interpretation in the sense of *Being and Time*. Thus the second Hölderlin lecture course asserts that Hölderlin's turn to the Fatherland and to the ownmost [*Eigenen*], and with these to the way toward a new union through the "holy," cannot at all be comprehended "theologically" since all "theology" already presupposes the *theos*, God, "and this so certainly, that wherever theology arises God has always already begun to take flight." "Neither the theologians of the 'German Christians,' nor those of the Confessional Front [*Bekenntnisfront*], nor the Catholic ones, can find the holy of the Fatherland. They are in the same situation as the biologists, the pre-historians, and the art historians; supposedly in touch with reality, they pursue and blindly carry on a kind of 'intellectualism' which not even the much-maligned nineteenth century can match. In an age when the world threatens to fall out of joint, the ownmost is not to be snatched up so cheaply."[13]

When in the course of his critical confrontation with Nietzsche, Heidegger concretely pictured the fundamental tendencies of the age, he could no longer assume that great creators display the truth of Being in a work for a historical community or people. The sketches for overcoming, or recovery from, metaphysics define the Führer as the functionary of a total mobilization who can capture the "instinct" for the ordering and securing of the whole in a plan and can thus, for example, combine the directing of literary efforts in the cultural sector with the general directing of pregnancy and breeding. Not the great creators but these functionaries define the age; not works but machinations; not peoples but the totalitarianisms in an alienated struggle for world domination. In spite of this, Heidegger stays with the task of seeking other beginnings for the future from out of the ownmost origin, so that perhaps the truth of Being may once again be experienced as the imprescribable claim of the holy. In the process Heidegger, like Nietzsche and like Hölderlin, reaches back to the form humanity took on after the neolithic revolution and before industrial culture. As the outbreak of World War II threatened, Heidegger prematurely closed his Nietzsche lecture course of summer 1939 with Hölderlin's verses about the shepherd who dwells apart on the green slopes in holy shadows. In his third Hölderlin lecture course Heidegger discussed the hymn in which Hölderlin names the Ister—the upper Danube valley, Heidegger's homeland. He supplemented the manuscript of the lecture with the following remark, not included in the published text: "Perhaps the poet Hölderlin must become a destiny of decisive confrontation for a thinker whose grandfather was born at the same time the 'Ister Hymn' and the poem 'Andenken' originated—according to the records, in the sheepfold of a dairy farm in Ovili, which lies in the upper Danube valley near the bank of the river, beneath the cliffs. The hidden history of Saying knows no accidents. Everything is dispensation [*Schickung*]." To one of the grandchildren of the shepherd spoken of by Hölderlin (Heidegger wants to say) fell the task of asking, by way of an "occidental conversation" with Hölderlin, how man can once again become "the shepherd of Being" and win back a homeland. If one excludes the great politicizing pseudo-myths, it will be difficult to find many examples in our century of such self-mythologizing.

II

To what sort of philosophy does a thinking lead which, like Heidegger's, sees itself called to politics but fails in its concrete engagement? In the present context this question can be directed toward only one of Heidegger's works, the *Beiträge zur Philosophie* of 1936–38, which may well be considered his main work. These *Beiträge* follow the new point of departure to which Heidegger found his way in 1929–30; they seek to experience the truth of Being as *Ereignis,* as that clearing for the self-concealing which can then become a "pathmark" [*"Wegspur"*] to the holy. Heidegger sees himself as unique and alone in following this pathmark, far ahead of his age. Thus, against the "contemporaries" he directs that polemic formerly associated with the "They" and then with the "average citizen." In philosophy these contemporaries take refuge in "new" themes, and by introducing the "political" and the "racial" they busy themselves with dressing up old set pieces from academic philosophy, though they don't admit it. They are hardly worth mentioning even in turning away from them toward the thoughtful grounding of Dasein as the moment-site of the truth of Being in which man, "far away and beyond," as the most distant is once again in the service of what is nearest, the fleeing away [*Flucht*] of the gods (5 [BP 5/18]). Heidegger analyzes an age in danger of bypassing every essential decision, an age which renounces the fight for standards, and names its basic tendencies: calculation, which shows itself in the priority of organization; hurried living, which is caught up in the highest achievements of mechanical enhancement and does not know the stillness of growth; the awakening of "mass-ness" [*"Massenhaften"*], which wants to make everything common and does not acknowledge what is rare (the schooling required here is just the opposite of the genuine School as leisure and reflection); the exposing, publicizing, and vulgarization of emotion through amplified stimulation; the wholly unquestionable character of all machinations; the tritest sentimentality which is always sniveling about "experiences" (82, 83 [BP 57, 58/119–124]). On the basis of baselessness the various world-views contend for priority: Christianity asserts God's transcendence, which nevertheless is available for securing salvation; the appeal to a "people" denies this transcendence; liberalism takes ideas and values as transcendence—not such as to live or die for, but to be actualized through culture. Any two of these transcendences, or all three, can be mixed together: the idea of a people and Christianity, the idea of a people and cultural politics, Christianity and culture (7 [BP 7/24–25]).

What had developed in Germany, however, was for Heidegger only an example of that which prevailed in this historical hour generally. Thus of science, which is becoming mere specialization and as "positive" comprehends what is pregiven, Heidegger says that it may as easily be put into service Bolshevistically as liberalistically, politically, or in the name of a people. Only a thoroughly modern "liberal" science, with its postulate of the priority of procedure over the things themselves, can subjugate itself to various ends: to the technicity in Bolshevism as well as the four-year plan and political education in National Socialism. In this situation talk of a crisis of science is indeed mere chatter; what really counts is whether, for example, the "Volkish" or the "Americanistic" organization has the greater means and powers at its rapid and complete disposal. Wanting to present itself as a business and striving for the appropriate Institutes in the Kaiser Wilhelm Society, history in this context becomes journalistic reportage or else that sort of historical apologetics which can be traced back to Augustine's *Civitas dei* (101 [BP 76/148, 152–154]). The idea of "world-view," which was first applied to "poet-philosophers" like Nietzsche, becomes a total faith or a total politics and so apologetics or propaganda; in every case it stands in contrast to the "authoritative" [*"herrschaftlich"*] knowing of philosophy as the ability to question (14 [BP 14/38, 41, 36]).

The question about, and reflection upon, who we ourselves are comes to conflict with that "self-certainty," the "innermost essence" of "liberalism," which takes world-view, personality, genius, and culture as theater props and values to be actualized. As the end form of Marxism—a West European possibility having nothing to do with Judaism or even Russianness (in which a not yet developed spiritualism slumbers)—Bolshevism colonizes this same territory of certainty concerning humanity. Heidegger tries to reduce the slogans of the time to absurdity: to the extent that the rule of reason as the equality of everyone is the consequence of Christianity, and this is at bottom (according to Nietzsche's idea of the slave rebellion in morality) Jewish in origin, Bolshevism is indeed Jewish; but then Christianity is also at bottom Bolshevistic. Most likely Heidegger did not know that Dietrich Eckart, the poet who especially inspired Hitler, unfolds these lines of thought in full seriousness, and that Hitler in his table-talk followed him. But the abysmal lack of understanding which Nietzsche (or the young Marx in his work on the Jewish question) brought to the Old Testament is not improved upon by Heidegger in his desire to pave the way toward "a justification of the West from its history" (19 [BP 19/53–54]).[14]

In a cursory way *Being and Time* had already related the fate of the individual to the destiny of a people; still, one could interpret the talk of Existentials as supposedly giving an account of atemporal structures of Dasein in general. Here, in contrast, Heidegger raises the questions of "who" we "ourselves" authentically are, and of how to speak about the characteristics of this Da-sein, in a new way. These characteristics are related to a historical situation, to that decision which divides an end from another beginning and so requires those "designated ones" [*"Gezeichneten"*] whom Heidegger addresses as the "futural ones" [*"Zukünftigen"*]—those few individuals who are open and exposed for the grounding of the moment-site of the truth of Being. This grounding gets related to poetry, thinking, deed, and sacrifice; but when Heidegger comes to specify who these individuals are his reference is to Hölderlin, Nietzsche, van Gogh—and there is no longer any talk of politicians. With these few individuals belong the "countless allies" who carry forth the grounding of the few, and the many who are related to one another by way of a common origin (45 [BP 45/96]). If one must talk of a people, then this is never something given (neither race nor class), but first becomes such by hearkening to a common call, the voice of the people, of which Hölderlin spoke (15, 221 [BP 15/42, 196/319]).

Heidegger does not deny that a first step can even lie in organizing the masses; it is a kind of cease and desist order which stands up to progressive deracination (25 [BP 25/62]). However, in the fact that with "cinema and trips to the beach" those "cultural goods" which until now remained closed to most people are available to everyone, Heidegger sees a settling into nihilism. It unites the closed eyes in the face of aimlessness, the "joiner's" evasion of decision, the anxiety before the disclosure of a realm of decision, and the gigantic arrangements for passing over anxiety by the vacuous but pervasive talk of "providence" and the "lord God." On the basis of what it accomplishes socially, then, this decisionlessness in regard to Being and the holy can claim to be the "most christian Christianity." Heidegger maintains that this decisionlessness itself is the criterion of nihilism, not whether churches and monasteries are destroyed or whether, on the other hand, this is not done and Christianity is allowed to go on its way (97 [BP 72/139]). But this shows that the idea of the participation of everyone in a common task remains just as foreign to Heidegger as the conviction that there is a human "right" to freedom of belief and security of life and that philosophy is foremost to defend this right. With Nietzsche, Heidegger emphasizes the "order of rank," the division of human Being into masters and slaves, and even the distinction of the "eminent ones" ["*Vornehmen*"]. In this context, however, the question of the "order of rank" is understood as a "transitional question," namely, as the necessity for distinction and "uniqueness, in order to accomplish the disclosure of Being" (139 [BP 114/224]).

Heidegger traces the basic tendencies of the present age back to the confluence of "machination" ["*Machenschaft*"] and "experience," and he identifies steps toward this goal in the distinction between *poiesis* and *techne,* the determination of entities as *ens creatum,* and the modern recourse to the subject. What has been called "disenchantment" (European rationalism in Max Weber's sense) is in truth enchantment and bewitchment through the unquestionability of machination in calculation, utility, breeding, regulation, and even "taste" (84 [BP 59/124]). Experience, in the various forms of subjectivity, can ally with this enchantment since for its part it suppresses every genuine decision. But merely to distinguish the Greek polis from every total world-view and total politics is not enough; the moment-site of the truth of Being must be experienced anew for the future.

Thus the *Beiträge* concludes with two sections on "The Futural Ones" and the "Passing [*Vorbeigang*] of the Ultimate God." The futural ones ground the There [*Da*] of the truth of Being as clearing for the self-concealing and thus as pathmark for the holy; they accomplish "history" in a unique sense of the word. If the moment as maturation of time is fulfilled in the encounter with the holy or divine, then it gains the freedom to be able to withdraw; time as history wheels around into eternity. This eternity is no longer thought as *aeternitas* (not even as *sempiternitas* or as eternal return), but as "passing." Here Heidegger joins up with the phenomenology of religion, for which the numinous is the fleeting, the transitory which has its appointed hour. In his first lecture course on Hölderlin he appeals to the preliminary drafts of *Friedensfeier,* where the divinities are called the fleet transients. It is significant that in Hölderlin this characterization refers to Christ. Due to his current anti-Christian sentiments, Heidegger suppresses this reference by quoting a text variant: Christianity, which has absorbed Platonism and the modern orientation toward certainty, is taken as the consummate opposite to that experience which elevates the essence of the divine into the highest and the "ultimate" of God, into the passing and its imprescribability. When the final version of *Friedensfeier* was discovered in the fifties, Heidegger showed sympathy for the thesis that Peace, as the Prince of the Festival, was Napoleon, or at least bore some resemblance; but by that time he took Hitler's "silly comparison of himself to Napoleon" to be a stumbling block to the reenactment of Hölderlin's poetry.[15]

As a thinking which prepares the way (or as formal-indicating hermeneutics, as Heidegger said in the 1920s), philosophy can only produce a kind of readiness within the realm of political or religious decision; it can neither anticipate this decision nor relieve anyone of it. In the lecture course from winter 1937–38 Heidegger quotes the definition of philosophy from paragraph 16 of the *Beiträge:* "Philosophy is the immediately useless but nonetheless authoritative knowing of the essence of things." (Curiously, while the editor does mention that Heidegger's marginal comment to the lecture—that "the passing of the ultimate God" had to remain unsaid—alludes to the *Beiträge,* he does not indicate that the lecture in many places repeats popular and didactic maxims from the *Beiträge* and that indeed the original plan called for doing this to a greater extent than turned out in fact to be possible.) Philosophy is "authoritative" because it returns to origins and thus preserves the higher rank of the originary and free as opposed to the late and fallen; yet in so doing it discovers that the authoritative belongs to those who have foundered: to Antigone, Hölderlin, Nietzsche, van Gogh. Furthermore, philosophy is useless, that is, not to be placed directly in the service of historical self-assertion (as Heidegger still tried to do in 1933). Such philosophy is the opposite of, and resistance to, National Socialism which at the time was arming itself for the struggle for world domination and thus precisely was not seeking reflection but the unquestionability of a total world-view and a total politics. Nevertheless, this philosophy knows itself to be bound up with the "uniqueness" of National Socialism in the determination of the historical task of the Germans: to confront, at this historical high noon, the urgent press of modernity revealing itself to be deracination by means of universal technology, and so to overcome and recover from the spread of technology through the full experience of that which is.

This definition of the task of philosophy is not false because it proposes the self-concealing as a limit on the relation of knowing to openness; in this respect the definition does justice to reality and is not by itself a "demonization" of Being and truth. It is false because it is understood in a one-sided speculative, "authoritative," way. Heidegger is certainly justified in claiming that the creative poet cannot succeed in his poetic venture on the basis of the arrangements of an art league or a citizens group, or on the basis of cultural political instructions, viz., the directives of a Stalin or a Goebbels. But the task of philosophy (let alone politics!) is not to be defined solely by analogy with such poetry. Because a philosophizing in the manner of the *Beiträge* genuinely recognizes neither the Other (except for a partnership with poetry) nor others who think differently, it cannot even enter into a process of critical testing with respect to itself (which of course cannot lead to an absolute knowledge, as it does in Hegel's *Phenomenology*).[16]

III

In the remarks about his rectorship from the years 1945–46, Heidegger attributes the real guilt to those who, in the decisive years around 1930, failed to recognize the mounting nihilism and did not see the national revolution as a possible countermovement which had to be kept free from the abuses of the National Socialist racial doctrine and the instrumentalization of knowledge and spirit. For Heidegger, the fact that the Second World War fundamentally altered the political constellation of the world was not enough for it to be considered epoch-making. It decided nothing essential (i.e., in the confrontation with nihilism), though it did decisively inaugurate total mobilization (ultimately through the deployment of the atom bomb as a means of war and as a threat for the future). Spengler had once been powerfully effective by introducing the language of "decline" into the age, a challenge which Heidegger immediately took up. The theology which tried to find the eternal in the moment saw the challenge as well. Thus in a 1920 article, "Between the Ages" ["Zwischen den Zeiten"], whose name subsequently became that of an important journal, Friedrich Gogarten wrote: "Today is a time of decline. We are seeing the disintegration in everything." Since the end of the twenties, through Nietzsche's tragic world experience and through the Greeks, Heidegger sought to view the decline in a new way. Thus, under the title "The Futural Ones," the *Beiträge* could formulate our historical hour as "the generation of decline." After 1945, with Trakl, Heidegger spoke of a decline which would lead to separation; in trying to translate Lao-Tse he wandered, as did the latter according to the famous legend, out beyond his own land.[17]

On April 8, 1950, Heidegger wrote to Jaspers that the current lack of a homeland [*Heimatlosigkeit*] was not without event; it conceals an advent whose distant sign we are perhaps experiencing. "The matter of evil is not at an end, but only now entered upon a worldwide phase. Stalin no longer needs to declare war; every day he wins a battle. There can no longer be any evasion. Each word and each writing is to be a counterattack, if not in the political sphere which has long since been trumped by other relations of Being and continues to lead only an illusory existence." Apparently, the presupposition for experiencing the "distant sign" was that one abstained from every mere restoration. When Reinhold Schneider experienced the consequences of his uncompromising refusals Heidegger, who had no ties to Schneider, personally professed himself to be in sympathy. In a discussion on the "zero-meridian" of nihilism, Heidegger cautioned Ernst Jünger against any premature hope. In the addenda to *Der Arbeiter* Jünger had written: "In coprophagous palaces one generation after another fattens on the excrement of its precursors. One does not thrive only on the accomplishments of the fathers, one also thrives on their outrages." He saw the German's indecisiveness in the fact that in 1813, 1848, and 1918 he neither established himself in the principles of 1789 nor dismissed them and their forms in a believable way. "In 1933 the last opportunity was let slip. Since then it has gone as with every decision too long put off: it became irrelevant."[18]

Heidegger sought to think in broader horizons; his demand for a "turn" was presented on the basis of what he had once taken up into his "Freiburg National Socialism," i.e., the reflections on Heraclitus and on the origin of the work of art, made public without their one-time political context. Hölderlin was heard through his echo in Trakl. If the *Beiträge* spoke of "the" history and anchored the essence, the "ultimate," of the divine in this history or indeed in the passing, these paradoxical ways of speaking are now set aside, and Heidegger comes to ask after possible paths in the *plural*. The decisive challenge is advanced technology through which the totalitarianism of National Socialism, with its lesser technology, appears as the possible prelude to a far worse future. Is there still "that which saves" [*"Rettendes"*]? In his reflections on Klee (especially on viewing the collection of paintings now shown in Düsseldorf) Heidegger specified which function art in the age of technology could have. Klee's art does not copy the image of any visible thing; instead it unfolds the possibilities for formation out of itself and thus makes visible what then might also exhibit a correspondence with something real (for example, a star or tree). In so doing, such art absorbs into itself the essence of the technical which, even in cosmological or biological knowledge, is to construct the real from its own formative powers. But art ties this construction and reconstruction back to fateful finitude which (already in the "lyrical" captions to the paintings) is brought to expression together with it. Thus it brings the spread of technology to a stand, whereas political revolutions and reforms for the most part merely make unreflective use of it.

Heidegger's thinking provided the first decades after the Second World War with decisive impulses, and Heidegger observed these developments closely; but his own thinking had nothing more to do with such effects. The theological discussion which took off from Bultmann remained as foreign to him as the revival of metaphysics, the rehabilitation of practical philosophy, and the working out of hermeneutic phenomenology. Sartre's engagement had already implicated Heidegger in a new protest movement. Wasn't Heidegger's critique of totalitarian tendencies the best he had to offer to political philosophy? Heidegger's thinking, which had stood in proximity to National Socialism, was linked to the Resistance as a defense of the ancestral homeland. Was it not simply a macabre accident that with his authentic "breakthrough" Heidegger fell into proximity with Hitler, spoiling everything that was expected from him, while a writer like Saint-Exupéry, for example, could become a hero and martyr of the Resistance against Hitler's totalitarianism? If one opens the writings of Saint-Exupéry, which Heidegger indeed loved, one finds trains of thought in which fascistoid tendencies are at least as glaringly evident as in Heidegger's occasional remarks on political questions. Was it not thus perfectly understandable that Heidegger got involved with the French Resistance fighter to whom, immediately after the war, some people made pilgrimages as to a kindred spirit? Heidegger even dedicated his book *On the Way to Language* to René Char with the sentence: "Is the beloved Provence the mysterious invisible bridge from the early thoughts of Parmenides to the poems of Hölderlin?"[19] In *Der Spiegel*'s interview he made reference to a conversation with René Char, the "poet and Resistance fighter": "Rocket installations are now being built in Provence, and the countryside is being unimaginably desolated. The poet, who certainly cannot be accused of sentimentality and glorification of the idyllic, said to me that this continuing deracination of man going on there is the end, unless thinking and poetizing once again ascend to nonviolent power." When the partisan Resistance turned into a resistance against existing alienation in the name of a utopia, reform Marxism could produce variants incorporating Heidegger in the search for socialism with a human face. Indeed when, starting in Paris, it finally came to a battle against logocentrism as Eurocentrism, one appealed to Heidegger.

After Heidegger's death, when *Der Spiegel* published an interview with the philosopher from the year 1966, there was a rude awakening for those, at least, who had drawn upon Heidegger in discussing philosophy and politics. Heidegger rejected concrete political efforts in favor of the dictum: "Only a god can save us now." That meant a god such as had presided over Athenian life from the Parthenon and such as belonged to Cézanne's efforts to bring the original and the simple into an image. Furthermore, Heidegger formulated a consistent renunciation of all hopes that were placed in democracy (which admittedly had been cast in a dubious light at the time through false "demands for democratization"). Heidegger referred to the summer 1935 lecture course in which he had spoken of the uniqueness of National Socialism and had, through an inserted remark, determined this uniqueness as an encounter with planetary technology. The intervening thirty years had supposedly made it clearer "that the planetary movement of modern technology is a power whose history-determining magnitude can hardly be overestimated." Thereupon Heidegger said unmistakably (to the extent that one can attribute something said in an interview entirely to him): "For me the decisive question today is how this technological age can be subjected to a political system, and to which system. I know no answer to that question, but I am not convinced that democracy is the way." When

Karl-Heinz Volkmann-Schluck, for example, refers to Tocqueville's warning about the tyranny of the majority and expounds the tendency to more equality and participation as the law of our history, one may well resist the wholesale manner in which a schema of the "history of being" covers over the differentiated juristic argumentation. That such a conception could see itself as following along Heidegger's path would be hard to dispute, however.[20] If Heidegger said with all decisiveness, at least in conversations, that in 1933 he had been thoroughly deluded and that nothing could excuse this delusion, he also lends support to efforts to avoid such delusions in the future.

Of course, one must always ask oneself whether Heidegger doesn't speak a language which has become impossible. Thus the conclusion to the little story "Der Feldweg" refers to the "stillness" surrounding the path, castle, and church, and says: "It reaches up to those who were sacrificed before their time through two World Wars." Heidegger did not use Hölderlin's words to speak of death for the Fatherland of course, but of self-sacrifice, yet without the least sense for how often such self-sacrifice made the business of concentration camps possible. Not a word about that which even Ernst Jünger himself had said early on, in the paper "Der Friede," about the extermination camps: "These murderous caves will be fixed in man's memory for ages; they are the authentic memorials of this war, as earlier were the Douaumont and Langemarck." It would certainly be philosophically justified to prosecute Antigone's deed in an age which, though driving Germans and Frenchmen to their graves together, nevertheless argues over Katyn, and in worldwide propaganda measures wants to deprive the former of their dead who, as "Germans," are accused of exterminating millions without graves.[21] The argument that total mobilization also produces corpses may not ignore the fact that the dead in Siberia and Auschwitz were killed before their death, namely in the murder of their dignity, while the dead of Hiroshima were not. Nevertheless, one of those who escaped the gas chambers wrote that the survivors of an atomic war could be so affected that "if the gas chambers still existed" they "would line up voluntarily before their gates." Ernst Tugendhat perceived a "frankly fantastic Atlantic ethnocentrism" in the fact that the existence of humanity was put at risk in order to preserve a "political system." Such argumentation overlooks the fact that total mobilization of the powers of production in a political system where the authorities absolutize the denial of participation by withholding information brings with it great dangers even, for example, in the "peaceful" use of atomic energy. Heidegger would like to work in opposition to such systems, but not on a path within the political sphere.

Doesn't the politically unconcretized thesis of "technology" as the ultimate "metaphysics" repeat the abstract emphasis on "the" worker? And doesn't this abstractness plainly call out to be appropriated by very different political options? Heidegger, for example, in his word of greeting to the 1974 Heidegger Symposium in Beirut, restricted himself to a sketch of his last great theme, "Contemporary Natural Science and Modern Technology"; and he was then able to address an American colloquium with almost the same words.[22] But Beirut is not the Black Forest; there it was not possible to disregard contentions, for example, that 120 million Arabs awaited the new prophets. In its second report the Club of Rome had recommended to the oil sheiks that they invest their capital in major scientific-technical projects of their own, e.g., in undertakings to gather solar energy from the desert and make it transportable. But is it possible to adopt the natural sciences, engineering, and biological sciences without at the same time developing the human sciences? While Europe (particularly in the Jewish and Christian tradition) made its religious origin into a matter for free research, as Buddhistically influenced religiosity had similarly done since time immemorial, in the Islamic world questions of biblical criticism are widely prohibited. But even in our context can one dismiss the human sciences with Nietzsche's thesis that a historical phenomenon is dead if it is fully "dissected"? It was certainly astonishing to see texts by Hölderlin in Arabic script. Where does the national rebirth lead which Hölderlin was supposed to represent (while in the meantime in Europe he represented complete refusal)? Kemal Ataturk had secularized Turkey instead of building up the Medresen universities, but the new scientific-technical world remained empty of meaning and so people wanted to recover their own origin too, at least through compromises. In other Islamic lands it was just those intellectuals who had studied in Europe and had caught cold from its alienations who made up the ranks of the fanatics seeking a breakthrough to what was authentically their own. But in these fanatics Europe encountered only itself: having cut itself off from its origin through the development of science and technology it had then, in a self-destructive awakening, compelled the pincers in which it lay to do their work.

Was it not the duty of philosophizing to learn from these experiences? Continental European philosophy after the Second World War arrived at a rehabilitation of practical philosophy into which many Heideggerian impulses also entered. Philosophy was no longer to join up with political tendencies blindly and without orientation; no longer would it offer a radicality divorced from reality, to be led around by the nose in any desired direction by some political party or other. There is no doubt that Heidegger supported efforts of this sort when they exhibited a certain reflectiveness. Thus, already in his 1955 contribution to the Festschrift for Ernst Jünger, he wrote that one has a mistaken idea of thinking if one subjects it to the "presumptuous demand" that it "know the solution to the riddles and bring salvation." "In the face of this it deserves full agreement when you point out the necessity of letting all still untapped springs of power flow and of bringing every aid to bear in order to hold one's own 'in the wake of nihilism.'" If this is the way Heidegger encouraged his students or visitors before shutting the door behind them, he himself nevertheless stuck by that radicality which could find hope only in a transformation of the fundamental ground itself.

In his long letter to Jünger, Heidegger quite rightly warned of the illusion in thinking that one has already passed over the zero-meridian of nihilism and once again has a rich field before one's eyes. "Perhaps the zero-line is suddenly emerging before us in the form of a planetary catastrophe. Who will then cross it? And what can catastrophes do? The two World Wars neither checked the movement of nihilism nor diverted it from its course." Heidegger supposed that he could countenance political nihilism, which neither maintains anything definite nor brings anything to completion, because he wanted to set himself upon a path through the radical recovery from nihilism and thus would initially be content merely with "constructing the path." But then is it not shocking that Heidegger returned to that point of departure with which he had once served Hitler, viz., that he traced Nietzsche's struggle for domination of the earth back to the Polemos of Heraclitus, to the confrontation over the truth of Being which first lets gods and men, freemen and slaves appear?[23] Is not even Hölderlin's poetry turned into its opposite by the use Heidegger makes of it? At least in his final shattering efforts Hölderlin's concern had been to learn to endure patiently the night of the loss of meaning; it was not this loss of meaning that was for him the danger —as Heidegger supposed—but rather that immediate nearness of the divine such as is sought in breakthrough and awakening. One wonders whether the tragic greatness which Heidegger demanded did not, at least sometimes, stand closer to the tragedy of Thomas Mann's Dr. Faustus than it did to Hölderlin or Sophocles.

Heidegger rightly points out that the "polis" is worlds apart from that totality of the political which was sheltered within the ideologies of our century. If the polis is the site of struggle, then for Heidegger this also meant that Hölderlin is not one among others, that he does not even belong with Goethe and Schiller, and thus only after a hundred years did his greatest poems find ears to hear them. But doesn't the radicality with which Heidegger seeks confrontation and differentiation dismiss without discernment what had been built up over centuries, e.g., the "metaphysics" which is merely to be overcome now, or the despised "civic spirit" ["*Bürgerlichkeit*"]? Since Marx and Nietzsche, and since movements like the youth movement, it is no longer thought necessary to ask what civic spirit once was and how in different forms it remains a task for the future. When the polis was no longer taken merely as something established by an individual like Theseus but seen as a communal issue for free men, one spoke of the *koinonia politike,* and later this expression was rendered as "civil society." Hegel could link the expression to experiences characteristically found in the communes of the northern European trade and commerce cities; thus he could newly define civil society in terms of economics and posit its relation to the sphere of the state in a different way. If it was subsequently shown that the mutual understanding of the citizens over common issues again and again became frozen into unjustified privileges and thus fell to open-ended history as a task, this did not demand abandoning altogether the point of departure in the heritage of civic account-giving concerning the administration of common issues. On the contrary, in the divergent tendencies which link themselves to the name "democracy" one may see attempts to win back the covenant of the citizenry. The participation of all in the administration of common concerns, which lies beyond the distinction between bourgeois and worker, the working out of the corresponding social structures, the accord over basic rights which was accomplished through history, belong to these attempts.

Heidegger remained consistent with his very different convictions: in 1933, when he had assumed responsibility in the sphere of the University, he eliminated the traditional self-administration and collegial system in favor of the *Führerprinzip;* in 1966, in *Der Spiegel's* interview, he once again declared his conviction that democracy was not a political system able to deal with the problems of technological world civilization. Concerning his 1933 involvement Heidegger alleged that the jumble of parties in which the Weimar Republic ended up was the best indication of the necessity for following other paths. Are today's parliaments able to do anything about the arms race and rampant overpopulation? Alternatively, one must ask of Heidegger whether he did not dangerously misunderstand the autonomy of the political sphere by, on the one hand, demanding too much of it (a transformation from its very ground) and, on the other, by conceding it too much (the risk in the actions of a Führer or, the opposite side of the coin, the refusal vis-à-vis everything existing).

Is the citizen despicable because he seeks to come to mutual understanding only about those things for which one does not live or die? The bourgeois movement does in fact live by renouncing the desire to solve metaphysical questions about death or salvation, instead seeking compromises about what is achievable and a minimal consensus. Realistically, with Luther, *Being and Time* had still left it open whether man was "drunk" with sin; but the political consequences were never drawn, viz., that therefore politics cannot stake everything on the transformation of man, but must accept the fact that out of fear of the consequences of their actions human beings must submit these actions to norms. This mutual understanding based on fear is thoroughly compatible with openness for the new, but it will require a legitimation for the assumption of risks and will not allow the actions of the politician the freedom which can be granted to the creative artist in his field. Admittedly, the development of technology has made political problems more acute in ways never before known. The possibility Heidegger had in view is genuine, viz., that Stalinism and National Socialism, with their relatively primitive technology, could be merely the prelude to a far more destruc-

Otto Pöggeler

tive future. But does this permit one to see structures in the new hege-
monic powers which, beneath the political drapery, tread the path to
battle over world domination, not with reason but with power alone,
having long since eliminated the distinction between war and peace? If
there is that European responsibility upon which Heidegger in his way
insisted, then this responsibility lies, after the self-destruction of Europe
as the one-time center of the world, in pointing to those limited changes
for a prudent politics which in spite of everything may well remain.

Translated by Steven Galt Crowell

Notes

1. See Martin Heidegger, *Einführung in die Metaphysik* (Tübingen, 1953),
p. 36 (*Introduction to Metaphysics,* translated by Ralph Manheim [New York:
Doubleday, 1961], p. 39); Martin Heidegger, *Hölderlins Hymne "Der Ister"*
(Frankfurt a.M., 1984), p. 68f. The quote from Thomas Mann's diary in what
follows is from the lecture "Der Nationalsozialismus als Versuchung" by Fritz
Stern, in Fritz Stern and Hans Jonas, *Reflexionen finsterer Zeit* (Tübingen,
1984), p. 48. On Heidegger and Kroner, see the article, "Ein Faktum," in
Frankfurter Allgemeine Zeitung, January 2, 1984. Further, see Martin Heidegger, *Hölderlins Hymnen "Germanien" und "Der Rhein"* (Frankfurt a.M., 1980),
pp. 26ff. On National Socialist "politics" with regard to the Jews, see the
summary of research on the topic in Andreas Hillgruber, *Zweierlei Untergang.
die Zerschlagung des Deutschen Reiches und das Ende des europäischen Juden-
tums* (Berlin, 1986), pp. 75ff.
2. Martin Heidegger, *Hölderlins Hymnen "Germanien" und "Der Rhein,"*
p. 254; Martin Heidegger, *Parmenides* (Frankfurt a.M., 1982), pp. 227ff. On
the following, see Martin Heidegger, *Unterwegs zur Sprache* (Pfullingen, 1959),
p. 190 (*On the Way to Language,* translated by Peter D. Hertz [New York:
Harper and Row, 1971], p. 84).
3. Weizsäcker's report is found in G. Neske, ed., *Erinnerung an Martin
Heidegger* (Pfullingen, 1977), p. 245f. On the most recent discussions, see my
review "Den Führer führen? Heidegger und kein Ende," in *Philosophische Rundschau* 32:26–67, 1985. On the *Beiträge,* see the quotations from this book in
my *Der Denkweg Martin Heideggers* (Pfullingen, 1963, 1983) (*Martin Heidegger's Path of Thinking,* translated by Daniel Magurshak and Sigmund Barber
[New York: Humanities Press, 1989]) and further the summary report in my
essay "Heidegger und die hermeneutische Theologie" in the Festschrift for Gerhard Ebeling, *Verifikationen,* edited by E. Jüngel (Tübingen, 1982), pp. 475–

498. (Translator's note: When the present essay was written the *Beiträge zur Philosophie* had not yet been published. It is now available as volume 65 of the *Gesamtausgabe*, edited by F. W. von Herrmann [Frankfurt: Klostermann, 1989]. In section II of the present essay Pöggeler quotes from the unpublished manuscript, which is divided into numbered sections. As von Herrmann indicates in the editor's afterword to the published version, his rearrangement of the manuscript material meant that the numbering of the sections no longer corresponded exactly to the unpublished version. Thus, Pöggeler's references to these sections, given in the body of the essay, do not correspond to the numbers in the *Gesamtausgabe*. Where such references occur I have adopted the convention of first listing the number which Pöggeler gives, following it in square brackets with the published number, a slash, and the relevant page numbers, e.g., (82 [BP 57/ 119]).) On the following, see Martin Heidegger, *Heraklit* (Frankfurt a.M., 1979), pp. 107f., 123, 181, 204, 209, 203; Martin Heidegger, *Was Heisst Denken?* (Tübingen, 1954), pp. 65ff. (*What is Called Thinking?*, translated by J. Glenn Gray [New York: Harper and Row, 1968], pp. 66–67; translation modified). On Nietzsche and Russia, see D. Tschizewskij and D. Groh, eds., *Europa und Russland* (Darmstadt, 1959), pp. 512ff. Also see below, n. 12. (Translator's note: Passages from Friedrich Nietzsche, *Twilight of the Idols*, are taken from *The Portable Nietzsche*, translated by Walter Kaufmann [New York: Viking, 1968], p. 543.)

4. There is a report on Hegel's lost letter to von Uexküll in Karl Rosenkranz, *G. W. F. Hegels Leben* (Berlin, 1844), p. 304. Bismarck's prognosis is cited from A. Hillgruber (see n. 1 above), p. 73. The corresponding statement from Marx is in Ernst Nolte, *Deutschland und der Kalte Krieg*, 2d ed. (Stuttgart, 1985), pp. 29ff. Cf. Alexis de Tocqueville, *Über die Demokratie in Amerika* (München, 1976), pp. 478f., 289ff., 393 (*Democracy in America*, translated by George Lawrence [Garden City, N.Y.: Doubleday, 1969], p. 339).

5. On Jaspers, see Baumgarten in K. Piper and H. Saner, eds., *Erinnerungen an Karl Jaspers* (München/Zürich, 1974), p. 127. That in 1933 Jaspers supported Heidegger on his path toward the Rectorate is due to that political blindness which is evident in several respects. Cf. the recollections of Werner Ehrengberg and Heinrich Liepmann in the previously cited volume, pp. 40f. and 51f. On the concept of *Volk* in *Being and Time*, p. 384 (Martin Heidegger, *Being and Time*, translated by John Macquarrie and Edward Robinson [New York: Harper and Row, 1962], p. 436). The early text on Abraham of Santa Clara is now in Martin Heidegger, *Denkerfahrungen* (Frankfurt a.M., 1983), pp. 1ff. If Heidegger proceeded from Lueger to F. Naumann, it is well known that Hitler also admired, for different reasons, the demagogic power of Lueger, which also availed itself of petty bourgeois anti-Semitism. Hitler called Lueger "the most forceful German mayor of all time" and "the last great German of the *Ostmark.*" Cf. Joachim C. Fest, *Hitler* (Frankfurt a.M./Berlin/Wien, 1973), pp. 67ff. On what follows, see Martin Heidegger, *Die Grundbegriffe der Metaphysik*

Otto Pöggeler

(Frankfurt a.M., 1983), pp. 255, 103ff.; Heidegger, *Hölderlins Hymnen "Germanien" und "Der Rhein,"* pp. 136, 290ff.; Martin Heidegger, *Nietzsche* (Pfullingen, 1961), Bd. I, p. 124.

6. See Martin Heidegger, *Die Selbstbehauptung der deutschen Universität/Das Rektorat 1933/34* (Frankfurt a.M., 1983), p. 24f. ("The Self-Assertion of the German University: Address, Delivered on the Solemn Assumption of the Rectorate of the University of Freiburg" and "The Rectorate 1933/34: Facts and Thoughts," translated by Karsten Harries, *The Review of Metaphysics* XXXVIII(3):484f., 1985); Ernst Jünger, *Sämtliche Werke*, Bd. 7 (Stuttgart, 1981), p. 118 ("War Front" and "Labor Front"). Further, Bd. 7, p. 17. Cf. Martin Heidegger, *Hölderlins Hymne "Andenken"* (Frankfurt a.M., 1982), p. 181. Cf. Heidegger, *Nietzsche*, Bd., 2, p. 21; Martin Heidegger *Wegmarken* (Frankfurt a.M., 1967), p. 218 (*The Question of Being*, translated by Jean T. Wilde and William Kluback [New Haven: Twayne, 1958], p. 43).

7. On the German situation prior to 1933, see Andreas Hillgruber, *Die Last der Nation* (Düsseldorf, 1984), pp. 32ff. On the sentence cited from Heidegger, see the interpretation given by Walter Bröcker in a letter to the editor of the *Frankfurter Allgemeine Zeitung*, April 14, 1984: "For 'precepts' read 'the National Socialist party program,' and for 'ideas' (in quotation marks!) read 'the National Socialist world-view.' . . . Heidegger's attempt to play Hitler off against the party did not go entirely unnoticed, of course, and turned the party against him." On the following, see, concerning Jaeger, H. W. Petzet, *Auf ein Stern zugehen. Begegnungen mit Martin Heidegger 1929 bis 1976* (Frankfurt a.m., 1983), p. 34. Concerning Jaspers, see Karl Jaspers, *Notizen zu Martin Heidegger* (München/Zürich, 1978), p. 13. On the place of Baden university politics in the revolution of the times, see Bernd Martin, "Heidegger und die Reform der deutschen Universität 1933," *Freiburger Universitätsblätter* 92:49–73, 1986.

8. See Heidegger, *Die Selbstbehauptung*, p. 25 ("Self-Assertion," p. 474). On the lecture course of summer 1934, see Heinrich Buhr in *Erinnerung an Heidegger* (n. 3 above), p. 55. On the following: Heidegger, *Hölderlins Hymnen "Germanien" und "Der Rhein,"* p. 134. On Eucken, see Hugo Ott, "Martin Heidegger als Rektor der Universität Freiburg 1933/34," *Zeitschrift für die Geschichte des Oberrheins* 132:343–458, 1984. On Heraclitus, see also Heidegger, *Die Selbstbehauptung*, p. 28f. ("Self-Assertion," p. 488f.); C. Ochwadt and E. Tecklenborg, eds., *Das Mass des Verborgenen. Heinrich Ochsner zum Gedächtnis* (Hannover, 1981), p. 38.

9. See Heidegger, *Hölderlins Hymnen "Germanien" und "Der Rhein,"* pp. 151, 214, 134, 210. On the following, see Heidegger, *Einführung in die Metaphysik*, pp. 112ff. (*Introduction to Metaphysics*, pp. 123ff.). Rudolf Bultmann's essay, "Polis und Hades in der Antigone des Sophokles," is reprinted in *Glauben und Verstehen*, Bd. 2 (Tübingen, 1961), pp. 20–31.

10. See Heidegger, *Einführung in die Metaphysik*, pp. 28, 35f., 41 (*Introduction to Metaphysics*, pp. 31, 38f., 44). The remark about Carnap is in the new

edition of this lecture in the *Gesamtausgabe* series (Frankfurt a.m., 1983), p. 228f. On the following, Martin Heidegger, *Grundfragen der Philosophie* (Frankfurt a.m., 1984), pp. 53ff., 4.

11. See Martin Heidegger, *Schellings Abhandlung über das Wesen der menschlichen Freiheit (1809)* (Tübingen, 1971), pp. 27ff. Carl Ulmer communicated the omitted passage in *Der Spiegel*, May 2, 1977. On the following, see Heidegger, *Einführung in die Metaphysik*, p. 152 (*Introduction to Metaphysics*, p. 166). According to his oral communications and letters, Walter Bröcker claims to remember with certainty that in his oral delivery of the lecture Heidegger said neither "of National Socialism" nor "of this movement," but rather "of the movement." "The Nazis, and they alone, used 'the movement' for National Socialism. Hence Heidegger's 'the' was for me unforgettable." On the following, see also Heidegger, *Nietzsche*, Bd. 2, pp. 145, 165, 198.

12. See Heidegger, *Hölderlins Hymne "Der Ister,"* pp. 98, 106, 118. On the following: Heidegger, *Parmenides*, p. 127. It was Spengler who predicted a "Russian" world-millennium. Max Weber, on the contrary, wrote to a friend: "America's world domination was as inevitable as, in ancient times, was Rome's after the Punic War. In these circumstances it is to be hoped that it is not shared with Russia. *This* is the goal of our future world politics, for the Russian danger is now in check only for the moment, not forever." Quoted in Wolfgang Mommsen, *Max Weber. Gesellschaft, Politik und Geschichte* (Frankfurt a.M., 1974), p. 93.

13. See Heidegger, *Hölderlins Hymne "Andenken,"* p. 132f. On the following, see Martin Heidegger, *Vorträge und Aufsätze* (Pfullingen, 1954), pp. 89ff. ("Overcoming Metaphysics" in *The End of Philosophy*, translated by Joan Stambaugh [New York: Harper and Row, 1973], pp. 109ff; also p. 105f.). Heidegger, *Nietzsche*, Bd. I, p. 657f. The supplement to Heidegger's lecture course on Hölderlin's Ister-Hymn is reproduced in my essay "Heidegger's Begegnung mit Hölderlin," *Man and World* 10:13–61, 1977.

14. On Dietrich Eckart, see Ernst Nolte, *Der Faschismus in seiner Epoche* (München/Zürich, 1979), pp. 403ff. On the philosophical explication of the Jewish world-experience, see my essay "L'interprétation hégélienne du Judaisme" in my book *Études Hégéliennes* (Paris, 1985), pp. 37–85. In the *Beiträge* (110 [BP 85/174]) Heidegger writes that "signs" like Chamberlain and the emerging predominance of the metaphysics of Richard Wagner indicate that the creatively accomplished end of Western metaphysics in Nietzsche is once again being covered over.

15. See Petzet, *Auf einen Stern zugehen*, p. 93f. On eternity as "passing," see Heidegger, *Hölderlins Hymnen "Germanien" und "Der Rhein,"* pp. 54ff. 110f. On the following, see Heidegger, *Grundfragen der Philosophie*, p. 3.

16. Without doubt Hegel took on new significance for Heidegger in the 1930s. Yet in the end Heidegger was already beyond Hegel's joining together of history and metaphysics and thus cannot be understood in terms of Hegel or

German Idealism. On this, see the chapter on "Philosophie und Geschichte" in my *Hegels Idee einer Phänomenologie des Geistes* (Freiburg/München, 1973), pp. 299ff. Karl Löwith early on pointed out the existential implications in Heidegger's philosophizing, but over Heidegger's protest and incorrectly he wanted to see this philosophizing as an existential one in general. In spite of this, Löwith by and large correctly rendered Heidegger's political self-understanding at the time of the *Beiträge's* composition. During a reunion in Rome in 1936, Löwith said that Heidegger's partisanship for National Socialism was not to be divorced from his philosophy (as Staiger had maintained), but rather belongs to the essence of that philosophy. Löwith reports: "Heidegger agreed with me without reservation and explained that his concept of 'historicity' was the basis for his political 'engagement.' He left no doubt about his belief in Hitler; the latter had underestimated only two things: the vitality of the Christian Church and the difficulties in the way of the annexation of Austria. He was still convinced that National Socialism was the prescribed way for Germany; one need only 'hold out' long enough. Only the measureless organization at the expense of vital powers appeared suspicious to him." To Löwith's remark that [this partisanship] meant that Heidegger occasionally had to share a table with individuals of J. Streicher's ilk, Heidegger answered with the familiar argument that everything would have gone even worse had not a few knowing ones [*Wissende*] gotten involved, etc. "One need waste no words over Streicher; the *Stürmer* is nothing but pornography. [Heidegger] did not understand why Hitler did not rid himself of this fellow; he probably had some dread of him." To this, Löwith correctly remarks: "In actuality, however, the program of this 'pornography' was entirely fulfilled in November 1938 and became German reality, and no one can deny that on just this particular point Streicher and Hitler were as one." *Mein Leben in Deutschland vor und nach 1933. Ein Bericht* (Stuttgart, 1968), p. 57f.

17. The quotation from Gogarten is taken from Alexander Schwan, *Geschichtstheologische Konstitution und Destruktion der Politik. Friedrich Gogarten und Rudolf Bultmann* (Berlin/New York, 1976), p. 155. Concerning Heidegger, Löwith reports (*Mein Leben*, p. 29): "In 1925 there seemed to him to be spiritual life only in theology, in Barth and Gogarten." On Trakl, see Heidegger, *Unterwegs zur Sprache*, pp. 37ff. (*On the Way to Language*, pp. 159ff.); on the translation of Lao-Tse, *Erinnerung an Heidegger*, pp. 121ff. Concerning Heidegger's teaching activities during the last years of Nazi rule, even those who participated in them said that they were a form of "resistance." The lecture courses published since then confirm this conception in some of its elements. A majority of Germans can claim "resistance" as a diffuse basic mood during these years (though precisely not as concrete activity). A minimum of honesty, however, requires that resistance of this sort be differentiated, or placed in quotation marks, to distinguish it from that of those who acted with clear consciousness of the alternatives and in many cases paid for it with their lives. On the following,

see Jaspers, *Notizen zu Martin Heidegger*, p. 288f.; on Reinhold Schneider, Ochwadt and Tecklenborg, eds., *Das Mass der Verborgenen*, p. 296. It is well known that Heidegger got involved in the "struggle against atomic death."

18. Jünger, *Sämtliche Werke*, Bd. 8, pp. 322, 349. On the following, concerning Heidegger's relation to Paul Klee, see my book, *Die Frage nach der Kunst* (Freiburg/München, 1984), pp. 26ff.

19. See Martin Heidegger, *Vier Seminare* (Frankfurt a.M., 1977), p. 149. In the seminar of September 1969, it is said that the recent "American interest in the question of Being" conceals "from the view of those interested the reality of the country: the collusion between industry and the military (between economic development and the armament which it requires)." The question is raised: "Did the slogans of May 1968 against the consumer society get to the point of recognizing in consumption itself the *then-current* face of Being?" (pp. 97, 107).

20. See Karl-Heinz Volkmann-Schluck, *Politische Philosophie. Thukydides, Kant, Tocqueville* (Frankfurt a.M., 1974). On other attempts to construct a new practical or political philosophy on the basis of Heidegger, see my essay, *Philosophie und Politik bei Heidegger* (Freiburg/München, 1972, 1974). In the Heidegger issue of the *Freiburger Universitätsblätter* (see above, n. 7), Max Müller maintained: "The *Spiegel* interview was for me the greatest disappointment" (p. 19). He traced Heidegger's "Führer-ideology" back to the orientation toward "concrete knowing action" which is rooted in the responsibility of a single individual for the "work" to be created. Concerning Heidegger's "antidemocratic" attitude Müller still today claims: "He most likely never gave it up" (p. 20).

21. See Jünger, *Sämtliche Werke*, Bd. 7, p. 203. In 1933 Heidegger saw anticipatory being towards death in the "sacrifice" of Albert Leo Schlageter who, according to Heidegger, died the "hardest death" and, while his nation was being humiliated, was alone in presenting "to the soul the image in himself of the future awakening of the people to its honor and greatness." When in 1934–35 Heidegger subsequently glossed his own isolation with Hölderlin, he had a new way of moving from the idea of sacrifice to the situating of the "mortals" before the divinities, who appeared as gods of the people or the homeland. After 1945 Heidegger spoke no public word about the extermination of the Jews and others. May one not therefore conclude that Heidegger's thinking remained unable to make connections with reality? Cf. Emil L. Fackenheim, *To Mend the World* (New York, 1982), pp. 189ff. It has been seen as inexcusable that Heidegger did not speak of these things even when visited in 1967 by the German-Jewish lyric poet Paul Celan; however, see the particulars on this matter in the chapter "Todtnauberg" in my book, *Spur des Wortes. Zur Lyrik Paul Celans* (Freiburg/München, 1986), pp. 259ff. On the following, see Ernst Tugendhat, *Rationalität und Irrationalität der Friedensbewegung und ihrer Gegner. Versuch eines Dialogs* (Berlin, 1983), p. 35.

22. It is necessary, wrote Heidegger after Beirut, to recognize *one* thing in its full scope: what is distinctive of modern technology, though historically con-

sidered it appears later, is neither a consequence of modern science nor merely the application of it, but rather determines this latter through its own self-concealing essence in which Being holds sway. That which has the power to save in the face of the danger—the sustaining staying of poetry, of the arts, of reflective thinking—must no longer be falsified into an instrument of the civilization industry. The thinking which questions is itself an action and must not—understood as mere theory—be prematurely delivered over to an unthinking praxis. Cf. also the word of greeting to the Chicago Heidegger Conference of April 1967 in John Sallis, ed., *Radical Phenomenology. Essays in Honor of Martin Heidegger* (Atlantic Highlands, N.J., 1976), pp. 1ff. On the encounter with the Islamic world, see Joachim Ritter, "Europäisierung als europäisches Problem," in *Metaphysik und Politik* (Frankfurt a.M., 1969), pp. 321ff. Oskar Becker, Heidegger's path companion, offered a different determination of art, mathematics, and technology. See my summary essay "Hermeneutische und mantische Phänomenologie," in Otto Pöggeler, ed., *Heidegger. Perspektiven zur Deutung seines Werkes* (Königstein/Ts., 1984), pp. 321ff.

23. For the letter to Jünger, see Heidegger, *Wegmarken*, pp. 234, 222, 251, 252 (*The Question of Being*, pp. 73, 49, 105, 103). Contemporaries and students of Heidegger's have tried in different ways to learn from the things they had to experience together. Hannah Arendt's reconciliation with Heidegger is not acceptable if it presupposes that the philosopher's thinking must misconstrue concrete political matters and the kind of judgment necessary in that realm (as Plato and Heidegger—two altogether different examples!—are supposed to show). Leo Strauss attempts to overcome nihilism, which he sees culminating in Hegelianism and historicism, through a recourse to classical philosophy in which philosophy's own task is taken to be aid and training for an open-ended history. In contrast, Hans Jonas has insisted that "ethics for technological civilization" confronts a new and unique task (*Das Prinzip Verantwortung* [Frankfurt a.M., 1979, 1984]). Emmanuel Levinas seeks to anchor Heidegger within a metaphysics of identity and totality, thus within the war between totalities and mythologies, and to break this devil's circle through the experience of the Other (and of a messianic peace). In his Levinas essay, "Violence and Metaphysics," Jacques Derrida asks, with Eric Weil, whether the accentuation of otherness does not also bring with it an irreducible finitude and thus violence (*Die Schrift und die Differenz* [Frankfurt a.M., 1972] [*Writing and Difference*, translated by Alan Bass (Chicago: University of Chicago Press, 1978)]). Does the mere call for "anarchy" arrive at a political philosophy worthy of the name? Keiji Nishitani (who in Japan became entangled in discussions of his political engagement similar to Heidegger's) defends himself on the basis of his Zen Buddhist position against the absolutizing of finitude and the claim to a chosenness in the Iranian-Jewish-European tradition. On the contradiction between Levinas and Nishitani, see the remarks in my book, *Heidegger und die hermeneutische Philosophie* (Freiburg/München, 1983), pp. 359ff.

13

HEIDEGGER'S IDEA OF TRUTH

Ernst Tugendhat

Introduction

"Heidegger's Idea of Truth" is a précis of the concluding arguments of Tugendhat's monumental (regrettably, as yet untranslated) study of phenomenological epistemology, *The Concept of Truth in Husserl and Heidegger* (Berlin: de Gruyter, 1967).

Prima facie, Tugendhat's analysis would seem to bear little or no relationship to the problem of Heidegger and politics. Instead, the highly specific focus of the present essay concerns Heidegger's attempt to go beyond the traditional phenomenological (i.e., Husserlian) theory of truth in section 44 of *Being and Time*. At issue is Heidegger's reconceptualization of truth as "disclosedness" (*"Erschlossenheit"*) or "uncon-cealedness" (*"Unverborgenheit"*). Whereas Tugendhat correctly locates this revision of the traditional correspondence theory of truth (*veritas est adaequatio rei et intellectus*) already in *Being and Time*, it is a tendency that is further accentuated in Heidegger's subsequent writings of the early 1930s, such as "On the Essence of Truth" (1930). Here, a crucial way station for Heidegger's abandonment of the traditional concept of truth is his essay on "Plato's Doctrine of Truth," which dates from 1931–32. For it is at this point that Heidegger's critical engagement with traditional theories of truth is radicalized, such that it borders on wholesale rejection. In this essay, Heidegger, in a fashion reminiscent of Nietzsche, identifies the "fall" of Western metaphysics with Plato's relocation of truth in the supersensuous sphere of "ideas." For Heidegger, Platonism thus represents the fatal move away from things themselves—

Ernst Tugendhat, "Heidegger's Idea of Truth" ("Heideggers Idee von Wahrheit") appeared in Otto Pögggeler, ed. *Heidegger: Perspektiven zur Deutung seines Werkes* (Königstein: Athenäum, 1984), pp. 286–297.

that is, as they naturally show and reveal themselves—and toward a "subjectivization" of the concept of truth—truth as what can be thought by "man"—from which metaphysics up until now has never fully recovered. His subsequent fascination with the Greek notion of *physis* as a precursor of his own concept of "Being" and turn toward the pre-Socratics as thinkers in possession of a more "primordial" standard of truth—truth as *aletheia*—is only explicable on this basis.

For Tugendhat, the central problem with Heidegger's concept of truth stems from its "overgeneralization," as it were. In Tugendhat's estimation, Heidegger, in seeking to surpass Husserl and correspondence theory, in essence "extends the concept of truth to *all* uncovering and *every* disclosedness." The result is that the difference between a "true" uncovering or disclosedness of entities—that is, one that would capture the entity *as it is in itself*—from uncovering or disclosedness *as such* is effaced. Thus, in seeking after an ontologically more primordial stratum of truth, which foreshadows Heidegger's own idea of truth as "clearing" ("*Lichtung*") or "being-cleared," the philosopher, in his radicality, in point of fact risks regressing behind both the Greek and phenomenological conceptions of truth. And thus, for both of these philosophical schools, truth signifies not an arbitrary or indeterminate uncovering or disclosure of entities, but an "essential" disclosure that, qua true, offers the entity to us in a "superior" mode of givenness.

Tugendhat's interpretation and criticism of Heidegger's concept of truth is of sufficient intrinsic merit that, even were it of merely tangential import in relation to Heidegger's political involvements, it would still be important to make it available to an English-speaking readership. Yet, in point of fact, its relation to Heidegger's political thought is far from irrelevant. For it stands to reason that if Heidegger's political thought is grounded in his philosophy, then it, too, would stand in an integral relation to his theory of truth. And thus, Tugendhat's critique points to a crucial aspect of Heidegger's theory of truth as it is developed in the 1930s: the ontological entanglement of truth with *error (das Irrnis)*. For in his essays of the early 1930s, "error" is deemed to be equiprimordial with "truth." All of which raises what is, for the purposes of our inquiry, the crucial question: does this putative "overgeneralization" of the concept of truth on Heidegger's part, as well as the subsequent ontological conflation of "truth" and "error," impinge in an essential way on his capacities to make cogent political judgments? More specifically: does this elemental epistemological confusion leave him intellectually—and morally—defenseless in face of the evils of National Socialism?

Unfortunately, in the present context it is not possible to provide a satisfactory answer to the extremely suggestive questions that have just been raised. However, in his book, *Heidegger and the Tradition,* the philosopher Werner Marx has offered some constructive reflections as to the lines along which any future consideration of these themes might proceed:

Heidegger conceived the institution of the *polis* in the first [i.e., the Greek] beginning, on the basis of *aletheia,* as an occurrence of truth in which man is violently involved. Likewise, in the "basic event of the realization of the National Socialist State" he saw an "incipient" foundation of a state, a "state-founding act," which he expressly characterized in the essay on the work of art (1935) as one of the ways in which "truth essences." That the "National Socialist Revolution" as the "total transformation of our German Dasein" could take place only violently, and that it was pervaded by evil as well as by error and sham, for Heidegger might thus have simply resulted from "an occurrence of truth." And it might have for him been merely a consequence of the *coordination* of evil and good in the clearing of Being, such that the founders of the state followed the directives of evil without [Heidegger] being able to hold them guilty on the basis of "moral considerations."

These references touch on the difficult and disturbing problem of the relationship of this thinker to National Socialism and the effect of his related speeches, writings, and actions insofar as they cast doubt on the often heard view that he "erred" with regard to the violence and evil of the National Socialist Revolution. On the contrary, he must have a priori assessed it correctly, since he viewed it as an "occurrence of truth."

These considerations are especially appropriate in bringing to light the extremely perilous character of Heidegger's concept of truth. They forcefully raise the question of whether Heidegger actually viewed the matter correctly when he recognized not only "the mystery" but also error, sham, and evil as equal partners within the occurrence of truth.[1]

Notes

1. Werner Marx, *Heidegger and the Tradition* (Evanston, Ill.: Northwestern University Press, 1971), pp. 250–251.

. . .

Heidegger is perhaps the only philosopher of our time who has tried to productively continue the classical tradition of ontological-transcendental philosophy. Certainly, the fact that this continuation was presented as an "overcoming" ["*Überwindung*"] in which philosophy in the end seems to dissolve has made it suspect. Criticism of Heidegger, however, has mostly been conducted on a plane which, for its part, is not that of the ontological-transcendental tradition. Assuming it is still meaningful today to adhere to the formal idea of ontology or transcendental philosophy as a desideratum, then Heidegger's efforts must be critically considered with respect to the idea by which he himself was guided so that we might orient ourselves concerning our own possibilities.

The concept of truth takes on special meaning in this context. Roughly speaking, one might say that to the extent that it inquires about beings as a whole the philosophy of the classical tradition is universal; on the other hand, it proceeds from that which is somehow assumed to be most primordial [*Ursprünglichsten*]. For metaphysics of the old school, this was an absolute entity. In modern transcendental philosophy, on both sides of the equation the standpoint of knowledge—and thus, that of truth—steps to the forefront. At issue are the conditions of possibility of all being, insofar as the latter can be thought as true; and what is most primordial—to which this question refers back—is not so much an absolute entity, but instead something that is given absolutely. It is in this way that Husserl understands his transcendental philosophy: namely, as a phenomenological clarification of everything that can be posited truly by transcendental subjectivity, whose distinguishing feature consists in its absolute self-givenness—that is, in its character as absolute evidence, and thus in a fulfilled relation to truth. Heidegger adheres to the idea of something that is most primordially given, and in this measure he formally remains in the tradition of transcendental philosophy. However, the self-givenness of subjectivity is for him no longer an absolute. Rather, as the ecstatic temporality of Dasein, it is already mediated by a prior openness—its "world" as "history"; and to this extent, the transcendental approach has been superseded. Let us term this position metatranscendental in order to have a name which suggests both the continuity as well as the break. What is most primordially given is no longer identified through absolute subjectivity qua "evidence," but instead through the disclosedness of finite Dasein; which means—insofar as this disclosedness is projected in an open region—through the clearing of this region itself.

Rather than offering an interpretation of Heidegger's basic position, I would instead like to ask: what does it mean that Heidegger, while abandoning the standpoint of certainty and evidence, for his part understands the recourse to a transformed transcendental dimension as most primordial truth. Thus, in *Being and Time*, he characterizes the disclosedness of Dasein as "the most primordial phenomenon of truth" (p. 221). Correspondingly, in the later writings, he characterizes the clearing of the world as the "truth of Being." Such claims are not immediately comprehensible from the standpoint of our normal understanding of truth, for they already presuppose Heidegger's own theory of truth, in which the latter is defined as "disclosedness" and "unconcealment." Hence, this theory must be interpreted if one wants to understand the validity and meaning of the fact that Heidegger chooses precisely the word "truth" to characterize his recourse to a metatranscendental dimension.

In order to keep the interpretation within a manageable frame, I will limit myself to a specific passage, section 44 of *Being and Time*. Here, Heidegger develops his concept of truth for the first time. To be sure, not all aspects of his view are as yet delineated, and the conception as a whole undergoes a distinct modification during the so-called "turn." But in the passage in question the essential decisions that remain fundamental for all that follows are already made and can be best understood.

The definition of the concept of truth is completed in two steps. In paragraph (a) Heidegger treats truth as assertion and arrives at the conclusion that it must be understood as "uncovering" (or, as Heidegger later says, "unconcealing"). This result permits him in paragraph (b) to extend the concept of truth to all uncovering and every disclosedness. And since it has already been shown in *Being and Time* that all uncovering of worldly entities is grounded in the disclosedness of the world, the latter proves in the end to be the "most primordial phenomenon of truth." Paragraph (b) will thus return us to our opening question as to how Heidegger can make truth into a fundamental philosophical concept. However, the decisive step in the argument of section 44 is the thesis of paragraph (a) that the truth of an assertion lies in its "Being-uncovering." Once this is admitted, everything else follows deductively, as it were. Hence, our first task is to interpret more precisely the analysis of truth as assertion.

That Heidegger proceeds here from the idea of truth as assertion, as in the only later detailed development of his concept of truth, "On the Essence of Truth," is a methodological necessity. Whereas the philosophical definition of a basic term need not limit itself to the normal understanding of the term, it must, however, proceed from it. And while for our customary understanding, truth as assertion is certainly not the only meaning of the word "truth," it is nevertheless the most frequent. Hence, although perhaps not much is to be gained from the fact that a concept of truth measures up to the idea of truth as assertion, this is still the minimal condition which it must fulfill for it to qualify as a concept of truth in general.

Heidegger did not acknowledge the stringency of this requirement since he was of the opinion that truth as assertion only rose to prominence with Plato and Aristotle (probably the obverse could be shown: even Homer generally speaks of truth only in relation to assertions; and Heidegger could arrive at his conception of truth only insofar as he allows his comprehension of the pre-philosophical Greek understanding of truth to be guided less by actual linguistic practice than by a loose interpretation of etymology). Be that as it may, Heidegger accepts the truth of assertion as that which is primary for us, and so it is an idea in relation to which a new concept of truth must prove itself. Thus, we certainly do not violate his own intentions here by taking him at his word.

He adheres to another maxim of hermeneutics insofar as he proceeds not only from the customary understanding of words, but also relies on traditional philosophical definitions; namely, the well-known principle: *veritas est adaequatio rei et intellectus*. Now how is the agreement that is intended here, Heidegger asks, really to be understood?

The answer is arrived at via a critique of various contemporary conceptions of truth, in particular the so-called copy theory: if we inquire about the truth of intention [*Meinung*], then it is not a matter of an agreement of an immanent representation with a transcendent Being [*Sein*]; instead, we are already oriented toward the entity in the mere intention itself. And the intention or assertion is true if it designates the entity "as it is in itself"; that is, if the entity "is in its self-sameness just as it gets pointed out and uncovered as its being in the assertion."

In a footnote to this passage, Heidegger appeals in this passage to the "phenomenological theory of truth" as Husserl had developed it in the sixth of his *Logical Investigations*—and rightly so. Just as Heidegger's critique of the copy theory merely repeats Husserl's argumentation, so his positive determination of the concept of truth appears in the first instance only to recur to that of Husserl. Because of his specific phenomenological problematic and his novel distinction between objective contents and their intentional modes of givenness, Husserl had arrived at a refutation of the copy theory as well as at a promising interpretation of the "adaequatio" doctrine. By differentiating various modes of givenness of the same object he was able to recognize that that which, in accordance with the "adaequatio" doctrine, is supposed to stand in agreement with the thing is neither—as this doctrine erroneously suggests—the subject, nor another thing—say, a sentence as a physical event—but instead the same thing, only in another mode of givenness. On the one side stands the thing as we relate to it intentionally in its so-called signitive givenness; on the other side the same thing as it is itself. This self-sameness of the thing is not something that is transcendent to our experience; rather, it is itself only a corollary of a distinct mode of givenness: the thing as it is itself is the thing as it shows itself if it is self-given to us.

Thus, if Heidegger says that the truth of an assertion consists in the fact that the entity is pointed out and uncovered "just as it is itself," one could initially think that he has simply restated Husserl's theory. In this case, however, one will succeed in grasping the specific nature of his concept of truth only if one asks how and why he differentiates his theory from that of Husserl. Heidegger himself tells us nothing about this expressly. We thus run up against the—in the first instance, purely external—peculiar nature of Heidegger's exposition. He develops his concept of truth in a debate with other contemporary theories; yet, only with those which Husserl had already refuted a quarter of a century earlier. What Heidegger obtained through his *argumentation* is thus only the position of Husserl. The decisive step beyond Husserl is no longer substantiated through argumentation; indeed, it is not even recognizable as an independent step.

The way in which Heidegger's theory differs from Husserl's can only be discerned from the different yet equivalent variants that he places alongside the first definition. The first definition reads: the assertion is true if it points out and uncovers the entity "just as it is in itself." Here, this "just as" ["*So-Wie*"] is emphasized by Heidegger. Clearly, this "just as" is essential for the truth relation, for it denotes the agreement between the entity *just as* it is uncovered in the assertion with the same entity "*as* it is in itself is."

It is all the more surprising that Heidegger, without rational justification, now advances a formulation in which the "just as" is absent. He says, "To say that an assertion is true means: it uncovers the entity in itself" (p. 218). The reformulation is however completely legitimate; it corresponds, moreover, entirely to Husserl's theory. For since the agreement, if it is correct, is an identity, if the assertion points out the entity as it is itself, one can simply say: it points out the entity in itself. The "just as" is implicit in the "in itself."

However, in a third formulation Heidegger now carries the simplification one step further: he also expunges—once more without rational justification—the "in itself." That an assertion is true now merely means: it uncovers the entity. Thereby, the following thesis is reached: "The Being-true (truth) of the assertion must be understood as Being-uncovering" (p. 218). With the use of this latter expression, Heidegger has clearly distanced himself from Husserl and attained his own concept of truth—which he henceforth maintains only in this formulation. It is all the more curious, therefore, that precisely this small, yet decisive step receives no further commentary. How are we to make sense out of it?

When it was first claimed that an assertion can be considered true if the intended entity "is in its self-sameness just as it gets pointed out and uncovered as its being," no special emphasis appeared to be placed on the word "uncovered." Heidegger understands an assertion in general as pointing out and uncovering (see *Being and Time*, section 33); and what constitutes the truth of the assertion appears not to be the fact that the entity is uncovered by the assertion, but rather *how* it is uncovered by it —namely, "as it is in itself." In the final formulation, however, it is apparent that precisely this qualification—which appeared to be the essential one—becomes dispensable for Heidegger, and that truth consists in pointing out and uncovering as such.

Heidegger's characterization of assertion as a pointing out and an uncovering in point of fact constitutes an essential step beyond Husserl. The only question is whether this new theory of the assertion thus renders any further qualification in defining the truth of the assertion superfluous. Husserl understood the act of assertion as a mode of intentionality statically, as it were: as the self-presentation of a determinate objectivity, as representation. Because Heidegger goes beyond Husserlian intentionality altogether with the concept of "disclosedness," he now understands assertion dynamically, so to speak, as a mode of disclosedness: as an uncovering and specifically as a point out (*apophansis*). Through the idea of disclosedness Heidegger attempts to thematize man's "Being-cleared" [*"Gelichtetsein"*] as such, something that is only implicit in Husserlian intentionality and the conceptual tradition that corresponds to it. Being-cleared is not assumed as a finished condition; instead the question is raised as to how it is achieved. Disclosedness is therefore understood as an event which is actively related to its counterpart—closedness or concealedness. In the specific case of the assertion, it clarifies things to say that wherever it emerges concretely in the context of life or science, it should not be understood as the functionless and rigid self-presentation of an objectivity, but instead dynamically as that which allows us to see: an allowing-to-see in which we point out something as something, and thereby remove it from concealment for ourselves and for others, as it were; so that now, as Heidegger says, it is "un-concealed."

And now we can also understand why Heidegger in defining the truth of the assertion allows that additional "as it is in itself" to fall out of account. As long as one understands the assertion statically as a representing or an intending, one cannot of course say: an assertion is true if it "intends" the entity in question; for the way in which it intends the entity can also be false. One must therefore already say: the assertion is true if it means the entity as it is in itself. If, conversely, we understand the assertion as a pointing out and an uncovering, then it appears to suffice if it uncovers the entity; for if the assertion is false, it doesn't uncover the entity at all, but instead "hides" and "conceals" it.

Thus uncovering as such, if it is really an uncovering, must already be true.

Heidegger certainly would have argued this way if he had made the attempt to justify why the "as it is in itself" became superfluous for him. However, as soon as one carefully analyzes the unspoken conviction underlying Heidegger's thesis, its weak point is already apparent. This lies in the ambiguity with which Heidegger employs the word "uncovering."

In the first instance, uncovering stands for pointing out (*apophaines-thai*) in general. In this sense every assertion—the false as well as the true—can be said to uncover. Nevertheless, Heidegger employs the word in a narrow and pregnant sense according to which a false assertion would be a covering up rather than an uncovering. In this case it goes without saying that the truth lies in being-uncovered; however, what does uncovering now mean if it no longer signifies pointing out in general? How is *aletheia* to be differentiated from *apophansis*?

Heidegger gives no answer to this question. For in contrast to Aristotle, whom he otherwise invokes (p. 219), he fails to expressly differentiate between these concepts: that is, between the broad and the narrow meaning of uncovering. Consequently, after he arrived at the initial conclusion that truth consists in Being-uncovering, he can again immediately speak of "uncoveredness as a mode of appearance" (p. 222). In this case, the thesis of truth as being-uncovered would only be intelligible if one insisted on the fact that a false assertion fails to uncover. Instead, Heidegger now says that in a false assertion the entity "is in a certain sense uncovered and yet disguised" (p. 222). Consequently, the covering up of the false assertion does not exclude a specific uncovering. But in which sense then does the false assertion uncover and in which sense does it cover up? Since Heidegger fails to qualify more precisely both the uncovering of the true assertion as well as the covering up of the false assertion, the only solution remaining for him is that of a quantitative definition: in the false assertion the entity is "not fully concealed" (p. 222). Should we therefore say that in the false assertion the entity would be partly uncovered and partly concealed? But then the false would be comprised partly of the truth and partly of the unknown. Of course, that is not what Heidegger meant. However, if one limits oneself to the concepts of unconcealment and concealment, there is no possibility of determining the specific meaning of true and false.

The characterization of what is false as a concealing is undoubtedly an advance; yet, this concealing is neither simply a degenerate form of that concealedness on the basis of which the *apophansis* derives its capacity to point out, nor a combination of concealedness with unconcealedness. The false assertion really conceals—but what does it conceal and how? One would have to say: it conceals the entity as it is in itself, and it does this in that it uncovers it in another way than the way it is in itself. At the same time, there exists no possibility of differentiating uncovering in the narrower sense—which accounts for the truth of the assertion—from uncovering in the broader sense of *apophansis,* such that the entity would be uncovered as it is in itself. In characterizing the assertion as true one is unable to get around having to add "as it is in itself"; and the definition of uncoveredness, which is supposed to make this addition avoidable, must for its part make use of it if it intends to be a definition of truth at all.

Also in the shorter writings that followed *Being and Time,* Heidegger time and again ignores this aspect which is essential for truth as he tries to refer the truth of an assertion back to unconcealedness. Thus, in "On the Essence of Truth," "The Essence of Reason," and "The Origin of the Work of Art," the entity must show itself as unconcealed in order for the assertion to be directed toward the entity. Thus, the truth of entities as unconcealedness would underlie the truth of an assertion as correctness. That one calls that aspect of the entity to which the true assertion directs itself "the truth" makes sense and also corresponds to the customary sense of the word. If we say, for example, "we are inquiring about the truth," then we clearly do not mean: we are inquiring about the correctness of an assertion; instead: we are inquiring about the way the entity is in itself. For Husserl, too, the primary meaning of truth lay in the truth of the entity. However, one cannot then view the self-manifestation or unconcealedness as such as that toward which the true assertion is directed. For even a false assertion is directed toward something that shows itself. Even appearance [*Schein*] is unconcealed.

To be sure, one could respond that appearance does not constitute true unconcealedness. Yet, we thereby encounter the same ambiguity that emerged in *Being and Time* with respect to uncovering, one which Heidegger nowhere explains. Thus, we are forced to conclude that a true assertion is not directed at the entity as it shows itself immediately, but instead at the entity as it is in itself. This difference intrinsic to self-manifestation [*Sich-Zeigen*] between an immediately apparent givenness and the thing itself is not taken into consideration by Heidegger. Whereas he thus deepens Husserlian intentionality and givenness with his concepts of uncovering and unconcealment, the difference between givenness in general and self-givenness escapes him. Heidegger justifiably views the characteristic feature of the Husserlian as well as, in a slightly different respect, the Platonic-Aristotelian concept of truth in terms of the fact that truth is understood as a type of self-manifestation and givenness. However, he immediately bypassed this idea in order to broaden this givenness as such and to inquire into its conditions of possibility, without taking cognizance of the fact that, for both Husserl and Greek philosophy, truth does not mean givenness as such but the possibility of a superior mode of givenness.

Perhaps Heidegger thought that in Husserl's discussion of self-givenness there was still a covert relation to an absolute, transcendent being-in-itself. But that is not the case. Self-givenness or "evidence" is for Husserl nothing other than the—ultimately only partial—fulfillment of a signitive intention, and thus always remains relative to the latter. The given has in itself a depth dimension; and thus what is initially given points as it were beyond itself.

If, conversely, instead of explaining the moment of self-givenness as something that is immanent to experience, one wanted to avoid it entirely, one would consequently be forced to relinquish the concept of truth. Only the wanton ambiguity in the discussion of uncovering can deceive us about this fact. Were unconcealedness to exhaust itself in the fact that it raises the entity out of concealedness into light, we would have no occasion at all to speak of truth and untruth. Such an occasion is provided only because our relation to the entity is peculiarly mediated, such that though the entity is not usually given to us as such, we are, nevertheless, able to intend it, and, *for this reason,* also intend it otherwise than it is. If the assertion as an act of pointing out is, as Heidegger has shown, dynamically directed from concealedness to unconcealedness, then at the same time, if its *telos* is not only *apophansis,* but also the truth, it is directed from the thing as it factically shows itself to the self-manifestation of the thing; and this second meaning of being-directed is in a certain sense even opposed to the first, in that its aim is not to bring the thing to givenness, but instead to measure the givenness against the thing. Only by way of this second meaning of being-directed does the first gain an additional dimension such that unconcealing, which would otherwise be arbitrary, is directed toward the self-givenness of the thing. If, conversely, one allows unconcealing to be directed toward givenness as it *shows* itself, one has thereby sanctioned arbitrariness. Self-sameness is the critical measure of unconcealedness. Only if this second meaning of being-directed is recognized in its autonomy can it profitably be clarified with the help of the first; so that one can say that the false assertion covers up the entity and that only the true assertion genuinely unconceals the entity—that is, as it is in itself.

On the one hand, were it only adequately supplemented, Heidegger's new conception of assertion as an uncovering and unconcealing appears thoroughly suited to deepen the idea of truth as assertion. The functional-*apophantic* theory of assertion is superior to the static intentional theory. Specifically, this dynamic conception makes comprehensible not only the completed true assertion, but also the character of "Being-underway" that truth as unconcealing of the object possesses—and thus its character as a "truth-relation" (not as truth!).

On the other hand, in the form in which Heidegger has factically implemented it, this theory leaves out of account precisely the phenomenon of truth in its specificity. To be sure, it is, however ambiguously, intended; but precisely for this reason it is not conceptually set in relief. Thus, in uncovering as *apophansis,* the specific meaning of truth is, so to speak, lost. Even the specific meaning of untruth is not simply left out by Heidegger. Instead, both in *Being and Time* and "On the Essence of Truth" it is belatedly taken into consideration, so that the opposition to it can no longer become essential for the meaning of truth. Instead, untruth now becomes an aspect of truth itself—which is only logical if truth means *apophansis.* The specificity of the problem of truth is passed over—although not in such a way that it simply falls by the wayside and thereby remains an open question. Instead, insofar as Heidegger adheres to the word "truth" itself, yet displaces its meaning in such a way that its real meaning still resonates, one can no longer even perceive that something has been left out.

What Heidegger gains with his new definition of truth as assertion first becomes apparent in paragraph (b) of *Being and Time,* section 44. Here Heidegger arrives at an unusual extension of the concept of truth beyond the realm of assertion. This occurs in two steps.

In order to understand the first step, one must keep in mind that in *Being and Time* the word "uncover" terminologically stands for every disclosedness of worldly entities: and thus not only for the disclosedness of the assertion which "points out," but also for the circumspect dis-closedness of concern [*Besorgen*] (see *Being and Time,* section 18). Now Heidegger returns to this point. If the truth of the assertion lies according to paragraph (a) in uncovering, then it follows, he concludes, that all encounters with worldly entities are actually "true" (p. 220). One sees that Heidegger has understood the thesis reached in paragraph (a) con-cerning the truth of uncovering—which is still comprehensible as long as one understands the word "truth" in the narrow sense—immediately in the wider sense; otherwise he could never have reached the conclusion he does. Only because, for Heidegger, even the truth of the assertion does not lie in how it uncovers, but in the fact that it uncovers in general, can he now without further justification transpose truth to all disclosed-ness as such. The question now is not whether, just as there are true and false assertions—a corresponding difference is evident in the case of circumspective concern; instead, insofar as it uncovers, concern as such is characterized as a mode of truth.

The fact that Heidegger has extended disclosedness beyond intention-ality and beyond the representation of objectivity is a significant and decisive step. What is thereby gained for the problem of truth, however, would have to be shown by investigating the details: whether it would be meaningful to differentiate between truth and untruth in the case of non-theoretical modes of disclosedness; or whether the mode of dis-closedness that is related to truth gains in distinctness by contrasting it with other modes of disclosedness. However, it is precisely questions such as these—which are only made possible as a result of the level of questioning reached by Heidegger—that Heidegger obstructs as a result of the fact that he simply equates truth and disclosedness. By equating the concepts of uncovering, disclosedness, and unconcealedness as such with truth there results an overall loss, despite the real gain in insight which these concepts contain in and for themselves. This is true not only because in the case of truth as assertion, something that is already known loses its clarity. In addition, the new possibilities for broadening the truth-relation which this standpoint has opened up remain unutil-ized: instead of broadening the concept of truth itself, Heidegger has given the word truth another meaning. The broadening of the concept of truth, from truth as assertion to all disclosedness, becomes trivial if all that one sees in truth as assertion is the fact that it discloses in general.

The consequences that result from this move are only apparent from the second step, which now follows. All uncovering of worldly entities is grounded, as was shown earlier (*Being and Time*, section 18), in the disclosedness of the world. Therefore, Heidegger can now conclude, the disclosedness of Dasein itself as Being-in-the-world—as the disclosedness of its world (p. 220)—is "the most primordial phenomenon of truth." At this point we are on the verge of answering our opening question as to how Heidegger can identify as the "most primordial truth" that which for him is the most primordial givenness—despite the fact that the latter is not characterized by "evidence" ["*Evidenz*"]. This definition results logically from Heidegger's characteristic conception of truth as assertion. It follows therefrom that here, as in the first case, what Heidegger calls truth does not really mean the specific phenomenon of truth. In fact, for Heidegger, this primordial disclosedness or clearing is the occurrence of a temporal leeway [*Zeitspielraums*] which renders possible every self-manifestation of being—every self-manifestation, and not only ones that are "true." That Heidegger can speak of truth in this context is only made possible by the fact that he already refers to self-manifestation itself as truth.

Is it perhaps—one then might ask—not merely a question of terminology? Heidegger's question is, however, more comprehensive. Since it is questionable how far one can differentiate between truth and untruth in respect to the disclosedness of world in general and in understanding our historical horizon of meaning— as one can in respect to assertions about facts—is it not therefore legitimate to understand the opening up of a world as such already as an occurrence of truth? Pointedly not, insofar as thereby the question as to whether and how the disclosedness of the world can specifically be related to truth is covered up.

Here, it is no longer a specific error of omission that is at issue, but instead an error that affects the problem of truth in its entirety: if all assertions of truth concerning worldly entities are relative to the horizons of our historical understanding, then the entire problem of truth is concentrated on these horizons, and the decisive question must therefore now be: in which way can one inquire after the truth of these horizons, assuming the question of truth can be applied to these horizons at all? This question ceases to be relevant for Heidegger, insofar as he considers all understanding qua disclosedness to be already in and for itself a truth. In this way, the conclusion is reached that, on the one hand, we can still speak of truth when understanding and its horizons are at issue; on the other hand, that it is no longer necessary to inquire after the truth of these horizons, insofar as this would mean inquiring about the truth of a truth.

Indeed, here, the same ambiguity repeats itself that was already present in the case of the assertion. However, in the case of the assertion the difference between *apophansis* and *aletheia* is already sufficiently clear such that no one who already calls *apophansis* as such true would for this reason decline to inquire after the truth of an assertion. Conversely, in the case of the meaning-horizons of understanding, it would first be necessary to investigate the basis for the posing of questions of truth.

Insofar as our horizons are never given to us transparently, what is in fact immediately given unavoidably refers beyond itself to the thing itself —though, clearly, in other ways than does the assertion. This fact permits us to say: if we inquire after the thing itself in the case of a given meaning, we seek to clarify it. An untrue assertion is false, an untrue meaning is confused or one-sided. The truth of an elementary assertion is decidable, for it consists in a meaning that is correctly understood "in itself"; in the case of the clarification of meaning, conversely, the Being-in-itself of truth, the "as it is in itself" that is attained in the full transparency of evidence, is only a regulative idea of critical questioning.

These rough indications suffice to show that in the sphere in which Heidegger correctly seeks to ground truth, the clarification of the specific nature of the truth-relation would encounter new difficulties. Even the factical questioning about truth would be unsatisfying insofar as clear evidence and certainty—and thus a positive claim to truth—would be unattainable; and thus the meaning of the truth-relation would consist in its negative-critical aspect. Would it not in point of fact seem tempting to understand truth simply as disclosedness itself—and thus to resolve the problem like a Gordian knot? If so, then even the demands of criticism could be suspended in the name of truth; this could then be understood as a consequence of a subsequent historical narrowing in the scope of truth which would not have been contained in the original meaning of the truth-relation. If truth means unconcealedness as Heidegger understands the word, then everything depends on the fact that an understanding of the world actually opens up, not that we scrutinize it critically. What must have appeared so liberating about this conception was that, without denying the relativity and lack of transparency of our historical world, it once again made possible an immediate and positive relation to truth: an alleged relation to truth that no longer stakes a claim to certainty, yet which also no longer poses a threat to uncertainty.

In this way, the specificity of truth-relatedness appears not only as surpassed, but also transformed into its opposite. One would have to demonstrate the way in which this surrender of the idea of critical consciousness presents and works itself out in detail in relation to the later writings—especially already in the lecture "On the Essence of Truth." However, our interpretation of Heidegger's concept of truth in *Being and Time* already allows us to set forth the following thesis: that the way in which Heidegger makes the word "truth" into a basic concept already bypasses the problem of truth. The fact that already he refers to disclosedness in and for itself as truth leads to its being screened off from the truth instead of related to it.

This result is not merely negative, however. It leaves intact the essence of the position through which Heidegger distances himself from Husserl's transcendental approach. The question thus arises whether Heidegger, as a result of his renunciation of critical consciousness, did not give his approach a direction that does not necessarily inhere in it, and to this extent, leaves other possibilities open. Heidegger's thinking is not as homogeneous as it appears to be; and today we are gradually gaining a distance from it which permits us, instead of global partisanship for or against, to critically differentiate the cul-de-sacs from what should not be lost.

Since Heidegger calls what according to him is the most primordially given—the disclosedness of Dasein, or, later, the clearing of Being— "the truth," yet thereby means something opposed to truth in the traditional, specific sense of the word, we are thus provided with incentive to connect this most primordial givenness with the truth. This most primordial given—"world" in the sense of the clearing of Being—is of course not the world in the sense of our determinate, substantive horizons;

instead, it is an open region [*Spielraum*]: not of beings, but rather, of these horizons themselves. Correspondingly, disclosedness does not exhaust itself in any specific conception of the world. If one now reflects on the specific meaning of truth, then one could no longer call disclosedness itself, or the clearing, truth. However, one could say that disclosedness is, according to its essence, directed toward truth; although it can also (according to Heidegger's concept of "insistence" ["*Insistenz*"]) obstruct the question of truth. The clearing is a realm whose depth dimension refers to truth; and thus he who stands within it is obligated to inquire after the truth not only of beings, but also of the aforementioned horizons.

In this way one could preserve Heidegger's radicalization of Husserl's transcendental position: eliminating as its point of departure a self-certain subjectivity that believes itself in possession of ahistorical, absolute evidential certainty, without, however, giving up Husserl's *concept* of evidence as the idea of the specific mode of givenness of truth. With Heidegger's posing of the problem, evidential certainty does not lose its meaning; instead, as is already the case at least in part with Husserl, it must be understood—of course, along with truth—as a regulative idea. In this way, the immediacy of evidential certainty would be surmounted; and nevertheless, instead of ceding to a new, precritical concept of the immediacy of truth, a critical consciousness would be maintained, while brought into the state of balance that constitutes its essence.

In Heidegger's metatranscendental position—in which the most primordially given is neither substance nor subject, but instead, an open region—critical consciousness could have been able to find its proper balance. Here, at the point at which transcendental not only takes in history, but also opens itself to it and renounces the support of an ultimate ground, arose the possibility of radicalizing and developing anew the idea of critical consciousness; yet also thereby the danger of surrendering this idea and giving preference to a new immediacy. But in fact the open region did not yield that proper balance; for without the depth dimension of truth, it was thought only as a region of *immediacy* (be it the immediacy of projection or the immediacy of the destining [*Geschick*] of unconcealedness). The step from the "uncanniness" ["*Unheimlichkeit*"] of *Being and Time* to the "hominess" ["*Heimischwerden*"] of the "Letter on Humanism" is only a small one: for the moment of reflection, which is constitutive for the question of truth, remained from the outset on the margins.

As a result, Heidegger was compelled to develop his position as an "overcoming" [*"Verwindung"*] of the modern philosophy of reflection —whereas it might have just as easily been a radicalization of the latter. Heidegger had associated the philosophy of subjectivity with the dogmatism of self-certainty. However, with respect to the *idea* of certainty as a regulative idea, modern philosophy only served to radicalize the Socratic requirement of critical justification—that is, of theoretical responsibility. Thus, the task would be to develop in its full breadth that concept of truth which Heidegger suggested with the concept of disclosedness, without denouncing the regulative idea of certainty and the postulate of critical justification.

Translated by Richard Wolin

14

BACK TO HISTORY:
AN INTERVIEW

Pierre Bourdieu

Introduction

The revelations concerning Heidegger's political misconduct presented in Victor Farias' *Heidegger et le nazisme* must have been received by Bourdieu as a delayed confirmation of theses that he originally elaborated in a little-known 1975 monograph, *L'ontologie politique de Martin Heidegger*. (Although Bourdieu's book was translated into German in 1976, it took another twelve years for it to be reissued in France.) For in that work, Bourdieu attempted to demonstrate the limitations of an exclusively intra-philosophical reading of Heidegger's texts. The latter could not be fully understood, he argued, unless they were situated in relation to a field of like-minded, non-philosophical texts that were produced in the 1920s by Germany's so-called "conservative revolutionary" writers: Moeller van den Bruck, Carl Schmitt, Oswald Spengler, Ernst Niekisch, and Ernst Jünger. Otherwise, Bourdieu claims, the historical and cultural radicalism of Heideggerian fundamental ontology—the summons to "decisiveness," "authenticity," "choosing one's hero," and so forth—would remain unappreciated. In this respect, Bourdieu's analysis coincides with a number of themes raised in Karl Löwith's essay, "The Political Implications of Heidegger's Existentialism."

Bourdieu's approach, grounded in the tradition of the sociology of knowledge, represents a thoroughgoing challenge to claims concerning the autonomy of philosophy. Heidegger's thought thus represents, as it were, the ideal test case for Bourdieu's approach, for its ideal of "the

Pierre Bourdieu, "Back to History: An Interview," appeared in *Libération*, March 10, 1988.

piety of thinking" claims a radical separation from the merely "conditioned" sphere of everyday historical life. What emerges above all in the
interview that follows, therefore, is the enormity of the methodological
stakes involved. Here, the point of departure is the sociologist's endemic
mistrust of the traditional notion of "prima philosophia" or "first philosophy": an approach to knowledge that betrays a superioristic disdain
for the "concrete" realms of history and society, as well as a concomi-
tant aversion to truth claims that are empirically verifiable, insofar as
such claims are said to pertain to the nether sphere of "facticity."

. . .

Robert Maggiori: At the moment, there is, to cite your own expression, an "unhealthy turmoil" surrounding Heidegger. Don't you fear
that the edition of your book [*L'ontologie politique de Martin Heidegger*] will contribute further to this turmoil.

Pierre Bourdieu: For a long time I resisted proposals to republish this
1975 text. Farias' book [*Heidegger and National Socialism*], while it
does not add anything extraordinarily new from a historical standpoint,
and though it remains external to [Heidegger's] work, and in this respect
represents a step backward in comparison with what I have tried to do,
has had the merit of forcing the Heideggerians to come down from the
lofty remove to which they had withdrawn. But this having been said,
the debate began very badly, just as in 1964,* something which belongs
almost exclusively to the logic of the process. Beginning from the moment where the parties are only concerned with "judging" and taking
sides, everyone can participate without knowledge of the texts and their
contents. And those who are in the greatest haste to "defend philosophy"
are naturally those whom one would least take to be philosophers and
who will let no favorable opportunity slip by, with the help of the charge
that they are being "attacked," to claim membership among that class.
But that is not the whole story: paradoxically, the constant reference to
the Holocaust, which via the philosopheme of "absolute evil" is rapidly
made into a *topos,* has led to the *dehistoricization* of the thought and

---

*Translator's note: Most likely Bourdieu is referring to the 1966–67 debate in the
journal *Critique*, set off by a review essay by François Fédier, "Trois attaques contre
Heidegger," in the November 1966 issue (no. 234). Responses by Robert Minder, Jean-
Pierre Faye, and Aimé Patrie appeared in the February 1967 issue (no. 237), followed by a
rejoinder by Fédier in July of the same year (no. 242).

the thinker; just as in Heidegger's case, the strategy of passing over to the extreme—which Heidegger himself so often exemplified—once again plays a role. When I hear people say that Heidegger alone makes it possible for us to think the Holocaust—but perhaps I am insufficiently postmodern—I think I must be dreaming . . .

M: But doesn't a debate of this nature run the risk of discrediting philosophy? Your book suggests quite expressly the question of the blindness of the philosopher . . .

B: It does not call into question philosophy and philosophers in general—which makes no sense—but instead a specific philosophy of philosophy; or, more precisely, a social use of philosophy that assumes its extreme form with Heidegger and the Heideggerians, and which is, alas, very widespread among philosophy professors. This type of professional posture leads professors of philosophy—the "queen of the sciences"—to draw prophetic conclusions from the philosophical legacy. Probably there are specific works—just as in music—that are more suitable than others for great virtuoso performances. This is the case with Heidegger's work. This is the basis of his success among many. It tirelessly sets in motion the entire register of prophetic effects which certain philosophy professors have long associated with philosophical activity: denunciation of common sense, of "doxa," of the "they" ["*das Man*"]; the claim of a hermetic divide between a thinking that is worthy of the name, ontology, and the customary, vulgar anthropological thinking of common sense and of the human sciences. Yet, other works that are intrinsically more rebellious—those of Marx, for example—led during the 1960s, especially with regard to the separation between "ideology" and "science," to an entirely similar set of practices. In this way certain philosophy instructors derive pleasure in repeating again and again, before their forty impressionable apprentices, the same theses.

M: There you exaggerate. . . . I cannot allow you to say that!

B: Once again, it's not a matter of calling into question philosophy in general, but rather, of identifying a certain misuse of symbolic power: preemptory judgments about the sciences, condemnations of scientism, positivism, historicism, of all sins against philosophical orthodoxy.

I must say that if this philosophy and these philosophers were drawn into the tumult over Heidegger's thought, it would in my eyes be no great loss. All the more so insofar as—and this brings us back to

Heidegger—it is arrogance that engenders the blindness. When Gadamer mentions Plato and Dionysus of Syracuse in Heidegger's defense,* he has no idea of how truthfully he speaks: the philosopher-king ended up as a slave of the tyrant; the philosophical Führer makes himself into the advocate of the Führer. The principle of these immense political errors, and of so many other smaller and apparently excusable errors, which have sent on their way "small prophets in the employ of the state," is the aristocratism of the poor man, who thereby proceeds to cut himself off from everyday experience, which he in turn mocks if one is concerned with real housing problems, instead of contemplating "dwelling" ["*das Wohnen*"]; and who must keep his distance from the human sciences and at the same time constantly borrows from them in secret; since one is concerned with avoiding every compromise with the century, and thus claiming one's separateness, one's *différence*—be it with an "e" or an "a"—especially from the historical and social sciences, which results in one's walling oneself off into a type of ghetto. At the end there is blindness, the "great blunder" ["*grosse Dummheit*"], as Heidegger allegedly said of his support of Nazism. There has been much critical discussion of the fact that he never disavowed this support. But how could he have when it was a question of acknowledging—and self-acknowledgment—that the "thinker" had never been able to think the essential; that "it"—as is said of his "great blunder"—was stronger than he himself had been; that his id, his unthought—that of an "ordinary university professor"—and the entire train of social phantasms had led around by the nose this small bearer of a cultural capital, Heidegger, the philosopher of "*Entschlossenheit*," of free decision, whose "fixed assets" were in danger?

M: We need to take a look at the method which you apply in your study. You dismiss the questions that have been customarily been posed: was Heidegger a Nazi? Why didn't he say anything about the Holocaust? Is it correct to say that your intent is to transcend the opposition between an internal and an external reading (which is, by the way, what Derrida calls for in his interview with the *Nouvel Observateur*)?

B: I actually found it rather comical that Derrida, who knows my 1975 book on the subject quite well—he read it, and I presented it in

* Translator's note: See Hans-Georg Gadamer, "Back from Syracuse?," *Critical Inquiry* 15(2):427–430, 1989.

one of his seminars, where he raised no objections—in order to dismiss the sociological analysis, conjures up a type of analysis which is supposed to overcome the opposition between internal and external reading; a program that I announced a long time ago and that I was apparently successful in. But one must realize that the Heidegger debate had placed him in considerable difficulty.

But to come to the method that I have sought to apply to other realms —to literature, in the case of Flaubert, to painting, in that of Manet, to law, etc.—this means in the first instance reintegrating the history of philosophy—which is said to belong to a separate sphere which normal historians dare not enter—with history. This is a difficult undertaking because, as always, social divisions are also mental divisions, principles of separation, and categories of the professorial understanding; and because the new way of investigating the history of philosophy that I am proposing presupposes that one knows how to combine things that our conception of culture separates with an insurmountable barrier. And thus, the academic concept of culture (which today is defended in a more or less regressive way by the homo academicus who has been wounded by the student protest movement—I am thinking especially of Allan Bloom—and also by media essayists who make their living by attacking the business of culture) has constituted itself by attacks against politics, economics, and all trivial realities of the normal world which the average professor doesn't care to familiarize himself with. To undertake a history of philosophy that actually integrates philosophy with history, within which and against which philosophy has often developed, means combining fire and water. The service rendered by Heidegger—that "pure" and ahistorical thinker par excellence, who explicitly denies that thought is related to the thinker and his biography, not to mention to the economic and social relations of his age; and who has always been read in a totally dehistoricized way—consists in forcing us, as a result of his "great blunder," to rethink the relationship between philosophy and politics. This is the meaning of the title which I gave to my study: the ontology is political and the politics becomes ontological.

M: Yes, but the relation you seek to establish between philosophy and history differs from Marxist analyses, be they those of Lukács, Adorno, or Goldmann. You allow for the mediation of what you call the "philosophical field": the microcosm, as you say, which is immersed in the social cosmos, and yet which is relatively independent, where the operations of philosophers, their social as well as philosophical—or, in Heidegger's case, ontological as well as political—strategies unfold.

B: Exactly. In order to understand Heidegger—of course, here I can't summarize my entire analysis—one needs to understand not only the "received ideas" which were in the air, in newspaper editorials, university speeches, in forewords to historical or philological works, in the conversations between university professors, and so forth, and which everyone—the essayists Spengler, Jünger, and Niekisch—propagated in his own way. One must also understand the specific logic of the philosophical field itself, in which the great professionals debated, which, at the time, meant neo-Kantians (who were of course all divided into various factions), phenomenologists, neo-Thomists, and so forth.

M: What one discovers through reading your book is that this philosophy, which seems to have originated from nowhere, cannot be separated from the existence of a field to which Heidegger belongs and in which he was formed philosophically.

B: Yes. The difficulty with Heidegger is that his philosophy has a dual basis; and that, in order to read it, two cultures that are rarely united with one another must be mobilized and made to function in an entirely new way which, for the most part, contradicts the themes that have determined the philosophy's reception. If the Heideggerians have not reached the Master's heights, it is because they make use of it in a way I would call mystico-literary, and, in a way that is far from professional, of a highly technical philosophy before the "Turn" (it suffices, for example, to read *Identity and Difference,* which is dedicated to a discussion of Hegel, in order to be convinced of this). In fact, one must be highly professional in order to introduce a "conservative revolution" into philosophy: it is a question of making something philosophically unnameable, distasteful—or even something that is in the eyes of a neo-Kantian opponent like [Ernst] Cassirer simply obscene—nameable, socially acceptable.

M: Why "highly professional"? Why don't you go so far as to say that one must be a very great philosopher?

B: One must dispose over extraordinary powers of invention, that is, an extraordinary philosophical capital (in this connection, see Heidegger's virtuoso performance in *Kant and the Problem of Metaphysics*) and over an extraordinary capacity to maintain forms, which presupposes a practical mastery of the totality of positions present in the field, and have an incredible sense for the game of philosophy. (In passing, one sees that the historicization of thought is not "reductionist," but the opposite.) In contrast with the essayists like Jünger and Spengler, who mix everything together, Heidegger *integrates* philosophical positions, which were previously thought to be irreconcilable, into a new position. This mastery of the space of what is possible, which characterizes professionals, is never so clear as in the case of the second Heidegger, who constantly defines himself in relation to others, who, through his prophylactic denials, constantly contradicts the ideas that one could have on the basis of other, present or past positions.

M: In your view, what is required for the real understanding of philosophy?

B: In opposition to the common view, the understanding of a philosophy requires neither a dehistoricization through eternalization that the timeless reading of canonical texts as "philosophia perennis" produces, nor simply the anachronism of adapting such texts to "the taste of the day"—as in: "Heidegger enables us to think the Holocaust." On the contrary, such understanding derives from a real historicization that returns to the principle of the work itself by reconstructing the problematic, the space of what is possible, in relation to which it has been constructed. In point of fact, one must speak of a double historicization: historical reconstruction presupposes the objectivation of historicity from a present-day standpoint, on whose basis it occurs. However, this would lead us too far afield.

M: But does the sociologist apply this procedure to himself? One could accuse him of not making the same type of inquiries when it is a question of his own abode.

B: If the sociologist disputes the philosopher's claim to extraterritoriality, to trans-historicity, then it is not in order to accord these privileges to himself and to assume the mantle of the philosopher-king. He applies to himself the same treatment that he applies to the philosopher: he strives to determine his specific "unthought," the social philosophy that haunts the concepts employed as well as the words most frequently used in the discourse about the social world. Sociology possesses the privilege of being able to turn its instruments of thought against itself—

which means against its own instruments of thought. And in case it should forget, the fact that it attempts to place other disciplines in question condemns its own questions to rebound with redoubled force against it.

Translated by Richard Wolin

15

FRENCH HEIDEGGER WARS

Richard Wolin

I believe one's point of reference should not be to the great model of language (*langue*) and signs, but to that of war and battle. The history which bears and determines us has the form of a war rather than that of a language: relations of power, not relations of meaning.

—Michel Foucault, "Truth and Power"

Few events in recent memory have shaken the world of French letters as the appearance of Victor Farias' book, *Heidegger et le Nazisme*. Through an extremely thorough and painstaking (and for French Heideggerians, clearly painful) labor of documentation, Farias has single-handedly given the lie to all the inventive rationalizations contrived by Heideggerians— as well as those set forth on several occasions by Heidegger himself— over the course of the last four decades trivializing the Master's alacritous participation in the "National Awakening" of 1933. It is no secret that since the collapse of the two previously dominant intellectual paradigms of the postwar era, existentialism and structuralism, Heideggerianism, as a philosophy of "difference," has enjoyed unquestionable pride of place. Yet, his work has enjoyed a remarkably *dehistoricized* reception in France, such that Heidegger, qua critic of "technology" (*"Technik"*), has been able to emerge as a major intellectual antagonist of modern industrialized democratic society. And in this respect, from a structural point of view, Heideggerianism has been able to fill an important void in the discourse of the French left following the timely demise of Marxism in the 1970s; a situation that, conversely, could have no parallel in German cultural life, where an analogously dehistoricized reception of his work would be impossible, insofar as his intellectual filiations with the Nietzschean-inspired tradition of "conservative revolutionary" *Kulturkritik* (Carl Schmitt, Oswald Spengler, Ernst Jünger) have always been considered self-evident.

It is no small irony, then, that Farias' book, while hardly a theoretical tour de force, may well have paved the way for a new epistemological break in the volatile world of Parisian cultural life, one whose stakes concern the problematic of a *rehabilitation of subjectivity*. And thus, as a pair of French commentators have observed, "the 'Farias affair'. . . displays an essential dimension of the French intellectual universe, and a clarification of this uproar in the French intelligentsia should afford greater insight into the lines of force (or weakness) that structure this universe."[1] For in many respects, the systematic unmasking of the intellectual lacunae proper to Heideggerianism—an unmasking whose foremost target has been "anti-humanism" as the necessary precondition of an anti-democratic political predisposition (and in this respect, the differences between the "early" and "later" Heidegger appear less significant than one might initially suspect)—offers strong parallels with the fate of French Marxism in the 1970s.

Yet one outcome of the tumultuous events surrounding Farias' book may be discerned already: from this point hence, in France and elsewhere, intellectuals in all walks of life will never be able to relate to Heidegger's philosophy "naively," that is without taking into consideration the philosopher's odious political allegiances. And thus, the debate spawned by *Heidegger et le Nazisme* is destined to become an inescapable point of reference for all future discussions of Heideggerianism and its merits. Were the relationship between the philosopher and his politics non-integral, if one could make a neat separation between the philosophical oeuvre and the political engagement, then this outcome would be prejudicial. All persons—great thinkers included—are capable of errors of political judgment, even egregious ones. However, the more one learns about Heidegger's relations with National Socialism, the more one is ineluctably driven to conclude that the philosopher himself perceived his Nazi involvements not as a random course of action, but as a *logical outgrowth of his philosophical doctrines*. A careful correlation of the early philosophy with the political speeches of the 1930s[2] leaves no doubt concerning the fact that Heidegger himself viewed his National Socialist activities as a concrete exemplification of *eigentliches Dasein* or authentic existence. That is, Heidegger himself makes a great effort to justify his participation in the Nazi movement in terms of categories carefully culled from his magnum opus of 1927, *Sein und Zeit.*

Why Heidegger? Why in France? Why now? Have the true intellectual stakes of the debate been exaggerated beyond reason by an unprecedented degree of media hype (in newspapers, journals, and highly publicized television debates)? Or is it true that beneath the layers of publicity surrounding the controversy, the Farias revelations have indeed unleashed questions of major intellectual import?

Paris was the logical staging ground for such a debate if one takes seriously the oft-quoted maxim: "Today, Heidegger lives in France." That is, without question, the major repercussions of the debate stand to be felt in Parisian intellectual circles where Heideggerianism has been so dominant in the postwar years.

The repercussions of Heidegger's philosophical preeminence can be described with a fair degree of precision. His influence has, first and foremost, hastened the demise of the paradigm of "subjectivity." As such, it has laid the groundwork for an unsparing theoretical rejection of the categories of meaning, intentionality, experience, and human volition. Ironically, the predominance of this paradigm in France in the 1940s and 1950s was largely attributable to the influence and impact of a very different Heidegger—the Heidegger of *Being and Time,* who, qua representative of *Existenzphilosophie,* was received through the influential phenomenological writings of Sartre and Merleau-Ponty. But in the course of what one might call the second French Heidegger reception of the 1960s, the later Heidegger—the critic of anthropocentrism and the philosopher of "Being"—was played off against the early "existential humanist" Heidegger (i.e., the Heidegger of Sartre's influential essay, "L'existentialisme est un humanisme"); a maneuver which, significantly, coincided with an analogous assault on the categories of philosophical subjectivity undertaken by the leading exponents of French structuralism —Claude Lévi-Strauss, Jacques Lacan, Louis Althusser, and Michel Foucault.

Hence, it would seem plausible to conclude that when the final balance sheet is drawn concerning the theoretical stakes of the current debate, a reevaluation of the legacy of philosophical subjectivity—as a programmatic component of a revitalized ethos of "democratic humanism"—will likely figure among the most important long-term consequences. For there is no avoiding the fact that, insofar as totalitarianism has rightfully been perceived as the major dilemma of political modernity, and, correspondingly, the idea of "human rights" has undergone a sweeping and dramatic revivification, a philosophy that parades under the banner of "anti-humanism" such as Heidegger's can hardly remain above suspicion.[3] Especially now that the unsavory details of his political involvements of the early 1930s have become a matter of public record, one cannot help but suspect that his thoroughgoing critique of philosophical humanism—for example, in the influential "Letter on Humanism" (1946)—represents a thinly disguised continuation of anti-democratic politics by other means. Here, we see the reason why those philosophers allied with "deconstruction" have been so dismayed by recent developments; for in the wake of what we now know regarding Heidegger's political loyalties, the deconstruction of the "subject" can hardly seem an entirely innocent affair.

Moreover, in order to gauge the truly explosive impact of Farias' indictment, one must also consider the fact that two of the major cultural and political *événements* in France during the 1980s were both Holocaust-related: *Shoah,* Claude Lanzmann's magisterial epic about the death camps (1985); and the trial of Klaus Barbie, which received intensive media coverage since his return to France in 1983 and sensational trial in 1987. Further, now that the myth of intrepid French resistance to the Nazi occupation has been blown apart by American historians such as Robert O. Paxton,[4] and given the rise of Jean-Marie Le Pen's neo-fascist National Front, the French media has, in a certain measure, attempted to restore the tarnished national honor by dramatic revelations concerning "Nazis and/or collaborators still among us." Heidegger seems to have fallen victim to this (to be sure, in part exaggerated) logic of compensation.

Finally, despite the fact that significant debates over Heidegger's Nazi past have surfaced in France on at least two previous occasions,[5] Farias' documentation incorporates the pathbreaking revelations of the Freiburg historian Hugo Ott;[6] and it is principally the additional materials brought to light by Ott's archival work in Freiburg that has, as it were, transformed quantity into quality: as a result of Ott's researches, the full extent of Heidegger's dedication to the National Socialist cause has attained the status of an undeniable fact; whereas previously, the incomplete documentation of the case, coupled with Heidegger's own disingenuous accounts of his activities, made it fairly easy for his devoted supporters to parry any possible blows to the Master's reputation.[7]

Thus, with the appearance of the Farias book,[8] French perceptions regarding Heidegger's political loyalties in the early thirties have definitively changed: his zealous involvement with the NSDAP, which could formerly be denied or trivialized, has now assumed the status of a permanent taint. The traditional contingent of French Heidegger defenders is at present scrambling to salvage what can be salvaged; and his long-standing detractors are basking—at least momentarily—in the glory of schadenfreude, since what they have been suggesting all along now seems a proven fact.

At the center of the recent French controversy is of course the book by Victor Farias. On the one hand, Farias deserves credit for having ignited a long overdue debate over the tabooed theme of the political dimension of Heidegger's work. On the other hand, his argument concerning Heidegger's Nazi ties is so brazenly tendentious, that he has in the end ironically undermined his own case. For Farias, there are no gray areas, the question of Heidegger and Nazism is an open and shut case. National Socialism was not a political credo that Heidegger adopted opportunistically and then abandoned when it proved a political liability. Instead, for Farias, Heidegger was *born* a Nazi and remained one until the end of his days. To be sure, Farias is able to muster an impressive amount of evidential support to show that: a) Heidegger's provincial-Catholic background in the German town of Messkirch predisposed him toward a "national revolutionary" solution to the evils of modernity; and b) his partisanship for Nazi principles continued long after the point when his enthusiasm for the historical movement itself had waned (at least into the early forties). But to accept the results of Farias' inquiry at face value would be to conclude that both Heidegger's life and thought are so irredeemably colored by Nazi convictions that nothing "uncontaminated" remains worth salvaging. In this respect, the book is truly a "livre à thèse," and this proves to be its ultimate undoing. It is so negatively disposed toward its subject that the outcome—a rousing condemnation of Heidegger qua dyed-in-the-wool Nazi—is a foregone conclusion. Various commentators have compared Farias' strategy of argumentation—which frequently consists of juxtaposing the pro-Nazi sentiments of Heideggerian intimates or associates with those of the Master himself—with the tactic of "guilt by association"—by no means an unfair accusation. In this respect, Farias has done a great disservice to his own cause. There is really little objective need for exaggeration or hyperbole: the facts of the case are disturbing enough and speak for themselves. The strategy of unnuanced, wholesale condemnation has left Farias extremely vulnerable to attacks from the Heideggerian faithful, who have been able to seize on the prejudicial character of his inquiry as a clever way of de-legitimating his efforts and avoiding coming to grips with the troubling substantive concerns that have in fact arisen.

The "thèse" of this "livre à thèse" is fairly simple: that Heidegger was not merely a Nazi, but a *radical* Nazi, by which Farias means a supporter of the Röhm faction or SA. As he comments in the opening pages of his book: "Martin Heidegger's adherence to the NSDAP in no way resulted from an improvisational opportunism or tactical considerations. . . . Heidegger opted for the wing represented by Ernst Röhm and the SA and sought to place this variant of National Socialism on a proper philosophical footing, in open opposition to the biological and racial faction led by Alfred Rosenberg and Ernst Krieck" (pp. 16–17). Were Farias to make this argument stick, he would thereby also rather handily dispel some evidence that might prove troubling to a more simplistic attempt to equate Heidegger with National Socialism; for example, the fact that Heidegger was at a later point the object of calumnious attacks by the ideologists Rosenberg and Krieck (the Nazi Rector-Führer at Frankfurt University, who was also a philosopher). Hence, by aligning Heidegger with the SA, Farias can plausibly explain his later difficulties with certain Nazi authorities such as Rosenberg and Krieck by claiming that such polemics were a result of Heidegger's former SA allegiances.[9] Farias tries to prove his case by showing that Heidegger, on numerous occasions, cultivated especially close ties with the various German student associations in the early 1930s, which were at this point *"gleichgeschaltet"* and closely allied with the SA. However, the evidence Farias offers on this score is largely circumstantial and far from convincing. As Hannah Arendt has shown in her contribution to the Festschrift for Heidegger's eightieth birthday,[10] the philosopher always had a large student following, dating back to his Marburg years in the early twenties. Moreover, since he was apparently convinced of the retrograde character of the German university system (as is suggested by his polemics against "so-called academic freedom" in the early thirties), it follows logically that he would look to the German youth of the period as a possible source of revitalization. Of course, there is no sidestepping the fact that in 1933, it was a "Fascist youth" to whom Heidegger directed his not infrequent appeals on the subject of national rejuvenation.

In any event, Farias' contention that Heidegger was a radical Nazi and Röhm adherent is far from persuasive. Although an interesting sidelight on the Heidegger-SA theme is shed in a remark by Heidegger in "The Rectorship, 1933–34: Facts and Thoughts,"[11] where he claims to have relinquished any and every illusion concerning the authenticity of the National Socialist movement as of June 30, 1934, the "Night of the Long Knives." What is fascinating about Heidegger's admission is that it can be interpreted in either of two ways: either the brutality of the Röhm purge was the event that finally enlightened him concerning the base realities of National Socialism; or else the destruction of the SA signaled for him the defeat of National Socialism in its radical, heroic strain. The fact that in 1935 Heidegger could still counterpose the "inner truth and greatness of the National Socialist movement" to the "works that are being peddled about nowadays as the philosophy of National Socialism,"[12] suggests that he himself continued to distinguish (as he would in the *Der Spiegel* interview some thirty years later) between the movement's original historical potential and its later bastardization, which subsequently accounted for Heidegger's own withdrawal of active support. Yet, even if Heidegger's political sympathies indeed lay with the Röhm faction, the case for Heidegger as a hard-core SA adherent is one for which Farias has failed to provide adequate proof.

A final illustration of the manner in which Farias undermines the credibility of his own argument (and one frequently cited by his opponents) pertains to the eighteenth-century prelate Abraham à Sancta Clara, a native son of Heidegger's own Messkirch. A prolific writer who gained a position of tremendous influence at the court of the Habsburgs (as well as the model for the Capuchin preacher in Schiller's *Wallenstein*), Abraham was also a virulent anti-Semite. It so happens that the first published writing of the young Heidegger in 1910 was composed on the occasion of a monument erected in the honor of this local hero. Farias devotes an entire chapter (pp. 39–55) to this otherwise uninteresting bit of Heidegger juvenalia. That Heidegger has no special words of praise for Abraham's anti-Semitism is to Farias a matter of indifference. However, Farias pursues the tenuous connection between these two sons of Messkirch relentlessly, ending his book with a discussion of a 1964 speech delivered by Heidegger at Messkirch once again in honor of the eighteenth-century monk. In his speech, Heidegger quotes an observation by Abraham that "our peace is as far from war as Sachsenhausen from Frankfurt" (Farias, p. 293). Of course, by invoking Sachsenhausen, Abraham (and Heidegger) are referring to the district of Frankfurt. But Farias cannot let pass the opportunity for some ruminations on the workings of Heidegger's unconscious, by linking the Frankfurt quarter with the concentration camp of the same name outside of Berlin. Farias' amateur Freudianism suggests that Sachsenhausen is a metonymic trope for Auschwitz, the logical historical outgrowth of Abraham's anti-Semitism; and thus, that Heidegger's statement is merely a sinister instance of parapraxis. But such feeble efforts at lay analysis fall short of producing the resounding indictment Farias has been seeking for some 300 pages.

Finally, the Farias book is extremely weak from a philosophical standpoint. This would not be a damnable failing if the author had been content to stick primarily with biographical themes. But instead, he chooses to indict not only Heidegger the man—who, following the researches by Ott, has become an easy target—but also Heidegger the thinker. At this level of analysis, the questions at issue become decidedly more complex, and Farias lacks the intellectual wherewithal to broach these matters with the requisite degree of prudence and sophistication. Because Heidegger as a man may have been rotten to the core does not mean one can, *mutatis mutandis,* make the same argument concerning his philosophy. If the canon of great works were to be decided on the ad hominem grounds of the ethical character of the authors, we would conceivably be left with little to read. On occasion, Farias concocts specious parallels between Heidegger's work and his politics, but these insights for the most part have the status of unsystematic afterthoughts. Yet, when the stakes are so high, offhanded remarks won't do. Farias leaves us with the impression that there is a necessary link between Heidegger's thought and his Nazism; and that as a result, Heideggerianism as a philosophical enterprise is essentially flawed or invalid. While the relationship between thought and politics in Heidegger's case may well turn out to be of paramount importance, Farias has not shown us wherein this linkage consists, nor the reason why it may be fatal to the Heideggerian project. The conclusions are suggested instead by insinuation and innuendo.

For certain French Heideggerians, the Farias book will forever be viewed as a small-minded and rancorous assault on a great philosophical legacy.[13] Or as Heidegger himself was fond of saying: "When they can't attack the philosophy, they attack the philosopher." The philosopher and Heidegger translator Pierre Aubenque asks plaintively: "What is the *ethical* status, as far as our traditional judgments about inquisition and censure are concerned, of a book that openly presents itself as an enterprise of denunciation, and especially the denunciation of a thinker, above all, when this denunciation is in a large measure calumnious?" François Fédier attempts to explain the hue and cry concerning Heidegger's Nazi ties psychologically, as an instance of "ressentiment": it is reducible to "the rage of mediocrities against Heidegger—I've seen it at work my entire life."[14] Henri Crétella contends that there can be no integral relation between Heidegger's thought and Nazism, since the latter was predicated "on a refusal to think." He then seeks to turn the tables on Farias by claiming that "there are two ways to declare a taboo on thinking: a vociferous, frenzied way, and another, gently anesthetizing way." Whereas the former mentality, which Crétella identifies as the "historical meaning" of Nazism, has been vanquished, the second, which is the "essential meaning" of Nazism, survives in inquiries such as that of Victor Farias.[15]

On the other hand, many commentators have been genuinely disturbed by the recent facts that have come to light about Heidegger's National Socialist past, recognizing that to harp ceaselessly on Farias' purported methodological failings is to beg the major question at issue, viz., to what extent might Heidegger's personal misdeeds jeopardize the legacy of his philosophical project? A common theme among those who have chosen to acknowledge the gravity of Farias' revelations relates to the philosopher's obstinate refusal to utter the barest word of contrition about his Nazi past or about the Holocaust in general.[16] As Maurice Blanchot observes: "each time that he was asked to recognize his 'error,' he maintained a rigid silence, or said something that aggravated the situation. . . . It is in Heidegger's silence about the Exterminations that his irreparable error lies" (Blanchot goes on to cite Heidegger's arrogant remark to the effect that Hitler had failed *him* by reneging on the original radical potential of National Socialism).[17] In a similar vein, the philosopher Emmanuel Levinas observes: "Does not this silence, even in peace-time, about the gas chambers and the death camps—something beyond the realm of 'bad excuses'—attest to a soul that is in its depths impervious to compassion [*sensibilité*], is it not a tacit approval of the horrifying."[18] Even Heidegger's most talented and original disciple, Hans-Georg Gadamer, has freely admitted that in his political engagement, "Heidegger was not a pure and simple opportunist"—rather, "he 'believed' in Hitler."[19]

Equally fascinating have been a series of related discoveries that have surfaced as unintended outgrowths of the main debate itself.

The most momentous of these "spillover" disclosures concerns the man who for 35 years was France's most stalwart Heidegger advocate, Jean Beaufret. Beaufret, a Heidegger translator, intimate, and interlocutor—as well as a former Resistance fighter—who published several volumes of his *Conversations with Heidegger* before his death in 1982, is perhaps best known to the English-speaking world as the addressee of Heidegger's important "Letter on Humanism"—a 50–page rejoinder to a series of questions posed by Beaufret in 1945 on the relationship between fundamental ontology and humanism (Heidegger's response is also a pointed rebuttal of Jean-Paul Sartre's defense of the humanist tradition in "Existentialism is a Humanism"). Whenever questions had been raised in years past concerning Heidegger's unsavory political allegiances, Beaufret had always been in the forefront of his defenders; and his credentials as an ex-*Résistant* seemed to lend an aura of unimpeachable moral sanctity to his pro-Heideggerian proclamations. After all, when a Resistance figure defends an alleged Nazi, his motives must certainly be beyond reproach.

But not in this case. As it turns out, Beaufret seems to have had a hidden agenda: he was a covert supporter of Robert Faurisson, the French historian who denies the existence of the gas chambers specifically and the Holocaust in general.[20] In two letters dated November 22, 1978 and January 18, 1979 (recently made available in Faurisson's journal, *Annales d'histoire revisioniste*), Beaufret expresses adamant support for Faurisson's "project" and sympathizes with him for the criticism he received from the press. At one point Beaufret observes: "I believe that for my part I have traveled approximately the same path as you and have been considered suspect for having expressed the same doubts [concerning the existence of the gas chambers]. Fortunately for me, this was done orally."[21] That the major French Heidegger interpreter of the postwar era was a closet supporter of Faurisson's thesis concerning the nonexistence of the Nazi death camps casts serious doubt (to say the least) concerning his "objectivity" as an intrepid Heidegger champion.

Another disturbing circumstance that has recently come to light concerns Heidegger's long-standing friendship with Eugen Fischer, who in 1927 became director of the notorious "Institute of Racial Hygiene" in Berlin. Fischer was one of the principal architects of the National Socialist racial theory, and thus in essence laid the intellectual groundwork for the "Final Solution." Born in 1874, Fischer established his credentials in 1913 with a book on the "problem of the bastardization of the human species." This work drew important lessons from German colonial racial legislation in Southwest Africa, where, as of 1908, marriages between Europeans and natives were forbidden, and those that had already been contracted were declared null. However, the true solution to the problem of miscegenation envisioned by Fischer was the "disappearance" of those of mixed race through a diabolical "process of natural selection."

Fischer was active in the early years of Nazi rule, helping to promulgate legislation aimed at "protection against the propagation of genetic abnormalities," on the basis of which over 60,000 forced sterilizations were performed in 1934 alone. His institute in Berlin was also the inspiration behind the Nuremberg racial laws of 1935, forbidding intermarriage (as well as sexual contact of any sort) between Jews and non-Jews. A leading theorist of eugenics and a forceful proponent of "a biological politics of population," Fischer has been described as "one of the linchpins of the execution of the bureaucratic and ideological methods that facilitated [Nazi] genocide." It may help put things in perspective to add that Dr. Joseph Mengele was a "researcher" at Fischer's institute.

Relations between Heidegger and Fischer were loose, but for that reason nonetheless interesting. Both hailed from the same region in

Baden. Both participated in a Leipzig congress in November 1933 to promote the cause of "German science." The two remained in contact for the duration of Heidegger's rectorship. And it may have been in no small measure due to Fischer's influence that the racial measures promoted by Heidegger during his tenure as rector that have been chronicled by Farias—a questionnaire concerning racial origin distributed to all professors; an obligatory lecture for all instructors on the importance of racial purity; the establishment of a "department of race" at the university run by the SS—followed a model set forth by his fellow Schwarzwalder.

In 1944, at the age of 55, Heidegger had been drafted into the *Volksturm*—a reserve unit comprised of older German men—as was not uncommon for men his age during the war's later stages. Only a personal telegram sent to the Gauleiter of Salzburg spared Heidegger from service. The sender of the telegram was none other than Eugen Fischer. It read: "With all due respect for the imperatives of the hour and those of the *Volksturm* . . . I am in favor of freeing from armed service Heidegger, an exceptional and irreplaceable thinker for the nation and the Party."[22]

That ties between the two remained cordial over the years is suggested by the fact that in 1960, Heidegger sent Fischer a copy of his book *Hebel, der Hausfreund,* with the inscription, "For Eugen Fischer, with warm Christmas greetings and best wishes for the New Year" (Farias, p. 79).

It would certainly be unfair to judge Heidegger by the company he kept, no matter how sinister. Yet the Heidegger-Fischer episode is of interest insofar as it suggests that, because of his ties with Fischer, the philosopher may well have been aware of the Nazi preparations for genocide (as well as other crimes) at a relatively early date—something his supporters have always denied.

Two of the leading French Heideggerians, Jacques Derrida and Philippe Lacoue-Labarthe, have been in the forefront of the philosophical debate concerning the question "whither Heideggerianism?" in the aftermath of the Farias controversy. Unlike the base Heidegger apologists (Fédier, Aubenque, Crétella), who have seized on the purportedly tendentious nature of Farias' study to avoid confronting the disturbing facts of the case in the hope of fostering a return to "business as usual," Lacoue-Labarthe and Derrida have been willing to confront these troubling biographical themes head-on (Derrida, for example, speaks of Heidegger's "terrifying silence" about the past in the February 9, 1988 issue of *Le Monde*). Their intention, however (the methodological validity of which can hardly be denied), is to allow the vultures to feed on Heidegger the contingent, empirical individual (what *is* an author, anyway?), while saving the philosophical oeuvre itself—especially Heidegger's work following *die Kehre* (the "Turn"); where—so the argument runs—Heidegger freed himself from the vestigial anthropocentrism that is still so prominent in *Being and Time*.

Ironically, both Lacoue-Labarthe and Derrida published book-length "responses" to Farias well before his manuscript ever appeared: they are respectively entitled *La fiction du politique* and *De l'esprit: Heidegger et la question* (both appeared in 1987).[23] Both Lacoue-Labarthe and Derrida had heard tell of the troubling revelations from the other side of the Rhine (Ott's work being the major source) and decided to stake out a position on the philosophical implications of these findings in advance of the storm that would soon be unleashed. Since these two books contain the major *prises de position* on the question of Heidegger and politics by the two leading representatives of Heideggerianism working in France today, they are worth discussing at some length.

La fiction du politique is simultaneously an unflinching arraignment of Heidegger's Nazism and a bold endorsement of (post-"Kehre") Heideggerian orthodoxy. Unlike the tiresome apologists, who would give anything to go back to "life before Farias," Lacoue-Labarthe pulls no punches when addressing the fatal interrelation between philosophy and politics that led to Heidegger's 1933 "engagement." His approach is characterized by a refreshing willingness to seriously weigh the continuities between Heidegger's early philosophical writings and his National Socialist convictions in the early thirties. His assertion that "contrary to what has been said here and there, Heidegger's engagement is *absolutely coherent* with his thought" (p. 22; emphasis added), apparently leaves little room for equivocation. But what Lacoue-Labarthe gives with one hand, he takes away—cleverly—with the other: the insight just cited pertains only to the pre-1935 Heidegger. The post-1935 Heidegger emerges virtually unscathed.

Lacoue-Labarthe's argument—which parallels Derrida's in its essentials—proceeds as follows. The problem with the early Heidegger is that he suffers from a *surfeit of metaphysical thinking*. Even though he has gone to great lengths to distance himself from the tradition of Western metaphysics in *Being and Time* and other early works, insisting that this tradition must be subjected to the purifying powers of *Destruktion,* the break proves in the end to be insufficiently rigorous. Metaphysical residues abound—most notably, in the Dasein-centered paradigm of *Being and Time,* where, when all is said and done, a human subject—albeit, a non-Cartesian, existentially rooted subject—once again provides privileged access to ontological questions. Thus, in the last analysis, *Being and Time,* despite the profound insight with which the book opens (the question concerning "the Being of beings"), simply relapses into conventional onto-theological modes of thought; its anthropomorphic demarche is really little more than a warmed-over version of traditional metaphysical humanism. Now that Nietzsche's insight concerning the death of God has been acknowledged, the topographical locus of the metaphysical *arche* has merely shifted: a transcendent dwelling-place has merely been exchanged for an immanent one, and Dasein, in its "decisive resolve toward authentic Being-for-Self," has become the new focal point of metaphysical inquiry. The fact that the second volume of *Being and Time* was never written can thus be explained by the fact that Heidegger, circa 1935, came to view the entire existential framework of his 1927 work as essentially flawed; that is, as perilously beholden to the paradigm of metaphysical humanism he had been at such pains to counteract.

What, however, do such ethereal philosophical questions have to do with Heidegger's attachments to the *base* realities of Nazi politics? Everything in the world, according to Lacoue-Labarthe and Derrida. Through a brilliant piece of hermeneutical chicanery, they intentionally seek (unlike the blatant apologists) to link up the philosophy of the early Heidegger with his pro-Nazi phase in order the better to save him: the early Heidegger, whose thought is in any case overly saturated with superfluous metaphysico-humanist residues,[24] can be safely jettisoned in order that the post-humanist Heidegger—the Heidegger of the Nietzsche lectures and the "Letter on Humanism"—can be redeemed unscathed. And thus by an ingenious interpretive *coup de maitre,* the troubling "question" of Heidegger and politics can be neatly brushed aside, since the post-1935 Heidegger abandoned the philosophical paradigm that led to his partisanship for Hitlerism in the first place. Lacoue-Labarthe, for example, specifies the lineages between National Socialism and humanism in the following passage, which has been the cause of not a few raised eyebrows:

Nazism is a humanism in that it rests on a determination of *humanitas,* which is, in its eyes, more powerful, i.e., more effective, than any other. The subject of absolute self-creation, even if it transcends all the determinations of the modern subject in an immediately natural position (the particularity of race), brings together and concretizes these same determinations (as does Stalinism with the subject of absolute self-production) and sets itself up as *the* subject, absolutely speaking. The fact that this subject lacks the universality that seems to define the *humanitas* of humanism in the usual sense does not, however, make Nazism an anti-humanism. Quite simply, it fits Nazism into the logic, of which there are many other examples, of the realization and concretization of "abstractions."[25]

The "defense" proffered by Lacoue-Labarthe and Derrida is certainly not without its merits. It therefore behooves us to examine it in a bit more detail before passing judgment on its worth. Above all, I would like to focus on what is perhaps the linchpin of the argument: the counter-intuitive claim that it was an *excess of metaphysical thinking,* or an allegiance to "humanism," that led to Heidegger's Nazism.[26]

At the same time, it is important to note the extent to which this reading of Heidegger conforms verbatim with the philosopher's self-interpretation of his intellectual/political trajectory. Hence, it is a strikingly orthodox reading of Heidegger. In this respect, the Lacoue-Labarthe/Derrida interpretation is of a piece with Heidegger's reevaluation of his own philosophy in his Nietzsche lectures of 1936–41. Previously, Heidegger had accepted Nietzsche's work at face value, viewing the latter as Nietzsche had understood himself: as a great subverter of metaphysical humanist nostrums and a critic of that "nihilism" to which traditional Western values inevitably led. It was fundamentally the debacle of Heidegger's Nazi experience that led him to reconceptualize his previous, uncritical relationship to Nietzsche. For just as Heidegger understood Nietzsche's efforts toward a "transvaluation of all values" as a *philosophical* answer to nihilism, he had greeted the National Socialist Revolution as a *political antidote* to nihilism. In viewing the

Nazi movement through a Nietzschean frame of reference, Heidegger endowed it with all the attributes of a salutary, world-historical challenge to Western nihilism and to the "decadent" values that are its necessary historical accompaniment: liberalism, individualism, philosophical subjectivism, mass society, techne, value-relativism, and so forth; in short, he perceived it as that panacea for the aporias of modernity allusively prophesied by Nietzsche's Zarathustra. The Nazis were the heroic "new barbarians" that would save the West from a seemingly irreversible process of Spenglerian decline.

In fact, it is fascinating to note that Heidegger maintained this perspective until the end of his life. That he never "renounced" the National Socialist experiment was neither an accident nor an oversight. Instead, if one examines "The Rectorship: 1933–34," the 1966 *Der Spiegel* interview, as well as *An Introduction to Metaphysics,* it is clear that Heidegger continued throughout his life to distinguish the debased historical actuality of Nazism from its true historical potential. He originally developed this distinction in the last-named work where, as we noted earlier, he takes pains to differentiate between "the inner truth and greatness of the National Socialist movement" and the inauthentic "works that are being peddled nowadays as the philosophy of National Socialism." The former he defines in terms of "the encounter between global technology and modern man"; that is, the "inner truth and greatness" of Nazism is to be found in its nature as a world-historical alternative to the technological-scientific nihilism bemoaned by Nietzsche and Spengler. What is shocking about this claim that "the inner truth and greatness of the movement [lies in] the encounter between global technology and modern man" is that the second half of this sentence was added parenthetically to the text of the 1953 re-edition of these lectures of 1935. Thus, not only has Heidegger refused to omit the original distinction between the "historical" and "essential" forms of Nazism in the later edition, he has in fact *re-emphasized the value of this distinction eighteen years later* by adding a clarification (concerning the "encounter between global technology and modern man") through which he seeks to *re-enforce* the original distinction itself.

His dogmatic non-repentance is further illustrated by his long-standing conviction that the National Socialist movement (and he personally) had been "betrayed" by the Führer himself. That is, it was Hitler who, owing to a failure of nerve, ultimately abandoned the original "anti-nihilistic" thrust of the movement (which was its raison d'être, according to Heidegger), by curbing its more radical tendencies. Thus, according to the testimony of the writer Ernst Jünger, Heidegger claimed after the war that Hitler would be resurrected and exonerate Heidegger, since he (Hitler) was guilty of having misled him.[27] That Heidegger never made a profession of guilt concerning his role in the "German catastrophe" follows logically from this reasoning, since, in the last analysis, *the fault lay with the National Socialist movement itself*—which had failed to live up to its true historical potential—*rather than with him*. This whole "strategy of denial" on Heidegger's part is fully consistent with the rather exalted mission he assigns to the National Socialist *Führer-Staat* in his Rectoral Address of 1933, where the latter is hailed as a bellicose re-invention of the Greek polis. Since the National Socialist state failed to live up to the metaphysical goals Heidegger had set for it, it was the Nazis, not Heidegger, who were ultimately at fault.[28]

To return to the Lacoue-Labarthe/Derrida contention that it was a "surplus of metaphysical thinking" that accounted for Heidegger's National Socialist leanings: according to this argument, Heidegger finally came around to realizing in the late 1930s that Nietzsche, instead of having delivered a deathblow to Western metaphysics, was in truth *the last metaphysician*. The post-Cartesian version of metaphysics largely consisted of an exaltation of human will; and Nietzsche's thought, for all its criticisms of philosophical humanism, was ultimately of a piece with this tradition, since its central category—"the will to power"—is likewise a glorification of will. It is precisely such an exaltation of "will" that is, according to Heidegger, at the root of Western *techne* and the triumph of modern technology. This celebration of will is at the very heart of the modern cultural project of "human self-assertion" (Blumenberg). Hence, National Socialism, which originally presented itself in Heidegger's eyes as a countermovement to the nihilism of the Western "will to *techne*"—and thus as a world-historical alternative to the "nihilism" so reviled by Nietzsche—in the end proved to be only a different historical manifestation of that same nihilism, in the same way that Nietzsche's strident critique of metaphysics itself ultimately rests on metaphysical foundations. The equation according to which Heidegger proceeds, therefore, is: National Socialism = Nietzscheanism = metaphysics. If it was an infatuation with Nietzsche (more specifically, with the latter's critique of nihilism) that led to Heidegger's embrace of National Socialism, then it was ultimately Western metaphysics that was at fault, since this was the intellectual framework that stood behind Nietzsche's thought. Heidegger had been misled and duped (first by Nietzsche, then by the Nazis), but he was not "responsible for," let alone "guilty of" any misdeeds.

A similar interpretive strategy of containment is pursued by Derrida in *De l'esprit*. Derrida, unlike Lacoue-Labarthe, believes that he can succeed in getting the *early* Heidegger partially off the hook. The sticking point is the key word in Derrida's title, *"l'esprit"* (or *"Geist"*). Derrida argues that the frequent positive allusions to "spirit" in the political speeches of 1933 indicate a sharp departure from *Being and Time*, where this category is systematically criticized. For a "metaphysics of spirit" was a Hegelian trope, a tell-tale metaphysical residuum that Heidegger the philosopher had long since renounced. Therefore, the utilization of this outmoded philosophical rhetoric was by definition discontinuous with the philosophy of *Being and Time*, despite the fact that the latter remained partially beholden to prejudicial Cartesian nostrums (above all, in treating Dasein as the *arche* through which the "question of Being" could be unlocked). As Derrida himself explains the rationale behind his "spirited" defense of Heidegger: one must preserve the "possibilities of rupture" in a "variegated Heideggerian thought that will remain for a long time provocative, enigmatic, worth reading." In his Rectoral Address, "Heidegger takes up again the word 'spirit,' which he had previously avoided, he dispenses with the inverted commas with which he had surrounded it. He thus limits the movement of deconstruction that he had previously engaged in. He gives a voluntaristic and metaphysical speech [whose terms] he would later treat with suspicion. To the extent that [Heidegger's discourse] celebrates the freedom of spirit, its exaltation [of spirit] resembles other European discourses (spiritualist, religious, humanist) that in general are opposed to Nazism. [This is] a complex and unstable skein that I try to unravel [in *De l'esprit*] by recognizing the threads in common between Nazism and anti-Nazism, the law of resemblance, the fatality of perversion. The mirror-effects are at times vertiginous."[29]

The far-fetched and illogical conclusion we are left to draw from the

line of argument pursued by both Lacoue-Labarthe and Derrida is that
it was a surfeit of metaphysical humanism (later abandoned) that drove
Heidegger into the Nazi camp! But in the end, this interpretive tack
amounts only to a more sophisticated strategy of denial. The entire
specificity of the relationship between Heidegger's philosophy and National Socialism is theorized away once the distinction between "humanism" and "anti-humanism" is so readily blurred. The "Volk" for which
Heidegger became the spokesman in 1933 is an eminently particularistic
entity, unlike the category of "mankind" or "humanitas" with which
one associates traditional humanism. In addition, any trace of personal
or German national responsibility is conveniently effaced once the triumph
of National Socialism is attributed to a nebulous, impersonal force such
as "planetary technology," "metaphysical thinking," "nihilism," or the
"will to will."[30] Since Nazism proves in the last analysis to be merely a
particular outgrowth of the rise of "planetary technology," which itself
is a mere "symptom" of the "forgetting of Being" that has victimized
the history of the West since Plato, the historical specificity of the Hitler
years becomes, in the overall scheme of things, *a minor episode.* From
this perspective, it would be presumptuous of Martin Heidegger, the
lowly "shepherd of Being," to assume culpability for a metaphysical
process (the forgetting of Being) for which he can hardly be held responsible. If you want someone to blame, knock on Plato's door. He's the
one, after all, who, by distinguishing between the forms and the sensi-
bles, kicked off the entire onto-theological muddle in the first place. In
fact, Heidegger deserves our ceaseless praise for attempting to *reverse*
this odious process; albeit within the limits of *"Gelassenheit"* or "releasement" (which substitutes for the overly "voluntaristic" category of
"Entschlossenheit" in the later Heidegger), according to which matters
can only be made worse if men and women assert their "wills" to try to
change things. As Heidegger confesses in the *Der Spiegel* interview (in a
line that theologians have ever since cited with glee), at this point in
history, the domination of "will," "metaphysics," and "techne" has
gone so far that "only a god can save us!"

That the "anti-humanist" philosophical framework of the later Heidegger can hardly be deemed an unqualified advance, as Lacoue-Labarthe and Derrida would have it, is indicated by a telling remark made
by Heidegger in 1949 (well after his alleged *Kehre*): "Agriculture today

is a motorized food industry, in essence the same as the manufacture of corpses in gas chambers and extermination camps, the same as the blockade and starvation of countries, the same as the manufacture of atomic bombs."[31] This cynical avowal—by the man who has staked a claim to being the leading philosopher of our time—is by no means an unrigorous aside, but pertains to the very crux of Heidegger's later philosophy as a critique of "techne." That the Freiburg sage can simply equate "the manufacture of corpses in gas chambers and extermination camps" with "mechanized agriculture" is not only a shockingly insensitive affront to the memory of the victims of the Nazi death camps—whose extermination in the remark just cited is treated as in essence no different from the production of higher-yield crops. It is not only a gruesome equation of incomparables. It serves once more to deny the specifically German responsibility for these crimes by attributing them to the dominance of an abstract, supervening, world-historical process. It suggests, moreover, that other Western (as well as non-Western) nations who engage in mechanized food production, "blockades," and the manufacture of nuclear weapons, are in essence no different than the SS lieutenants who herded Jews into the gas chambers. It illustrates an extreme myopia concerning the various uses to which technology can be put in the modern world, an incapacity to distinguish between its beneficial and destructive employment. It is in sum a simplistic *demonization of technology.* That the later Heidegger's philosophy is to such a great extent predicated on a demonization of "technique," as exemplified by the 1949 observation just cited, suggests a glaring flaw in his theoretical framework.

Hence, it comes as a surprise if, turning to Jean-François Lyotard's contribution to the debate, *Heidegger et "les juifs,"* a paramount relationship is established between Heideggerian thought and "the Jews." For according to Lyotard, in the history of the West, the Jews represent "the Other"—the "dissimilar," which, in its "difference," remains forever unassimilable to the dominant *ratio* or *logos.* Heideggerianism, as a thought of "ontological difference," allows us to *think* the Other with the requisite subtlety and profundity.[32] The fate of the Jews in Western culture has been one of "forgetting" and "repression." And thus, for Lyotard, the *"Vernichtung"* ("annihilation") of the Jews by the Nazis is in point of fact only a massive instance of *"Verleugnung"* ("denial"; p.

57). In it is inscribed the secret of Western thought, of all thought in fact: the extirpation of otherness, the suppression of "non-thought" or what is "Other" to thought. Heideggerianism, as a philosophy of re- membrance (*Andenken*), must be enlisted in the struggle to undo such forgetting.

Lyotard's analysis, moreover, coincides with that of Derrida and Lacoue-Labarthe on a number of essential points—concerning the value of "humanism," for example. Thus, humanism, he argues, is useless for our attempts to think the Holocaust, insofar as, qua mode of represen- tation, it is conducive only to what Freud called "secondary repression": by virtue of its platitudes and truisms, we "remember" all the better to forget (p. 52). Moreover, in its superficial attempts to name the unname- able and speak the unspeakable, humanism commits the sacrilege of transgressing the Jewish proscription against graven images. Hence, the affectations of shock and dismay with which the "dossier" concerning Heidegger's "case" has been received is a monumental instance of *tartuf- ferie*. For in truth, his Nazism merely points to the Machiavellian nature of politics as such, which necessitates that the "good" always remain a "lesser of evils" (p. 94).

At the same time, Lyotard emphatically takes issue with one of the central theses of Lacoue-Labarthe's analysis: the claim that National Socialism is best understood as a "national aestheticism" (or as Lacoue- Labarthe remarks at one point: "Racism—and anti-Semitism in partic- ular—is primarily, fundamentally, an aestheticism"[33]); that is, as the radical culmination of the Western discourse of *techne* or "art" that begins with the Greeks. In support of this claim, Lacoue-Labarthe lays great stress on the famously untranslatable bon mot from Thucydides' account of Pericles' Funeral Oration: "We cultivate the beautiful in its simplicity, and the things of the mind, without losing our firmness."[34] For (and herein lies the major thesis of his book concerning the essential interrelationship between "politics" and "fiction") it is this quintessen- tially Greek understanding of the relation between "form" and "politics" that initiates a discourse of "mythopoesis," a "logic of aesthetico-politi- cal immanentism," which subsequently becomes determinative for West- ern political thinking in general—which Lacoue-Labarthe refers to as "archaeo-politics." As he observes: "How then could we not see that in this [Periclean] utterance, which brings together art and philosophy to say what constitutes the specific quality and the heroic singularity of the Athenian *polis,* there is, not the founding charter of our 'democracies,' but the program of something which had a horrific fulfillment of which we are, so to speak, the . . . heirs."

According to Lacoue-Labarthe—who, once again, offers us a strikingly *orthodox* Heideggerian reading of the "destiny of the West"—this mythopoetic discourse exalts the powers of human self-formation and self-affirmation (*Selbstbehauptung*) to the point of apocalyptical self-annihilation. Predicated on the self-deluded metaphysical ideal of *self-positing subjectivity* (just as qua "humanism," Nazism is the "absolute subject of self-creation"), the goal of this discourse would be a state of pure and total "immanentism"—that is, a "state" that would be devoid of "exteriority," and hence, essentially *totalitarian.* As such, National Socialism qua national aestheticism is the logical culmination of the Western metaphysic of *Gestell* (enframing) that was first realized with the Greek ideal of the "state as a work of art" (Hegel)—the ultimate *ergon* (product) of workmanship or *techne* fashioned by the philosopher-king qua master craftsman—which, as filtered through the metaphysical lens of Descartes, becomes *techne* qua modern *Technik,* or "man" totally reduced to the status of *animal laborans.* Or, as Lacoue-Labarthe concludes: "It is, moreover, because from Plato to Nietzsche and Wagner and through to Jünger—and even to Heidegger who, at least as the reader of Trakl, actually taught us this—such an eidetics [of self-fashioning subjectivity—R. W.] underpins mimetology in the form of what I have felt might be called an onto-typology, that an entire tradition (the one that culminates in Nazism) will have thought that *the political is the sphere of the fictioning of beings and communities.*"[35]

But for Lyotard, despite such inventive ontological-historical (*seinsgeschichtlich*) analyses and acrobatics, Lacoue-Labarthe remains nevertheless fully unable to account for the chief victims of National Socialism qua "national aestheticism"—"the Jews"—and thus for the inner logic and specificity of Nazism itself. Further, one is in all honesty compelled to inquire whether the "fictional," mythopoetic striving after "total immanentism"—the Periclean connection, as it were—identified by Lacoue-Labarthe as a type of metaphysical *Ur-Grund* of Nazism can realistically be considered as one of its proximal causes; or, by the same token, whether, following Heidegger, we must necessarily view

National Socialism in the first instance as an *essentially metaphysical phenomenon*—a product of the "destining of Being." For don't we risk by virtue of such forms of argumentation "spiritualizing"—and thus explaining away—a series of diabolical historical circumstances that possesses in truth a very different, concrete, this-worldly etiology?

In *Heidegger and Modernity*, Luc Ferry and Alain Renaut have radically called into question the main interpretive strategy of Heidegger's French defenders, namely, the idea that it was an atavistic attachment to the world-view of metaphysical anthropocentrism that best explains Heidegger's mistaken belief in the "inner truth and greatness of National Socialism." They plausibly argue that to insinuate, as does Philippe Lacoue-Labarthe, that "Nazism is a humanism" contravenes virtually all the inherited meanings of *humanitas*, which suggests the intrinsic worth of all human persons rather than the superiority of one race or Volk. Instead, they seek to explain Heidegger's partisanship for National Socialism in terms of an attitude of *resolute anti-modernism* that resulted in the search for a "third way" between the twin evils of "Bolshevism" and "Americanism" (or, as we read in an *Introduction to Metaphysics*: "From a metaphysical point of view, Russia and America are the same: the same dreary technological frenzy, the same unrestricted organization of the average man").[36] In this respect, Heidegger viewed Nazism as a type of "postmodern" social formation, that is, as a form of political life that was truly appropriate to the age of technology. Or, in Heideggerian parlance, Nazism was a legitimate harbinger of "an other beginning." However, its leaders ultimately proved unable to rise to the epochal challenge to which they were summoned, and the movement eventually relapsed into inauthenticity—to a state of "technological frenzy" and nihilism that was essentially no different than what was already happening in the East or West.

Hence, Ferry and Renaut attempt both to reduce the "surfeit of humanism" argument of the French Heideggerians to the status of a pseudo-explanation and to set forth an alternative account of Heidegger's enthusiasm for German fascism based on his unremitting *hostility toward modernity*. In fact, it is precisely this charge—that of a "forgetting of modernity," where "modernity" signifies an appreciation of the

values of autonomy, right, and the "democratic invention"—that Ferry
and Renaut view as most damning. The accusation of "anti-modernity"
is of course one that is potentially most threatening to the apostles of
postmodernism, who seem to share the sweeping indictment of modernity qua unmitigated dominance of technological reason set forth by
Heidegger (see, for example, Lyotard's equation of "reason" with "terror" in "What is Postmodernism?").[37] For Ferry and Renaut, however,
it is the simplifications of this critique of modernity that are most troubling. For the Heideggerian-inspired vogue of anti-humanism that has
swept France since the 1960s[38] errs in depicting modernity as a rigidly
homogeneous continuum; a view that proceeds in fatal disregard of the
highly differentiated character of modern societies as well as what might
be called the "normative core of modernity": the triumph of an egalitar-
ian-democratic ethos, one that has been recently reconfirmed by the
revolutions in Eastern Europe of 1989. In their estimation, it was in the
first instance Heidegger's disregard of this normative core that led to his
"great blunder" [*"grosse Dummheit"*] of the 1930s; and it is a theoretical misstep that also haunts the political program of the so-called post-
modernists.

By the same token, Ferry and Renaut by no means wish to fall into
the opposite trap of simply proffering apologies for the contemporary
triumph of neo-liberalism. Instead, they seek to wage a war on two
fronts, as it were. On the one hand, as we have suggested thus far, they
seek to disqualify an "extrinsic" criticism of modernity, which, in its
antipathy to the values of democratic egalitarianism, would be tanta-
mount to regression. This fear underlies their criticisms of both Heideggerian "anti-modernism" and neo-Heideggerian "postmodernism." On
the other hand, they seek to promote the project of an "internal" criticism of modernity, a type of criticism of modern democracy by democratic means. In contrast to the currently fashionable undifferentiated
indictment of modernity that simply equates "reason" with "domination," Ferry and Renaut favor a more nuanced position, according to
which the excrescences of instrumental rationality (the devastation of
the environment, the predominance of an achievement ethos, and a
society of consumption) would be tempered by a rational reflection on
ends. Hence, their major disagreement with the neo-Heideggerian equa-

tion of "reason," "metaphysics," "technology," and "nihilism" suggests the paramountcy of laying the groundwork for a critique of modernity *from within.*

Perhaps the key question one might pose to them is, ironically, a Heideggerian one: what would be the constituents of a new "theory of the subject" that would succeed in refashioning this notion without succumbing to the historically familiar antinomies of "bourgeois subjectivity"—a self-legislating, "functional" monad that devalues intersubjectivity, sensuality, and otherness. The "success" of their program would seem to hinge on the answer given to this question; and it is by no means clear that the results yielded thus far are entirely satisfactory.[39]

Essentially, Heidegger is a philosopher who is not at home in the modern world. Thus, it comes as little surprise that, when pressed by his interlocutors during the course of the *Der Spiegel* interview for a tidbit of philosophical wisdom concerning a possible solution to the dilemmas of the modern age, Heidegger can only answer emphatically in the negative: whatever the solution may be, "it is not democracy"; instead, "only a god can save us." His devaluation of the modern project of human autonomy is so extreme, that he will only admit to a deus ex machina solution—in the most literal sense of the term. The powers of human intelligence and volition are so thoroughly downplayed, the modern ideal of self-fashioning subjectivity is so far devalued, that all we are left with is an appeal to myth that is abstract, irrational, and sadly impotent.

Notes

1. Luc Ferry and Alain Renaut, *Heidegger and Modernity* (Chicago: University of Chicago Press, 1990), p. 9.

2. The most important of these speeches have been included in part I, "Political Texts, 1933–1934."

3. Of course, the equation of "Heideggerianism" with "anti-humanism" is a far from uncontroversial assumption. A spirited debate in the English-language reception of Heidegger has emerged precisely over this question. For a defense of the "meta-humanistic" implications of Heidegger's theories, see Fred Dallmayr, "Ontology of Freedom: Heidegger and Political Philosophy," *Political Theory* 12:207–224, 1984; and John Caputo, *Radical Hermeneutics* (Blooming-

ton: Indiana University Press, 1987), pp. 209ff. For a critique of this position, see Richard Bernstein, "Heidegger on Humanism," in *Philosophical-Political Profiles* (Philadelphia: University of Pennsylvania Press, 1986), pp. 197–220.

4. Michael Marrus and Robert O. Paxton, *Vichy France and the Jews* (New York: Basic Books, 1981).

5. See the debate in the 1946–1947 issues of *Les Temps Modernes* that was spurred by Karl Löwith's essay, "Les implications politiques de la philosophie de l'existence chez Heidegger" (November 1946), reprinted in this volume. See also the further discussions of this theme by Alphons de Waelhens and Eric Weil in the July 1947 issue of *Les Temps Modernes*. The second debate, which occurred in the Parisian journal *Critique*, was provoked by a review essay by François Fédier that attacked three books critical of Heidegger: Guido Schneeberger's *Nachlese zu Heidegger* (Bern: Suhr, 1962), Theodor Adorno's *Jargon der Eigentlichkeit* (Frankfurt: Suhrkamp, 1964), and Paul Hühnerfeld, *In Sachen Heidegger* (Hamburg, 1959). Fédier's essay, which appeared in the February 1967 number, was rebutted in articles by Robert Minder, Jean Pierre Faye, and Aimé Patri, all of which appeared in *Critique* in July of the same year. An overview of this debate can be found in Beda Allemann, "Martin Heidegger und die Politik," in Otto Pöggeler, ed., *Martin Heidegger: Perspektiven zur Deutung seines Werk* (Königstein: Athenäum, 1969), pp. 246–260.

6. Among Ott's researches, the most important are as follows: "Martin Heidegger als Rektor der Universität Freiburg," *Zeitschrift für die Geschichte des Oberrheins* 132, 1984; "Martin Heidegger also Rektor der Universität Freidburg i. Br.—die Zeit des Rektorats von M. Heidegger," *Zeitschrift des Breisgau-Geschichtsvereins* 103, 1984; and "Martin Heidegger und die Universität Freiburg nach 1945," *Historisches Jahrbuch* 105:95–128, 1985. Most of Ott's findings have been incorporated in his recent book, *Martin Heidegger: Unterwegs zu seiner Biographie* (Frankfurt: Campus, 1988).

7. Heidegger's own accounts of his rectorship can be found in "The Rectorship 1933–34: Facts and Thoughts," translated by Karsten Harris, in *Review of Metaphysics* (1985):481–502; his "Letter to the Rector of Freiburg University, November 4, 1945"; *Der Spiegel* interview of May 1976: "Only a God Can Save Us." The latter two documents have been reprinted in part I of this volume.

8. It is of more than passing interest to note that Farias first tried repeatedly to publish his manuscript in Germany—the country that has been his home for a number of years now; he himself is a former Heidegger student and currently lives in Berlin where he teaches at the Free University—but met with rejection from all quarters. That the renewed debate over Heidegger's past has exploded in France has been no small source of embarrassment to German intellectuals, who are only now beginning to formulate their own interpretations concerning "Der Fall Heidegger."

9. The disagreements fall into the category of unpleasant harassment rather than anything more serious. Krieck—with whom Heidegger made common

cause in the spring of 1933 in the interest of the *Gleichschaltung* of the Association of German University Rectors—published several public attacks on Heidegger's philosophy as being ultimately incompatible with National Socialist doctrines. Rosenberg seems to have been interested in suppressing the publication of a 1942 Heidegger essay, "Plato's Doctrine of Truth." The essay was eventually published, very likely owing to the intervention of Benito Mussolini(!), who was informed about the matter by the Italian philosopher Ernesto Grassi. For more on the Heidegger-Mussolini connection, see *Heidegger et le Nazisme*, pp. 273–282 ("Heidegger et il Duce"). See also the extremely informative interview with Ernesto Grassi in *Libération*, March 2, 1988, pp. 40–41.

10. "Heidegger at Eighty," reprinted in Michael Murray, ed., *Heidegger and Modern Philosophy* (New Haven: Yale University Press, 1978), pp. 292–303.

11. See n. 4 above.

12. Heidegger, *An Introduction to Metaphysics*, p. 197.

13. For comments on the part of the most loyal Heidegger devotées, see the contributions by Pierre Aubenque, Henri Crétella, and François Fédier in the dossier published in *Le Débat* 48 (January-February 1988). For a countervailing perspective, see the observations by Stéphane Moses and Alain Renaut in the same dossier.

14. Cf. Fédier's contribution to the *Nouvel Observateur* dossier on "Heidegger et la pensée Nazie," January 22–28, 1988, p. 50. See also his diatribe against Farias, *Heidegger: l'anatomie d'un scandale* (Paris: Laffont, 1988).

15. Cf. n. 13 above.

16. Paul Celan, in his poem "Todtnauberg," tells the story of his pilgrimage to the philosopher's Schwarzwald mountain ski hut and of his disappointment over Heidegger's refusal to utter a single word upon being asked about the Holocaust. A similar tale has been recounted by the theologian Rudolph Bultmann, who upon suggesting after the war that Heidegger publicly recant his Nazi past, received only a cold, silent stare in return (cf. the article by Robert Maggiori in *Libération*, October 16, 1987).

17. *Nouvel Observateur*, January 22–28, 1988, pp. 43–45. Blanchot's comments, "Thinking about the Apocalypse," have been translated in *Critical Inquiry* 15(2):475–480, 1989.

18. *Nouvel Observateur*, January 22–28, 1988, p. 49. An English translation of Levinas' article, "As If Consenting to Horror," may be found in the issue of *Critical Inquiry* cited in n. 26, pp. 485–488.

19. *Nouvel Observateur*, January 22–28, 1988, p. 45. An English translation of Gadamer's article, "Back from Syracuse?," may be found in the issue of *Critical Inquiry* cited in n. 17, pp. 427–430.

20. Faurisson's argument is largely based on the fact that he has personally never met a Jew who actually *saw* the gas chambers. That Jews who did see the inside of the chambers were asphyxiated within three to four minutes might go

far toward explaining the peculiar lack of eyewitness accounts Faurisson has encountered.

21. Cf. the report by Robert Maggiori in *Libération*, January 7, 1988, p. 43.

22. See Michel Tibon-Cornillot, "Heidegger et le chainon manquant," *Libération*, February 17, 1988, pp. 41–42, for a comprehensive treatment of the relations between Heidegger and Fischer. In a follow-up letter the next day, Fischer would write: "The faculty defends [Heidegger] as a spiritual Führer and a thinker. . . . We really do not have many great philosophers, let alone National Socialist philosophers." The fact that the papers of both Heidegger and Fischer are closed to public viewing represents a significant obstacle to a more detailed investigation of their relations.

23. Both have recently been translated into English. Jacques Derrida, *Of Spirit: Heidegger and the Question* (Chicago: University of Chicago Press, 1989) and Philippe Lacoue-Labarthe, *Heidegger, Art and Politics* (Oxford: Blackwell, 1990).

24. Cf. Derrida's essay, "The Ends of Man," in *Margins of Philosophy* (Chicago: University of Chicago Press, 1982).

25. Philippe Lacoue-Labarthe, *La fiction du Politique* (Strasbourg, 1987), p. 81.

26. This contention has been subjected to a thoroughgoing rebuttal by Ferry and Renaut in *Heidegger and Modernity*.

27. Cited in "Neue Forschungen und Urteile über Heidegger und Nationalsozialismus," *Der Spiegel*, August 18, 1986, p. 167.

28. See the remarks by Jean-Michel Palmier cited in ibid.

29. Cf. "Heidegger, l'enfer des philosophes" (interview with Jacques Derrida), *Nouvel Observateur*, November 6–12, 1987, pp. 171–172; also in part III above.

30. The category of the "will to will" dominates Heidegger's critique of traditional metaphysics and its nihilistic implications in his *Nietzsche*, 2 vols. (Pfullingen: Neske, 1962). A four-volume English translation has recently appeared from Harper and Row.

31. Cited in *Der Spiegel*, August 18, 1986, p. 169.

32. Jean-François Lyotard, *Heidegger et "les juifs"* (Paris: Galilée, 1988), pp. 45–47; English translation: *Heidegger and the Jews* (Minneapolis: University of Minnesota Press, 1990).

33. Lacoue-Labarthe, *La fiction du politique*, p. 61.

34. Ibid., p. 82.

35. ibid., p. 71; emphasis added. See also the following remarks (pp. 61–62): "The infinitization or absolutization of the subject, which is at the heart of the metaphysics of the Moderns, here finds its strictly operational outcome: the community creating, the community at work creates and works itself, so to speak, thereby accomplishing the subjective process par excellence, the process of self-formation and self-production. This is why that process finds its truth in

Richard Wolin

'a fusion of the community' (in festival or war) or in the ecstatic identification with a Leader who in no way represents any form of transcendence, but incarnates, in immanent fashion, the immanentism of a community. And this is also why a will to immediate effectuation or self-effectuation underlies national-aestheticism. This will to immediacy is precisely what has been caesur-ed, for it was, ultimately, the crime—the boundless excess—of Nazism."

36. Heidegger, *An Introduction to Metaphysics*, p. 37.

37. Jean-François Lyotard, *The Postmodern Condition* (Minneapolis: University of Minnesota Press, 1984), pp. 63–64, 81–82.

38. See Ferry and Renaut, *French Philosophy of the Sixties: An Essay on Antihumanism*, translated by Mary Cattani (Amherst: University of Massachusetts Press, 1990).

39. See, for example, the recent book by Renaut, *L'ère de l'individu: Contribution à une histoire de la subjectivité* (Paris: Gallimard, 1990). See also the review essay by Alexander Nehamas, "The Rescue of Humanism," in *The New Republic*, November 12, 1990, pp. 27–34.

MARTIN HEIDEGGER
AND POLITICS:
A Bibliography of Secondary Literature

Adorno, Theodor W. *The Jargon of Authenticity.* Translated by Kurt Tarnowski and Frederic Will. Evanston: Northwestern University Press, 1973.

Allemann, Beda. "Martin Heidegger und die Politik." In Otto Pöggeler, ed., *Heidegger: Perspektiven zur Deutung seines Werkes.* Königstein: Athenäum, 1984.

Altwegg, Jurg, ed. *Die Heidegger Kontroverse.* Frankfurt: Athenäum, 1988.

Baudrillard, Jean. "Zu spät!" *Die Zeit,* February 5, 1988.

Bernstein, Richard. "Heidegger on Humanism." *Praxis International* 5:95–114, 1985.

Blitz, Mark. *Heidegger's Being and Time and the Possibility of Political Philosophy.* Ithaca, N.Y.: Cornell University Press, 1981.

Bourdieu, Pierre. *L'Ontologie politique de Martin Heidegger.* Paris: Editions de Minuit, 1988. (English translation forthcoming from Stanford University Press.)

Chytry, Joseph. *The Aesthetic State: A Quest in Modern German Thought.* Berkeley: University of California Press, 1989.

Dallmayr, Fred. "Heidegger and Marxism." *Praxis International* 7:207–224, 1987.

Dallmayr, Fred. "Ontology of Freedom: Heidegger and Political Philosophy." *Political Theory* 12:204–234, 1984.

Dallmayr, Fred. *Twilight of Subjectivity: Contributions to a Post-Individualist Theory of Politics.* Amherst: University of Massachusetts Press, 1981.

Davidson, Arnold I., ed. "A Symposium on Heidegger and Nazism." *Critical Inquiry* 15(2):407–488, 1989.

Derrida, Jacques. *Of Spirit: Heidegger and the Question.* Chicago: University of Chicago Press, 1990.

Edler, Frank H. W. "Philosophy, Language, and Politics: Heidegger's Attempt to Steal the Language of the Revolution in 1933–34." *Social Research* 57: 197–238, Spring 1990.

Farias, Victor. *Heidegger and Nazism.* Edited, with a foreword by Joseph Margolis and Tom Rockmore. Translated by Paul Burrell and Gabriel Ricci. (Philadelphia: Temple University Press, 1989).

Fédier, François. *Heidegger: Anatomie d'un scandale*. Paris: Laffont, 1988.

Ferry, Luc, and Alain Renaut. *Heidegger and Modernity*. Chicago: University of Chicago Press, 1990.

Forum für Philosophie Bad Homburg, ed. *Martin Heidegger: Innen-Aussenansichten*. Frankfurt am Main: Suhrkamp Verlag, 1989.

Franzen, Winfried. "Die Sehnsucht nach Härte und Schwere." In Annemarie Gethmann-Siefert and Otto Pöggeler, eds., *Heidegger und die praktische Philosophie*. Frankfurt: Suhrkamp, 1988.

Franzen, Winfried. *Von der Existenzialontologie zur Seinsgeschichte*. Meisenheim am Glan: Anton Heim, 1975.

Gadamer, Hans-Georg. "Review of Pierre Bourdieu." *Die politische Ontologie Martin Heideggers. Philosophische Rundschau* 26:143–149, 1979.

Gethmann-Siefert, Annemarie, and Otto Pöggeler, eds. *Heidegger und die praktische Philosophie*. Frankfurt: Suhrkamp, 1988.

Goldmann, Lucien. *Lukács and Heidegger*. Translated by William Q. Boelhower. London: Routledge and Kegan Paul, 1977.

Habermas, Jürgen. "Martin Heidegger: Nazi, sicher ein Nazi!" (interview with M. Hunyadi). In Jurg Altwegg, ed., *Die Heidegger Kontroverse*. Frankfurt: Athenäum, 1988.

Habermas, Jürgen. *The Philosophical Discourse of Modernity*. Translated by Frederick Lawrence. Cambridge, Mass.: MIT Press, 1987.

Habermas, Jürgen. "Work und Weltanschauung: The Heidegger Controversy from a German Perspective." In Shierry Weber Nicholsen, ed. and trans., *The New Conservativism: Cultural Criticism and the Historians' Debate*. Cambridge, Mass.: MIT Press, 1989.

Harries Karsten. "Heidegger as a Political Thinker." In Michael Murray, ed., *Heidegger and Modern Philosophy*. New Haven: Yale University Press, 1978.

"Heidegger et la pensée Nazie." (Contains texts by Maurice Blanchot, Hans-Georg Gadamer, Philippe Lacoue-Labarthe, François Fédier, and Emmanuel Levinas.) *Le Nouvel Observateur*, January 22–28, 1988:41–49.

"Heidegger, la philosophie, et la Nazisme." (Contains texts by Pierre Aubenque, Henri Crétella, Michel Déguy, François Fédier, Gérard Granel, Stéphane Moses, and Alain Renaut.) *Le Débat* 48:113–176, 1988.

Herf, Jeffrey. *Reactionary Modernism: Technology, Culture, and Politics in Weimar and the Third Reich*. New York: Cambridge University Press, 1984.

Hühnerfeld, Paul. *In Sachen Heidegger: Versuch über ein deutsches Genie*. Hamburg: Hoffman und Campe, 1959.

Janicaud, Dominique. "Heidegger's Politics: Determinable or Not?" *Social Research* 56:819–849, Winter 1989.

Janicaud, Dominique. *L'Ombre de cette pensée: Heidegger et la question politique*. Paris: Jerome Million, 1990.

Jaspers, Karl. *Notizen zu Martin Heidegger*. Edited by Hans Saner. Munich: Piper, 1988.

Jaspers, Karl. *The Philosophy of Karl Jaspers.* Edited by P. A. Schlipp. La Salle, Ill.: Open Court, 1981.

Krockow, Christian Graf von. *Die Entscheidung: Eine Untersuchung über Ernst Jünger, Carl Schmitt, Martin Heidegger.* Stuttgart: Ferdinand Enke, 1959.

Lacoue-Labarthe, Philippe. *Heidegger, Art, and Politics.* Translated by Chris Turner. Oxford: Blackwell, 1990.

Losurdo, Domenico. "Heidegger et la démission de la philosophie allemande." *L'homme et la société* 97:103–118, 1990.

Löwith, Karl. *Heidegger: Denker in dürftiger Zeit. Sämtliche Schriften.* Vol. 8. Stuttgart: J. B. Metzler, 1984.

Löwith, Karl. *My Life in Germany Before and After 1933.* New York: Columbia University Press, 1992.

Lukács, Georg. *The Destruction of Reason.* Translated by Peter Palmer. London: Merlin Press, 1980.

Lyotard, Jean-François. *Heidegger and the Jews.* Minneapolis: University of Minnesota, 1990.

Marcuse, Herbert. "Heidegger and Politics: An Interview with Frederick Olafson." In R. Pippen et al., eds., *Marcuse: Critical Theory and the Promise of Utopia.* South Hadley, Mass.: Bergin and Garvey, 1987.

Marcuse, Herbert. "The Struggle Against Liberalism in the Totalitarian View of the State." In *Negations.* Boston: Beacon, 1968.

Marten, Rainer. "Heideggers Geist." *Allmende* 20:82ff., 1988.

Marten, Rainer. "Ein rassistisches Konzept von Humanitat." *Badische Zeitung,* December 19–20, 1987.

Martin, Bernd, ed. *Martin Heidegger und das "Dritte Reich."* Darmstadt: Wissenschaftliche Buchgesellschaft, 1989.

Megill, Allan. *Prophets of Extremity: Nietzsche, Heidegger, Foucault, Derrida.* Berkeley: University of California Press, 1984.

Neske, Günther, and Emil Kettering, eds. *Martin Heidegger and National Socialism: Questions and Answers.* Translated by Lisa Harries. New York: Paragon House, 1990.

Ott, Hugo. "Der junge Martin Heidegger: Gymnasial-Konviktszeit und Studium." *Freiburger Diozesan-Archiv* 104:315–325, 1984.

Ott, Hugo. "Martin Heidegger als Rektor der Universität Freiburg 1933/34." Part I. *Zeitschrift für die Geschichte dès Oberrheins* 132:343–358, 1984.

Ott, Hugo. "Martin Heidegger als Rektor der Universität Freiburg i. Br. 1933/34." Part I. *Zeitschrift des Breisgau-Geschichtsvereins* 102:121–136, 1984.

Ott, Hugo. "Martin Heidegger als Rektor der Universität Freiburg i. Br. 1933/34." Part II. *Zeitschrift des Breisgau-Geschichtsvereins* 103:107–130, 1984.

Ott, Hugo. "Martin Heidegger und der Nationalsozialismus." In Annemarie Gethmann-Siefert and Otto Pöggeler, eds., *Heidegger und die praktische Philosophie.* Frankfurt: Suhrkamp, 1988.

Ott, Hugo. "Martin Heidegger und die Universität Freiburg nach 1945: Ein Beispiel für die Auseinandersetzung mit der politischen Vergangenheit." *Historisches Jahrbuch* 105:95–128, 1985.

Bibliography

Ott, Hugo. *Martin Heidegger: Unterwegs zu seiner Biographie.* Frankfurt: Campus, 1988.

Petzet, Heinrich Wiegand. *Auf einen Stern zugehen: Begegnungen und Gespräche mit Martin Heidegger, 1929–1976.* Frankfurt: Societät Verlag, 1983.

Pöggeler, Otto. "Besinnung oder Ausflucht: Heideggers ürsprunglicheres Denken." In Forum für Philosophie Bad Homburg, ed., *Zerstörung des moralischen Selbstbewusstein: Chance oder Gefährdung.* Frankfurt: Suhrkamp, 1988.

Pöggeler, Otto. "Den Führer führen? Heidegger und kein Ende." *Philosophische Rundschau* 32:26–67, 1985.

Pöggeler, Otto. *Martin Heidegger's Path of Thinking.* With an afterword to the second edition. Translated by Daniel Magurshak and Sigmund Barber. Atlantic Highlands, N.J.: Humanities Press, 1987.

Pöggeler, Otto. *Philosophie und Politik bei Heidegger.* Freiburg: Alber, 1972.

Rorty, Richard. "Taking Philosophy Seriously." *New Republic,* April 11, 1988, 31–34.

Schneeberger, Guido. *Ergänzungen zu einer Heidegger Bibliographie.* Bern: Suhr, 1960.

Schneeberger, Guido. *Nachlese zu Heidegger.* Bern: Suhr, 1962.

Schürmann, Rainer. *Heidegger on Being and Acting: From Principles to Anarchy.* Translated by Christine-Marie Gros. Bloomington: Indiana University Press, 1987.

Schürmann, Rainer. "Political Thinking in Heidegger." *Social Research* 45, 1978.

Schürmann, Rainer. "Principles Precarious: On the Origin of the Political in Heidegger." In Thomas Sheehan, ed., *Heidegger: The Man and the Thinker.* Chicago: Precedent, 1991.

Schwan, Alexander. "Martin Heidegger, Politik und praktische Philosophie." *Philosophisches Jahrbuch* 81:148–171, 1974.

Schwan, Alexander. *Politische Philosophie im Denken Heideggers.* With an afterword to the second edition. Opladen: Westdeutscher Verlag, 1988.

Schwan, Alexander. "Zeitkritik und Politik bei Heideggers Spätphilosophie." In Annemarie Gethmann-Siefert and Otto Pöggeler, eds., *Heidegger und die praktische Philosophie.* Frankfurt: Suhrkamp, 1989.

Sheehan, Thomas. "Heidegger and the Nazis." *New York Review of Books,* June 15, 1988, 38–47.

Sluga, Hans. "Metadiscourse: German Philosophy and National Socialism." *Social Research* 56:795–818, Winter 1989.

Steiner, Georg. "Heidegger Again." *Salmagundi* 82–83:31–56, Spring-Summer 1989.

Stern, Gunther. "On the Pseudo-Concreteness of Heidegger's Philosophy." *Philosophy and Phenomenological Research* 9:337–370, 1948.

Sternberger, Dolf. "Die grossen Worte des Rektors Heidegger: eine philosophische Untersuchung." *Frankfurter Allgemeine Zeitung,* March 2, 1984.

Strauss, Leo. "Philosophy as Rigorous Science and Political Philosophy." In *Studies in Platonic Political Philosophy*. Chicago: University of Chicago Press, 1983.

Tertulian, Nicholas. "Quand le discours Heideggerien se mue en prise de position politique." *La Quinzaine Litteraire* 499:22–24, December 1987.

Vietta, Silvio. *Heideggers Kritik am Nationalsozialismus und an der Technik*. Tübingen: Niemeyer, 1989.

Wolin, Richard. "Heidegger et le nazisme." *L'homme et la société* 97:119–131, 1990.

Wolin, Richard. *The Politics of Being: The Political Thought of Martin Heidegger*. New York: Columbia University Press, 1990.

Wolin, Richard. "Recherches récentes sur la relation de Martin Heidegger au national socialisme." *Les Temps Modernes* 495:56–85, 1987.

Zimmerman, Michael. *Heidegger's Confrontation with Modernity*. Bloomington: Indiana University Press, 1990.

Zimmerman, Michael. "The Thorn in Heidegger's Side: The Question of National Socialism." *Philosophical Forum* 20(4):326–365, 1989.